LEO STRAUSS AND EMMANUEL LEVINAS

Leo Strauss and Emmanuel Levinas, two twentieth-century Jewish philosophers and extremely provocative thinkers whose reputations have grown considerably over the last twenty years, are rarely studied together. This is due to the disparate interests of many of their intellectual heirs. Strauss, or at least a popular neo-conservative interpretation of his work, has influenced political theorists and policy makers on the right, whereas Levinas has been championed in the humanities by different cadres associated with postmodernist thought.

In *Leo Strauss and Emmanuel Levinas: Philosophy and the Politics of Revelation*, Leora Batnitzky brings together these two seemingly incongruous contemporaries, demonstrating that they often had the same philosophical sources and their projects had many formal parallels. Batnitzky situates Strauss in the context from which he emerged – early twentieth-century German-Jewish thought – to reveal that he was a far more complex and nuanced thinker than both his enemies and allies currently recognize. Her fresh reading of Levinas questions those who see in his work the revival of the Jewish tradition in an overtly postmodern framework. While such a comparison is valuable for a better understanding of each figure, it also raises profound questions in the current debate on the definitions of "religion," suggesting new ways that religion makes claims on both philosophy and politics.

Leora Batnitzky is Associate Professor of Religion at Princeton University. She is the author of *Idolatry and Representation: The Philosophy of Franz Rosenzweig Reconsidered* and editor of the forthcoming *Martin Buber: Schriften zur Philosophie und Religion*. She is co-editor of *Jewish Studies Quarterly*.

Leo Strauss and Emmanuel Levinas

Philosophy and the Politics of Revelation

LEORA BATNITZKY

Princeton University

CAMBRIDGE
UNIVERSITY PRESS

CAMBRIDGE UNIVERSITY PRESS
Cambridge, New York, Melbourne, Madrid, Cape Town, Singapore, São Paulo

Cambridge University Press
32 Avenue of the Americas, New York, NY 10013-2473, USA

www.cambridge.org
Information on this title: www.cambridge.org/9780521861564

First published 2006
Reprinted 2006

Printed in the United States of America

A catalog record for this publication is available from the British Library.

Library of Congress Cataloging in Publication Data
Batnitzky, Leora Faye, 1966–
Leo Strauss and Emmanuel Levinas : philosophy and the politics of revelation / Leora Batnitzky.
p. cm.
Includes bibliographical references and index.
ISBN-13: 978-0-521-86156-4
ISBN-10: 0-521-86156-X
1. Philosophy, Jewish. 2. Strauss, Leo. 3. Lévinas, Emmanuel. 4. Philosophy, Modern –
20th century. 5. Political science – Philosophy. 6. Cohen, Hermann, 1842–1918. I. Title.
B5800.B38   2006
181'.06–dc22   2005022907

ISBN   978-0-521-86156-4 hardback

To Bob, with gratitude and love

Contents

Acknowledgments

Earlier versions of a number of parts of this manuscript were published else-where and I gratefully acknowledge permission to reprint material here. An earlier version of parts of Chapter 1 was published as "Jewish Philosophy after Metaphysics," in *Religion after Metaphysics*, edited by Mark Wrathall, Cambridge University Press (2003), pp. 146–65. The first half of Chapter 2 was published in an earlier version as "Encountering the Modern Subject in Levinas," *Yale French Studies*, 104 (2003) special issue on "Encounters with Levinas," edited by Thomas Trezise, pp. 6–21. An earlier version of the first half of Chapter 3 was published as "Franz Rosenzweig's Philosophical Legacy: Levinas or Strauss?" in *The Legacy of Franz Rosenzweig: Collected Essays*, edited by Luc Anckaert, Martin Brasser, and Norbert Samuelson, Leuven Univer-sity Press (2004), pp. 109–18. And parts of Chapter 6 were published as "Leo Strauss's Disenchantment with Secular Society," in *New German Critique*, spe-cial issue on "Secularization and Disenchantment," edited by Peter Eli Gordon and Jonathan Skolnik, 95 (winter 2005), pp. 106–26.

I also presented early versions of parts of this book at Arizona State Uni-versity, Brandeis University, The Jewish Theological Seminary of America, Pennsylvania State University, the University of California at Los Angeles, the University of Toronto, the University of Virginia, and Yale University. I am grateful for the questions, comments, and criticism I received from these different audiences and would like especially to thank Norbert Samuel-son, Eugene Sheppard, Jack Werthheimer, Kenneth Reinhard, Daniel Con-way, Claire Katz, David Novak, Robert Gibbs, Chuck Mathewes, and Steven B. Smith for their invitations to speak.

Many people were also generous enough to comment on different parts of the manuscript or on the project more generally. For their thoughts on Strauss and Levinas and related matters, I'd like to thank Lawrie Balfour, Zachary Braiterman, Peter Gordon, Kenneth Hart Green, Eric Gregory, Martin Kavka,

George Kateb, Claire Katz, Steven Kepnes, Mark Larrimore, Robert Lebeau, Olga Litvak, Samuel Moyn, David Myers, David Novak, Bill Plevan, Elliot Ratzman, Howard Rhodes, Stanley Rosen, Eugene Sheppard, Meir Soloveitchik, Jeffrey Stout, Cornel West, and Michael Zank. I am especially grateful to Martin Kavka, Samuel Moyn, David Novak, and Cornel West for reading what became the penultimate manuscript and for offering their criticism, advice, and encouragement at different stages of the project. A very inadequate special thanks goes to Sam Moyn, who saved me from many errors, big and small, for his incredible intellectual generosity that has only been matched by his patience for commenting on this project.

I also received a lot of institutional assistance while writing this book, for which I am very thankful. Much of the preliminary work on this project was made possible by a generous leave that I received for the academic year 2001–2 from Princeton University's Center for Human Values and the Richard Stockton Bicentennial Preceptorship. I continue to be grateful for the supportive and stimulating environments of Princeton University's Department of Religion and Program in Judaic Studies. I'd especially like to thank my colleagues Martha Himmelfarb, Peter Schäfer, Jeffrey Stout, and Cornel West for their support and encouragement as I have worked on this book over the last years, as well as Lorraine Fuhrmann, Pat Bogdziewicz, and Kerry Smith for their continuous help and good cheer.

My editor, Andrew Beck of Cambridge University Press, has made the editorial process of the publication of this book a pleasure. I am grateful to him and to his assistant Faith Black for their professionalism, attentiveness, and good advice. I would also like to thank Christine Dunn for her help with the copyediting of this book and Alexis Wichowski for her help with the index.

Finally, a thank you of an entirely different order goes to my family, without whom this book, and just about everything else, would not be possible. For unusual patience and support, especially as I finished this book, I'd like to thank my husband Bob and our sons Jonathan, Gabriel, and Eli.

List of Abbreviations

WORKS BY LEVINAS

AM   "L'actualité de Maïmonïde," *Paix et Droit* 15(4) (April 1935).

AQ   *Autrement qu'etre ou au-delà de l'essence.* The Hague: Martinus Nijhoff, 1974.

AT   *Alterity and Transcendence.* Michael B. Smith, trans. London: The Athlone Press, 1990 ; M. Nijhoff, 1974.

AUP   "Totalité et infini." *Annales de l'Université de Paris* 31 (1961): p. 386.

BV   *Beyond the Verse: Talmudic Readings and Lectures.* Gary D. Mole, trans. London: The Athlone Press, 1982.

CPP   *Collected Philosophical Papers.* Alphonso Lingis, trans. Dordrecht: Martinus Nijhoff, 1988.

DE   *De l'évasion.* Montpellier: Fata Morgana, 1992.

DF   *Difficult Freedom: Essays on Judaism.* Seán Hand, trans. Baltimore: Johns Hopkins University Press, 1990.

DH   *Discovering Existence with Husserl.* Richard Cohen and Michael B. Smith, trans. Evanston, IL: Northwestern University Press, 1998.

DI   *De Dieu qui vient à l'idée.* Paris: Librairie Philosophique J. Vrin, 1986.

DL   *Difficile Liberté, Essais sur le judaisme.* Paris: Albin Michel, 1963.

DU   *Du Sacré au Sainte.* Paris: Les Editions de Minuit, 1977.

EI   *Ethics and Infinity: Conversations with Philippe Nemo.* Richard A. Cohen, trans. Pittsburgh: Duquesne University Press, 1985.

LR   *Levinas Reader.* Seán Hand, trans. New York: Blackwell, 1990.

NP   *Noms propres.* Paris: Livre de Poche, 1987.

NTR   *Nine Talmudic Readings.* Annette Aronowicz, trans. Bloomington: Indiana University Press, 1990.

OTB   *Otherwise than Being or Beyond Essence.* Alphonso Lingis, trans. The Hague: Martinus Nijhoff, 1981.

PN   *Proper Names.* Michael B. Smith, trans. London: Athlone Press, 1996.

RHW   Review of H. A. Wolfson's *The Philosophy of Spinoza.* In *Revue des Éstudes Juives* 51 (1–2) (1937), pp. 114–19.

RPH   "Reflections on the Philosophy of Hitlerism." *Critical Inquiry* 17 (1990), pp. 62–71.

TeI   *Totalité et Infini. Essai sur l'extériorité.* The Hague: Martinus Nijhoff, 1961.

TI   *Totality and Infinity: An Essay on Exteriority.* Alphonso Lingis, trans. Pittsburgh: Duquesne University Press, 1969.

TIHP   *The Theory of Intuition in Husserl's Phenomenology.* Andre Orianne, trans. Evanston, IL: Northwestern University Press, 1987.

TN   *In the Time of the Nations.* Michael B. Smith, trans. Bloomington: Indiana University Press, 1994.

TO   *Time and the Other.* Richard A. Cohen, trans. Pittsburgh: Duquesne University Press, 1987.

US   "Useless Suffering." In *The Provocation of Levinas,* R. Bernasconi and D. Wood, eds. London: Routledge, 1988, pp. 156–67.

WORKS BY STRAUSS

AAPL   *The Argument and Action in Plato's Laws.* Chicago: University of Chicago Press, 1975.

CCM   Leo Strauss and Karl Löwith. "Correspondence Concerning Modernity." Susanne Klein and George Elliot Tucker, trans. *Independent Journal of Philosophy/Unabhängige Zeitschrift für Philosophie* 4 (1983), pp. 105–19.

CCWM   Leo Strauss and Hans-Georg Gadamer, "Correspondence Concerning *Wahrheit und Methode.*" *The Independent Journal of Philosophy/ Unabhängige Zeitschrift für Philosophie* 2, pp. 5–12.

CLS   "Correspondence of Karl Löwith and Leo Strauss." George Elliot Tucker, trans. *Independent Journal of Philosophy/Unabhängige Zeitschrift für Philosophie* 5/6 (1988), pp. 177–92.

CM   *The City and Man.* Chicago: University of Chicago Press, 1978.

EW   *Leo Strauss: The Early Writings (1921–1932).* Michael Zank, trans. and ed. Albany: State University of New York Press, 2002.

FPP   *Faith and Political Philosophy: The Correspondence between Leo Strauss and Eric Voegelin, 1934–1964.* Barry Cooper, trans. Columbia: University of Missouri Press, 2004.

GN   "German Nihilism." *Interpretation* 26(3) (spring 1999), pp. 353–78.

GS 1   *Leo Strauss Gesammelte Schriften. Band 1, Spinozas und zugehörige Schriften.* Heinrich Meier, ed. Stuttgart, Germany: Verlag J. B. Metzler, 2001.

GS 2   *Leo Strauss Gesammelte Schriften. Band 2, Philosophie und Gesetz Frühe Schriften.* Heinrich Meier, ed. Stuttgart, Germany: Metzler, 1997.

GS 3   *Leo Strauss Gesammelte Schriften. Band 3, Hobbes' politische Wissenschaft und zugehörige Schriften – Briefe.* Heinrich Meier, ed. Stuttgart, Germany: Verlag J. B. Metzler, 2001.

IPP   *An Introduction to Political Philosophy.* Detroit: Wayne State University Press, 1989.

JPCM   *Jewish Philosophy and the Crisis of Modernity.* Kenneth Hart Green, ed. Albany: State University of New York Press, 1997.

LAM   *Liberalism Ancient and Modern.* Chicago: University of Chicago Press, 1995.

MIPT   "The Mutual Influence of Theology and Philosophy." *Independent Journal of Philosophy/Unabhängige Zeitschrift für Philosophie* 3 (1979), pp. 111–18.

NCP   "Notes on the Concept of the Political." In *Heinrich Meier, Carl Schmitt and Leo Strauss: The Hidden Dialogue.* J. Harvey Lomax Meier, trans. Chicago: University of Chicago Press, 1995.

NRH   *Natural Right and History.* Chicago: University of Chicago Press, 1952.

OT   *On Tyranny.* Chicago: University of Chicago Press, 2000.

PAW   *Persecution and the Art of Writing.* Chicago: University of Chicago Press, 1988.

PG   *Philosophie und Gesetz: Beiträge zum Verständnis Maimunis und seiner Vorläufer.* Berlin: Schocken, 1935. As reprinted in GS 2.

PL   *Philosophy and Law.* Eve Adle, trans. Philadelphia: The Jewish Publication Society of America, 1995.

RCPR   *The Rebirth of Classical Political Rationalism.* Thomas Pangle, ed. Chicago: University of Chicago Press, 1989.

RMF   "Some Remarks on the Political Science of Maimonides and Farabi." Robert Bartlett, trans. *Interpretation* 18(1) (fall 1990), pp. 3–30.

SA   *Socrates and Aristophanes.* Chicago: University of Chicago Press, 1996.

SCR   *Spinoza's Critique of Religion.* Chicago: University of Chicago Press, 1997. Translation of *Die Religionskritik Spinozas als Grundlage*

seiner Bibelwissenschaft Untersuchungen zu Spinozas Theologisch-
Politischem Traktat. Berlin: Akademie-Verlag, 1930.

SPPP   Studies in Platonic Political Philosophy. Thomas Pangle, intro.
Chicago: University of Chicago Press, 1983.

WPP   What Is Political Philosophy and Other Studies. Chicago: University
of Chicago Press, 1988.

Preface

Talk of the crisis of the west and of the future of western civilization has only increased in recent years, as the horrors and destruction of the twentieth century continue to extend into the twenty-first century, albeit in new forms. This book is a study of two twentieth-century thinkers who, writing immediately prior to and after the Nazi genocide, consider the parameters of the west to restore what both claim is western civilization's universal glory and moral importance. Significantly, the philosophies of Leo Strauss (1899–1973) and Emmanuel Levinas (1906–95), while particular to their place and time, both have contemporary resonance in present debates about the crisis and status of "the west." Strauss, especially, has become, depending on one's political commitments, the hero or the villain of the United States' war on terror.[1] This is the case despite the fact that Strauss's thought in no way concerns concrete public policy. Less in public political debate, but more in academic political debates, Levinas's thought, or the purported implications thereof, has become a rallying cry against the arrogance of the powerful oppressing weaker "others" precisely because the powerful are unable, or unwilling, to affirm the "alterity" of the "other."[2] And this is the case despite the fact that Levinas, far more than Strauss, defended "the west" against its "oriental" others.[3] This study questions both of these views of Strauss and Levinas, not only because, as I will argue, they are incorrect, but also, and in fact more so, because the philosophies of Strauss and Levinas deserve greater attention for their contemporary significance.

From the very brief description of Strauss's and Levinas's rather different current receptions, it should be clear already that they aren't often considered together. One of the main arguments of this book is that Strauss and Levinas ought to be studied together because their projects bear a broad formal similarity to each other and not accidentally so. Strauss and Levinas emerge from the same intellectual context: the interwar period of Weimar Germany. While Levinas was born and raised in Lithuania and Strauss in rural Germany, their shared intellectual coming of age took place under the tutelage of Edmund Husserl and Martin Heidegger. As importantly, both experienced as Jews the trauma of the Second World War. The respective exile imposed on both, the question of Jewishness as it relates to the Second World War, and the meaning of European civilization generally became paramount to Strauss's and Levinas's intellectual development. While Strauss went on to become one of the most important voices in political philosophy in America in the twentieth century and Levinas one of the most important philosophers in the French phenomenological tradition, the center of each of their respective intellectual projects, I will argue, consists in grappling with the meanings of persecution generally, and Jewishness, particularly. And while both remain in the throes of Husserl and Heidegger, even when they try to transcend them, they each grapple with these questions in dialogue with previous Jewish thinkers, including first and foremost Moses Maimonides, Baruch Spinoza, Hermann Cohen, and Franz Rosenzweig.

Recognizing Strauss's and Levinas's shared intellectual horizon, I argue, allows us to appreciate and, in fact, understand their respective thoughts differently and, I contend, better than they have been understood until now. My claim is historical and philosophical. While it remains a common place of much of the study of philosophy and political theory that historical contextualization is at best complementary and at worst irrelevant to philosophical understanding, my claim in this study is that historical contextualization helps us to understand philosophy and to philosophize better. In this, I follow Strauss's view that contemporary readers all too often assume that they can understand an author better than he understood himself and in doing so only impose their own view of the world onto the great texts of the past. Historical contextualization is a first step to philosophical thinking because to understand the problems of the present we need to understand our own assumptions, which we can only begin to recognize by appreciating assumptions other than our own.

To be sure, the relation between philosophical thinking and historical study is not as easily resolved as the preceding might imply. Indeed, Strauss shares with Levinas an aversion to "historicism," by which both mean the view that philosophical truth is inextricably imbedded within history. In fact, the formal philosophical similarity of Strauss's and Levinas's respective projects begins here: with each of their attempts to consider the possibility of a nonhistoricist, that is an acontextual, morality after the Nazi genocide. One of the aims of this study is to clarify Strauss's and Levinas's respective moral criticisms of the challenge of *historicism*, a complex and contentious term whose relevance has only increased in academic and popular debate.[4]

When I began working on this project a number of years ago, I described some of my ideas to a rather well-known political theorist who has some interest in Strauss. He responded with great enthusiasm, followed by the exclamation that "now Strauss's thought will be exposed for what it really is: ethnic pride." A similar assumption sometimes operates among Levinas's interpreters, who seem to fear that if the place of Judaism in Levinas's thought is central, his philosophy might be rendered ineffective or even untrue. These assumptions and conclusions could not be farther from the argument and intention of this study. An appreciation of the importance of Judaism in both Strauss's and Levinas's thoughts coheres with what I am claiming is a central part of their intellectual task, which is to insist on the historical and spiritual importance of Judaism (and not of particular Jewish people) for understanding the development and indeed the vitality of western civilization. If some find this claim suggestive of "ethnic pride," I suggest they examine the details of Strauss's and Levinas's philosophical, historical, and philological claims and develop their objections on this basis. The assumption that an interest in the intellectual and historical importance of Judaism for understanding western civilization is *by definition* suspect bespeaks a powerful prejudice (both thinking and unthinking) against which Strauss and Levinas consciously argue.

It is well known that classical Jewish texts and themes are important to both Strauss and Levinas. But Levinas increasingly is thought of as a defender of the veracity of Jewish revelation, while Strauss continues (with a few notable exceptions) to be thought of an atheist who clearly chose, to uses Strauss's terms, Athens over Jerusalem. Levinas emphasizes the harmonious interchange between Judaism and philosophy. Strauss, on the other hand, famously claims that "Jews of the philosophic competence of Halevi and Maimonides took it for granted that being a Jew and a philosopher are mutually exclusive."[5]

In the following pages, I argue in great detail that the particular readings of Levinas as a philosophical defender of revelation and Strauss as a defender of philosophy against revelation are imbedded in a post-Christian philosophical framework in which the tasks of philosophy and revelation are fused together. It is true that Levinas emphasizes the harmonious interchange between Judaism and philosophy, while Strauss emphasizes their profound if not irreconcilable tension. But, I argue, Levinas appears as a philosophical defender of revelation only because there is an unacknowledged assumption about the mutuality between philosophy and revelation. The first contention of this study is that we ought to rethink this assumption about the fusion of philosophy and revelation philosophically, theologically, historically, and politically. Once we do so, it becomes clear that the argument between Levinas and Strauss is an argument about the status of modern philosophy.

And by implication, much of the contemporary philosophical discussion of "religion," especially in continental philosophical circles, is less about the meaning of "religion" than about the meaning and scope of philosophical inquiry in the modern world. Only once we recognize this central concern with the status of contemporary philosophical thought can we begin to appreciate the implications of Levinas's and Strauss's arguments (as well as many arguments within continental philosophy) about not just Judaism but religion generally.

Levinas, I will argue, is a defender of a particular modern philosophical project that endows philosophy with social and political capabilities, while Strauss is a critic of this project. It is for this reason, I will show, Levinas ultimately fails to defend the philosophical possibility of *Jewish* revelation, for his arguments remain mired in a faith in philosophy. But as importantly, Levinas ultimately fails to defend the possibility of philosophical rationalism. Levinas throws out what he doesn't like about liberal modernity and modern rationality, but because he is tied to a modern faith in philosophy, he is unable to save philosophy for critical purposes. The result is that Levinas's philosophical program cannot maintain a coherent conception of philosophy, revelation, or politics.

To be sure, part of the difficulty of the arguments that follow in this book is that they go against the grain of some of Levinas's own self-presentation and the interpretations of his followers. I attempt to offer a suggestively fresh reading of Levinas, thereby calling into question the three dominant strands of Levinas interpretation: the first that sees him as a reviver of a Jewish philosophical tradition, the second that understands him in strictly phenomenological terms, and the third that views him as a postmodern philosopher. While Levinas's engagement with German-Jewish philosophy, and the philosophy of Franz Rosenzweig in particular, is better known than Strauss's, the straightforward acceptance of his claims by his interpreters about this relation continues to obscure Levinas's more complex relation to this body of thought and his complicated relation to the German metaphysical tradition more broadly defined. Seen in these contexts, I maintain that Levinas emerges not as a philosophical defender of "Judaism," but as a defender of the need for philosophical activity for social and political purposes after Heidegger. Levinas's *messianic* (a term he uses) faith in philosophy renders his philosophical relation to Judaism and a "Jewish philosophical tradition" problematic. At the same time, the tensions, if not contradictions, in his social and political claims for philosophical activity make it difficult to view him strictly from within the phenomenological tradition and his attempt to restore the modern subject after Heidegger calls into question his affinity with postmodernism.

A reconsideration of Levinas's thought is significant not only in and of itself but also, if not more so, because of the appeal his thought has for so many. This appeal derives from the very impetus that drives it: despair with liberal politics and strictly rational modes of analysis in an only increasingly violent world and the subsequent rejection of politics in favor of nonpolitical, what Levinas calls *ethical*, ways of being. In this sense, Levinas's thought coheres with late-twentieth-century despondency about politics generally, coupled with the simultaneous desire to respect others as "other" by way of interpersonal relations. However, Levinas's philosophy, like much of late-twentieth-century thought, remains mired in the very premises it seeks to overcome. The result is not merely philosophical incoherence, but a weakening of the critical potential to speak meaningfully about concrete political realities and also the lived realities of religious life.

While I am critical of Levinas's project, the task of this study is not to defend Strauss's positions, but rather to present his thought as important and challenging, philosophically, theologically, and politically. In terms of his political relevance, Strauss, of course, has many proponents (many of whom bitterly disagree with one another) and, increasingly, many foes. But I argue that a full appreciation of the relevance of Strauss's view of politics requires a deeper understanding of the centrality of religion, and of Judaism in distinction to Christianity, to Strauss's project. This is not to imply that Strauss was a believer in biblical revelation, but only (and sufficiently) that his own arguments show that this possibility cannot be denied philosophically.[6] At the same time, Strauss's own view of philosophy suggests a fundamental limitation to philosophy in and of itself, not just from a social or political perspective, but from a philosophical one also. I suggest that Strauss's claim for a fundamental limitation to philosophy increases the critical import of philosophy, while the overinflated claims for what philosophy can accomplish that Strauss criticizes only diminish what is philosophy's truly critical potential. While Drucilla Cornell has suggested that Levinas's philosophy can contribute to contemporary legal interpretation as a "philosophy of the limit,"[7] I argue that the problem with Levinas's thought, despite his contention that his thought overcomes a "totalizing" image of philosophy, is that it doesn't recognize a limit to philosophy and thereby has difficulty making a critical contribution to arguments about religion and politics.

Following Strauss I maintain that the possibility of philosophical, religious, and political rationalism depends on the *analytic separation* and subsequent *practical coordination* of philosophy and revelation, which concerns addressing primarily the question of political arrangements in general and the authority of law in particular. In this context, I examine what I take to be Strauss's model of religious rationalism from the perspective of contemporary Jewish law (i.e., law that lacks a political dimension), and suggest that Strauss's thought should be the starting point for Jewish philosophical thinking in the late twentieth century because Strauss gives a better account of the scope and nature of Jewish thought, of the content of Jewish thought, and the needs of post-Emancipation Jewry than other contemporary thinkers who are actually engaged in constructive Jewish thought. This isn't to argue for the veracity of Strauss's positions, however complicated they may be, but rather to claim that any constructive attempt to articulate a Jewish philosophy in the twenty-first century must begin by responding to the questions and framework raised by Strauss's thought.

Finally, given what only seems to be increasing controversy about Strauss – about whom perhaps the one thing that everyone can agree on is that there is no agreement – a few more words are in order about the perspective I take in this book. Despite claims to the contrary, I do not believe that Strauss's views are hidden and mysterious. As I will argue in great detail in the chapters that follow, Strauss's interest is in problems and not solutions. This is particularly ironic given that he is so often presented, with sometimes contradictory characterizations, as the dogmatist par excellence. Some of the continued perplexity about Strauss may be due to the fact that he insists on the complexity of the human predicament, maintaining that there are multiple human goods whose competing claims are not easily if even possibly resolved. Strauss's writing on many different subjects and in many different contexts reflects an engagement with this multiplicity. This makes Strauss a challenging writer and thinker, but not one who is given easily to simplification or, as importantly, one who is impossible to understand.[8]

Like Strauss's own project, this book is not a constructive attempt to erect a system of philosophy, theology, or politics. Instead, following Strauss, my aim is to raise questions about a number of assumptions in contemporary academic life, some of which rightly spill over into discussion of contemporary politics, ethics, and theology. These include first and foremost questions about the relations among philosophy, religion, and politics, in some of their historic and current constructions. Appropriately then, we begin to examine in Chapter 1 Strauss's and Levinas's conceptions of Athens and Jerusalem.

PART ONE

∾

PHILOSOPHY

∾

Strauss and Levinas between Athens and Jerusalem

*W*HILE THEY ARE RARELY CONSIDERED TOGETHER, THE INTELLEC-
tual biographies of Leo Strauss (1899–1973) and Emmanuel Levinas
(1906–95) are remarkably similar. Both attempt to rethink the philosophical possibility of morality after the Nazi genocide and they use many of the
same philosophical resources to do so. Both studied with Edmund Husserl
and Martin Heidegger in the 1920s, both argue against what each maintains is
the amorality of Heidegger's philosophy, and both claim the German-Jewish
philosopher Franz Rosenzweig as a, if not the, major influence in so doing. The
exegesis of classic Jewish texts matters greatly to both of them, and each claims
to be returning to Plato. Both have had significant Catholic receptions and
both continue to have important influences on contemporary discussions of
ethics and politics. Nevertheless, despite these striking historical similarities,
from the perspective of their contemporary and ever-growing receptions, one
might think that Strauss and Levinas do not have much in common, philosophically or politically, with one another. And if one made this claim, it would
be based largely on yet another remarkable similarity between Strauss and
Levinas, which are their respective constructions of the relation between what
Strauss calls "Athens" and "Jerusalem" and what Levinas calls "Greek" and
"Hebrew."

As has been argued by a number of recent interpreters, the crux of
Levinas's philosophy is his reorientation of "Greek" by way of "Hebrew."
Understood as such, Levinas is thought to be a Jewish philosopher whose
achievement is to have revived the Jewish tradition philosophically. In contrast, with the exception of a few recent interpretations, Strauss has been
viewed largely as a political philosopher for whom revelation is, at best,
of instrumental significance. While Strauss maintained that what he called
"Athens" is in necessary tension with what he called "Jerusalem," many if not
most of Strauss's interpreters continue to argue that Strauss comes down

largely on the side of Athens. As such, Levinas's decidedly Hebrew thought would seem to be opposed philosophically to Strauss's decidedly Greek thought.

In this chapter, I begin to attempt to dismantle these assumptions. I argue that there is a formal philosophical affinity between Levinas and Strauss precisely in regard to their arguments about the philosophical *possibility* of revelation. Once we appreciate this philosophical affinity we must rethink the view of Strauss as an affiliate of Athens and of Levinas as an affiliate of Jerusalem. The difference between Levinas and Strauss, I claim, ultimately reflects a disagreement about the status of modern philosophy. Levinas emerges as a defender of a particularly modern philosophical project that ascribes social and political status to philosophy, while Strauss is a critic of this very project. I suggest in the conclusion of the chapter that rethinking the place of Athens and Jerusalem in Levinas's and Strauss's philosophies may provide us not only a fuller understanding of their respective arguments, but also an opportunity to rethink the basic if unspoken premises that inform much contemporary philosophical discussion about the relation between philosophy and revelation, or between Athens and Jerusalem.

To begin to appreciate the similarities and then differences between Levinas and Strauss, I turn first to a, if not the, quintessential question in considering the relation between Athens and Jerusalem. This question concerns the very possibility of something we might call "Jewish Philosophy." Section 1.2 of the chapter considers Strauss's and Levinas's shared attempt to retrieve different forms of Platonism after Heidegger's philosophically devastating criticism of the Platonic tradition and its aftermath. Significantly, Strauss and Levinas share not only the attempt to reread Plato after Heidegger, but both also maintain that the medieval Jewish philosopher, Moses Maimonides, holds the key to doing so. This isn't to deny, of course, Strauss's and Levinas's radically different readings of Plato and Maimonides. Rather, by understanding the formal similarities of their projects it is possible to understand the root cause of their differences. In Section 1.3 of the chapter, I argue that this difference concerns their respective definitions of philosophy. In Section 1.4, I suggest Strauss's and Levinas's different conceptions of philosophy are ramified in their shared attempt to rethink human nature. In Section 1.5, I begin to develop the implications of these different views of philosophy as they relate to the definitions of Judaism particularly and religion more generally. The conclusion, Section 1.6, considers the relation between Strauss's and Levinas's conceptions of philosophy and the problem of evil.

1.1. JEWISH PHILOSOPHY BETWEEN ATHENS AND JERUSALEM

Neither Strauss nor Levinas attempts to harmonize Judaism and philosophy. For Strauss, such a harmonization is impossible because Judaism and philosophy represent two fundamentally opposed attitudes toward the world. Though they both seek wisdom, the beginnings of the wisdom of biblical religion and the beginnings of the wisdom of philosophical reflection are in marked contrast to one another. Philosophy for Strauss is the search for wisdom that begins with the thinker's unending quest for the nature of the good.[1] In contrast, Judaism is rooted in revelation, which begins not in thought, but in obedience to God and the revealed law.

Strauss argues that we must *choose* between Jerusalem and Athens not only because they are fundamentally different but also because they are in basic opposition to one another. This doesn't mean that one can't be a Jew interested in philosophy or a philosopher interested in Judaism. Indeed, as Strauss puts it, "every one of us can be and ought to be either . . . the philosopher open to the challenge of theology or the theologian open to the challenge of philosophy."[2] But this formulation only underscores Strauss's well-known statement that "being a Jew and a philosopher are mutually exclusive"[3] because such an identity is self-contradictory.

Levinas, like Strauss, does not believe in the harmonization of Judaism and philosophy, not because they are fundamentally opposed, but because they are fundamentally alike. In Levinas's words, "I have never aimed explicitly to 'harmonize' . . . both traditions. If they happen to be in harmony it is probably because every philosophical thought rests on pre-philosophical experiences, and . . . the bible has belonged to these founding experiences."[4] Judaism and philosophy are thus similarly oriented, according to Levinas. Both Judaism and philosophy approach the goodness beyond being embodied in what Levinas calls the responsibility for the other.

As Levinas puts it, "philosophy derives [*dérive*] from religion. It is called for by religion adrift [*en dérive*], and in all likelihood religion is always adrift."[5] Philosophy and religion exist in a relation of mutuality, for Levinas. Philosophy derives from religion, but philosophy also gives direction and purpose to religion. Judaism and philosophy do not need to be harmonized for Levinas because they are already in fundamental harmony with one another. Judaism or what Levinas calls elsewhere "religiosity" ("*le religieux*") is the prephilosophical stuff out of which philosophy arises. Judaism and philosophy are thus organically connected. From Levinas's perspective, Jewish philosophy is impossible because it is redundant.

Jewish philosophy is thus impossible for both Levinas and Strauss, but for opposite reasons. Because Judaism and philosophy ultimately mean the same thing, the notion of Jewish philosophy is at best superfluous for Levinas. In contrast, the notion of Jewish philosophy is incoherent for Strauss because such a notion betrays the meanings of both Judaism and philosophy.

We have seen that from a formal perspective at least there is an important, if at first unlikely, affinity between Levinas and Strauss on the question of the impossibility of Jewish philosophy. I suggest that this affinity is significant because it rests on a deeper *philosophical* agreement about the philosophical *possibility* of the truth of Judaism. While Levinas and Strauss each make a claim for the impossibility of Jewish philosophy, each also claims at the same time that "Judaism" somehow makes not Jewish philosophy possible, but philosophy possible.

Simply put, the shared claim of Levinas and Strauss is that Judaism understands something that philosophy *anticipates but cannot quite articulate* on its own terms. Significantly, Levinas and Strauss each make this point with reference to Plato. For both, Plato anticipates revelation. In *Totality and Infinity*, Levinas maintains that the true universality of reason is predicated upon Plato's conception of discourse, which "implies transcendence . . . [and] the revelation of the other to me."[6] It is this Platonic anticipation of revelation that defines ethics as first philosophy, for Levinas. *Totality and Infinity* is, as its subtitle indicates, "an essay on exteriority." Philosophy, for Levinas, anticipates the exteriority of revelation. As such, philosophy is bound to revelation, which reorients philosophy. *Totality and Infinity* ends with a succinct summary of this reorientation:

Freedom is not justified by freedom. To account for being or to be in truth is not to comprehend nor to take hold of . . . , but rather to encounter the Other without allergy, that is, in justice.[7]

Freedom, for Levinas, which includes philosophical freedom, cannot justify itself on its own terms. My freedom is justified by the other, by the other's revelation to me.

Strauss, from a formal perspective at least, makes this very argument about philosophy's bondage to revelation. Note Strauss's very Levinasian formulation in *Philosophy and Law*, in which he argues that philosophy's "*freedom depends upon its bondage. Philosophy is not sovereign. The beginning of philosophy is not the beginning simply.*"[8] While *Philosophy and Law* is admittedly a transitional work for Strauss, the theme of philosophy's dependence on and anticipation of revelation marks Strauss's mature work. Recall, for instance,

Strauss's argument in *Natural Right and History* that: "Philosophy has to grant that revelation is possible. But to grant that revelation is possible means to grant that philosophy is perhaps not the one thing needful ... or that philosophy suffers from a fatal weakness."[9] The notion that philosophy requires and anticipates revelation is a constant theme throughout Strauss's writings, a theme that, from a formal perspective at least, parallels Levinas's own arguments. Of course, the objection to this statement will be, in its strongest form, that Strauss rejects Jerusalem for the sake of Athens or, at the very least, that we don't know where Strauss comes down on the question of Jerusalem or Athens. In my view, this often stated objection (whatever its form) misses the mark and here the parallels with Levinas are not only important but also decisive.

But before turning to the implications of comparing Strauss with Levinas for understanding Strauss's view of revelation, it is important to note that even on "Straussian" terms the question about Strauss's "own" view of revelation skews the *philosophical* question that Strauss poses in regard to revelation. As Strauss puts it in regard to Nietzsche, "Through judging others, Nietzsche had himself established the criterion by which his doctrine is to be judged."[10] While a full treatment of Straussian hermeneutics and even more so debates about Strauss's hermeneutics are beyond the scope of this chapter (but will be discussed in greater detail in Part 3 of this book), it is important to mention that among the criteria by which Strauss is to be judged is Strauss's own claim that "the problem inherent in the surface of things, and only in the surface of things, is the heart of things."[11] As Strauss puts it in his discussion of the tension between Jerusalem and Athens, "If we wish to understand Plato, we must take him seriously. We must take seriously in particular his defense of Socrates."[12] Just as Strauss urges us to take seriously Plato's defense of Socrates if we are to take Plato seriously, if we are to take Strauss seriously we must take seriously Strauss's philosophical arguments about revelation. A comparison with Levinas, I suggest, allows us to appreciate the serious philosophical nature of Strauss's arguments about revelation.

If I am right, as I have argued that Jewish philosophy is as impossible for Levinas as it is for Strauss, then what we are able to see is that Levinas and Strauss make very similar claims about the *philosophical status of revelation.* Indeed, both of their arguments concern not the philosophical veracity of "Judaism" and revelation – for both Levinas and Strauss, such a proof would be impossible – but the inadequacy of philosophy conceived without "Judaism" or revelation. Indeed, Strauss, like Levinas, poses a fundamental question about philosophy's need to recognize its own possible bondage to something outside of philosophy. Understood in this way, it does not matter what Strauss's "own" views of revelation actually are for the *philosophical* question remains the same: does philosophy require the philosophical possibility of revelation?

To begin to answer this question, let us return to Strauss's treatment of Plato. Like Levinas, Strauss makes his argument about the philosophical need of revelation with reference to Plato. For Strauss, it is the Plato of the *Laws* and not of the *Republic* (or as Levinas argues in greater detail in *Totality and Infinity*: the Plato of the *Phaedrus*) that is definitive for recognizing philosophy's anticipation of revelation. While I do not mean to discount the different conceptions of ethics and politics that emerge from Strauss's and Levinas's respective interpretations of Plato, note the striking formal similarity of Strauss's and Levinas's use of Plato. Each uses Plato to argue for philosophy's anticipation of revelation. Strauss argues that in the *Laws*:

Plato transforms the 'divine laws' of Greek antiquity into truly divine laws, or recognizes them as truly divine laws. In this approximation to the revelation without the guidance of the revelation we grasp at its origin the unbelieving, philosophic foundation of the belief in revelation.... Platonic philosophy had suffered from an *aporia* in principle that had been remedied only by the revelation.[13]

Here Strauss's argument is in the service of establishing an analysis of the life world of medieval Jewish philosophy in which "before *all* philosophizing the fact of revelation remains firm."[14] Like Levinas, Strauss attempts to describe the prephilosophical life world out of which philosophy arises. As Levinas does for the Bible, Strauss does for medieval Jewish philosophy. Levinas's and Strauss's analyses of these respective premodern "Jewish" life worlds are in the service of establishing the *possibility* of the truth of revelation, a possibility that for both Levinas and Strauss must alter our very conceptions of ethics and politics in the contemporary world. As Levinas puts it in the outline of his doctoral thesis, which became *Totality and Infinity*, ethics:

is not a byproduct of self-knowledge. It is completely heteronomous.... To state that the Other, revealed by the visage, is the first intelligible ... is to affirm also the independence of ethics with regard to history.... To show that the first signification emerges in morality ... is a return to Platonism.[15]

1.2. AFTER HEIDEGGER: MAIMONIDES BETWEEN ATHENS AND JERUSALEM

Levinas's and Strauss's shared interest in returning to Plato is historically specific. Both respond to the Nazi genocide by searching for a way to speak with authority about morality and both consider a return to Platonism the possibility for doing so. While Strauss's interest in a philosophical turn to Plato took place in the 1930s (as we will see in the following discussion of *Philosophy and Law*), his mature reading of Plato developed in the context of his attempt to respond to the rise of National Socialism. There were also philosophical seeds of Levinas's interest in returning to Plato in the 1930s. But like Strauss's developed thought, Levinas's mature understanding of Plato took place in the context of an attempt to respond to the moral challenge posed by National Socialism. In their mature attempts to return to Plato, both respond philosophically first and foremost to Martin Heidegger's effort to put an end to the metaphysical tradition. For both Strauss and Levinas, in declaring an end to metaphysics Heidegger also declared an end to absolute claims about morality.

In a 1957 lecture titled "The Onto-theological Constitution of Metaphysics" (a lecture that concluded a course on Hegel's *Science of Logic*), Heidegger argued that the western philosophical tradition is onto-theological in nature. Onto-theology is the metaphysical quest to ground the being of entities in the being of a highest entity, but onto-theology also characterizes what Heidegger contends is the western philosophical tradition's fundamental forgetfulness of Being. Heidegger maintained that theology's quest to ground the being of entities in the being of a highest entity is made possible by the error of metaphysics, which is the inability to distinguish between the being of entities and the being of Being. The overcoming of metaphysics, for Heidegger, is thus by definition also the overcoming of theology (which he understands as always being "onto-theology"), as it has been known historically.

From Levinas's and Strauss's perspectives, Jewish thought does not fit into Heidegger's category of onto-theology because it is *not* concerned primarily with onto-theological issues (such as foundational or metaphysical *proofs* of God's existence). But this doesn't mean, however, that Jewish thought is not concerned with metaphysics. The possibility of a return to metaphysics for Levinas and Strauss is not fundamentally ontological in character. Rather, Levinas and Strauss both maintain that Jewish thought is concerned with a kind of metaphysics that is not utilized for the purpose of ontological grounding, but rather for its ethical or political implications.

To be sure, it is important to distinguish Levinas's notion of ethics from Strauss's notion of politics. The former concerns, as Levinas might put it, being for the other, while the latter concerns, as Strauss might put it, the collective pursuit of the good life, or justice.[16] There is no doubt that the rhetoric of Levinas's descriptions of ethics and Strauss's descriptions of politics are exceptionally different. Yet the definitions of what Levinas calls ethics and what Strauss calls politics are in a significant sense remarkably similar. We can appreciate this similarity by turning briefly to Maimonides's discussion of the relation between the perfection of the body and the perfection of the soul, a discussion to which neither Levinas nor Strauss refers, but which, I suggest, nonetheless illuminates this important overlap in their thoughts.

Levinas's view of ethics is captured in the phrase he is fond of quoting from Rabbi Israel Salanter, the sage of the nineteenth-century Mussar movement: "The other's material needs are my spiritual needs."[17] In keeping with Maimonides, I suggest, Strauss's view of politics is also predicated on the notion of the just fulfillment of the physical needs of others. Maimonides maintains in the *Guide of the Perplexed* that:

It is obvious that this ultimate perfection [of the soul] does not carry with it any actions or moral qualities ... [yet] this glorious ultimate perfection cannot be attained unless the first form of perfection [of the body] has been achieved. ... The true law, which, as we have explained, is the only and unique one, namely the law of Moses, has been given so as to bestow upon us the two kinds of perfection [of the body and the soul] together. It [the perfection of the body] provides for the improvement of human relationships by removing injustice and inculcating good and generous habits.[18]

For Maimonides, the political good involves, as Levinas would have it in terms of ethics, the fulfillment of physical needs, of "food and other requisites of his body, such as shelter, baths, etc."[19] Beyond rhetoric, Strauss's conception of the requirements of politics parallels Levinas's conception of the requirements of ethics. Politics for Strauss, and ethics for Levinas, concerns the physical needs of other people.

Where Levinas differs from Strauss is in insisting that there is no equal or higher good than meeting the physical needs of others.[20] As Strauss puts it, in a statement that very much parallels, but does not cite Maimonides, "The philosopher is the man who dedicates his life to the quest of knowledge of the good, of the idea of the good; what we would call moral virtue is only the condition or by-product of that quest."[21] For Levinas, meeting the physical needs of the other constitutes ethics. One of the tasks of this book is to consider more deeply the implications, and indeed the *ethical* implications, of this difference between Levinas and Strauss. In Part 3 of this book we will deal with these implications more fully. Here, however, we need first to appreciate the formal similarities between Strauss's and Levinas's thought to begin to gauge their real differences.

Both Levinas and Strauss claim that it is necessary to reread Plato after Heidegger and Jewish revelation, and particularly the philosophy of Mai-monides, makes it possible to do so. As Heidegger remarked in his Nietzsche lectures, ". . . all Western philosophy is Platonism. Metaphysics, Idealism, and Platonism mean essentially the same thing . . . Plato has become the prototypal philosopher."[22] In an early work defining his philosophical agenda, Levinas revalues this very assertion of Heidegger's, declaring that "all philosophy is Platonic."[23] Levinas, like Strauss, seeks to resuscitate Plato after Heidegger has declared an end of metaphysics. For both Levinas and Strauss, it is not just *biblical revelation*, but more specifically the coordination of Athens and Jerusalem or Greek and Hebrew, *in Maimonides's thought*, which holds the key to rereading Plato after Heidegger.

Like Levinas, Strauss argues that Maimonides is truly a Platonist. It is striking that in 1935, the year Strauss published *Philosophy and Law* in which he first begins to make his arguments about Maimonides and Plato and their possible relevance for contemporary debates, Levinas published an article entitled "The Currency of Maimonides" in which he praised Maimonides for his fight against paganism in his synthesis of Judaism and philosophy.[24] As Levinas succinctly put it in a later work, "Judaism feels very close to the West, by which I mean philosophy. It is not by virtue of simple chance that the way towards the synthesis of the Jewish revelation and Greek thought was masterfully traced by Maimonides. . . ."[25] Levinas's and Strauss's respective readings of Maimonides in the mid-1930s would provide the seeds for each of their mature philosophies. Whereas Levinas saw himself as continuing what he regarded as Maimonides's "medieval synthesis," Strauss understood himself as furthering Maimonides's deep insight that Athens and Jerusalem cannot be synthesized (though again they can and must be coordinated).

This disagreement about the possibility of a medieval synthesis is, of course, the fundamental difference between Levinas's and Strauss's reading of Maimonides, a difference that is noted by Levinas in a comment whose referent seems to be Strauss. Levinas states that

Maimonides is not an accident of Holy History. . . . [I]n Maimonides himself, to whom rational knowledge of God, metaphysical knowledge, is the supreme good of the human person . . . everything culminates in the formation of the negative attributes. But the possibility of this knowledge is maintained as the ethical behavior of goodwill (*hesed*), judgment (*mishpat*), and fairness (*tsedeqah*), as 'for the other.' The imitation of God! The love of one's neighbor is at the summit of a life devoted to supreme knowledge. *This is a remarkable reversal, unless we are to question the sincerity of this teacher, suggesting that he may have spoken otherwise than he thought, to avoid unsettling pious minds.*[26]

In what Levinas calls Maimonides's "remarkable reversal," we find a summary of Levinas's own philosophical project: to present what he calls metaphysical

knowledge that is not fundamentally ontological in nature, but is ethical. It is
Strauss who has, in Levinas's words, questioned "the sincerity of this teacher,"
a position that Levinas dismisses.

Levinas's one published reference to Strauss comes by way of his discussion of the question of whether there is anything positive to be learned from
Spinoza's legacy. There is no reason to conclude that Levinas necessarily read
Strauss because this one reference to him refers to Strauss as "an American
philosopher," and also, more importantly, because Levinas's remarks come
in the context of his appreciative comments of a 1965 book on Spinoza by
Sylvain Zac that deals with Strauss.[27] What is relevant for our purpose is that
in his brief statements about Strauss, Levinas offers a fairly standard reading
of Strauss, a reading that this book seeks to complicate. Levinas writes:

Does Spinoza, in his *Tractatus Theologico-Politicus*, hide his real thought and
the mortal blows, visible to anyone who can read, dealt to the authority of the
Scriptures and the religions they found? The American philosopher Leo Strauss
has in fact invited us to see a cryptogram in the whole of philosophy, even in the
work of Maimonides, in which Reason secretly fights against religion.[28]

Even if he is not referring directly to these essays, the context of Levinas's
remarks about Spinoza and Maimonides is Strauss's 1948 essay on Spinoza,
"How to Study Spinoza's Theologico-Political Treatise," and his 1941 essay,
"The Literary Character of *The Guide for the Perplexed*."[29] Here however,
we must simply note that in his 1941 Maimonides essay, Strauss argues that
contrary to the general consensus that in the *Guide* Maimonides attempts to
reconcile philosophy and revelation (a view put forward by Maimonides), the
argument of the *Guide* is that philosophy and revelation are irreconcilable.[30]
But much to the perplexity of his own interpreters, Strauss, in this essay
and later ones on Maimonides, never explicitly states what he takes to be
Maimonides's view of the implications of this argument. We see that Levinas
infers from Strauss's suggestion that philosophy and revelation are irreconcilable that Maimonides must therefore have been insincere in writing to his
readers.

Whether Strauss considers Maimonides insincere is a matter not only of
interpretations but also of speculation. And one's interpretation of and speculation about this question will depend in large part on whether one accepts or
rejects Strauss's basic premise, which is that revealed religion and philosophy
are fundamentally irreconcilable. We should be clear first that *this irreconcil-
ability doesn't mean for Strauss that revealed religion is irrational and that philosophy is rational.* For Strauss, the tension between revelation and philosophy
is not one between irrationality and rationality, but between fundamentally

irreconcilable criteria for what constitutes the *starting point* of truth. Philoso-phy begins and ends for Strauss with the philosopher's sense of wonder, while revealed religion begins and ends with adherence to the divine law. Nonethe-less, in an important sense, the philosopher and the believer share more with each other than they differ from each other. Both begin with nonrational cri-teria, yet both subsequently move toward rationality in attempting to provide reasons for the life of the philosopher or believer.

The philosopher, Strauss maintains, believes that his own judgment is the starting point of all knowledge. Yet this can only be the case after the philoso-pher faithfully commits to the philosophical life.[31] However, Strauss contends that this common path poses no problem for revealed religion because the believer wholly acknowledges that his source of truth, revelation, comes from outside of himself: from God. Philosophy's weakness in regard to revelation lies here because the philosopher unlike the believer contends that the source and final authority of truth comes from the philosopher. Revelation's weak-ness in regard to philosophy, on the other hand, lies in the impossibility of making revelation wholly evident on the basis of human experience. Neverthe-less, despite this mutual tension between philosophy and revelation, between Athens and Jerusalem, "the Bible and Greek philosophy agree not merely regarding the place which they assign to justice, the connection between jus-tice and law, the character of law, and divine retribution. They also agree regarding the problem of justice, the difficulty created by the misery of the just and the prospering of the wicked."[32]

Strauss's contention about the difference between philosophy and revela-tion is rooted in his definition of philosophy: "philosophy is meant – and that is the decisive point – not as a set of propositions, a teaching, or even a sys-tem, but as a way of life, a life animated by a peculiar passion, the philosophic desire, or *eros*; it is not understood as an instrument or a department of human self-realization."[33] As a way of life, "the problems are always more evident than the solutions. All solutions are questionable. . . . Therefore, the right way of life cannot be established metaphysically except by a completed metaphysics, and therefore the right way of life remains questionable."[34] Referring to, but without citing, the response of the Israelites upon the receiving of the divine law – "*na'aseh v'nishma*," "we will do and (then) we will hear" (Exodus 24:27) – Strauss writes, "By saying that we wish to hear first and then to act to decide, we have already decided in favor of Athens against Jerusalem."[35] In Chapter 8, we will have occasion to discuss Levinas's interpretation, in one of his Talmudic readings, of this very verse from Exodus. Here, however, we need to recognize that the question of whether Strauss thought Maimonides was insincere, as many critics and fans of Strauss suggest, is the wrong question.

The question to be asking is whether the tension between the starting points of philosophy and revealed religion is *philosophically* irreconcilable. If one disagrees with Strauss's premise that these assumptions are irreconcilable, it is difficult to imagine that Strauss considers Maimonides philosophically sincere. On the other hand, if one takes Strauss's premise seriously – that the relation between revealed religion and philosophy is *philosophically,* though not politically, irreconcilable – then one might understand Strauss's reading of Maimonides as a reflection on what Strauss argues (and argues that Maimonides argues) is a, if not the, *profound* philosophical problem.

Where Strauss comes down on the question of "what Maimonides really thought" is a complicated topic beyond the scope of this chapter.[36] That said, I would venture to claim that Strauss does increasingly regard Maimonides's view of the truth of revelation as doubtful. Even if this is the case, it does not change, as Strauss says, the question of whether philosophy and revealed religion are philosophically irreconcilable. The question in regard to Strauss's interpretation of Maimonides then is not whether Maimonides is insincere or not, but whether Maimonides is a philosopher, in Strauss's sense of the term, which means one who begins and ends his reflection by virtue of his own sense of wonder and not by divine authority.[37]

As Kenneth Hart Green has shown, Strauss's attitude toward Maimonides's view of revelation shifted over time, but Maimonides nonetheless remained a central model for Strauss throughout his career. I'd like to add to Green's thesis about the importance of Strauss's engagement with Maimonides the view that it doesn't matter philosophically what Strauss thought Maimonides thought about revelation. Nor does it matter *philosophically* if Strauss was personally a nonbeliever. The *philosophical* issue that Strauss is interested in (and claims Maimonides is interested in) is the tension between philosophy and revealed religion. And part of taking this tension seriously for Strauss is an acknowledgement of the fundamental *limitations of philosophy* when it comes to grounding and articulating the bases of ethical and political life.

For Strauss, it is revelation, and not philosophy, that can ground ethical and political life. As he puts it in *Philosophy and Law,*

The necessary connection between politics and theology (metaphysics)... vouches for the fact that the interpretation of medieval Jewish philosophy beginning from Platonic politics (and not from the *Timaeus* or from Aristotelian metaphysics) does not have to lose sight of the metaphysical problems that stand in the foreground for the medieval philosophers themselves. And this procedure, so far from resulting in the underestimation of these problems, actually offers the only guarantee of understanding their proper, that is their human, meaning. If, on the other hand, one begins with the metaphysical problems, one misses ... the political problem, in which is concealed nothing less than the foundation of philosophy, the philosophic elucidation of the presupposition of philosophizing.[38]

Once again, the form of Strauss's argument brings him closer to Levinas. The relation between Athens and Jerusalem for Strauss, as for Levinas, serves political and ethical ends, again understood as the fulfilling of the material needs of others. For both, Athens and Jerusalem exist in a necessary tension. Metaphysical speculation philosophically secures the ethical possibilities of society, but politics and ethics make metaphysics possible in the first place. As Strauss puts it, "the philosophic foundation of the law, in spite of outward appearances, is not *a* teaching among others but is the place in the system of the Islamic Aristotelians and their Jewish pupils where the *presupposition* of their philosophizing comes under discussion."[39]

1.3. THE SCOPE OF PHILOSOPHY

In regarding philosophy as asocial and religion as social Strauss is more Heideggarian than Levinas.[40] Strauss shares with Heidegger the notion that philosophy is grounded upon a prior sociality for which philosophy cannot account. And Strauss concludes with Heidegger that philosophy is incapable of transcending sociality. Instead of concluding too quickly that Strauss wants to maintain an illiberal elite-mass distinction (which still may be the case), we must first recognize that Strauss insists on a fundamental limitation of philosophy as it has come to be understood in the modern period. Strauss's view of the moral and political limitation of philosophy has everything to do with his association of "religion" with the public and social sphere. Strauss's argument in this regard is intimately connected to what is, historically, an accurate depiction of Jewish religion. Jewish religion, as opposed to Protestant religion, is concerned fundamentally (though not exclusively) with outer forms of social life, forms that are enacted primarily in public.[41]

Here the contrast with Levinas is instructive. Levinas wants to maintain that philosophy *can* ultimately account for the *truth* of religion and that this accounting has profound social implications (indeed, one could sum up Levinas's entire project with this one sentence). Contending that prophecy is the "fundamental fact of man's humanity," Levinas argues that "next to the unlimited ethical exigency, prophecy interprets itself in concrete forms. . . . In these concrete forms, become religions, men find consolations. But this by no means puts the rigorous structure I [Levinas] have tried to define back into doubt."[42] The rigorous structure that Levinas has in mind is the result of philosophical reflection. Levinas argues that religions offer consolation, while philosophy may not and that "a humanity which can do without these consolations perhaps may not be worthy of them."[43] Nevertheless, it is philosophy that articulates the truth of religion and marks what for Levinas is the deep structure of human existence, one that is "beyond every sacramental signification."[44] Philosophy does not overcome the truth of religion, for Levinas, but nonetheless articulates the ground of this very truth in a kind of transcendental reflection that has universal implications for human behavior.

Let us now turn back to the question with which we began in Section 1.1: is something called "Jewish philosophy" possible? I have argued that Levinas's and Strauss's arguments for the impossibility of Jewish philosophy are premised on a shared argument for the philosophical possibility of the truth of revelation. I would like to suggest that as such, when compared with one another, Levinas's and Strauss's philosophies do enact *philosophically* a type of late-twentieth-century Jewish philosophy. Jewish philosophy would here be defined only by the negative task of showing philosophically that Jewish revelation cannot be disproved philosophically and that this conclusion has profound implications *for philosophy*. Indeed, both Levinas and Strauss fit Strauss's description of Judah Halevi's argument in the *Kuzari*:

In defending Judaism, which according to him [Halevi], is the only true revealed religion, against the philosophers, he was conscious of defending morality itself and therewith the cause, not only of Judaism, but of mankind at large. His basic objection to philosophy was then not particularly Jewish, nor even particularly religious, but moral.[45]

The Jewish philosophy of Levinas and Strauss is thus in the service of defending morality to humanity at large. Part of the goal of this chapter has been to show not only that there is a profound, if at first unlikely, *philosophical* affinity between Levinas and Strauss but that Strauss's thought fits this characterization of Jewish philosophy.

If comparing Levinas and Strauss helps us to rethink Strauss's place within the context of the rubric of Jewish philosophy, the comparison also helps us to rethink Levinas in a number of other ways. Perhaps ironically, comparing Levinas and Strauss on the impossibility and possibility of Jewish philosophy shows Levinas to be more a defender of philosophy than Strauss. Indeed, this is the implication of their difference on the relationship between Judaism and philosophy. To return to Strauss's characterization of Halevi, Strauss writes:

by going so far with the philosophers . . . he [Halevi] discover[s] the weakness of the philosophic position and the deepest reason why philosophy is so enormously dangerous. For if the philosophers are right in their appraisal of natural morality, of morality not based on Divine revelation, natural morality is . . . *no morality at all*.[46]

Strauss emerges here as the defender of the moral necessity of revelation against Levinas who maintains that philosophy is not fundamentally agnostic and that therefore "at no moment . . . [does] the Western philosophical tradition in my eyes lose its right to the last word."[47] Whereas Strauss argues that philosophy qua philosophy cannot give the law (or revelation) to itself, the implication of Levinas's philosophy is that philosophy qua philosophy can come to revelation on its own terms.[48] Could it be then that, contrary to the petrified positions on Levinas and Strauss, Levinas is a modern defender of philosophy and Strauss is a defender of revelation?

As a preliminary answer, I would venture, "yes." Recall Levinas's statement, "philosophy derives [*dérive*] from religion. It is called for by religion adrift [*en dérive*], and in all likelihood religion is always adrift." While Levinas is critical of aspects of the western philosophical tradition, his task is to return this tradition to what he argues is its true meaning: Plato's notion of a good beyond being. As Levinas puts it in an interview, "Despite the end of Eurocentrism, disqualified by so many horrors, I believe in the eminence of the human face expressed in Greek Letters and in our own, which owe the Greeks everything. It is thanks to them that our history makes us ashamed."[49] One could argue that Strauss's task also is to return the western philosophical tradition to its former glory. While this is certainly one aspect of Strauss's project, the comparison with Levinas allows us to see that for Strauss, philosophy is much more limited when it comes to ethical and political matters than it is for Levinas. This isn't to deny the importance of philosophy for Strauss, but rather to emphasize the classical character of Strauss's understanding of philosophy as a way of life that by definition questions all purported solutions to the question of how the human being ought to live. For this reason, Strauss argues strongly that philosophy *itself* cannot articulate a universal ground for morality, while Levinas contends that it is a matter of finding the right philosophy to articulate this universal ground.

Strauss argues that philosophy is fundamentally limited, but he nevertheless reserves a role for philosophy in social and moral thought. Strauss argues perhaps most clearly in *Natural Right and History* that if philosophers acknowledge the philosophical relevance of the nonphilosophical foundation of revelation, philosophers have a clarifying role in deducing a social philosophy. Yet if philosophers do not acknowledge the possibility of revelation, philosophers can only have an adversarial role in regard to social and moral philosophy. This is because for Strauss philosophy is not fundamentally social in character.

Levinas assumes a social and political status for philosophy that Strauss puts into question. In Strauss's words:

In most of the current reflections on the relation between philosophy and society, it is somehow taken for granted that philosophy always possessed political or social status.... Here, we are touching on what, from the point of view of the sociology of philosophy, is the most important difference between Christianity on the one hand, and Islam as well as Judaism on the other. For the Christian, the sacred doctrine is revealed theology; for the Jew and the Muslim, the sacred doctrine is, at least primarily the legal interpretation of the Divine Law (*talmud* or *fiqh*). The sacred doctrine in the latter sense has, to say the least, much less in common with philosophy than the sacred doctrine in the former sense. It is ultimately for this reason that the status of philosophy was, as a matter of principle, much more precarious in Judaism and in Islam than in Christianity: in Christianity philosophy became an integral part of the officially recognized and even required training of the student of the sacred doctrine. This difference explains partly the eventual collapse of philosophic inquiry in the Islamic and in the Jewish world, a collapse which has no parallel in the Western Christian world.[50]

This long quotation comes from the introduction to Strauss's *Persecution and the Art of Writing*. In this context, Strauss maintains that awareness of the historical lack of social status of philosophy should alert us to the complex relation between esoteric and exoteric writing. While I have certainly not provided a comprehensive account of Strauss's view of esoteric writing, to be discussed in greater detail in Part 3 of this book, I have suggested in this chapter that Strauss's concern with esotericism is rooted in what he considers the profound philosophical problem of the relation between philosophy and revelation. Rather than focusing here on Strauss's account of esotericism, however, I would like to focus now very briefly on the philosophical and historical issues that Strauss raises here in regard to contemporary conceptions of what philosophy "is."

While Levinas and Strauss share with Heidegger the notion that philosophy's most fundamental insight begins in and does not transcend our natural attitude toward the world, Levinas maintains a role for philosophy that is closer to Husserl's than it is to Heidegger's.[51] As such, Levinas is a defender of a particularly modern, philosophical project: to articulate a universal, philosophical account of what it means to be human. No doubt, the endpoints of Husserl's and Levinas's projects are different. For Husserl, the task of phenomenology is to "know thy self."[52] For Levinas, the task of phenomenology is recognition of how the other constitutes me. Nonetheless, Levinas understands his philosophy as continuous with the Husserlian project. As Levinas puts it, my philosophy would consist in seeing that the identity of the *me* and of this "I think" is not equal to the task of encompassing the 'other man,' precisely because of the alterity and irreducible transcendence of the other. . . . The framework of Husserlian phenomenology may have been broken open in the course of the transcendental analysis, but the 'destruction' of the dominant *me* in which it was anchored is not some step along the way to the insignificance of the person. . . . The 'discovery' of others (not as *datum* exactly, but as a face!) subverts the transcendental approach of the *I*, but retains the egological primacy of this *I* that remains unique and chosen in its incontestable responsibility.[53]

Much like Heidegger, Strauss maintains that philosophy cannot ground or even articulate, on its own terms, social practice.[54] Levinas, in contrast, argues that the modern philosophical project of providing a transcendental description of the self – albeit a self who is beholden to another – is one worth maintaining, preserving, and revitalizing.

1.4. BACK TO NATURE?

We can begin to appreciate Levinas's and Strauss's different conceptions of philosophy by turning once again to another remarkable parallelism between their projects, which is their shared interest in articulating a conception of human nature in response to the Nazi genocide. In keeping with the general argument of this chapter, my suggestion is that once we appreciate the similarity of Levinas's and Strauss's quests to rethink human nature, we can also appreciate their profound difference, which concerns philosophy's relation to human nature. Strauss's concern with the possibility of rethinking nature after Spinoza and Hobbes is well known, though not necessarily well understood given the disputes between various "Straussians" especially on this matter.[55] There is, of course, much more to be said about Strauss on natural right, which I turn to in greater detail in Chapter 6, but in this context we need only note the general contours of his central occupation with rethinking "nature" to bring to focus Levinas's less acknowledged, though actually more obvious and definite, attempt to resurrect a very particular conception of "nature."

Strauss's concern with "nature" is with human nature.[56] As he puts it in *Natural Right and History*: "For, however indifferent to moral distinctions the cosmic order may be thought to be, human nature, as distinguished from nature in general, may very well be the basis of such distinctions . . . the fact that atoms are beyond good and bad does not justify the inference that there is nothing by nature good or bad for any compounds of atoms, and especially for those compounds we call 'men.'"[57] Note that Strauss does not write that human nature *does* provide the basis for the distinction between good and bad, but only that it *may*. Despite the way in which he is often interpreted, Strauss does not provide a final definition of nature. Rather, the question of nature is precisely a question. Strauss's concern is not with final definitions, but with the question of what is lost and gained for the meaning of what it is to be human by *not* asking questions about the nature of human beings. Describing his Walgreen Lectures (published as *Natural Right and History*) in a letter to Eric Voeglin in 1950, Strauss wrote "I do nothing more than present the *problem* of natural right as an unsolved problem."[58]

While Levinas does not explicitly announce his intention to rethink human nature as Strauss does, the definitive and detailed attempt to consider the nature of human being is in an important sense more specific to his project than it is to Strauss's. Many, if not most, of Levinas's central motifs for describing "the ethical" are taken from "nature." For instance, Levinas describes the ethical relation as "paternity," "maternity," "senescence," and "fraternity." As he puts it, "The biological human brotherhood – conceived with the sober coldness of Cain – is not a sufficient reason for me to be responsible as a separated being. The sober coldness of Cain consists in conceiving responsibility as proceeding from freedom in terms of a contract. But responsibility for another comes from what is prior to my freedom. . . . Responsibility does not come from fraternity, but fraternity denotes responsibility for another, antecedent to my freedom."[59] Notice that Levinas does not deny biology, but rather maintains that biology has a deeper, ethical meaning. Put another way, Levinas contends that our natural being is our ethical being.

Levinas's view of the "naturalness" of ethics is expressed perhaps most basically in his understanding of our natural condition, which is that we age.[60] For Levinas, the passivity of senescence, the natural condition par excellence, mirrors the ethical relation. "In the patience of senescence what is unexceptionable in proximity is articulated, [which is] the responsibility for the other man."[61] Levinas's argument is that the fact that I am, as a human being, by nature a being who ages, despite myself, points to the nature of the ethical relation in which I am passively for the other. While there is much to be said here about Levinas's contentions in *Otherwise than Being*, and how they relate to his earlier claims in *Totality and Infinity*,[62] what we need to note for our purposes is the increased intensity with which Levinas equates the natural state of being a human being with ethics. His argument is that the natural *is* the ethical.

This claim will no doubt be surprising to some familiar with Levinas's work because Levinas is actually often at pains to criticize what he calls "nature." But I want to point out that when Levinas uses the term *nature* negatively he does so, as he acknowledges, with a post-Hobbesian view of nature in mind.[63]

Yet, rather than a dismissal of the relevance of nature for conceiving ethics, Levinas's philosophy is a rethinking of nature to articulate the meaning of ethics. Describing his terms as deriving from biology, Levinas writes:

If biology furnishes us the prototypes of all these relations, this proves, to be sure, that biology does not represent a purely contingent order of being, unrelated to its essential production. But these relations free themselves from their biological limitation. The human I is posited in fraternity: that all men are brothers is not added to man as a moral conquest, but constitutes his ipseity.[64]

Ethics does not concern the moral conquest of nature for Levinas. Rather ethics is the moral *meaning* of nature.

Levinas's use of the term *fraternity*, in *Totality and Infinity* onward, is infused with the attempt to claim an ethical meaning for a concept of nature. Fraternity is for Levinas the generalized relation of responsibility for the other that stems from the unique relationship between father and son. As such, fraternity concerns both equality and unique responsibility. In Levinas's words:

The unique child, as elected one, is accordingly at the same time unique and non-unique. Paternity is produced as an innumerable future; the I engendered exists at the same time as unique in the world and as brother among brothers. I am I and chosen one, but where can I be chosen, if not among other chosen ones, among equals? The I as I hence remains turned ethically to the face of the other: fraternity is the very relation with the face in which at the same time my election and equality, that is, the mastery exercised over me by the other are accomplished.[65]

Levinas's explication of the ethics of fraternity is rooted in the "natural" model that he presents. My brother is my brother only by virtue of my uniqueness, which concerns my father's relationship to me.[66] We are equal in that we are brothers, yet our equality derives from an asymmetrical relation in which my father is uniquely responsible for me. Levinas's notion of fraternity is not a liberal notion of natural equality. On the contrary, the equality of fraternity for Levinas concerns, as he states, "the mastery exercised over me by the other." We are all equal in our unique responsibility, Levinas argues, but this implies not my independence from the other but the servitude I owe him:

Thou shalt not kill' – that means then 'Thou shalt cause thy neighbor to live.' Events of sociality prior to all association in the name of an abstract and common 'humanity.' The right of man, absolutely and originally, takes on meaning only in the other man. A right with respect to which I am never released![67]

We see then that while their conceptions of "nature" are no doubt different from one another, Levinas shares with Strauss the attempt to rethink the meaning of the *nature* of the human being. Indeed, Strauss's and Levinas's attempts to rethink nature are coeval with their arguments about the nature of human obligation. If the liberal notion of natural equality implies corresponding rights that we have as human beings,[68] Strauss and Levinas both contend that our obligations precede and make possible our rights. As Strauss puts it, "Hobbes had to . . . deny sin because he did not recognize any primary obligation of man that takes precedence over every claim *qua* justified claim, because he understood man as by nature free, that is, without obligation. . . ."[69] And as Levinas puts it, "The Other is not transcendent because he would be free as I am; on the contrary his freedom is a superiority that comes from his very transcendence."[70]

Once we have appreciated this further formal similarity between Levinas and Strauss, we can also begin to appreciate their profound difference, which concerns the relationship of philosophy to human nature. Ironically, we see that Levinas actually has a more overdetermined *philosophical* view of "nature" than Strauss does. For Strauss, the concept of nature acts as an impetus for ongoing critical reflection. Nature, however, is not a fixed and final result of critical reflection. For Strauss, critical reflection divorced from politics, culture, and religion is by definition weaker than it is for Levinas. As Strauss puts it, "Socrates implied that disregarding the opinions about the nature of things would amount to abandoning the most important access to reality which we have, or the most important vestiges of truth which are within our reach."[71] Only by recognizing the limitations of critical reflection for grounding moral and political life, that is, only by recognizing that philosophy begins in and, *from a moral and political perspective*, cannot transcend moral and political life, can philosophy have a critical and indeed moral function within society. This recognition, Strauss maintains, embodies Socrates's break with his predecessors: "In contradistinction to his predecessors, he [Socrates] did not separate wisdom from moderation. In present-day parlance one can describe the change in question as a return to 'common sense' or to 'the world of common sense.'"[72] Most basically, while Strauss maintains that philosophy can never finally resolve the question of the meaning of human nature, Levinas believes that a philosophical articulation of human nature is precisely what is needed.

1.5. THE PHILOSOPHICAL RETURN TO RELIGION OR THE RELIGIOUS TURN TO PHILOSOPHY?

I have argued in this chapter that, in different ways, Levinas and Strauss both claim that the Jewish philosophical tradition, and the medieval Maimonidean tradition in particular, is philosophically relevant to the possible late-twentieth-century reinvigoration of western philosophy and rethinking of human nature. In terms of the form of their respective arguments, I have suggested that the basic argument between Levinas and Strauss is not so much about "revelation" *but about philosophy*. Although Levinas is today often considered a philosophical defender of Jewish revelation, I have suggested that Levinas's project is to defend the possibilities of western philosophy for directing social and political life. In contrast, I have suggested that while Strauss argues that philosophy has a clarifying role in society, he is critical of what he argues is the modern premise that philosophy has the ability to direct social and political life. As such, when compared with Levinas, Strauss emerges as a defender of the philosophical *possibility* of revelation.

A comparison and dialogue between Levinas and Strauss raises a number of basic questions about contemporary philosophical discussions about the possibilities of "religion after metaphysics." The assumption that religious truths are fundamentally "metaphysical" or "onto-theological" in character is in tension with at least some dominant aspects of the historical Jewish tradition's primary (but not exclusive) emphasis on the social and political forms of religious life. We should appreciate that the very story about "religion *after* metaphysics" so popular now in continental and increasingly American philosophical conversations may be a very particular, if not misleading story. This story is infused with what I would suggest is a particular Protestant narrative (which may not do justice to the full array of the Protestant tradition) that disassociates "religion" from public life. While it is, of course, all too simple to call this Protestant caricature, and what is likely a caricature of Protestantism, symptomatic of modernity, I'd like to suggest that there is some truth to this claim. Could it be that the dissociation of religion from public life goes hand in hand with a particularly modern claim that philosophy is capable of grounding social and political life? And could it be that a rejection of this modern role for philosophy opens up the possibilities of conceiving religion as a public, and not only private, matter?[73]

These questions are no doubt complex and will be taken up in greater detail throughout this book. Yet I would like minimally to suggest that just as the debate between Levinas and Strauss concerns the status of philosophy, contemporary debate about "religion after metaphysics" or "religion after onto-theology" reveals more about the current status (or lack of status) of philosophy than it does about religion. I am in agreement here with Hent de Vries who, in his very interesting book, *Philosophy and the Turn to Religion*, attempts "to demonstrate the philosophical relevance of the religious without resorting to the axioms or the types of argumentation of either *metaphysica specialis* (that is, ontotheology) or its mirror image, the empirical study of religion as an ontic or positive (cultural, anthropological, social, psychological, linguistic) phenomenon."[74] Yet is de Vries, or Derrida for that matter, on his own terms, justified in claiming (purportedly against Heidegger) that "one can – or, perhaps, cannot but be – on both sides of the line at once, that is to say, that this line dividing the philosophical and the theological was never given (certain or theoretically justifiable) in the first place."[75] As Derrida argues in relation to Levinas (in "Violence and Metaphysics") does not the claim that the "line dividing the philosophical and the theological" fall back to the philosophical?[76] When de Vries, following Derrida, states that in regard to religions, he is interested "less in their theological message than in the structural inflection of what is commonly held to be possible and what not," is this not a philosophical question?

If, as I have argued, questions about the "turn to religion" in much of recent continental philosophy are largely questions about the status of philosophy, what is the philosophical question that is at stake here? There are certainly strictly philosophical reasons to question the modern status of philosophy, but there are also pressing existential reasons, the most important of which are the perceived evils of the twentieth century. If philosophy in the late twentieth century has turned to religion, it did so largely in response to these particular horrors. As Derrida, drawing on Kant, writes in "Faith and Knowledge," "The possibility of *radical evil* both destroys and institutes the religious."[77] It is an attempt to respond to evil – and specifically to the evil of the Nazi genocide – that is at the heart of both Levinas's and Strauss's philosophical projects.

1.6. PHILOSOPHY AND THE PROBLEM OF EVIL

By way of conclusion, let us consider briefly Levinas's discussion of the first murder recorded in the Bible, Cain's murder of his brother Abel. We will turn then to how Strauss might interpret this story. Levinas makes much of the meaning of Abel's murder in *Totality and Infinity* and in some earlier essays now published in *Difficult Freedom*.[78] Cain's murder of Abel represents for Levinas the *moral*, though obviously not actual, impossibility of murder. As Levinas puts it:

For in reality, murder is possible, but it is possible only when one has not looked the Other in the face. The impossibility of killing is not real, but moral. The fact that the vision of the face is not an *experience*, but a moving out of oneself, a contact with another being and not simply a sensation of self, is attested to by the 'purely moral' character of this impossibility. A moral view [*regard*] measures, in the face, the uncrossable infinite in which all murderous intent is immersed and submerged. This is precisely why it leads us away from any experience or view [*regard*]: it is not *known*, but is in *society* with us. The commerce with beings begins with 'You shall not kill' does not conform to the scheme of our normal relations with the words, in which the subject knows or absorbs its object like a nourishment, the satisfaction of a need. It does not return to its point of departure to become self-contentment, self-enjoyment, or self-knowledge. It inaugurates the spiritual journey of man. A religion, for us, can follow no other path.[79]

It was only possible for Cain actually to murder Abel, Levinas argues, because he did not look at his brother's face. Here Levinas emphasizes a point made by many traditional commentaries on the narrative of Cain and Abel.[80] When Cain meets Abel in the field, the biblical text reports no verbal exchange between them. Levinas maintains that this silence between Cain and Abel results from Cain's refusal to look at his brother's face. According to Levinas's analysis, had Cain looked at his brother's face, had he listened and spoken to him, he would not have been able to murder his brother.

What is most significant for our discussion of the ultimate difference between Levinas and Strauss is the implication of Levinas's position that morality is not something that needs to be taught because it is part of our very makeup as human beings. Philosophy is not responsible for morality in the sense that it posits moral rules because as Levinas states again and again, morality is not a cognitive matter.[81] Nevertheless, philosophy can articulate on its own terms the meanings of the human face. Such a philosophical articulation is the goal of Levinas's phenomenological analyses. To use Levinas's own words, "ethics is first philosophy."

As regards religion and the veracity of any conception of divine law, Levinas's argument is that philosophy articulates the human, ethical meaning of religion and law. Levinas reads the story of God's dialogue with Cain in this way:

The personal responsibility of man with regard to man is such that God cannot annul it. This is why in the dialogue between God and Cain – 'Am I my brother's keeper?' – rabbinical commentary does not regard the question as a case of simple insolence. Instead it comes from someone who has not yet experienced human solidarity and who thinks (like many philosophers) that each exists for oneself and that everything is permitted. But God reveals to the murderer that his crime has disturbed the natural order, so the Bible puts a word of submission into the mouth of Cain: 'My punishment is greater than I can bear.' The rabbis pretend to read a new question to this response: 'Is my punishment too great to bear? Is it too heavy for the Creator who supports the heavens and the earth'?[82]

Rather than understanding God's question to and punishment of Cain as an indicator of a divine law above human will, Levinas understands these as indicating the primacy of interhuman relations and human responsibility. Levinas reads the rabbis as making precisely this point. Cain's punishment is meant as a human rebuke to God rather than a divine rebuke to the human. Cain can only recognize that the murder of his brother "disturbed the natural order" when he recognizes the centrality of human, and not divine, nature.

Levinas's faith is in the human and more narrowly in the ability of philosophy to articulate, without recourse to history, culture, or religion, what it means to be human. And it is on both of these points that Strauss parts with Levinas. The reality of evil for Strauss means that we should have faith neither in the human being who is capable of creating such suffering nor in philosophy divorced from its complex relationship to politics, culture, and religion. Philosophy in itself cannot, in the end, give an account of the necessary strictures of divine law. As I will show in greater detail in Chapter 6, from his early writings on Jewish themes to his broad argument in *Natural Right and History*, philosophy, for Strauss, can articulate a local morality, but not a universal one. Cain needs God to tell him that he is his brother's keeper. Strauss does state in *Natural Right and History* that "'the experience of history' and the less ambiguous experience of the complexity of human affairs may blur, but they cannot extinguish the evidence of those simple experiences regarding right and wrong, which are at the bottom of the philosophic contention that there is a natural right."[83] Yet, as I will argue in greater detail in Chapter 6, this contention is significantly qualified by Strauss's claim that "it is unfortunate for the defenders of justice that it is also required for the preservation of a gang of robbers: the gang could not last a single day if its members did not refrain from hurting one another, if they did not help one another, or if each member did not subordinate his own good to the good of the gang."[84] Strauss does not deny that we can know right and wrong, but he does question strongly whether philosophy in and of itself can defend a universal morality beyond that of a closed city or society.[85]

As Strauss puts it elsewhere, "only revelation can transform natural man into 'the guardian of his city,' or, to use the language of the Bible, the guardian of his brother."[86] In the absence of a particular society, Cain's murder of his brother Abel points for Strauss to the necessity of divine law for a *universal* morality.[87] The divine law teaches the human being how to act morally. This is not something that the human being can know by himself and it is not something for which any phenomenological analysis can account. For Strauss, moral education, if it is to have any universal application, as opposed to a more limited application within a closed society, begins with stepping out of the human order. This is God's lesson to Cain: God is watching. You are your brother's keeper. For Levinas, in contrast, no education is necessary for we already are moral beings. What is necessary is a philosophical articulation of our fundamental nature.

In Chapter 2 we will explore this difference between Levinas and Strauss more deeply. There I take up in more detail my claim that Levinas is a defender of a particularly modern philosophical project, while Strauss is a critic of it. To do so, I focus particularly on Levinas's and Strauss's respective analyses of Descartes. While Levinas's ethical philosophy certainly is an attempt to reformulate the modern notion of the autonomous subject, it nonetheless affirms the truth of the modern and specifically Cartesian view of a separate and separable human subject. We turn now to this topic and its significance for understanding the meanings of the philosophies of Levinas and Strauss.

Levinas's Defense of Modern Philosophy:
How Strauss Might Respond

L EVINAS IS MOST FAMOUS FOR HIS CLAIM THAT "ETHICS IS FIRST philosophy." By this he means to criticize primarily the priority given to ontology, to the question of being as such, particularly in Martin Heidegger's philosophy and more generally in the western philosophical tradition. Levinas aims to show that my obligation to another person constitutes the starting point of all truth. Philosophy cannot fully grasp what Levinas calls the "face of the other." Philosophy can, however, by way of a phenomenological retrieval, recover what ontology – the quest for the meaning of being – has forgotten: namely, the way in which the subject has already been "called" into responsibility by the revelation of the other's moral authority. In this sense, Levinas's thought challenges the "totalitarian" impulse of western ontology, which constitutes much of the western philosophical tradition. And it is Jerusalem, or Hebrew, as opposed to Athens, or Greek that, Levinas maintains, allows him to challenge philosophy's hegemony from within.

This description of Levinas's project not withstanding, I argue in this chapter that Levinas's relation to the western philosophical tradition, and to the modern philosophical tradition beginning with Descartes, is far more complex than Levinas's interpreters have allowed. While Levinas certainly does claim that the western philosophical tradition is "totalizing," he also maintains that various figures in this tradition – including first and foremost Plato and Descartes, Heidegger's villains par excellence – articulated key aspects of the ethical philosophy that he, Levinas, seeks to retrieve. I focus in this chapter on Levinas's retrieval of Descartes's philosophy to show that despite his arguments about the inability of philosophy to grasp the face of the other, Levinas's project is nothing short of a defense of the modern philosophical project after Heidegger.

My evidence for this argument is Levinas's texts and *Totality and Infinity* most particularly, in which Levinas boldly and blatantly claims that he is drawing on a number of profound Cartesian insights. Despite these obvious statements by Levinas, the scholarly literature on Levinas and Descartes is surprisingly sparse. Some attention has been given to Levinas's use of Descartes's conception of infinity and some attention has been given to Levinas's use of Descartes's evil genius in arguing for a goodness that is "beyond being."[1] Our focus in this chapter, however, is on Levinas's appropriation of Descartes's philosophy to argue for a separable, independent self.[2] Levinas's claim about ethics thus rests upon his elucidation of the subject of ethics, the "I" who is uniquely responsible. If postmodern philosophy takes as its villain the subject of the cogito, the reading of Levinas presented in this chapter calls into question the view of Levinas as a postmodern thinker. It is the separate, independent, indeed atheistic self that Levinas means to affirm in *Totality and Infinity*.

Yet surely, one might quickly reply, Levinas's subject is not Descartes's subject. I argue in what follows, however, that the subject described by *Totality and Infinity* is, according to Levinas, none other than Descartes's so-called modern subject. In an important sense, this claim isn't even a claim because Levinas says as much. If Heidegger, in *Being and Time*, takes Descartes to have expressed and determined the modern dichotomy between subject and object, Levinas seeks nothing less than to reaffirm such a distinction. To appreciate Levinas's arguments, as well as their impetus, we must turn to Levinas's debt to and reliance on Husserl's view of the ego. To be sure, Levinas completely transforms Husserl's egology into an ethics of the other. Yet against Heidegger, Levinas turns to Husserl's account of the ego to offer his view of ethics. We will see, however, that in returning to Husserl Levinas returns (as he says) to Descartes. Whereas Husserl locates Descartes's mistake in claiming that the ego is "a piece of the world,"[3] Levinas reaffirms, against Husserl, Descartes's initial impulse.

The first half of the chapter (Sections 2.1 through 2.4) focuses on Levinas's defense of modern philosophy in light of his use of Descartes. The second part of the chapter (Sections 2.5 and 2.6) attempts to understand more broadly the *meaning* of Levinas's appropriation of Descartes in the context of how we might define the task of philosophy. Following Strauss, I argue that Descartes's innovation concerned not just the invention of the modern subject per se (epitomized by a dichotomy between subject and object), but more importantly the possibility of the invention of modern philosophy, which concerns the bracketing of social and political concerns from philosophy and a forgetfulness of philosophy's proper role and place within society. The second half of the chapter thus analyzes Levinas's defense of this project in the context of what I will suggest is his puzzling claim, especially in the context of Descartes, that philosophy must first bracket social, political, and religious concerns in order then to ground these very activities. The chapter concludes (Section 2.7) by reconsidering Levinas's and Strauss's respective arguments about the relation between philosophy and revealed religion and its implications for a conception of the relation between philosophy and politics.

2.1. THE ARGUMENT OF *TOTALITY AND INFINITY*

Totality and Infinity, Levinas's first major philosophical work, does not make a linear argument. Indeed, Levinas seems to move from claim to claim without any apparent attempt to alert his readers to a clear progression of thought. A number of interpreters of Levinas have commented that this lack of linear argument is part and parcel of Levinas's philosophical claim that ethics is first philosophy. These interpreters contend that Levinas's claims about ethics do not lend themselves to propositional argument.[4] Yet I would like to suggest that while there is certainly much to be said about Levinas's style and choice of structure, *Totality and Infinity* does make a philosophical argument, one that we can outline fairly clearly. I make this claim for two reasons. First, this view conforms to Levinas's own self-understanding. Levinas very much understands himself as a philosopher in the phenomenological tradition. As such, he must have an argument to present that can be questioned, for this is the business of philosophy. Second, by appreciating the actual argument of *Totality and Infinity* we can grasp Levinas's central *philosophical* claim, which is not, as many might believe, a claim about the self's obligation to the other. While this contention, of course, marks Levinas's entire philosophical project, his central argument in *Totality and Infinity* is for a separable, independent subject. If Levinas can adequately describe and argue for such a subject, then his claim about ethics follows.

I have set myself the not small task of explaining the structure of *Totality and Infinity*. Yet despite the book's complexity, there is a structure to the book and the book's argument emerges from this structure. To appreciate this structure, we should look first to the order of the book, which I reproduce here:

Totality and Infinity, Table of Contents

Section I. The Same and the Other
   A. Metaphysics and Transcendence
   B. Separation and Discourse
   C. Truth and Justice
   D. Separation and the Absolute

Section II. Interiority and Economy
A. Separation as Life
B. Enjoyment and Representation
C. I and Dependence
D. The Dwelling
E. The World of Phenomena and Expression

Section III. Exteriority and the Face
A. Sensibility and the Face
B. Ethics and the Face
C. The Ethical Relation and Time

Section IV. Beyond the Face
A. The Ambiguity of Love
B. Phenomenology of Eros
C. Fecundity
D. Subjectivity in Eros
E. Transcendence and Fecundity
F. Filiality and Fraternity
G. The Infinity of Time

We must recognize first that while the book has four sections, the first section is different from the other three. In Section I "The Same and the Other," Levinas lays out what will be the argument, to be made in greater detail, in the next three sections. Section I has four parts that mirror the structure of the book as a whole. Part A of Section I, "Metaphysics and Transcendence" describes the broad arguments that are developed in the next three parts (B–D). In Part A of Section I, Levinas lays out his general claim that ethics precedes ontology and that ethics is transcendence. The following three parts (parts B–D) make the argument that Levinas will make in Sections II through IV of the book. Part B, "Separation and Discourse," makes in short the argument of Section II, "Interiority and Economy." Part C, "Truth and Justice," makes the argument that Section III of the book, "Exteriority and the Face," will make in greater detail. And Part D, "Separation and the Absolute," introduces the argument that will be made in Section IV, "Beyond the Face."

What then is the argument? Once again, Levinas contends that ethics is first philosophy. My obligation to another person, Levinas claims, logically precedes anything that we can say about the nature of being. The most fundamental fact of my humanity concerns this obligation I have to another person. Levinas means to upset the equation between self and other, politics and ethics, and indeed between totality and infinity. By virtue of its own language, it is possible to read *Totality and Infinity* as establishing these dichotomies. Yet Levinas's philosophical goal is much more complex. Levinas intends to show not that there is a dichotomy between self and other, politics and ethics, or totality and infinity, but rather that the latter term in each of these pairs makes possible the former term, without subsuming the reality of the former term into itself. In the case of self and other, this means that Levinas argues not for altruism, which is in fact a view of ethics predicated upon a dichotomy between self and other, but for an ethics of infinite responsibility that makes truly independent selves possible. We will have occasion later in this chapter to discuss Levinas's view of the relation between politics and ethics, and totality and infinity. But these arguments, along with Levinas's radical claim about ethics grow out of Levinas's initial contention about the separable self. Indeed, Levinas's entire argument in *Totality and Infinity* hangs on his contentions about a truly separable, independent self.

Before turning to the specifics of Levinas's arguments, let us look once again at the structure of *Totality and Infinity*. The first subtitle of each of the four parts of Section I, "Desire for the Invisible," summarizes Levinas's broad claims. Ethics for Levinas is the movement beyond the visible. The face of the other, which would seem to imply visuality, is for Levinas not graspable by vision or thought. Desire for the invisible is for Levinas the desire for infinity. However, the desire for the invisible can only happen within the visible. Hence, an account of the invisible requires an account of the visible. An account of infinity requires an account of totality. If the desire for the invisible is the task of ethics (and Levinas begins his study by stating that it is) then he must first provide an account of the visible. This is the goal of Parts B–D of Section I. Again, these parts mirror the more detailed arguments Levinas makes in Sections II through IV. To appreciate the abbreviated argument of Parts B–D of Section I, let us turn to the first subtitle of each part: "Atheism or the Will," (Part B), "Freedom Called into Question," (Part C), and Part D has only one part and so we will consider its title "Separation and the Absolute."

Simply put, the argument of *Totality and Infinity* is as follows. If we desire the invisible (which Levinas defines as the ethical stance) then we must recognize what is necessary to make this desire possible. The first and, I will argue, most important element in Levinas's argument is an argument for "atheism or the will." In the detailed phenomenological descriptions of Section II of *Totality and Infinity* ("Interiority and Economy") Levinas sketches a picture of the atheistic self. If this sketch is successful, then his phenomenological descriptions of Section III of *Totality and Infinity* ("Exteriority and the Face") follow from it. Again, Levinas's arguments about my obligation to another depend philosophically upon whether he can describe successfully the atheistic self.

Section IV of *Totality and Infinity*, "Beyond the Face," is Levinas's attempt to bring his analysis of the self and the other, of the worlds of totality and infinity, into phenomenological relation with his descriptions of the world of social relations, defined here for him primarily by the relations of the family. Returning to Levinas's subtitle of Section I Part D, "Separation and the Absolute," it becomes clear that Levinas's attempt in Section IV is to describe the ways in which separate beings come together to create the ethical relation, which is for Levinas "the absolute." But Levinas's ethical relation is not one of mutuality. For Levinas, while the erotic encounter between two separate beings is not ethical, it can create the asymmetrical ethical relationship between parent and child.[5] Here we find the argument of Sections II and III repeated again in new form: separation (which the erotic relation, and any relation aiming for mutuality, cannot achieve) is necessary for a glimpse (not visual, of course) of the absoluteness of the ethical relation. In the conclusion of *Totality and Infinity*, Levinas considers the implications of his view of separation and the absolute for the concepts of religion and politics. These are themes that he continues to develop throughout his later work.

While there is, of course, too much more to be said about the structure and argument of *Totality and Infinity*, what I would like to make clear is that the central argument of *Totality and Infinity* is for the separable self. Levinas's radical claim about ethics rests neither on a philosophical argument for altruism nor even on a philosophical argument for ethics per se. Rather, I suggest that the philosophical claims of *Totality and Infinity* rest upon Levinas's attempt to affirm phenomenologically a picture of an independent, isolated, and separable subject.

2.2. HEIDEGGER AND HUSSERL

To appreciate Levinas's arguments about the self, we must discuss briefly Husserl's and Heidegger's respective views of the self. In affirming an isolated, separable subject Levinas moves back from Heidegger to Husserl. As is well known, in *Being and Time*, Heidegger denies precisely Husserl's view of the ego, claiming that Husserl presents an ontic self, not an ontological one. In simpler terms, Husserl argues for a view of the ego that can be distinguished from the historical self and the self's being in the world. Heidegger, in contrast, maintains that the self only gains its identity *through its being in the world.*

Significantly, Husserl makes his argument in *Cartesian Mediations* against Descartes's notion of the ego, which from Husserl's point of view is too much part of the world. As Husserl puts it against Descartes, "Just as the reduced Ego is not a piece of the world, so, conversely, neither the world nor any worldly Object is a piece of my Ego."[6] The notion that the ego is a piece of the world is for Husserl Descartes's great mistake, and while Descartes does at one point state that "sensation . . . is nothing but an act of consciousness,"[7] his claims about the ego's constitution remain too tied to sensibility for Husserl.[8] Husserl nonetheless believes that he has followed Descartes's method in describing what he calls the *transcendental ego*, which is defined by its *lack* of worldly attributes. Husserl thus affirms Descartes's *cogito*, but gives it a new twist: "To say, 'I am, *ego cogito*' does not therefore mean I, this human being, am."[9] While Husserl argues that the transcendental ego isn't subject to personal pronouns, he also claims that the transcendental ego is at once absolute and unique.[10] A discussion of the ways in which Husserl tried to work this tension out is beyond the scope of this chapter. What we need to appreciate, however, is that Husserl claims to be following Descartes in affirming a unique subject whose uniqueness derives from the stripping away (what Husserl called the "bracketing") of its historical and social situation. From Husserl's perspective, this further stripping away of the Cartesian cogito beyond any remnant of this world is consistent with, and in fact demanded by, the Cartesian method.

In *Being and Time*, Heidegger accepts Husserl's view of Descartes's legacy as epitomizing the modern, acontextual subject. When Heidegger criticizes the philosophical dichotomy between subject and object, he does so with Husserl and Descartes in mind. To show that from the perspective of being there are no absolutely separable subjects, Heidegger (perhaps somewhat ironically) returns the proper pronoun to the ego that Husserl had tried to deny. As Heidegger puts it, "Because *Dasein* has *in each case mineness*, [*Jemeinigkeit*], one must always use a *personal* pronoun when one addresses it. 'I am, you are.'"[11] But the effect of Heidegger's returning the personal pronoun to the ego is to show precisely that the ego cannot be described without reference to the ego's social and historical relations. The ego, for Heidegger, is fundamentally relational. That I am I is only possible because I exist in a web of relations. Outside of these relations, there is no subject. So while Heidegger, in arguing against Husserl, might seem to be returning personal identity to the ego, he is, from another perspective, also denying any notion of personal identity in the sense of absolute identity (which is what Husserl wants to affirm).

One might think that based on his view of the primacy of ethics that Levinas's notion of the self would be closer to Heidegger's than to Husserl's. But Levinas maintains, *contra* Heidegger, that identity is not wholly fluid but rather concrete. In this, he returns to Husserl's notion of a truly separable self, though this self for Levinas is not an ego in terms of cognitive function. Rather, he argues that the truly unique, separate self is one that can be encountered phenomenologically only by way of an appreciation of sense experience. Unlike Husserl's transcendental ego, Levinas's ego is not a thinking self, but a self that senses itself, by way of sensible experience, as uniquely separated from being. For Levinas, in order for the ego to think, it must first be separate from being, it must sense itself as itself.

It is the self's sense of itself *as a separable, independent self* that is the core philosophical argument of *Totality and Infinity*. Against Heidegger, Levinas maintains that there is a separable subject whose identity cannot be reduced to any web of relations. From Levinas's point of view, Heidegger's "mine" reduces the self to nothing, while Husserl's "mine" overly cognizes the identity of the ego. Levinas's attempt to make ethics first philosophy is captured in his "mine," which *contra* Husserl is not a cognitive matter and *contra* Heidegger transcends social and historical relations. Levinas's "mine" concerns my unique responsibility for the other person. This responsibility is "mine" alone and I am uniquely defined by it. I do not possess this responsibility; rather this responsibility *is* me. But in being me, my unique responsibility requires a self who experiences itself as unique, *a self who stands outside of the social and historical order*. To begin to posit such a self, Levinas turns back from Heidegger to Husserl. But as we will see in Section 2.3, it is from Husserl to Descartes that Levinas turns to describe a unique being who finds himself unique not in his cognitive existence, but in his sentient existence. We will leave for the conclusion the question of how this sentient being is linked to Descartes's "I think therefore I am."

2.3. LEVINAS AND DESCARTES

Jean-Luc Marion has noted the concurrence between Heidegger's and Husserl's views of Descartes, despite their fundamental disagreement about the status of the ego. As Marion puts it:

[T]his fundamental dispute with Husserl does not keep Heidegger from agreeing with him. . . . He consistently agrees to interpret Descartes's *cogito, ergo sum* in terms of intentionality, in terms of the displacement of ecstasy brings about, in terms of . . . the representation that runs through intentionality. Only one difference remains. At the point where Husserl acknowledged an anticipation of phenomenology, Heidegger denounces a form of metaphysics. But whether they approve or disapprove of intentionality, they give the *cogito, ergo sum* the same interpretation in terms of it. . . . [T]hinking, *cogitare*, is equivalent . . . to putting thought at a distance as an object.[12]

Marion shows that Descartes rejected the idea of intentionality that Husserl and Heidegger associate with his philosophy. Descartes, Marion argues, does not, as Husserl and Heidegger maintain, claim that every thought is accompanied by an "I think." As Descartes put it, this view of the cogito "is as deluded as our bricklayer's saying that a person who is skilled in architecture must employ a reflexive act to ponder on the fact that he has this skill before he can be an architect."[13] Marion follows Michel Henry in describing Descartes's cogito as "material phenomenology," by which he means to emphasize Descartes's focus not on intentionality and representation in grounding the "I," but on receptivity and sensation.

We cannot discuss here the complex philosophical and historical issues of Descartes scholarship in twentieth-century France. But this brief mention of Marion's discussion of Michel Henry's interpretation of Descartes provides us an important starting point for understanding Levinas's view of Descartes. It is interesting that Marion does not refer to Levinas in this essay, published first in 1990, on Henry's reading of Descartes. While Levinas certainly does not give a comprehensive account or reading of Descartes or even of the cogito, the general theme of receptivity is the key to understanding Levinas's construction of the self. For Levinas, the self is not one who represents itself to itself through thought (the view that Husserl and Heidegger both attribute to Descartes). Rather, Levinas's self senses itself as itself by way of sensible experience. While not systematic in its presentation, Levinas's discussion in *Totality and Infinity* of Descartes provides the framework for Levinas's phenomenological description of the separate and independent subject.

As I argued in the beginning of this chapter, Section II of *Totality and Infinity*, "Interiority and Economy," constitutes the core argument of the book, upon which the arguments in Sections III and IV are built. From the beginning, Levinas frames his effort in this section as an attempt to find a middle point of sorts between Husserl and Heidegger. Levinas criticizes Husserl's claim that every intentionality is founded upon representation, but states also that his goal is not to be "anti-intellectualist" like "the philosophers of existence" and Heidegger in particular in understanding the existent only in terms of doing and labor.[14]

Levinas's description of the self is a return to Husserl's view of a transhistorical self, but on Heidegger's terms. For all his analysis of the moods of *Dasein*, Heidegger, Levinas suggests, has not taken the mood of satisfaction seriously because he has reduced our understanding of things to their use. Levinas argues against Heideggerian phenomenology that hunger is not related just to the need for food, but also to the possibility of contentment.[15] In attempting a phenomenological analysis of contentment, which he also calls "enjoyment,"

Levinas stretches the limits of Husserl's notion of intentionality, claiming that the self senses itself as a separate, isolated, and independent self in a noncognitive way.[16] Significantly, Levinas attributes the possibility of this analysis to Descartes:

The profundity of the Cartesian philosophy of the sensible consists, we have said, in affirming the irrational character of sensation, an idea forever without clarity or distinctness, belonging to the order of the useful and not of the true.[17]

Levinas continues by stating that Kant follows Descartes's view of sensation in distinguishing between knowledge and sensible experience and was right to do so. Yet Kant's view of sensibility is ultimately too negative. Levinas means to return to what he claims is the fullness of the Cartesian view of sensibility, which he argues accesses a reality that cognitive knowledge cannot access. Sensibility, Levinas contends, grounds the self as self, "beyond instinct" and "beneath reason."

Sensibility does not constitute representation, which is the province of reason, but it does constitute what Levinas calls "the very contentment of existence," which is my unreflective sense of myself.[18] I do not possess sensibility but am constituted by it. Heidegger's *Da*, Levinas maintains, cannot account for sensibility: "It is not care for Being, nor a relation with existents, nor even a negation of the world, but its accessibility in enjoyment."

Before the self makes objects of the world, sensibility, for Levinas, is the receptive capacity of the self to bear and be shaped by the world in which it lives:

The bit of earth that supports me is not only my object; it supports my experience of objects. . . . The relation with my site in this 'stance' ['*tenue*'] precedes thought and labor. . . . My sensibility is here. In my position there is not the sentiment of localization, but the localization of my sensibility. . . . Sensibility is the very narrowness of life; the naïveté of the unreflected I, beyond instinct, beneath reason.[19]

Levinas claims that sensation is not the subjective counterpart to objectivity but is prior to objectivity. Sensibility is not muddled thought but gives access to a reality to which reason cannot reach. A reality that serves no theoretical or practical purpose, contentment and enjoyment are the location of the transhistorical, transcognitive self. Levinas calls this sense of self a "surplus" for it cannot be captured by reason, biology, or society. Again using the example of eating, Levinas writes:

Eating, for example, is to be sure not reducible to the chemistry of alimentation. But eating also does not reduce itself to the set of gustative, olfactory, kinesthetic, and other sensations that would constitute the consciousness of eating. This sinking one's teeth into the things which the act of eating involves above all measures the surplus that is not quantitative, but is the way the I, the absolute commencement, is suspended on the non-I.[20]

Throughout Section II of *Totality and Infinity*, Levinas provides detailed analyses of the ways in which the "I" separates itself from the world in the surplus produced by sensibility. The "I," Levinas insists, is a separate subject that cannot be subsumed into being or the objects of the world.

Again, Levinas claims to expand Husserl's notion of intentionality to describe a view of the self that cannot be reduced to its thought about itself or to the relations that constitute it. By turning to sensibility to describe how this self is constituted, Levinas also attempts to correct Husserl's correction of Descartes. While Husserl maintains that Descartes went wrong in understanding the ego as carrying with it a residual of the world, Levinas maintains that Descartes was right in grasping how the self as self is constituted by the world *before* it can begin to constitute the world. For Levinas, Husserl's aim for transcendental purity must be corrected by a return to this initial Cartesian insight. But this does not mitigate Levinas's notion that he is in keeping with Husserl's phenomenological method, which, unlike Heidegger's, is not, Levinas claims, antiintellectualist. Like Husserl and Descartes before him, Levinas does not object to but affirms reason's ability, to use Marion's words, to put "thought at a distance as an object." But unlike Husserl, and like Descartes, Levinas claims there is more to the self than this representational capacity. We will return to this point later. First, however, we need to focus on how Levinas's claims about the sensible self make possible his claims about ethics.

2.4. THE SEPARABLE SELF AND ETHICS OR DESCARTES ONCE AGAIN

Already in Section II, Levinas states the claim that will ground his argument about ethics in Section III, "Exteriority and the Face." Levinas writes:

The intentionality of enjoyment can be described by contrast with the intentionality of representation; it consists in holding on to the exteriority which the transcendental method involved in representation suspends. To hold on to exteriority is not simply equivalent to affirming the world; but is to posit oneself in it corporeally. . . . The body naked and indigent is the very reverting, irreducible to a thought, of representation into life, of the subjectivity that represents into life which is sustained by these representations and *lives of them*; its indigence – its needs affirm 'exteriority' as non-constituted, prior to all affirmation.[21]

Levinas's analysis of enjoyment has shown that the separable subject is made possible by the interiorization of sensible input. The separate self is, therefore, by definition a receptive self for Levinas. Yet we have seen that the self's interiorization of sensible experience does not mean for Levinas that the self is nothing but sensible experience. Levinas's analysis of nourishment, discussed in Section 2.3, suggests that beyond the science of sensibility (what he calls "biology") there is a remainder (what he calls a "surplus") that accounts for our very humanity. But for Levinas, the surplus that constitutes the separable, independent I from sensible experience does not produce a substantive I, but one whose very constitutedness and indebtedness to the exteriority that has made possible its interiority become ever more apparent.

It is in connection with this indebtedness to the exterior world that Levinas understands infinity and the ethical relation. Significantly, Levinas attributes this movement from the interiority of the self to the exteriority of the face of the other not just to Descartes's notion of infinity *but to the cogito itself*:

It is by reason of this operation of vertiginous descent unto the abyss, by reason of this change of level, that the Cartesian cogito is not a reasoning in the ordinary sense of the term or an intuition. Descartes enters into a work of infinite negation, which is indeed the work of the atheist subject that has broken with participation and that remains incapable of affirmation (although, by the sensibility, disposed for agreeableness) – enters into a movement unto the abyss, vertiginously sweeping along the subject incapable of stopping itself.[22]

The "movement unto the abyss" is for Levinas an indicator of infinity and the ethical relation. The atheistic self, both as a metaphysical construct and as a philosophical argument, leads to infinity. The very makeup of the atheistic self (its metaphysical constitution) is rooted in infinity. If, as Levinas argues, the cogito is grounded upon the exteriority that it has made interior, then the cogito is made possible by way of an exteriority for which it cannot account. It is for this reason that Levinas maintains that "the Cartesian cogito is not a reasoning in the ordinary sense of the term or an intuition." The Cartesian method marks a movement into the abyss of the exteriority that constitutes the ego. Against Husserl's and Heidegger's reading of the cogito, Levinas maintains that the true separateness of the subject, its interiorization of exteriority, gives way to the ethical relation.

Levinas's argument about the separable self and infinity are also apparent in the structure of *Totality and Infinity*. If Section II is philosophically successful, if Levinas has described adequately the phenomenological expression of the separate self, then Levinas's arguments about exteriority and the face in Section III follow from his initial argument about the separable self. Philosophically,

Totality and Infinity's structure suggests a transcendental argument of sorts. If we take as true the description of the separable self, then we must recognize that the separable subject is made possible only by way of its relationship to the face of another. Indeed, just as Kant argues in the transcendental deduction of the *Critique of Pure Reason* that the self's inner tracking of itself as self is made possible by an external world of objects (which we can't know anything about), so too Levinas maintains that the self's sense of its own interiority is made possible by the exteriority of infinity. While there surely are profound affinities between Levinas and Kant in their attempt to articulate a kind of ethical humanism, it is significant that in making his transcendental argument in *Totality and Infinity* that Levinas, following Husserl, retains the Kantian transcendental methodology while turning back to Descartes. For Levinas, Descartes's notion of sensibility and its relation to infinity show the way to a true understanding of transcendence, which Kant's transcendental idealism cannot fully apprehend. This isn't to say, however, that Levinas is claiming that Descartes's philosophy is identical to his. Rather, just as his teacher Husserl does, Levinas maintains that Descartes and the Cartesian methodology anticipate philosophically certain insights that he hopes to explicate further. Again like Husserl, and Descartes before him, Levinas's project in *Totality and Infinity* is a building of philosophical truth by way of a systematic methodology.

We can now appreciate Levinas's description in the preface of *Totality and Infinity* regarding the task of the book. *Totality and Infinity*, Levinas writes, "present[s] itself as a defense of subjectivity, but it will apprehend the subjectivity not at the level of its purely egoist protestation against totality, nor in its anguish before death, but as founded in the idea of infinity."[23] We have seen that Levinas's arguments about a subjectivity founded in the idea of infinity rest upon his reading of Descartes and his claim that Descartes's notion of the self can and must be rehabilitated for the purposes of contemporary philosophy. In contrast to the postmodern reading of Levinas, we see that Levinas's philosophical project is not to overcome assertions about the modern subject, but to reassert the truth of such a construction. We cannot deny that Levinas's "self" is different from what has become the conventional reading of Descartes's cogito. Nonetheless, we cannot ignore the fact that Levinas attempts to develop his own philosophy on the coattails of Descartes.

Before turning to the meaning of Levinas's use of Descartes, we must note that even from the perspective of Levinas's philosophy, Levinas might seem to give up his aspiration to rehabilitate Descartes. One might argue that even if we grant that *Totality and Infinity* makes an argument for the modern subject that in *Otherwise than Being* Levinas reverses himself in arguing for the other as the locus of identity. After all, Levinas's arguments, especially in what is perhaps the central chapter of that book, "Substitution," are attempts precisely to dislocate the modern self. Levinas's claim in *Otherwise than Being*, and especially in "Substitution," is that I do not constitute my own identity; the other does.

However, we should not be misled by Levinas's claims in *Otherwise than Being* about the passivity of the self into concluding that Levinas means to overcome the notion of a separable, isolated subject. Were we to accept a reading that posits such a dichotomy between *Totality and Infinity* and *Otherwise than Being* we would be overlooking the fact that Levinas's central argument in *Otherwise than Being* is an argument about the meanings of sensibility. We have seen that Levinas's claims about an isolated, separable self are based on his arguments about sensibility as a kind of intentionality above instinct and below reason. In *Otherwise than Being*, Levinas makes this very same argument. In a footnote he writes:

Inasmuch as an image is both the term and the incompletion of truth, sensibility, which is immediacy itself, becomes an image. This image is thus to be interpreted out of knowing. But our thesis is that sensibility has another signification, in its immediacy. It is not limited to the function of being the image of the true.[24]

"That sensibility has another signification" is the very argument that Levinas makes in *Totality and Infinity* about the separable subject. I have argued that if, in *Totality and Infinity*, Levinas has made his argument that there is an isolated, transhistorical self then his argument about ethics follows. In *Otherwise than Being* Levinas makes the same argument about sensibility that he makes in *Totality and Infinity*. The difference is that in *Otherwise than Being* Levinas begins with the ethical relation and not with the isolated subject. Nevertheless, Levinas nowhere denies the truth of the isolated subject and affirms the separate subject in his description of the ethical relation.

It is worth noting in this context the epigraph to Levinas's chapter on substitution. He quotes Paul Célan "Ich bin du, wenn ich ich bin," "I am you if I am I." In claiming that I am you (this is Levinas's argument about substitution), Levinas nonetheless maintains that I am I. Just as he argues in *Totality and Infinity* for the separable subject and for the authority of the other over the self, so he argues in *Otherwise than Being* for the other's authority over me and for my separable self. If Heidegger's motto in *Being and Time* is "Everyone is the Other and no one is himself,"[25] then Levinas's motto, following Célan, is that "the other is the other and the self is itself. Only thereby can I be for the other."[26] Both of these claims about the truly separable nature of the other and the self are made possible by Levinas's contention that sensibility has a meaning before and beyond cognitive representation. I sense myself in sensibility, but it is also by way of sensibility that the other comes to me. In neither case is this sensing cognitive in nature. Rather, Levinas claims, my sense of myself and my sense of the face of the other stem from the fact that I am a receptive and (in the language of *Otherwise than Being*) created creature. We have seen then that Levinas's contentions about ethics are thus grounded in his claims about sensibility. It is Descartes whom Levinas credits and claims to return to in making these arguments.

We are left with the question of whether Levinas has done justice to Descartes. The complexities of Descartes scholarship – their history and their contents – are beyond the scope of this book. Nevertheless, we should note that Marion's expositions of Descartes show that there is at least some textual and philosophical basis for Levinas's claims. Our concern in this chapter, however, is not with the accuracy of Levinas's reading of Descartes, but with the meaning of Levinas's use of Descartes for understanding the broader parameters of Levinas's project.

I suggest in Section 2.5 that, perhaps surprisingly, Strauss's analysis of Descartes allows us to think more deeply about the issue of sensibility in Descartes's and Levinas's philosophical relation to this issue. This is because Strauss's arguments about Descartes allow us to move beyond what might seem to be a fairly narrow discussion of sensibility into a broader discussion of the nature and scope of philosophy. I will suggest, following Strauss, that what we can glean from Levinas's use of Descartes is Levinas's affiliation with a particular modern philosophical project that Descartes, among others, instituted. Let us turn now to the meaning of this affiliation and its implications.

2.5. HOW TO UNDERSTAND LEVINAS'S USE OF DESCARTES: WHAT STRAUSS MIGHT SAY

We can begin to understand what would be Strauss's analysis of the meaning of Levinas's use of Descartes by turning to *Spinoza's Critique of Religion*, in which Strauss actually makes much of Descartes's view of sense experience. The context there is Strauss's discussion of Spinoza's critique of Maimonides's definition of prophecy. Maimonides maintains that the prophet is someone who has an overflow of both the intellectual and imaginative faculties. Spinoza argues in contrast that the prophet possesses an excess only of imagination. This definition of prophecy leads Spinoza to differentiate completely the intellectual and imaginative faculties. And Strauss argues, Spinoza's critique of religion follows immediately from this differentiation. As Strauss puts it:

Spinoza draws the conclusion. . . . Imagination and understanding exclude each other. All the more is the heightened activity of imagination, which is evident in all the prophets (and admitted by Maimonides also) an unmistakable sign that the prophets were particularly poorly endowed for purely intellectual activity (Tr., p. 15).[27]

Strauss attributes Spinoza's differentiation between imagination and understanding to Spinoza's acceptance of Cartesian science. The difference between Spinoza and Maimonides on prophecy concerns their respective acceptances of Cartesian or Aristotelian science.

Strauss argues that the Aristotelian view distinguishes the cognitive, sensory, and imaginative faculties, while the Cartesian view conflates the sensory and imaginative faculties. This difference, he argues, is the decisive point in understanding Spinoza's critique of Maimonides's view of prophecy. It is helpful to quote Strauss at length:

With Descartes's fundamental doubt, through which the final liberation from all prejudices, the final foundation of science is to be achieved, the notion of knowledge is posited from which Spinoza's critique of Maimonides's doctrine of prophecy follows. . . . [T]he decisive element in this doctrine is the conception of the imagination. Maimonides presupposes the Aristotelian analysis of imagination (*De anima, Gamma 3*) by which the relation of imagination to sensory perception and to intelligence is thus defined: in the first place, imagination is inferior to sensory perception and to the intellect, in that the latter are as such truthful, whereas imagination is in most cases deceptive. Secondly, imagination is superior to sensory perception in that imagination is capable of functioning without sensory perception, for instance during sleep. Imagination is thus essentially distinguished from sensory perception. Therefore critique of imagination is in no sense critique of sensory perception. Maimonides's critique of sensory perception is exclusively directed against the sensory conception of what is supersensory, against the conception of the incorporeal as corporeal, or necessarily linked to the body. The false conception is however not due to sensory perception, but to imagination. Further, since imagination can function independently of sensory perception, there exists the possibility that the intellect may force imagination into its service for perceiving the super-sensory: hence the possibility of prophecy.[28]

Because Spinoza operates with a Cartesian view of the imagination, he cannot but come to the critique of religion from the perspective of philosophy that he explicates in the *Treatise*. It is important to recognize that Strauss does not argue that Descartes's philosophy inevitably leads to the critique of religion. He explicitly leaves this question open.[29] What Strauss does argue is that the combination of Cartesian science with Maimonidean philosophy (which amounts to Spinoza) leads to the critique of religion.

Cartesian science rules out the possibility of Maimonides's view of prophecy because dreams, as part of the imagination, do not have any epistemological status. There is truth and there is illusion. But the reason that the critique of religion does not necessarily follow from Descartes's philosophy is that Catholic theology, Strauss asserts, still maintains a distinction between natural dreams and the grace of God. Even if all dreams are illusion from the point of view of knowledge, grace is still possible. In the context of Strauss's analysis, we have an explanation for what has come to be viewed as Descartes's famous (or infamous) voluntarism. In parts of *Meditations*, Descartes reserves, indeed posits, the primacy of God's will over rational knowledge.[30] While much of Marion's work is dedicated to showing that Descartes was not strictly a voluntarist because he denied that we know enough about God to separate his will from his reason,[31] Marion also emphasizes the central role of the will in Descartes's view of dreams:

If dreams achieve, 'on the level of reason,' some conceptual results that guarantee the autonomy of reason (self-interpretation, self-inspiration, *cogitatio*), how can we explain that they nevertheless inspire conclusions ('Spirits of Truth') and attitudes (pilgrimage to Loretto) that are clearly religious? The relation to the divinity is established at the end, and as a result, of the process of interpretation.... On this, Descartes has interpreted his dreams in a way that supports his own (later) philosophy: Whenever he faces a difficulty, he can draw a meaningful response from within himself.... The divinity therefore does not inspire dreams by means of enthusiasm, nor does it inspire their interpretation, as a warranty. It then becomes clear that as early as 1619, since the divinity only intervenes externally and as a mediator (as a warranty), the will (abstract and without content) becomes the only appropriate and possible relational mode between God and Descartes.[32]

Even if, as Marion suggests in some of his later work, Descartes presents a more nuanced voluntarism than he is often credited with, Levinas would nevertheless certainly reject Descartes's emphasis on God's will and, without mentioning this aspect of Descartes's philosophy, in effect does so in a number of ways. Most basically, Levinas affirms truth over will both in his conception of God and in his conception of individuals. This favoring of truth over will is for Levinas also a prioritizing of the good over the will. We see this type of argument in Levinas's critique in *Totality and Infinity* of labor. This same dynamic of favoring the good or the true over the will informs Levinas's fundamental distinction in *Otherwise than Being* between the saying and the said. In regard to God more particularly, Levinas very much aligns himself with an intellectualist tradition of religious thought that would posit the primacy of moral reason over God's will. Supernatural interventions of any sort are anathema to Levinas's conceptions of religion and ethics. Levinas argues again and again that the meaning of law, and religious law in particular, is only its ethical truth and in no way its positive origin in a supernatural, external source. Here Levinas uses one of Descartes's arguments to come to the opposite view of Descartes on the issue of voluntarism. Levinas's affirms Descartes's affirmation of the goodness of God in his use of Descartes's "evil genius." Like Descartes, Levinas argues that God by definition cannot be an evil trickster. Nonetheless, Levinas does not and will not go so far as Descartes in claiming that, in Marion's words, "the only appropriate and *possible* relational mode between God and Descartes" is the will.

Strauss notes that Maimonides doesn't have the option of supernatural grace; indeed, this is the core of his rationalist philosophy. We have seen that Levinas also would reject any notion of supernatural grace. Does Levinas then succumb to the same equation that leads Spinoza to his critique of religion? After all, if Strauss is right that the combination of a claim for the unity of knowledge and faith (what he argues in 1930 is Maimonides's view) and the Cartesian view of science leads to Spinoza's critique of religion, then don't Levinas's arguments lead to Spinoza's conclusions?

Strauss's reading of Spinoza as mediating between Maimonides and Descartes would suggest that Levinas's philosophy is ultimately in line with Spinoza's critique of religion. To be sure, Levinas would certainly reject this claim, but before turning to how Levinas might respond, let us lay out what would be Strauss's criticism.[33] Recall that *Spinoza's Critique of Religion* was written before Strauss's "change of orientation," which concerned his hermeneutical claims about the relation between esoteric and exoteric writing. In this 1930 book, Strauss takes not only Spinoza's claims at face value (in Strauss's words, he "understood Spinoza too literally because...[he] did not read him literally enough"[34]), but Maimonides's claims also. While Strauss's later work on Maimonides would emphasize the tension between Maimonides's view of philosophy and revelation, in *Spinoza's Critique of Religion* Strauss contends that Maimonides attempts to establish a unity between knowledge and faith (as Maimonides says he does). We saw in Chapter 1 that Levinas attempts to establish this very unity. Strauss contends that once this unity is assumed and once Cartesian science is accepted, the critique of religion cannot but follow.[35]

Simply put, Strauss's claim is that the unity of faith and knowledge denies any possibility of divine transcendence. Levinas, of course, claims precisely to be revitalizing a notion of transcendence. But from Strauss's point of view, Levinas's notion of transcendence would not do justice to what he argues is the meaning of revelation, which concerns for Strauss the possibility of divine interaction with humanity. In an important sense, Levinas would not disagree with this objection of Strauss's, for Levinas intends, as he says again and again, to show that any notion of the divine is ultimately relevant only for an appreciation of human ethics. God for Levinas can only be experienced through the face of another human being. As Levinas says, his philosophy is profoundly humanistic in this respect.[36]

From Strauss's perspective, however, the reduction of God to interhuman relations is a denial of the divinity of the divine. But we must recall at the same time that Strauss, like Levinas, is attracted to the medieval rationalism of Maimonides, who claimed that we cannot have positive knowledge of God. As Levinas does, Strauss agrees with Maimonides that knowledge of God is not possible from an epistemological perspective. Where Strauss and Levinas disagree in regard to Maimonides is on the issue of whether following the particularities of the divine law is a prerequisite for the experience of God. Strauss agrees with Maimonides that is; Levinas does not. The meaning of the particularities of the divine law is always ethics for Levinas and is always subordinate to ethics. Strauss's reading of Spinoza's critique of religion suggests that the modern critique of religion consists in reducing the divine to the human. And from Strauss's perspective, once the divine has been reduced to the human, the divine all but disappears.

In *The Election of Israel* David Novak makes a similar argument in regard to Hermann Cohen that I am suggesting Strauss would make in regard to Levinas.[37] Novak claims that Spinoza's rereading of the covenant as a human decision to choose God, rather than as a divine decision to choose humanity, marks Cohen's philosophy. Cohen, like Levinas, would be greatly offended by the claim that his philosophy rests on the same premises as Spinoza's philosophy does. Yet Cohen's reduction of a supernatural divine to interpersonal ethics, a reduction that Levinas repeats, is consonant with, if not derivative from, Spinoza's notion of the covenant (Israel's choosing God) and from what Strauss argues is Spinoza's critique of religion.

To be fair to Levinas, however, we must recognize that Levinas's claims are not in keeping with Spinoza's conception of the covenant. Levinas's ethics are oriented around the claim that I do not choose the other but the other chooses me. And as we have seen throughout this chapter, Levinas makes this claim philosophically based on his analysis of sensibility. Indeed, Levinas's analysis of sensibility, and his reliance on Descartes for this analysis, might even suggest that we need to rethink Strauss's claim about the wedding of an argument for the unity of knowledge and faith with Cartesian science as a recipe for the critique of religion. Would Levinas's discussion of sensibility call into question the argument that I have just made from Strauss's point of view? Could Levinas contend that sensibility gives us access to true transcendence, to true religion and that Descartes makes this argument? Indeed, might Levinas's analysis call into question Strauss's story about the modern critique of religion, suggesting that the very resources for true religion are found in, among other places, various modern philosophical projects, such as Descartes's and Kant's? Indeed, might Levinas not respond that, contra Strauss, true religion lies in the unity of faith and knowledge and not in their antithetical relation to one another? Doesn't Levinas's story about philosophy suggest that where modern philosophy has gone wrong is in separating, not in uniting, faith and knowledge?

2.6. THE DIFFERENCE BETWEEN LEVINAS AND STRAUSS OR ON DESCARTES YET AGAIN

Spinoza's reformulation of Maimonides's notion of prophecy provides us an entry way into these big questions. Again, Strauss claims that Spinoza's notion of prophecy is predicated on Cartesian science in which imagination and sensibility are conflated. Maimonides's view of prophecy, predicated on Aristotelian science, still left room for the possibility of prophecy because of the separation between imagination and sensibility. But for Spinoza, following Descartes, sensibility is associated with illusion and cognition is associated with truth. We have seen, however, that Levinas's argument is that there is another dimension to sensibility, unaccounted for by Husserl and Heidegger who, Levinas claims, misinterpret Descartes. This dimension, Levinas maintains, is above instinct and below reason. The truly separate subject resides in this sensibility and so does the other whose presence overflows my capacity for internalization. Levinas explicitly connects this argument about sensibility with Descartes's notion of the infinite. Levinas maintains that there is an alternative to traditional Jewish and Christian theological claims about transcendence that posit a supernatural reality on the one hand, and what became the accepted reading of Cartesian science that denies any such supernatural reality, on the other hand. Faith and knowledge are not really at an impasse, but meet in the experience of the other person.

On the questions of religion, God, and ethics, Levinas's claims in connection with Descartes are questionable at best. While Marion in particular has shown in great detail that there is more to Descartes than Husserl or Heidegger thought, this same careful work on Descartes has also led Marion to emphasize the complexity and indeed centrality of Descartes's voluntarism, as we saw in Section 2.5. At the same time, Marion also emphasizes Descartes's

general disinterest in the relations between God and people as well as between
people:

No texts of Descartes suggest that divine otherness even allows, not to mention
requires, the acknowledgment of finite otherness; the finite other does not cor-
respond, univocally or even analogically, to God in the relation of otherness, of
personhood, or of consciousness (moral or not).[38]

Yet Levinas's claim is not to have an accurate reading of what Descartes actually
said or intended to do, but to explore the *philosophical meaning* of Descartes's
insights. Levinas follows Husserl in using Descartes as a jumping-off point for
reinvigorating philosophy.

But Levinas wants to use Descartes for the express purposes that Descartes
rejected. Here I don't mean merely that he wants to use Descartes's solip-
sistic philosophy to ground an interpersonal ethics or that he wants to use
Descartes's notion of the infinite to argue for a God that does not will. In
these regards, Levinas may have free license to use Descartes's insights for
his own interpretive purposes (as Husserl does). But Levinas's reversal of
Descartes goes far deeper than a creative rereading or interpretation. Husserl
understood Cartesian science properly when he used Descartes to ground his
phenomenological method. The mark of Descartes's method is his bracketing
of all social, political, and religious questions from philosophy. Here Levinas's
appropriation of Descartes can only be understood in the context of
Heidegger's denial of an isolated subject and his subsequent focus on the
historicity of subjectivity and philosophy.

The fundamental tension within Levinas's philosophy is that on the one
hand, he wants to show that social, political, and religious questions are, in
their historical and cultural senses, separate from philosophy. But on the other
hand, Levinas wants to argue that philosophy can articulate the basis of social
life. Levinas's philosophical articulation of ethics is meant to provide the philosophical bases of society, politics, and religion. So Levinas means to affirm
the independence of philosophy that Descartes posited by bracketing social,
political, and religious concerns, which Levinas regards as always connected
to the sediments of culture and history. Yet, paradoxically, Levinas's argument
is that by bracketing these concerns we may return to the proper meanings of
society, politics, and religion. This tension between the bracketing of normative social, political, and religious concerns, on the one hand, and the claim
that philosophy grounds social, political, and religious practice, on the other
hand, is inherent in Levinas's thought.

Strauss's theoretical framework and also his comments about Descartes help
us to understand this tension better. Strauss argues that among the defining

features of what is called *modern rationalism* is the assumption that there is an essential harmony between society and thought. Levinas's philosophy shares in this assumption. Strauss, of course, argues that there is not a harmony between society and thought and he attributes this insight to Greek philosophy and the medieval Islamic and Jewish philosophers who received it. Significantly, however, Strauss notes that Descartes, one of the institutors of what would become modern philosophy, did not recognize any such harmony. Strauss refers specifically to the first two maxims of Descartes's *Discourse on Method*, which claim that "conformity with the opinions of the religious community in which one is brought up, is a necessary qualification for the future philosopher."[39] Strauss maintains that Descartes's writings were affected by the thought of persecution, as Descartes says they were.[40] Strauss does not offer an analysis of Descartes's writing style,[41] but his general point about Descartes is pertinent to our discussion of Levinas. While Descartes announces that the philosopher must accept the opinions of the religious community in which he was born, Descartes defines philosophy as the bracketing of such inherited opinions. Indeed, the Cartesian quest for certain knowledge is marked by the quest for the independence of philosophy.

Strauss's references to Descartes in *Persecution and the Art of Writing* point to the perhaps unintended consequence of Descartes's quest for the independence of philosophy. While Descartes was well aware of the necessity of accepting received opinion (whether sincerely or insincerely), those who followed Cartesian philosophy became increasing unaware of this necessity because political circumstances changed. When persecution for the philosopher was no longer a distinct possibility, philosophers dispensed with and forgot about the distinction between exoteric and esoteric knowledge. From Strauss's perspective, the elimination of this distinction was a disaster for both thought and society because modern rationalism eventually, and in Strauss's view, necessarily, disintegrated into radical historicism. As a consequence of this disintegration, society was denied the possibility of critical thought. Strauss's view of the disintegration of modern rationalism and its social consequences finds its expression in his critique of Heidegger.

We need not enter into discussion of Heidegger's philosophy to appreciate the relevant point for our consideration of Levinas. What is relevant for our purposes is Strauss's characterization of the modern philosophical project. According to Strauss, Descartes was keenly aware of the sociopolitical situation of philosophy, but the modern philosophical project forgets this sociopolitical condition and assumes an implicit connection between social progress and intellectual progress. The reception of Descartes as founder of modern foundationalism is based on this forgetfulness. Perhaps surprisingly,

Levinas, in his appropriation of Descartes, participates in this very forgetfulness.[42]

Strauss suggests that one consequence of the forgetfulness of what he argues
is the eternal tension between thought and society is the elevation of philosophy to *messianic* heights. Part of what classical philosophy recognizes is its own
inability to account fully or definitively *on philosophical grounds* for morality
or virtue. There is thus *a philosophical reason* along with a political reason for
the philosopher's interest in society. As we saw in Chapter 1, Strauss argues
that philosophy is unable to account on its own terms for society and politics.
Philosophy's critical power comes from its recognition of its fundamental limitation. Philosophy can direct social and political life, but philosophy cannot
account on its own terms for this life. Strauss argues that modern rationalism
elevates itself to religious and indeed messianic heights in assuming it can fully
articulate the meaning of humanity at large and in this sense direct social and
political life. However, as Strauss puts it, "a philosophy based on faith is no
longer philosophy."[43] In Thomas Pangle's words, "Strauss suggests ... that 'at
the bottom' of modern philosophy is the understandable impulse to resolve
the conflict between philosophy and faith, not by continuing the endless ten-
uous attempts of each protagonist to subsume the other, but by turning away
and transcending the plane of the whole controversy."[44]

Levinas's claims about ethics and philosophy are, as he says, messianic in
character and can thus be characterized, as we will see in greater detail in
Chapter 3, by Strauss's description of modern philosophy's religious claims
for itself. While Levinas at times is critical of the tradition of western philosophy through his emphasis on the ethics of the "Hebrews" as opposed to
the ontology of the "Greeks," his messianic claims for philosophy are – perhaps ironically – part and parcel of a particular modern philosophical project.
Despite his contentions that the task of ethics is infinite, Levinas's employment of philosophy and philosophical analysis suggests that philosophy can
provide society with a definitive answer to who we are as human beings.
Ironically perhaps, Levinas does present a "totalizing" image of philosophy,
despite his claims to the contrary. For these reasons, Levinas is right to see an
affinity between his philosophy and Descartes's philosophy. For philosophically speaking, Descartes, at the very least in his historical reception if not
intentionally, secures the possibility of the independence of philosophy and
its messianic potential.

We can now return to the tension in Levinas's thought that I have noted
in this section. As I have argued, Levinas follows Descartes in attempting to
secure a place for philosophical speculation outside of society, politics, and
religion. Yet Levinas reverses Descartes's separation between philosophy and

society in concluding from this move that philosophy, on its own terms, can actually articulate the ground of society, politics, and religion. Levinas, of course, would not see the tension that I am describing as a tension. But let me put the tension like this. Levinas claims that we can bracket out history, culture, and religion in his view of ethics *and* that this view of ethics then has the potential to direct social and political (if not religious) life. Levinas's first claim differentiates him from modern philosophers such as Hegel, Heidegger, and others who, in different ways, suggest that philosophy is inextricably intertwined with history and culture. But at the same time, Levinas's second claim differentiates him from modern philosophers, such as Kant or Rawls, who ground their claims for morality in notions of reason and cognition that Levinas's view of ethics explicitly rejects. We are left then with Levinas's puzzling claim for the ability of philosophy qua philosophy to articulate the meanings of public life on the basis of an argument about the privacy of experience, his account of sensibility, an argument that I would suggest is not and cannot be extended into the public realm.

As I argued in the first part of this chapter, Levinas's phenomenological claim about ethics, at least in *Totality and Infinity*, but arguably in *Otherwise than Being*, is based on what he argues is the true experience of personal identity. The sensible experiences of enjoyment and contentment produce a subjective interiority that points to my receptive capacities, but also ultimately to my inability to interiorize the other. While much of Levinas's later work is meant to emphasize the ways in which the interpersonal relation of ethics makes possible (from a transcendental perspective) public life, it is hard to know what he means by this. Levinas and many of his interpreters point out that his is not a practical ethics in the sense of telling us what we should do in particular cases, for this is the realm of politics. As Levinas succinctly puts it:

The order of politics – post-ethical or pre-ethical – which inaugurates the 'social contract' is neither the sufficient condition nor the necessary outcome of ethics. In its ethical position, the self is distinct from the citizen born of the City, and from the individual who precedes all order in his natural egoism. . . . The inter-human lies also in the recourse that people have to one another for help, before the marvellous alterity of the Other has been banalized or dimmed in a simple exchange of courtesies which become established as an 'inter-personal commerce' of customs. . . . [45]

Politics, society, and custom are by definition for Levinas the banalization of ethics.[46] From a philosophical perspective, it is hard then to know what Levinas intends by his messianic claims for philosophy, save for a heightened sense of the inner life and its dependence on our relations to others.

2.7. LEVINAS AND THE MESSIANIC ASPIRATIONS
OF PHILOSOPHY

The main problem with the messianic aspiration of modern philosophy according to Strauss is that it simply cannot do what it claims it can. Levinas's philosophy would be for Strauss a case in point. From Strauss's perspective, Levinas's philosophy eclipses the possibility of thinking critically about politics. When all is said and done, Levinas's philosophy has left the world the same as it found it. Ironically, this is because Levinas has given philosophy too much credit. Levinas's reliance on Descartes places him squarely in the arena of a particularly modern philosophical project not, as might be supposed, because he argues for the autonomy of the modern subject (though he does make this argument), but because he argues for the religious task of philosophy. Strauss's reading of Descartes suggests that Descartes, among others, initiated the messianic possibilities of modern rationalism. It has been the suggestion of this chapter that, once again, ironically perhaps, Levinas's project is best understood as the continuation of this modern religious project.

Strauss's contention, in contrast, is that philosophy can be useful only when it is recognized that philosophy is not in and of itself able to ground or even fully articulate the meanings of social and political life. Describing a postliberal view of justice, one that on the surface of things mirrors Levinas's account of giving to the other, Strauss writes in *Natural Right and History*:

Justice will then be the habit of benefiting others. The just man is he who gives to everyone, not what a possibly foolish law prescribes, but what is good for the other, i.e. what is by nature good for the other.... This being the case, there cannot be justice, i.e. giving to everyone what is by nature good for him, except in a society in which wise men are in absolute control.... [J]ust ownership is something entirely different from legal ownership. If there is to be justice, the wise rulers must assign to everyone what is truly due to him or what is by nature good for him. They will give to everyone only what he can use well, and they will take away from everyone what he cannot use well. Justice is then incompatible with what is generally understood by private ownership.[47]

Strauss may seem here to be elevating the position of the philosopher, or wise person, in insisting on a difference between legal and just ownership and positing that only wise rulers can know the latter. But this assertion is qualified in *Natural Right and History* by Strauss's contention that a written and indeed historic document written by wise people of the past, is the only guarantee that there may be (certainly not that there will be) wisdom in the present and future. While Strauss's claim about "wise rulers" might initially suggest an elevation of the philosopher in comparison with Levinas's claims about the "inter-human relation," Strauss's claim for philosophy is far more limited than Levinas's. For Strauss, wisdom requires politics, society, and religion. Both for the possibility for philosophy to exist and also for philosophy to be effective Strauss contends that the strength of the philosophical enterprise for philosophy and society begins with philosophy's recognition of its fundamental limitation in regard to politics, society, and religion. This recognition makes possible philosophy's critical function. Levinas, from Strauss's perspective, recognizes no such limitation on philosophy and thereby renders philosophy ineffective. But more than rendering philosophy ineffective Strauss's analysis would seem to suggest that by reducing philosophy to ethics, and indeed all human life to ethics, Levinas has in effect weakened not only the fullness of what it means to be human, but the moral enterprise.

To more fully understand this difference between Levinas and Strauss we must turn to a more detailed discussion of their respective views of how revelation, and specifically revealed religion, relates to the philosophical and moral enterprises. Once again, we can begin to appreciate their profound differences on the question of revelation only by first recognizing the common sources of their thinking. We turn now in Part 2 of the book to Levinas's and Strauss's shared relation to the German-Jewish philosophy of Franz Rosenzweig and Hermann Cohen. It is by way of their relation to these momentous figures that we can also more deeply appreciate Levinas's and Strauss's complex philosophical relations to Spinoza and Maimonides.

PART TWO

REVELATION

3

॰

'Freedom Depends Upon Its Bondage':
The Shared Debt to Franz Rosenzweig

*I*N PART 1 OF THIS BOOK I DESCRIBE LEVINAS'S COMMITMENT TO A particular modern philosophical project as embodied in his messianic claims for philosophy. We turn now in Part 2 to what I argue is Levinas's commitment to modern philosophy and Strauss's criticism of modern philosophy in the context of their claims about revelation and engagement with early-twentieth-century German-Jewish thought. Levinas and Strauss both profess a strong debt to the philosophy of the German-Jewish philosopher Franz Rosenzweig (1886–1929). Levinas's first major philosophical work, *Totality and Infinity*, includes the following now-famous note in its preface: "We were impressed by the opposition to the idea of totality in Franz Rosenzweig's *The Star of Redemption*, a work too often present in this book to be cited."[1] As both Robert Gibbs and Richard Cohen have shown, an appreciation for Levinas's claim about his debt to Rosenzweig takes us far in appreciating the theological-ethical import of his thought.[2] Although Steven Schwarzschild did remark some decades ago that "[T]he Rosenzweigian motivation for Strauss's work in general becomes quite clear and should be explicated by someone soon,"[3] far less attention has been paid to Strauss's debt to Rosenzweig. But Strauss dedicated his first major book, *Spinoza's Critique of Religion*, to Franz Rosenzweig's memory.[4] And as Strauss acknowledged more than thirty years after this dedication, in the preface to the English translation of his book, Rosenzweig's thought provided the impetus for the development of his own arguments about philosophy and revelation.[5]

But Levinas and Strauss have remarkably different readings of Rosenzweig. Levinas claims that Rosenzweig's thought makes, to use Levinas's words, "everything philosophy."[6] Strauss, in contrast, attributes to Rosenzweig the recognition that revelation signifies the rupture of philosophy and, therefore, the end of philosophy from the perspective of revelation. Perhaps even more basically, when Levinas writes that Rosenzweig's philosophy opposes totality he means by this that Rosenzweig opposes the historical constructedness of truth, both in regard to his view of the self and in regard to his notion of revelation. In contrast, Strauss faults Rosenzweig for being too much of a historicist and ultimately rejects his thought for this reason.

There is no doubt that a case can be made for both Levinas's and Strauss's reading of Rosenzweig.[7] Indeed, the significant tension between these two readings is found in Rosenzweig's philosophy.[8] While their readings of Rosenzweig are remarkably different, Rosenzweig, for both Levinas and Strauss, marks a break with both the western philosophical tradition and the tradition of modern Jewish thought. For both, Rosenzweig's philosophy in the *Star of Redemption* is a radical step toward taking revelation seriously from a philosophical point of view. The title of this chapter – "freedom depends upon its bondage" – comes from Strauss's *Philosophy and Law*. This phrase captures not only Strauss's view of the significance of Rosenzweig's thought, but of Levinas's thought also. Both credit Rosenzweig, whom Strauss knew briefly and whom Levinas did not, with provoking them to rethink revelation and hence the possibility of true freedom.

I argue in this chapter that the significance of Levinas's and Strauss's respective appropriations of Rosenzweig is that these respective interpretations at the same time reflect their broader hermeneutical approach to written texts, Jewish and philosophical. There is a profound link between Levinas's claim that ethics is first philosophy and his reading of Rosenzweig, while there is also such a link between Strauss's claim that politics is first philosophy and his reading of Rosenzweig. But perhaps most fundamentally, Levinas's and Strauss's respective readings of Rosenzweig reflect their basic premises about the meaning of "revelation." In investigating their respective assertions about Rosenzweig, we are thus at the same time investigating their respective contentions about what it means to make a truth claim in regard to revelation.

After exploring in the first two parts of this chapter Levinas's and Strauss's respective interpretations of Rosenzweig and the meaning of revelation, I argue in Section 3.3 that Levinas has a post-Christian view of revelation in which revelation is revealed through philosophy. Strauss in contrast maintains that philosophy cannot mediate revelation, which only divine law can. The conclusion, Section 3.4, considers the implications of this analysis for the question of the scope and meaning of Jewish thought.

3.1. LEVINAS'S READING: ROSENZWEIG'S OPPOSITION TO TOTALITY

Before appreciating Levinas's and Strauss's different interpretations of Rosenzweig, we must note the common claim that both make about his thought. Simply, Rosenzweig's philosophy represents for both of them the reintroduction of a notion of divine transcendence into the western philosophical tradition. When Levinas claims that Rosenzweig introduced an opposition to the idea of totality, he claims that Rosenzweig's system of philosophy undoes itself as a philosophical system by way of his claims about revelation. Indeed, we need but note the title to Stéphanè Moses's seminal work on Rosenzweig, *System and Revelation,* to which Levinas wrote the introduction.[9] From Levinas's perspective, Rosenzweig's consideration of revelation bursts what he claims is the totalizing and systematic tendency of western philosophy, which is the premise that reason can know everything. Revelation undoes reason for Levinas in that it ruptures our ability to cognize everything.

Yet revelation does not signify the end of philosophy for Levinas. Levinas attributes this insight also to Rosenzweig, claiming that Rosenzweig's philosophical opposition to the idea of totality not only does not diminish the relevance of philosophy, but signifies the beginning of an era in which "everything is philosophy." Levinas suggests that Rosenzweig's opposition to totality yields two significant metaphysical insights: the first that concerns the nature of the self and the second that concerns the relation between the self and another person. Levinas uses the term *metaphysics* to signify a basic structure of experience that makes possible and is the ethical relation. Rosenzweig's opposition to totality should, for Levinas, be understood in terms of ethics. I cannot cognize or assimilate another person into myself. The other person's rupture of my idea of totality is for Levinas the proper and true meaning of revelation. Ethics, for Levinas, is my response to the other person. The possibility of ethics rests on my irreducible uniqueness. Simply put, if I couldn't respond to another person, ethics would not be possible. So, while the other person ruptures my freedom from the perspective of my totality, this rupturing also truly frees me from the perspective of ethics.

From Levinas's perspective, Rosenzweig's views of the atheistic self prior to revelation and this same self in the throes of revelation give expression to what he argues are the metaphysical "facts" about human subjectivity. From the perspective of Levinas's philosophy, Rosenzweig's account of the metaethical self (in Part 2 of the *Star*) points to the radical distinctness of the irreducibly separate self. Levinas follows Rosenzweig in claiming that once the sediments of culture and history have been brushed away, an irreducible surplus remains of the self. As we saw in Chapter 2, Levinas claims that this irreducible separateness makes ethics, which he claims is the meaning of revelation, possible.

As is well known, Rosenzweig begins his discussion in the *Star of Redemption* of revelation by quoting the Song of Songs. He writes:

Love is strong as death. Strong in the same way as death? But against whom does death display its strength? Again him whom it seizes. And love, of course, seizes both, the lover as well as the beloved, but the beloved otherwise than the lover. It originates in the lover. The beloved is seized, his love is already a response to being seized.[10]

Before turning to Strauss's reading of Rosenzweig, let us explore briefly a number of Levinasian themes in this quotation. Rosenzweig's explication of "Love is strong as death" serves from Levinas's perspective as the quintessential response to Heidegger. Death displays its strength again him whom it seizes. From a Levinasian perspective, Rosenzweig's formulation here describes the limitation of Heidegger's view of the self and of death. The power of death is that it is the end of being oneself. This is what it means to die: to no longer be living. Love is as strong as death because love is as transforming as death is. But love, Rosenzweig, suggests, is more complicated than death. Love seizes both the lover and the beloved. For this reason, love breaks open the notion of totality even more profoundly than death does because love concerns the relation between two subjectivities, while death concerns only one subject.

From Levinas's perspective, Rosenzweig's account of the *dynamic* of revelation also describes the *dynamic* of the ethical relation, which is one of asymmetry. The experience of revelation, Rosenzweig claims, is a two-stage process that consists of two statements made by the beloved to the lover (who again is the initiator of love). These two statements are "I have sinned" and "I am a sinner." What Rosenzweig describes as the acknowledgement of sin in the present Levinas would describe as the ethical situation in which I transform my present (and not only recognize the error of my past) by virtue of my relationship to the other. Rosenzweig's description of the response of the lover to the beloved's second acknowledgement would seem to confirm Levinas's view. Rosenzweig claims that in response to my acknowledgment of my sin, the lover says to me "You are mine."[11] As Rosenzweig continues, this "is a sentence which does not have 'I' for a subject."[12] From Levinas's perspective, I am now for the other because I am now a "you." But in responding to the other, in becoming a "you," I truly become myself.

Levinas transforms Rosenzweig's consideration of divine revelation into an ethical theory. Calling what Rosenzweig describes as revelation "the Good," Levinas writes:

Has not the Good chosen the subject with an election recognizable in the responsibility of being hostage, to which the subject is destined, which he cannot evade without denying himself, and by virtue of which he is unique? A philosopher can give to this election only the signification circumscribed by responsibility to the other. This antecedence of responsibility to freedom would signify the Goodness of the Good: the necessity that the Good choose me first before I can be in a position to choose, that is, welcome its choice.[13]

Levinas understands himself as a philosopher and Rosenzweig as a philosopher also. Hence he contends that the meaning of revelation is "the necessity that the Good choose me first." That Levinas reads Rosenzweig philosophically or ethically does not mean, however, that Levinas does not have recourse to theological concepts. Indeed, Levinas is at times more theological than Rosenzweig, such as when he describes what I called Rosenzweig's two stages of revelation with reference to "incarnation."

The body is not only an image or figure here; it is the distinctive in-oneself of the contraction of ipseity and its breakup. This contraction is not an impossibility to forget oneself, to detach oneself from oneself, in the concern for itself. It is a recurrence to oneself out of an irrecusable exigency of the other, a duty overflowing my being, a duty becoming a debt and an extreme passivity prior to the tranquility, still quite relative, in the inertia and materiality of things at rest. . . . Here what is due goes beyond having, but makes giving possible. This recurrence is incarnation. In it the body which makes giving possible makes one *other* without alienating. For this other is the heart, and the goodness, of the same, the inspiration or the very psyche of the soul.[14]

Like Rosenzweig, Levinas describes the self's ability to respond to the other as a remaking of the self for the sake of the other. Levinas describes this process as incarnation to emphasize the concrete particularity of the self who is now for the other. Yet while Levinas appears to be far more theological than Rosenzweig in his choice of vocabulary, the important thing to notice is that while Rosenzweig suggests in his discussion of the Song of Songs that we can understand divine love through human love, Levinas's analysis reverses this order. For Levinas, we can understand ethics through theological concepts such as "incarnation." Again we can appreciate Levinas's articulation of his own project, which is to understand theology, revelation, and even incarnation *from the point of view of the philosopher.*

The reading I have just offered of Rosenzweig through Levinas (a reading that has a number of contemporary advocates) is not a claim for the historical accuracy of such a reading, both in terms of what Levinas says about Rosenzweig and in terms of what Rosenzweig actually says. As Samuel Moyn has shown, it is quite possible, if not likely, that Levinas projects his debt to Rosenzweig back onto his own philosophical claim about ethics.[15] What is interesting about this historical point, however, is that this fact would not make a difference from Levinas's point of view. And nor would the fact that Rosenzweig, in his discussion of revelation, may have meant something different from or even contradictory to Levinas's claims about interhuman relations. From Levinas's perspective, neither of these points would change what he claims is the *philosophical* significance of Rosenzweig's claims about revelation. It would, therefore, not be of philosophical relevance whether or not he gets Rosenzweig qua Rosenzweig right because, to use Strauss's phrase, Levinas maintains that it is possible to understand an author better than he understands himself.[16] It is here that we find the confluence between Levinas's reading of Rosenzweig and his own claims about the meaning of philosophy. It is the work of philosophy, from Levinas's perspective, to disregard extraphilosophical matters, such as historical, cultural, literary, or even theological context. The significance of Rosenzweig's philosophy, Levinas would maintain, is this philosophical insight, both about the content of philosophy, which for Levinas is the ethical relation, and the scope of philosophy, which for Levinas is to articulate clearly and definitively the ultimate meaning of our humanity (which he argues is ethics).

3.2. STRAUSS'S READING: GOD AS WHOLLY OTHER

Strauss's claims about Rosenzweig are significantly at odds with Levinas's claims. All of Levinas's work is oriented toward showing that relations between people have a divine element (what Levinas calls *trace*) to them and that anything divine we may speak of is centrally and ultimately of ethical significance. In contrast, from Strauss's perspective, Rosenzweig is concerned with the question of God's transcendence, not as evidenced only in human relations, but as evidenced by God's hold over us.

In his 1921 dissertation, "The Problem of Knowledge in the Philosophical Teachings of F. H. Jacobi," Strauss describes Jacobi's view of revelation as follows: "God is not only 'in us.' At the very least he is just as much 'over us.'"[17] The importance of Rosenzweig's philosophy for Strauss is the recognition of the necessity of thinking about God as wholly transcendent. It is in this sense philosophically significant that Strauss dedicated *Spinoza's Critique of Religion* to Rosenzweig's memory, for this is the book that he wrote after his dissertation. In his dissertation Strauss considered the relevance of Jacobi's notion of revelation for the problem of knowledge: what does Jacobi's view of revelation have to do with his theory of knowledge? In *Spinoza's Critique of Religion*, Strauss approached this same problem from the other side: what does Spinoza's theory of knowledge have to do with his denial of revelation? Rosenzweig, for Strauss, represents the Jewish philosophical challenge to Spinoza because Rosenzweig, unlike Spinoza, takes the possibility of revelation seriously for the problem of knowledge. As he would articulate more clearly in his 1965 preface to the English translation of *Spinoza's Critique of Religion*, Strauss dedicated his 1930 book to Rosenzweig's memory because Rosenzweig's attempt to take revelation seriously marked the *possibility* of showing that Spinoza's seemingly devastating critique of religion failed.

Taking revelation seriously for Strauss meant that Rosenzweig recognized the inherent weakness of philosophy. Whereas Levinas reads Rosenzweig as making "everything philosophy," Strauss reads Rosenzweig as exposing philosophy's fatal weakness in light of revelation. On Strauss's reading, Rosenzweig would agree with Levinas that philosophy is not revealed by philosophers, but for Rosenzweig this fact points not to philosophy's reinvigoration but to its ultimate weakness. Strauss's reading would find particular support in Rosenzweig's claim that it is revelation *and not philosophy* that makes communal truth possible. Rosenzweig argues in the *Star* and beyond that the purely philosophical quest for truth cannot provide an objective, public grounding of communal life, which only revelation can provide. As he puts it in the transition to Part 2 of the *Star* ("On the Possibility of Experiencing Miracle"): "And here the questionable aspect of the new philosophy [the philosopher of the *Weltanschauung*, the point of view] steps into plain view ... the bridge from maximum subjectivity to maximum objectivity is formed by theology's concept of revelation."[18] In this connection, Rosenzweig argues that miracles are possibly verifiable not through private, individual experience but through public, communal testimony. For Rosenzweig, the *possibility* of the truth of revelation and of individual miracles rests on the communal reception of such truths, and not on the individual's personal experience of them. In contrast, Rosenzweig maintains that philosophy can provide only the possibility of privately, and not publicly, verifiable truth.

In his own work Strauss agrees with Rosenzweig that philosophy by itself does not have the ability to provide a community of people with a common morality, while revelation does. Rosenzweig seems to agree with Strauss that Judaism, and revealed religion generally, is fundamentally *unphilosophical* precisely because it begins with accepted truths and not, as philosophy does, with the questioning of all such truths. Rosenzweig maintains that in relation to the old philosophy, "the new thinking" is fundamentally unphilosophical: "All philosophy has asked about essence [*Wesen*]. This is the question by means of which it differentiates itself from the *unphilosophical* thinking of common sense, which does not ask what a thing "actually" is."[19] The *Star of Redemption* is a philosophical argument for the necessity of the unphilosophical thinking of common sense.

Rosenzweig was a deep admirer of Judah Halevi and the reading of the *Star* that I have been offering here to illuminate Strauss's admiration for Rosenzweig has a profound affinity with Strauss's reading of Halevi's *Kuzari*.[20] According to Strauss, in the *Kuzari*, Halevi argues on *philosophical* grounds that the philosopher cannot deny the formal necessity of divine revelation for the moral life. It is worth quoting Strauss once again on Halevi, to apply his words to Rosenzweig. Strauss writes:

by going so far with the philosophers . . . he [Halevi] discover[s] the fundamental weakness of the philosophic position and the deepest reason why philosophy is enormously dangerous. . . . One has not to be naturally pious, he has merely to have a passionate interest in genuine morality in order to long with all his heart for revelation: *moral man as such is the potential believer* (emphasis added).[21]

Strauss's comment that "moral man as such is the potential believer" captures the thrust of Rosenzweig's argument about revelation in the *Star*. Rosenzweig would agree with Strauss that philosophy is "not a set of dogmas . . . but a method or an attitude."[22] Philosophy designates the attitude of questioning for oneself all that there is.

Rosenzweig argues that the philosophical attitude is both profoundly true and profoundly dangerous. Philosophical paganism, the denial of revelation, remains philosophically true. As Rosenzweig puts it in "The New Thinking," "paganism is . . . no more and no less than the truth."[23] In this sense, "Revelation does not in the least destroy genuine paganism."[24] Rosenzweig argues that the right kind of philosophy recognizes the necessity of revelation for the *practical* life, while the wrong kind of philosophy (both idealism and Nietzschean philosophy in Rosenzweig's case) denies or at the very least is indifferent to revelation's *practical* relevance. As Strauss argues in regard to Halevi's *Kuzari*, the *Star* is a philosophical argument for the practical need for revealed religion in general, and not for the philosophical truth of Judaism in particular. Indeed, this is precisely the view that Rosenzweig expressed in connection with his attempt to popularize his "new thinking" at his adult education center in 1923. Rosenzweig maintains that the arguments he presents are not ones in favor of Judaism, but rather ones that use certain Jewish notions to make an argument for the relevance of common sense.[25] While certainly not identical with revelation, common sense for Rosenzweig opens the door to the *possibility* of the experience of revelation, while "the old thinking" closes this very door. For this reason, according to Rosenzweig, "the new thinking" does not have any "special Jewishness" to it.[26] The recognition of the philosophical necessity of revelation *via the practical life*, and *not a proof of the philosophical veracity* of Jewish revelation per se, marks what Rosenzweig calls "the new thinking."

Despite his great admiration for Rosenzweig, Strauss recognizes that Rosenzweig's notion of revelation and claims about common sense are predicated on an argument about revelation's ultimate historicity and this is where he parts ways with Rosenzweig. It is true that Rosenzweig, like Strauss and Levinas, rejects the framework of a scientific historicism (e.g., *Wissenschaft des Judentums*) and the notions of scientific or moral progress this view entails. But Strauss and Levinas also reject the further claim that truth is created in and by history. Rosenzweig does not reject this claim and though he presented himself as an opponent of historicism, Rosenzweig meant by this more narrowly a kind of Hegelian historicism that charts reason's movement through history. Rosenzweig did not reject the inversion of this sort of historicism, which is a historicism nonetheless, that claims that truth is produced not in but *by* history.[27]

Rosenzweig maintains that while the philosophical attitude purports to be universal, it is particularistic precisely because it does not recognize its rootedness in its own transpired history.[28] Indeed, in this connection, the *Star* argues that a miracle is possibly verifiable through an appeal to transpired history:

the most cogent proof of the miracle is the appeal to the martyrs. . . . The testimony of oath and the testimony of blood . . . amalgamate and after several centuries both ultimately become a single proof in Augustine's famous appeal from all individual reasons to the present historical overall-manifestation, *the ecclesiae auctoritas*, without which he would not credit the testimony of Scripture.[29]

Miracles are possible, Rosenzweig argues, not because we may experience them individually, but because martyrs have publicly attested to their truth in the past and because subsequent generations have verified these received truths by risking their own lives for them. Martyrdom for Rosenzweig is not an event confined to the past, but an intensified illustration of the "present historical" need for a public and communal *affirmation of the past* for the sake of the present. In this Rosenzweig affirms the "historicity" that his immediate contemporary Heidegger advocates and it is this very position that Strauss and Levinas *both* reject in their post-Heideggerian philosophies.[30]

From Strauss's perspective, Rosenzweig's emphasis on the historicity of truth and meaning extends not just to his arguments about philosophy and revelation defined abstractly, but to his claims about how to read and indeed to reappropriate for modern Jews classical Jewish texts. Here Rosenzweig's notion of *transpired history*, a term he uses to describe the ultimate importance of the Bible, is intimately connected to his educational efforts and claims about how contemporary Jews must and can understand their tradition. Rosenzweig maintains that revelation gains its meaning by way of transpired history, which includes *the reception and verification* of revelation by future generations. As Strauss puts it in his preface to *Spinoza's Critique of Religion*:

Rosenzweig's return [to revelation] was not unqualified. The Judaism to which he returned was not identical with the Judaism of the age prior to Moses Mendelssohn . . . While opposing the old thinking, the new thinking was nevertheless its heir. . . . The new thinking is 'experiencing philosophy.' As such it is passionately concerned with the difference between what is experienced, or at least capable of being experienced, by the present-day believer and what is merely known by tradition; that difference was of no concern to traditional Judaism.[31]

Strauss continues to criticize Rosenzweig for distinguishing between what the "compilers of the canon meant" and "how the text affects the present-day believer." Strauss rightly recognizes that for Rosenzweig, "[t]he former is the concern of history as history which, if it regards itself as self-sufficient, is one of the decayed forms of the old thinking; the latter, if it is practiced with full consciousness, calls for the new thinking."

Although Strauss does not believe that history is self-sufficient, he agrees (against Rosenzweig and Levinas) with what he describes as "the old thinking" that the aim of interpretation is to understand a text in the way in which its author intended it to be understood. Just as Levinas's interpretative approach to Rosenzweig reflects his own philosophical program, Strauss's reading of Rosenzweig reflects his. Strauss claims that we must first understand an author as he understood himself and only then can we come to the ahistorical truth of a text. The truths of the great texts of western civilization, the philosophical canon and the Bible, reflect the contemplation of the timeless question of what is the best life. For Strauss, the Bible and its subsequent interpretations offer a different answer to this question than do the great texts of philosophy. But what these two traditions have in common, Strauss maintains, is the timeless question of what constitutes the good society. This question, Strauss claims, is the question of politics and this is the question that constitutes the very possibility of philosophical reflection. Strauss's claim about politics as first philosophy follows in part from his engagement with Rosenzweig. The philosophical possibility of revelation is the moral guard against the fundamental amorality of philosophy, for Strauss.

3.3. WHAT TO MAKE OF THIS DIFFERENCE: LEVINAS AS POST-CHRISTIAN PHILOSOPHER

We have seen that Levinas and Strauss have markedly different readings of Rosenzweig and that these readings bear directly on each of their views of the scope and nature of philosophy as it relates to revelation. For Strauss, philosophy simply cannot account for revelation, while for Levinas philosophy defines revelation's true meaning, which is ethics. Ironically, while Levinas views his philosophy as a continuation of Rosenzweig's views and Strauss views his philosophy as a break with Rosenzweig, Strauss's reading of Rosenzweig is truer to Rosenzweig's basic philosophical intention, which is to question the autonomy of philosophy with regard to *divine* revelation, which cannot by definition be articulated only in ethical terms. I would argue then that as an actual reading *of Rosenzweig*, Strauss's emerges as the stronger one because it takes greater care to understand Rosenzweig's fundamental premise, which is to rethink the meaning of *divine* revelation. In contrast, Levinas's reading of Rosenzweig is of a piece with his broader hermeneutical approach, which characterizes much of post-Kantian philosophy. This view suggests, using the words that Strauss attributes to Kant, that it is possible to understand an author better than he understood himself.[32] Levinas's interpretation of Rosenzweig is premised on the notion that the true meaning of Rosenzweig's thought does not begin with Rosenzweig's stated intentions but with a philosophical/ethical reading of Rosenzweig.

Levinas's interpretation of Rosenzweig is in this sense doubly ironic, first because, as noted in Section 3.1, he considers himself Rosenzweig's heir and second because rather than allowing revelation to call the autonomy of philosophy into question, as is Levinas's stated intention, his philosophy actually reasserts the modern domination of philosophy over revelation. In Part 1 of this book, I argued that Levinas is a defender of a particular modern philosophical project that ascribes, to use Levinas's own term, *messianic* aspirations to philosophy. Philosophy, for Levinas, can and ought to guide religion, society, and politics. I argue in what follows that Levinas's expansion of the task of philosophy – in which "philosophy" becomes "everything" and is revealed through nonphilosophers – is of a piece with a particular Christian and post-Christian philosophical project that historically does not, as is most often argued, securalize theology, but that makes philosophy theological.

Following Strauss, I suggest that the modern philosophical tradition ultimately eclipses the question of revelation in its religious claim that philosophy can redeem politics and society. As I will show in greater detail in Chapter 6, Strauss maintains that this tendency of much of the modern philosophical canon is linked historically and conceptually to medieval Christian attempts to fuse philosophy with theology. I add to Strauss's account of Christian approaches to the relation between philosophy and theology the historical analyses of Ian Hunter who, in his recent book, *Rival Enlightenments: Civil and Metaphysical Philosophy in Early Modern Germany*, shows the religious roots and even more importantly the *religious aspirations* of modern German philosophy.[33] I suggest that Levinas's philosophy, despite his claims to the contrary, reenacts this very Christianization of philosophy that defines German metaphysics and, again despite claims to the contrary, also marks post-Kantian moral and political philosophy. Levinas's reading of Rosenzweig and transformation of some of Rosenzweig's themes are an instance of this very Christianization of philosophy.

Let us begin by recalling Strauss's claim about the difference between Judaism and Islam on the one hand and Christianity on the other in regard to the sociology of philosophy. Once again, Strauss writes:

Here, we are touching on what, from the point of view of the sociology of philosophy, is the most important difference between Christianity on the one hand, and Islam as well as Judaism on the other. For the Christian, the sacred doctrine is revealed theology; for the Jew and the Muslim, the sacred doctrine is, at least primarily the legal interpretation of the Divine Law (*talmud* or *fiqh*). The sacred doctrine in the latter sense has, to say the least, much less in common with philosophy than the sacred doctrine in the former sense. It is ultimately for this reason that the status of philosophy was, as a matter of principle, much more precarious in Judaism and in Islam than in Christianity: in Christianity philosophy became an integral part of the officially recognized and even required training of the student of the sacred doctrine.[34]

As I suggested in Chapter 1, Strauss's assertions about Christianity are certainly not comprehensive. Nevertheless, even though they do not do justice to the full array of Christian traditions, Strauss's contention about the status of revealed theology for the Christian tradition is useful not only for understanding differences between Judaism, Christianity, and Islam, but also for understanding the development of modern metaphysics. While the standard story of the development of Enlightenment philosophy suggests that modern philosophers properly separate philosophy from revelation[35] and that medieval theologians do not make such a separation, the recent work of Hunter along with a number of other intellectual historians shows that that this misleading account of the historical circumstances in which the modern study of metaphysics arose is the outcome of how deeply imbedded we are in what has become and remains the *religious* aspiration of the development of the discipline of modern philosophy.

Hunter begins his study by noting that it was Martin Luther who called for the exclusion of university metaphysics. As Luther put it:

Virtually the entire *Ethics* of Aristotle is the worst enemy of grace. This is in opposition to the scholastics.... It is an error to say that no man can become a theologian without Aristotle. Indeed, no one can become a theologian unless he becomes one without Aristotle.[36]

Contemporary philosophers and historians of philosophy attack Luther for irrationalism,[37] but as Hunter notes:

As soon as we ... reinstate the specific anthropology underpinning Luther's ... position ... then the true character of the 'two truths' doctrine becomes apparent ... [Luther] was not irrationally rejecting philosophy. Rather he was attempting to exclude philosophers (university metaphysicans) from the role of mediating the Christian mysteries, treating their rationalist pursuit of salvation through ascent to transcendent knowledge as incompatible with the mode of acceding to salvation through biblical faith.[38]

Note the overlap between Hunter's historically oriented reconsideration of the intentions of Luther with Strauss's textually oriented claims about Halevi's, and by implication Rosenzweig's, arguments about philosophy. In the cases of both Luther and Halevi, the assumption of modern interpreters is that their claims for revelation must be irrationalist in character. But as both Hunter and Strauss point out in different ways, this assumption is predicated on a misunderstanding of the actual argument that concerns the *types* of claims made, and authorities appealed to, by revelation and philosophy. It is only because contemporary philosophers and historians assume that philosophy can and does provide a universal grounding of morality that they label any claim to the contrary as either fundamentally irrationalist (as in the cases of Luther and Halevi) or as fundamentally atheistic (as in the case of Strauss's thought, regardless of whether this is the case for Strauss the person).

We must note that Strauss's claim about Christian theology as the fusion of philosophy and revelation still holds, even in the case of Luther. For Luther, philosophy cannot account for revelation, but Christian theology can

articulate the Christian mysteries. Strauss argues, in contrast, defending both
Judaism and Islam, that divine law is the only possible rational mediation of
the divine.[39] We will discuss Strauss's conception of religious law as the basis
of religious rationalism in Chapter 5 and his broad claims about law in Part 3
of this book. Luther, of course, never claimed to be a rationalist (and neither did Halevi).[40] Luther nevertheless argued that the fusion of philosophy
and revelation in university metaphysics was a profound danger to Christian
faith.

Arguments against university metaphysics introduced by Luther were ironically defeated by the Protestant academy.[41] The Lutheran argument against
university metaphysics was taken up by civil philosophers such as Christian
Thomasius and Samuel von Pufendorf who, in advocating the separation of
politics from philosophical claims to the good, put forward an alternative
anthropology to what became the post-Kantian anthropological view of the
human being. These civil philosophers, historical critics of the rise of modern metaphysics, criticized the metaphysical school as sectarian because of its
commitment to a particular view of human nature. First and foremost this
metaphysical view of human nature implied, in the words of Thomasius, that
"it is within human capacity to live virtuously and happily."[42]

There is much to say about the historical conditions of the rise of German
metaphysics and the ways in which post-Kantian philosophers and intellectual historians have rewritten this history, but this is, of course, an enormous
subject beyond the scope of this book. However, two aspects of this historical
debate between the metaphysical and civil philosophers are directly relevant
for our consideration of Levinas and Strauss. The first aspect, on which we
have already touched, is the anthropological vision of the early German metaphysicians, which saw human beings as being able to create and sustain the
conditions for their own happiness. Clearly, this anthropological assumption remains at the core of Kantian and post-Kantian metaphysics and moral
philosophy. Along with this assumption, the civil philosophers were critical
of the metaphysical philosophers for also implying that the problems of all
human beings were the same and required the same solution.[43] Thomasius,
for example, rejected the premise of the metaphysical philosophers that "man
is a single species and that what is good for one [person] is good for another."[44]
This premise about the natural equality of all human beings and all human
problems is, of course, at the heart of what became the post-Kantian political
project.[45] As we have seen, it is this notion of natural equality as the *first* premise
of political, social, and ethical life that Levinas and Strauss both criticize in
their shared claim that obligations precede rights. As Levinas put it in the 1990
preface to the republication of his article "Reflections on the Philosophy of

Hitlerism," published first in 1934, "we must ask ourselves if liberalism is all we need to achieve an authentic dignity for the human being."[46]

In this connection, Levinas and Strauss would both seem to be critical of the implications of the development of modern metaphysics. Indeed, we already have noted many times throughout this book the ways in which their formal claims for the necessity of revelation for philosophy parallel one another. But it is in connection with a second theme related to the rise of German metaphysics that Levinas and Strauss differ from one another. And it is in connection with this second theme that I suggest Levinas shares in the implicit Christian assumptions, in both form and content, which went along with the development of German metaphysics.

As Walter Sparn argues, rather than attempting to free philosophy from the shackles of theology, the fusing of philosophy and theology in university metaphysics had theological aims and used theological tools to achieve these ends.[47] The basic goal of university metaphysics was not to rationalize theology (as most of its subsequent histories would have it), but to keep secular subjects within Christian academic culture. This historical point raises an important philosophical point that has been lost in most histories of the rise of German metaphysics. The metaphysical philosophers, rather than moving beyond theology, created a new theology of metaphysics. As Hunter succinctly put it, "the metaphysical philosophers regarded their 'natural theologies' as *new moral theologies for public life*, shifting the locus of salvation to metaphysics itself (emphasis added)."[48] Modern metaphysics arose as a spiritual exercise that recommended itself not just to individuals (as was the case for ancient philosophy) but to society at large. In arguing and eventually triumphing philosophically against the civil philosophers, the metaphysical philosophers championed a new vision of, to borrow a term from Levinas, a messianic future in which metaphysics as philosophy becomes "everything" and saves society.

Seen in historical context, Levinas's messianic claims for philosophy do not represent a break with the aspirations of modern metaphysics (and neither do, e.g., Derrida's religious claims for philosophy). Like the early modern German metaphysicians, Levinas regards philosophy as a spiritual exercise, which is designed to perfect not just our understanding of philosophical matters but the kind of people we may become. As Hunter puts it, "From a purely historical perspective . . . it is the *paideia* of metaphysics itself – inculcated in religious or academic institutions dedicated to grooming the spiritual elite – that is responsible for inducing the desire for metaphysical knowledge."[49] But a historical look at the development of early modern metaphysics also points to something more important than this common quest for spiritual improvement (common also to ancient and medieval philosophy) that much of the subsequent reception of the modern metaphysical tradition has eclipsed. Levinas's deepest formal affinity with the rise of modern metaphysics is in ascribing *moral and social authority* to, in Hunter's words, "the self-transformative function of university metaphysics."[50] Prior to the rise of modern metaphysics, moral and social authority came from the Church (and scholastic philosophy). The development of modern metaphysics historically transformed what had been the *social* function of Christian theology. In this sense, Levinas's positive use of the term *metaphysics* is akin with the historical function of Christian theology and with the historical function of what became post-Christian metaphysics.

But the kinship between Levinas's philosophy and Christian and post-Christian philosophy goes deeper than this formal structure of ascribing moral and social authority to university metaphysics. The content of Levinas's attempt to harmonize philosophy and theology is in keeping with the attempt of the early modern metaphysicians through Kant to keep secular knowledge within the orbit of what Levinas would call revelation and what I am suggesting would be more appropriately called Christian revelation, or Christian theology. Let us turn to one aspect of this historical objective that is particularly relevant for understanding the meaning of Levinas's philosophy in general and his transformation of Rosenzweig in particular.

According to Sparn and Hunter, the metaphysics of both Leibniz and Kant should be understood as a transformation, indeed a generalization, of Luther's metaphysical view of Christ's two natures.[51] Summing up Kant's employment of Luther's metaphysical doctrine, Hunter writes: "In fact Kant superimposes the Christological doctrine of Christ's divine and human natures onto the metaphysical doctrine of man's noumenal and phenomenal natures, thereby conceiving of moral renewal as a kind of secular spiritual rebirth taking place via philosophy within the person."[52] In this context, I'd like to suggest that Levinas's use of Christological terms, such as *incarnation*, is not insignificant. Hunter's description of the Kantian project as attempting a "moral renewal as a kind of secular spiritual rebirth taking place via philosophy within the person" could equally apply to the role that incarnation plays in Levinas's philosophy. Incarnation, for Levinas, is the way in which I am for the other. As the ethical relation, incarnation also fuses the human with the divine. The trace of the other is divine and the only meaning the divine trace can have, for Levinas, is an ethical meaning. In this important sense, ethics, Levinas's main theme, is the fusing of divine and human nature. Incarnation is my spiritual rebirth, but this rebirth is at one and the same time secular in that it can and does only concern human relations. For Levinas, as for Kant, philosophy is the mediating force that affects this spiritual change.

Levinas might reply that it is actually the other person and not philosophy that affects this change within me. But this reply would only beg the question of why Levinas finds the highly technical, metaphysical, and indeed philosophical language of phenomenology necessary for describing the ethical relation. And why also does Levinas in his confessional writings, as I will show in great detail in Chapter 8, insist upon recourse to philosophical points and arguments in attempting to articulate the true meaning of the Talmud? We need but mention once again Levinas's own dictum, taken not from his philosophical writings, but from his confessional writings: "Philosophy derives [*dérive*] from religion. It is made necessary by religion adrift [*en dérive*], and in all likelihood religion is always adrift."[53] There can be no question that Levinas ascribes to the philosophical, indeed metaphysical, enterprise the very prestige assigned to it by the university metaphysicians in the early modern German university. And while many subsequent histories of the modern metaphysical tradition, and many subsequent philosophies premised on these histories, continue to deny the *religious* claims of modern European philosophy, the continuity of Levinas's thought with this tradition can help us to rethink the reception of this history. Indeed, we might say that Levinas's very attempt to return philosophy to its ethical origins is a return to the origins of modern metaphysics.

3.4. MODERN PHILOSOPHY AND THE LEGACY OF CHRISTIANITY

There are, of course, significant differences between Levinas's project and that of the early modern and modern metaphysicians, and we turn to these and their implications in Chapter 4. For now, however, I would like to conclude by considering the implications of Levinas's appropriation of Rosenzweig in the context of this discussion of the Christian and post-Christian themes of the rise of modern metaphysics. That Levinas reads Rosenzweig as making "everything philosophy" tells us much more about Levinas than it does about Rosenzweig. I previously mentioned Moyn's historical claim that in responding to what he regarded as Heidegger's immoral turn in politics and philosophy, Levinas projects back a debt to Rosenzweig in his own work. I have tried to give this historical point additional conceptual credence in showing how Levinas's actual historical debt is to German metaphysics and, in important ways, to Kant especially.[54] This is relevant not only for the historical record but for appreciating the kind of claim Levinas makes. In returning to "metaphysics" after Heidegger, Levinas returns to Kant and his early modern predecessors in an attempt to affect a secular spiritual rebirth. While purporting to criticize the western philosophical tradition and the modern philosophical tradition in particular, Levinas repeats the very origins of this tradition, which is the attempt to subsume theology under the rubric of philosophy.

It is likely that Levinas and his defenders would not recognize the kind of argument that I am suggesting Strauss makes in contrast to him. Once again, the history of the reception of the modern metaphysical tradition is relevant. Just as many histories regard all the precursors to Kant as poor expressions at best of what would become Kant's philosophy, so Levinas might regard Strauss's philosophy as an archaic enterprise that has not advanced far enough conceptually. What is striking about this sort of claim is that it is simultaneously teleological and ahistorical. This chapter has been a small attempt to begin to rethink the history of post-Christian philosophy and how this relates to Levinas's project. In assuming that philosophy and revelation are basically in harmony with one another, we, in following Levinas, commit this fundamental historical and perhaps philosophical error. In Hunter's words, "In continuing to see metaphysics as the harmonization of philosophy and theology, its modern historians may remain more indebted to this objective [of keeping secular knowledge within the orbit of Christianity] than they realize."[55]

4

An Irrationalist Rationalism: Levinas's Transformation of Hermann Cohen

*L*EVINAS REJECTS THE NOTION THAT THE MEANINGS OF THE TEXTS OF the past – philosophical and religious – derive from the contexts of their own historical eras. Instead, Levinas contends, all philosophical truth derives its meaning from its ethical significance. In Chapter 3 we explored Levinas's philosophical relation to a particular trajectory of post-Kantian philosophy that presumes the inherent superiority of ahistorical philosophical reflection to historical truth and the harmonious interchange, if not overlap, between revelation and philosophy. In this chapter, we turn in greater detail to the interconnection between these two claims in Levinas's philosophy by comparing his thought to the great neo-Kantian and Jewish philosopher's, Hermann Cohen (1842–1918). Half a century before Levinas, in the context of an argument for modern philosophy's need of "Judaism," Cohen held the very positions about truth and history, on the one hand, and revelation and philosophy, on the other, that Levinas holds. The coincidence of their claims about Judaism, philosophy, revelation, history, and truth allows us an opportunity to probe more deeply into Levinas's relation to the German metaphysical tradition and to the different trajectories of modern Jewish thought.

Before turning to the relation between Levinas and Cohen, we should note that Levinas, in his published works, mentions Cohen only a few times by name and does not seem to have engaged directly with Cohen's work.[1] But despite this lack of historical influence, Levinas's claims about revelation, philosophy, and ethics repeat (albeit unconsciously) Cohen's earlier contentions. Most basically, Levinas and Cohen both claim that Jewish revelation reorients philosophy toward recognizing the unique ethical duties individuals have toward each other. Both also maintain that revelation brings to philosophical reflection the priority of interhuman obligations and that philosophy brings to revelation the clarification of the solely human significance of revelation.

For Levinas, this coincidence in thought would be no mystery because philosophical and ethical truths by definition transcend history and culture. For this reason, all great thinkers – philosophical and religious – have access to the same truths. In fact, on this point too we can appreciate another similarity between Levinas and Cohen. Levinas's relation to Cohen is in accord with Cohen's own notion of a "source." For Cohen, a source's relevance does not derive from its historical origins but from its conceptual authority. Cohen's title of his posthumous book, *Religion of Reason Out of the Sources of Judaism* reflects this notion of "source."[2] The ultimate import and veracity of both "religion of reason" and "the sources of Judaism" are for Cohen not reducible or even inextricably connected to the historical manifestations of Judaism or the Jewish people. Indeed, this is one reason Cohen insisted that the title of his book was "religion of reason" and not "the religion of reason." "Sources," then are in no way reducible to their particular historical manifestations. Instead, they are used to reason about timeless truths. If Levinas's philosophical arguments about history parallel Cohen's, they do so, from Levinas's perspective, because the relationship between philosophy and history is a timeless one: philosophy does and must stand above history. For Levinas, as well as for Cohen before him, a philosopher will come to the truth regardless of his or her own place in history and even more importantly regardless of the place in history of the great books of philosophy and the Bible.

While I argue in this chapter that Levinas's thought is very close to Cohen's there are also basic differences between them that remain essential for our discussion of the continued relevance of Levinas's and Strauss's philosophies. At the beginning of the twentieth century, Cohen trumpets a rational liberalism that Levinas's philosophical framework, at the end of the twentieth century, attempts to reject. To emphasize a notion of asymmetrical obligation, Levinas rejects the notion of natural equality as the first principle of ethics. While Cohen, in his posthumous *Religion of Reason*, reflects on the dynamics of uniqueness that make such an asymmetrical view of the self possible, his entire system, nevertheless, is founded on affirming a notion of symmetry and equality among all people. Indeed, Cohen's 1904 masterpiece *Ethics of Pure Will*[3] attempts to elucidate a concept of modern law that is derived from and gives concrete expression to symmetry and equality among people. Along with the affirmation of a liberal political and ethical framework, Cohen also affirms the role of reason – and indeed of *science* – in deducing equality among people. Levinas, we have seen, rejects the primacy of reason in assessing our relation to others and emphasizes instead the significance of sensibility and ultimately of affectivity in grounding the fundamental obligation of one person to another. Finally, Levinas's rejection of natural equality as the first principle of ethics and his emphasis on sensibility rather than on reason as the basis of ethics have their impetus in his attempt to take the reality of evil seriously. In contrast, Cohen's thought remains, to borrow a characterization from Strauss, "optimistic" in its belief in the ultimate unreality of evil and in the primacy of reason.[4] Indeed, in one of his few references to Cohen, Levinas maintains that his philosophy epitomizes the idealist denial of both evil and transcendence.[5]

I argue in what follows that the deep similarity, but also ultimate difference, between Levinas and Cohen allow us to appreciate what I contend are the irrationalist implications of Levinas's thought. If we understand "rationalism" simply as an insistence on providing *reasons* for embracing one view over another, I suggest that Levinas's thought is ultimately irrationalist in that he does not and cannot provide any such reasons. Moreover, these irrationalist implications are philosophically, theologically, and politically problematic. In each case, Levinas rejects what is best about liberal modernity – the priority of the rule of law and rights-based constitutionalism[6] – and affirms what is most problematic – its messianic faith in philosophy. Section 4.1 of the chapter outlines the broad similarities between Cohen and Levinas in terms of their conceptions of revelation, philosophy, truth, and history. Section 4.2 of the chapter turns to Cohen's and Levinas's remarkably similar criticisms of Spinoza in light of their shared premises. In Section 4.3, we turn to the ultimate difference between Cohen and Levinas, which concerns their different accounts of reason and sensibility. I conclude in Section 4.4 by considering the implications of this analysis for evaluating the rationality of Levinas's brand of rationalism, which I maintain is not rational, philosophically or politically.

4.1. FUTURE AND PAST, INSIDE AND OUT

To appreciate the interconnection between Levinas's and Cohen's shared claims about history and truth on the one hand and philosophy and revelation on the other, we must first turn to Cohen's view of history in greater detail. As David Myers has noted recently, Cohen was ambivalent with regard to history.[7] Drawing on the distinction between empirical (*historisch*) and *a priori* (*geschichtlich*) notions of history, Cohen maintained, in Steven Schwarszchild's words, that "only those facts deserve the dignity of that name [*geschichtlich*] which are consciously ordered with an eye toward the rational, i.e. ideal, end."[8] For Cohen, history's ideal end, its *geschichtlich* character, determines the pure will and action to transform the outer form of history, its *historisch* character. The important point here, as it pertains to Levinas, is that this doesn't mean

for Cohen that empirical history in the present conforms to the rational ideal
of history. Rather, Cohen maintains that history is always projected toward
the future. Not insignificantly, Cohen calls this projection toward the future
"messianism." Put simply, Cohen's claim is that the messianic future of history, indeed the messianic *judgment* of history, is the true and final meaning
of history, as opposed to the pure facts of history. Against a Hegelian notion
of history, Cohen contends that the future determines the past rather than the
past determining the future. And, at the same time, the future for Cohen is
itself unreachable; we approach the future, but it is in the end a limit concept
for the truth claims of the present and of the past.[9]

Levinas makes the very same argument as Cohen does about the true meaning of history. In *Totality and Infinity*, he writes:

The deepening of the inner life can no longer be guided by the evidences of history.
It is given over to risk and to the moral creation of the I – to horizons more vast
than history, in which history itself is judged. Objective events and the evidence
of philosophers can only conceal these horizons. If subjectivity cannot be judged
in Truth without its apology, if judgment, instead of reducing it to silence exalts
it, then there must be a discord between events and the good. . . .[10]

Like Cohen, Levinas contrasts the inner meaning of history, in Cohen's terms,
its *geschichtlich* character, to its outer meaning, its *historisch* character. The
latter concerns objective events and cannot by definition arrive at what Levinas
calls the truth of history. Levinas's and Cohen's shared claim that the future
determines the past, and not the other way around, coincides with their shared
contention that "there must be a discord between events and the good." The
deepening of the inner life is for Levinas a turn away from the external facts
of history and evidences of philosophy toward the good. And like Cohen,
Levinas maintains that this good of history – its inner life – determines the
final truth of history, both in a temporal and transcendental sense. As Levinas
puts it:

To place oneself beyond the judgment of history, under the judgment of truth,
is not to suppose behind the apparent history another history called judgment
of God. . . . The judgment of God that judges me at the same time confirms me.
But it confirms me precisely in my interiority, whose justice is more severe than
the judgment of history. . . . The deepening of my responsibility in the judgment
that is borne upon me is not of the order of universalization: beyond the justice
of universal laws, the I enters under judgment by the fact of being good. . . . The
inner life is exalted by the truth of being – by the existence of being in the truth of
judgment. . . . The judgment of consciousness must refer to a reality beyond the
sentence pronounced by history. . . .[11]

Levinas's use of the term *the inner life* bears a deep affinity to Cohen's thought even beyond their philosophies of history. As Dieter Adelmann has recently argued in great detail, Cohen's philosophical system is predicated on his teacher's, the linguist Heymann Steinthal, notions of inner and outer form.[12] Steinthal's view of language responds to the basic philosophical problem of the German idealist tradition: the relation between *a priori* and synthetic knowledge. Following some of his contemporaries (and August Boeckh in particular), Steinthal understood this philosophical problem in the context of philology as the problem of "knowledge of the detected one" ("*Erkenntnis des Erkannten*"). Adelmann convincingly shows that it is not possible to understand Cohen's philosophy outside of the horizon of what was for him contemporary philology (from Humboldt to Boeckh, with whom Cohen also studied, to Steinthal).[13] Adelmann argues that Cohen relies on Steinthal's notion of inner form in his transcendental method that attempts to account for the unity of consciousness, in his understanding of the relationship between Judaism and philosophy and in his argument about the relation between religion and ethics. Finally, Adelmann shows that Cohen's arguments about the correlation between Judaism and philosophy are based on Steinthal's earlier view that "the prophetic vision is the inner form of language [itself]."[14]

In Section 4.3 of this chapter we turn to some of the more technical aspects of Cohen's use of Steinthal's notions of inner and outer form in his transcendental method as it relates to his philosophy of law. Here, however, we turn to Cohen's argument about the relation between religion and ethics in his posthumous work, *Religion of Reason*, which I suggest, following Adelmann, must be understood in the context of Steinthal's notions of inner and outer form. Simply put, for Cohen religion is the inner form of reason, while ethics is the outer form of reason. This formulation captures *Religion of Reason* in which Cohen's task is to elucidate the share that religion has in reason. As Cohen puts the problem:

Ethics can recognize and give recognition to man only as a member of humanity. As an individual man he can only be a representative carrier of humanity.... Does ethics have the methodological means for establishing it, if its goal is the totality (*Allheit*) which is realized in humanity? Would not such a division and gradation lie in the general direction of plurality (*Mehrheit*) and thus be an aberration from ethics' unifying goal of totality?[15]

Cohen argues that inwardness (*Innerlichkeit*) produces true individuals and that only true individuals can form a plurality (as opposed to a totality). Inwardness is produced by way of confession and prayer, which must have a communal context. Hence, the inner form of confession directs the outer form of the congregation, which is true plurality. Religion's share in reason is the production of the plurality that supports the totality or outer form of ethics.[16]

We can now appreciate the confluence between Cohen's claims about history and truth on the one hand, and philosophy and revelation on the other. For Cohen, the inner source of philosophy is revelation, just as the inner source of the events of history is history's ultimate messianic judgment. In both cases, the tension between these inner and outer forms represents what Levinas calls "a discord between events and the good." I have suggested in Section 4.1 that the content of Levinas's claims about history and truth and about philosophy and revelation parallels Cohen's claims. As importantly, the form of Levinas's contentions also parallels the form of Cohen's contentions. For both, the inner form of revelation and the messianic judgment of history produce the outer forms of philosophical evidence along with actual historical events.

4.2. THE SHARED CRITICISM OF SPINOZA: A CASE STUDY

The content and form of Levinas's and Cohen's arguments converge in their remarkably similar criticisms of Spinoza. First, Levinas and Cohen criticize Spinoza's denial of, again to use Levinas's words, "a discord between events and the good." Second, Levinas and Cohen claim that Spinoza's criticism of Judaism was not philosophically but politically motivated. Both see Spinoza as a betrayer of Judaism. In these ways, Cohen and Levinas's shared criticisms of Spinoza conform not only to each other, but also to a particular post-Kantian hermeneutic for which the political and social context of philosophy are derivative of what are claimed to be the timeless truths of philosophy.

But the convergence of Levinas's and Cohen's views of Spinoza is significant beyond an example of an application of their shared claims about history and truth, on the one hand, and revelation and philosophy, on the other. Spinoza's philosophy and historical person, for Levinas and Cohen, embody what is wrong with the modern philosophical tradition and its conception of Judaism. At the same time, however, Levinas's and Cohen's relation to Spinoza is more complex than either allows. Their projects are in an important sense indebted to the modern philosophical tradition inaugurated by Spinoza. In considering the differences between Levinas and Cohen, Section 4.3 of this chapter turns to the ways in which Levinas and Cohen each transform Spinoza's liberal political project. Here, in Section 4.2, however, we turn to their shared criticisms of Spinoza and also to the ways in which they, perhaps unwittingly, share in a post-Spinozist philosophical project.

To begin with, although Levinas and Cohen each see themselves as philosophically opposed to Spinoza, the basis of their shared criticism of Spinoza
shares the form of the opening of Spinoza's *Ethics*. As is well known, Spinoza
begins his ethics by putting forward a number of definitions and axioms.
Based on these, he proceeds to deduce all that follows in the *Ethics*. Most
of Spinoza's philosophical interpreters have understood the relation between
Spinoza's *Ethics* and his political *Treatise* in this same way. That is, the dominant interpretation of Spinoza, with a few notable exceptions, is that his
politics follows from his philosophical presuppositions.[17] As we have noted a
number of times throughout this book, this very approach to philosophical
interpretation is based on a forgetfulness of the historical relation between
philosophy and society, a relation that, ironically enough, is at the heart of
Spinoza's work. In their criticisms of Spinoza, Levinas and Cohen both assume
that the external stuff of history and politics follows from the internal, timeless
truth of philosophy.

Levinas and Cohen implicitly criticize what they (rightly) take to be
Spinoza's central *philosophical* claim, which is one that follows from the first
axiom of the *Ethics*. There Spinoza writes: "All things that are, are either
in themselves or in something else."[18] A seemingly tautological statement,
Spinoza's first axiom leads to the denial of what Levinas and Cohen before
him take to be the fundamental truth of transcendence. Spinoza's second
axiom adds, "[t]hat which cannot be conceived through another thing must
be conceived through itself."[19] This leads to what he calls "infinite substance,"
which he also calls "God." "God," then, is the sum, albeit the infinite sum,
of all individual things. Levinas's and Cohen's philosophies insist, in contrast, that "infinite substance" can capture neither the significance of the term
God nor the sum of relations between individual people. Spinoza's notion
of God implies that God contains everything. But for both Levinas and
Cohen, God is fundamentally separate from humanity (and the rest of the
world) just as individual people are fundamentally separate from each other.[20]
This metaphysical disagreement connects to a disagreement about the meaning of ethics. Spinoza, according to both Cohen and Levinas, denies (using
Levinas's phrase again) "a discord between events and the good," which is (to
use a basic Kantian distinction) the difference between what is and what ought
to be.[21]

It is on the basis of this basic philosophical disagreement that Levinas and
Cohen both find a personal motivation for Spinoza's claims about Judaism.
Because of their own philosophical commitments, Levinas and Cohen do
not find Spinoza's claims about Judaism *philosophically* credible. They both

contend, therefore, that Spinoza's characterizations of Judaism are personally and politically motivated. Levinas repeats (again unconsciously) the form
and content of Cohen's early-twentieth-century criticism of Spinoza. In his
1915 essay, "Spinoza on State and Religion, Judaism and Christianity," Cohen
attacks the philosophical meaning of Spinoza's title *Theologico-Political
Treatise*. For Cohen, there is an "unnatural connection" between the literary critique of the Bible (the "Theologico" in the title) and the "publicist task"
(the "Political" in the title). Because Cohen does not find a logical connection
between these words, he concludes that these ideas – the theological and the
political – "stand only in a very loose connection with one another."[22] Based
on what he calls the "unnaturalness" of this lack of connection in the title,
Cohen argues that Spinoza titled his book as such and made the arguments
he made based not on "objective," true considerations, but on his subjective,
negative feelings about Judaism. Cohen's approach to Spinoza conforms to
his views of history and truth. Once again, for Cohen the outer form of history
follows from the inner form of philosophy (i.e., history's *historisch* character is
predicated upon its *geschichtlich* character). Cohen begins by considering the
inner form of Spinoza's argument (the logical meaning of the title) and then
moves to what he regards as the outer form of his argument (the historical
and personal particularities of Spinoza's character).

   For Levinas, as for Cohen, Spinoza's arguments are simply wrong philosophically. Beginning with this philosophical fact, Levinas, like Cohen, posits
a historical fact: that Spinoza was a betrayer of the Jewish religion and
the Jewish people. As Richard A. Cohen has recently put it rather boldly,
from Levinas's perspective, Spinoza simply did not understand Judaism or
the Talmud.[23] Summarizing Levinas's position (Richard) Cohen writes: "All
Spinoza's betrayals, his bad faith, and his misunderstandings – of reason, of
religion, of ethics, of politics – can thus be understood, according to Levinas,
to have one primary source, his profound lack of understanding of and appreciation for the different (or the superior) wisdom of the Talmud."[24] Spinoza's
mistake, according to Levinas, is first a philosophical one. This philosophical
error can account for what Levinas considers to be Spinoza's moral error.
Again, in Richard Cohen's words:

Spinoza's betrayal comes not only in attacking Judaism from a Christian perspective, but as well because that perspective derives neither from an actual nor an
historical Christianity, but rather from a completely idealized one. Very simply, Spinoza presents Judaism in the worst possible light, Christianity in the
best. His betrayal is thus compounded by bad faith. *Tractatus*, contrarty to its

self-proclaimed objectivity and independence from external theory, is in fact an 'apologia.' It is thus a theological *and* a political work in the worst possible sense: at once biased and self-serving and doubly distorted. Spinoza presents a falsified Judaism, one seen through the doctrinal and denigrating filter of a triumphal Christian supersessionism, reinforcing Marcionist tendencies in Christianity. And he presents a falsified Christianity, one seen through the rose-colored lens of Christian apologetics.[25]

It should be clear that Levinas's evaluation of Spinoza has a deep affinity with Hermann Cohen's evaluation. Both begin with a defined idea of what is philosophically true. Both agree most fundamentally that "philosophy" defines politics and religion. For both Levinas and Cohen, the Jewish tradition represents the proper philosophical understanding of politics and religion. That Spinoza did not begin with this philosophical understanding can mean only that Spinoza begins with a faulty philosophical understanding of Judaism (despite the obvious fact of Spinoza's deep Jewish education). Both Levinas and Cohen attribute this faulty understanding to a Christian philosophical stance, one which, both claim, Spinoza appropriates from the beginning and which can mark Spinoza only as a betrayer of Judaism and the Jewish people. From the "internal" truths of philosophy and Judaism, Levinas and Cohen both move to the "external" analysis of Spinoza's historical situation.[26]

Levinas and Cohen have a depolitized reading of both Judaism and philosophy that then leads them to a politicized reading of Spinoza the person. Levinas describes the Talmud as the depoliticized quest for truth. We should understand the Talmud, Levinas suggests, as the summation of the

efforts made over thousands of years to go beyond the letter of the text and even its apparent dogmatism, and to restore a wholly spiritual truth even to those passages in the Scriptures called historical or ritual or ceremonial or thaumaturgical.... And it is on this issue that they [the rabbis of the Talmud] part company with Spinoza.[27]

For Levinas, going beyond the letter of the law means leaving behind the sediments of history, culture, and politics. But this isn't to say that Levinas's depoliticized views of philosophy and Judaism do not have political implications that Levinas is interested in elucidating. As we have seen in the case of his interpretation of Spinoza, Levinas, as did Cohen before him, arrives at a political reading of Spinoza (as a betrayer of Judaism) by way of his initial philosophical evaluation. As we saw in connection with Cohen, we might say that Levinas moves from the inner form of philosophy to the outer forms of history and politics.

The only response to the continued violence and cruelty of the twentieth century, Levinas suggests, is a turn to inwardness:

We must – reviving the memory of those who, non-Jews and Jews, without even knowing or seeing one another, found a way to behave amidst total chaos as if the world had not fallen apart – remembering the resistance of the maquis, that is, precisely, a resistance having no other source but one's own certainty and inner self; we must, through such memories, open up access to Jewish texts and give new priority to the inner life. The *inner life*: one is almost ashamed to pronounce this pathetic expression in the face of so many realisms and objectivisms.[28]

By "inner life" Levinas means the coincidences of the true meanings of Judaism and morality. These true meanings, we have seen, exist outside of history, culture, and politics. As Levinas puts it "Judaism is humanity on the brink of morality without institutions."[29] Jewish law, far from reflecting the outer structure of communal and political life, is for Levinas the inner meaning not only of Judaism but of civilization and humanity as well:

But that condition, in which human morality returns after so many centuries as to its womb, attests, with a very old testament, its origin on the hither side of civilizations. Civilizations made possible, called for, brought about, hailed and blessed by that morality – which can, however, for its part, only know and justify itself in the fragility of the conscience, in the 'four cubits of the *Halakhah*,' in that precarious, divine abode.[30]

Levinas's suggestion (and Cohen's before him) that the inner life, which consists of, among other things, the priority of the proper truth of philosophy, is more in keeping with Spinoza's philosophy than either of them would admit or like. While Levinas and Cohen part with Spinoza in insisting that there is a harmonious interchange between philosophy and revelation, their shared position coheres with Spinoza's basic view that revelation simply cannot trump philosophy. Levinas and Cohen desire to give a positive philosophical spin to revelation – claiming even, as we have seen, that revelation is the inner origin of philosophy – but this positive spin affirms the assumption that they share with Spinoza, which is that philosophy defines the true meaning of revelation (that for Levinas and Cohen *as well as for Spinoza* is interhuman relations).

As I argued in Chapter 3, this messianic claim for philosophy is a par-ticularly modern claim. But here we must note that Spinoza does not make a messianic claim for philosophy. Unlike Cohen and Levinas, Spinoza does not believe that philosophy in and of itself can solve what are for him the eternal tensions inherent to human society and politics. Spinoza's innova-tion is to cut revelation out of the conversation with philosophy. As Strauss argues, Spinoza breaks with medieval rationalism by arguing that revelation cannot contradict philosophy and that philosophy speaks the first and last word about the meaning of revelation. But Spinoza does not make the subsequent move, made by the early modern German metaphysical tradition, and perhaps made in this context by Leibniz, that philosophy is available to all people as an instrument, if not the instrument, for political and social salvation. For Spinoza, like Descartes before him, the philosophical enterprise is in tension with politics and society. The philosophies of Levinas and Cohen, in contrast, are the product of the forgetfulness of what became philosophy's unquestionable status with the development of German metaphysics and the creation of the modern nation-state. Although profoundly aware of philosophy's precarious political status, Spinoza's argument that revelation cannot contradict philosophical truth led the way to the possibility of Cohen's and Levinas's philosophies. More than offering devastating criticisms of Spinoza, Cohen and Levinas remain very much his heirs.

4.3. THE DIFFERENCE BETWEEN COHEN AND LEVINAS: REASON VS. SENSIBILITY

I have argued in the last two sections that Levinas's philosophy has a deep affinity with Cohen's philosophy. After exploring these affinities in detail, we are now in a position to appreciate their profound differences. Once again, Cohen's and Levinas's relationship to Spinoza is significant. Whereas Spinoza was among the theoretical initiators of the modern liberal state, Cohen's philosophy develops a full-fledged theory of modern law to go with this state. Levinas, while never denouncing the liberal state, presents a postliberal view of politics and ethics in which affectivity, not reason, is the ultimate guiding force of politics and society. In Chapter 5, we turn to Strauss's criticism of Cohen's modern defense of the rule of law. Here, however, I contrast Cohen's rationalist defense of law as the basis of ethics with what I contend is Levinas's defense of sensibility as the basis of ethics. I suggest that whatever may be said of Cohen's thought his is a consistent liberal rationalism. Levinas, instead, presents an illiberal irrationalism, which I suggest is philosophically incoherent and politically dangerous.

To appreciate Cohen's arguments about law, we must turn back to his neo-Kantian framework. The hallmark of Cohen's particular brand of neo-Kantianism is the attempt to deprioritize the sensible component of the "synthetic" part of Kant's transcendental idealism. Most basically, Cohen argues that the grounding of the reality of an object takes place in thought and not in sensation. In the third edition of *Kant's Theory of Experience*, Cohen criticizes Kant for not balancing properly the relation between reality and sensation and for, thereby, obscuring his own transcendental principle. Cohen writes: "Instead of going on from the *reality of grounding,* which lies beyond extensive intuition, to sensation, Kant started from sensation and grounded reality in it, as a *degree* of sensation. Thus the transcendental center of gravity was shifted in favor of the principle."[31] As Andrea Poma summarizes Cohen's criticism of Kant in relation to Cohen's construction of his own critical philosophy, "Cohen re-established the correct relationship between reality and sensation, foregrounding the fact that the grounding of reality in the object does not lie *in* sensation, but *for* sensation, in the principle of intensive magnitude, and thus in thought."[32] But for Cohen, this is much more than a philosophically technical point because *Cohen's criticism of Kant's notion of sensibility is intimately linked to Cohen's argument for what he calls the science of law.*

There is a long and technical discussion to be had about how Cohen's "correction" of Kant's view of sensibility is linked to his attempt to posit a science of law, but the following remarks should suffice to make this link clear for our purposes. The fact that thought (and not sensation) grounds the reality of an object is also for Cohen the fact of the concept of law, which makes free individuality and ethics possible. Just as Cohen criticizes Kant's notion of sensibility, so Cohen criticizes Kant's view of law. As he puts it in his *Ethics:*

Kant . . . did not deduce ethics with reference to the science of law, as he had done for logic with reference to the science of nature. There can be no doubt that the consequence of this would inevitably be an irreparable error in the concept of the transcendental method. If it is true for logic, why should it not be true for ethics? . . . [I]t is still a question of knowledge . . . here lie the profound difficulties with Kant's system[33]

On a technical level, Cohen criticizes Kant for distinguishing morality from right. Cohen argues that Kant's distinction denies law the status of science. Cohen maintains that Kant is inconsistent in this regard on the basis of his own philosophical premises and blames Kant's inconsistency on what he argues are Kant's Pauline prejudices. Cohen writes:

Kant had made law the center of gravity of his ethics. And thereby he distinguished legality from morality. Morality is rooted in law; but it is not legality. . . . [These points] have in fact no legal and no philosophical source, but an unambiguous religious one. They originate in the polemic, in which Paul criticized the Mosaic teaching, which he called and characterized law.[34]

The point of Cohen's criticism of Kant is to suggest that if Kant were more consistent with his own principles, he would then recognize that it is law and indeed legality that grounds ethics. While, as we have seen, the individual's true "inwardness" (*Innerlichkeit*) comes by way of "religion," for Cohen, the possibility and indeed the content of this inwardness is made possible only by way of Cohen's rejection of the primacy of sensibility. In other words, the inner and outer forms of law (the former being "religion," the latter "ethics") are made possible by reason or thought. Cohen's claims about the inner form of reason are clearly linked then to the modern concept of law. As we have seen briefly, the concept of law for Cohen is the creation of free individuality. Cohen's criticism of the priority of sensation in grounding objects and the individuality of the human person are thus intimately linked to his commitment to a liberal notion of the fundamental equality of all persons. The inner workings of reason for Cohen thus affirm the possibility of free individuality. Cohen is right in recognizing that the positing of such free individuality was Kant's own philosophical goal. Cohen's critique of Kant's notion of sensation, far from being an obscure point of critical idealism, is the very basis of what Cohen (rightly) took to be the Kantian, transcendental-idealist project: the positing of autonomous individuality.

Levinas, as we saw in Chapters 1 and 2, rejects the notions of equality and freedom as the first principles of ethics to argue for the priority of the asymmetrical relation between one person and another as well as for the priority of sensibility for grounding the separate individual. Levinas's and Cohen's respective claims for or against the priority of sensibility in understanding the constitution of the individual self are inextricably linked for both of them to either the rejection or the affirmation of the priority of equality among individuals. In prioritizing reason or thought in the creation of the free individual, Cohen also prioritizes the liberal notions of equality and freedom. And in prioritizing sensibility or sensation in the creation of the separate individual, Levinas also rejects the notions of equality and freedom as first principles (though not as principles) of ethics.

The contrast between Levinas and Cohen allows us to see what I suggest is a profound inconsistency if not a disturbing aspect of Levinas's thought. Unlike Cohen's neo-Kantian method, Levinas's phenomenological consideration of the inner life does not affirm law, equality, and freedom as first principles. What is affirmed is a profound subjectivity of interpersonal relations. Levinas is well aware of this implication. He affirms this position, arguing that persecution and ethics are two sides of the same coin. "Every accusation and persecution ... presupposes the subjectivity of the ego ... which refers to the transference from the 'by the other' into a 'for the other'. ... [T]he absolute accusation, prior to freedom, constitutes freedom which, allied to the Good, situates beyond and outside of all essence."[35] My affectivity, simply put, makes me beholden to the other person, whether that person is a victim needing my help or someone literally torturing me. Levinas's affirmation of sensibility over reason makes it impossible for me to distinguish the two. There are no principles that can be applied to a particular situation that would help us to recognize the difference between the two. Ethics for Levinas is this very vulnerability.

Let us apply briefly a comment that Levinas makes about Kant to our discussion of Levinas's relation to Cohen. In *Totality and Infinity*, Levinas states that "[t]he role Kant attributed to sensible experience in the domain of the understanding belongs in metaphysics to inter-human relations."[36] We have already seen that Cohen's rejection of Kant's view of sensibility is linked to his arguments about the centrality of law. Perhaps the most basic issue in this regard is the very idealist conception of freedom. Cohen wants to claim that Kant's notion of sensibility is in tension with the idealist rejection of "nature" in that, from the critical idealist perspective, the will must be free from the constraints of nature. Levinas's project, like Strauss's project, is rooted in, as we saw in Chapter 1, the attempt to reinsert a notion of nature. Levinas clearly parts with Cohen in this quest. But like Cohen, Levinas claims that Kant needs to take his view of sensibility to its proper conclusion. For Levinas, if Kant were to do so, he would recognize that sensible experience constitutes the ethics of interhuman relations. Levinas's comment implies that Kant would also have to forgo his own commitments to the priorities of freedom and autonomy. A discussion of what Kant might say in response to Levinas or Cohen is, of course, beyond the scope of this book.[37] But I would like to suggest that Cohen is more in keeping with the idealist project in making reason and freedom, and not the constraints of nature and sensibility, the center of his project.

Clearly, Levinas is not an idealist. But he might have been better off had he been one if he truly means to claim for his philosophy the status of "rationalism." Without an idealist framework – that is, with the explicit rejection of reason as first principle – Levinas's philosophy cannot but beg the question of rationalism. Is Levinas's philosophy rationalist?[38] He certainly claims in places that it is, yet what meaning can this rationalism have when he attempts simultaneously, if not more basically, to reject the priority of reason *for philosophy and ethics* precisely to affirm the priority of sensibility? In one of his essays on Spinoza, Levinas criticizes Kant for not appreciating the non-rational character of obedience:

the incentives [*mobiles*] of obedience are not of a rational order. They are incentives of an affective order, such as fear, hope, fidelity, respect, veneration and love. Obedience and heteronomy, but not servitude.... Obedience comes not from constraint but from an internal and disinterested élan. Commandment and love do not contradict one another, contrary to Kant.[39]

Levinas's claim that "commandment and love do not contradict one another," a claim that we saw in Chapter 3 he draws from Rosenzweig's philosophy, is in keeping with Levinas's attempt to make obligation prior to freedom. Levinas's claim, to use Strauss's words, is that "freedom depends upon its bondage," or in his own words "commands are the political condition of freedom."[40] As Peter Atterton has recently argued in connection with Levinas and Kant, Levinas's philosophical argument amounts to claiming that:

A retreat upon the conditions that make autonomy possible regresses upon a condition that is also conditioned by what it conditions. Alternatively, we could say that the face is quasi-empirical to the extent that it is not entirely separate from the field of experience it makes possible. To be sure, from the point of view of the fundamental tenets of transcendental philosophy, such formulations are absurd... transcendental argument ultimately breaks down in connection with the Other in that it is incapable of regressing upon a condition that can be thought in terms of the intentional structure of consciousness governed by the unity of the 'I think,' the basis of all experience, according to Kant.[41]

While Atterton goes on to suggest that Levinas's position is in keeping with Kant's emphasis on practical reasoning, it should be clear that Levinas's philosophy cannot withstand, as he seems to acknowledge in places, the scrutiny of a wholly rationalist argument.[42] In a certain sense, Levinas wants to have it both ways. He wants to claim that the other comes from outside of me to challenge me, but to also claim that this burst of exteriority is subject to and even grounds rational principles.

It is important to recall here that Levinas's contention that a nonrational exteriority grounds the possibility of rationality is *not* an argument for the movement from opinion to truth, such as found in Plato, or even a claim suggesting that philosophy develops out of the muddled stuff of religion and culture, such as found in Hegel. Levinas also rejects, as we will see in more detail in Chapter 7, an Aristotelian distinction between theoria and praxis. The exteriority of the other is not for Levinas the muddled stuff of culture, history, religion, and politics. Rather, the exteriority of the other is *a metaphysical principle*. As we saw in Chapter 2, Levinas follows Descartes in claiming that philosophy consists not in the rational refinement of culture, history, religion, and politics but in the bracketing of these areas of life. Unlike Descartes, however, Levinas believes that after this bracketing – that is, after the phenomenological analysis of the metaphysical dimensions of the other's exteriority – that philosophy can turn back and direct these avenues of life.

I have suggested in this section that this tension in Levinas's thought is philosophically problematic and politically dangerous. To summarize why, I will briefly mention a few arguments from previous chapters. In Chapter 3, I suggested that ethics, Levinas's main theme, is the fusing of divine and human nature. Incarnation, for Levinas, is my spiritual rebirth, but this rebirth is at one and the same time secular in that it can and does only concern human relations. In Chapter 2, I described Levinas's relation to an intellectualist tradition of religious thought that posits the primacy of moral reason over God's will. This is the rationalist side of Levinas's philosophy. Yet we are now in a position to see that at the same time Levinas transfers a voluntarist tradition of Christian religious thought away from the divine and onto the human.[43] While Levinas affirms the primacy of moral reason over God's will, he also affirms the primacy of the other human being's will over reason. Levinas's view of the exteriority of the other is not unlike theological arguments that give all priority to God's will. While we saw in Chapter 2 that Marion complicates the question of Descartes' voluntarism, it is still helpful to use one aspect of Descartes' position to describe Levinas's claim with regard to ethics. Just as Descartes argues that God can make two plus two equal five, Levinas maintains that the will of the other person dictates the laws of reason. The theological voluntarist position is based on a claim for faith and not for reason. My claim here is that Levinas's contentions about the other cannot be regarded as rationalist, but are instead a leap of faith.[44] This leap is disturbing precisely because it is described by Levinas as the very ground for directing not only reason but social, political, religious, and cultural life. Put most simply, Levinas's position is politically and philosophically dangerous because it means that there are no criteria for judgment.

4.4. COHEN, LEVINAS, AND THE LEGACY OF KANT

I have suggested that whatever may be said of Cohen's thought, he clearly affirms the primacy of rationality and rationalism. Levinas rejects this primacy yet still claims not only that he is a rationalist but also that his philosophy of the other is ethical. But here we must wonder about a very basic question, which is whether the pursuit of justice requires first and foremost rational criteria to decide what is and is not just? Levinas's philosophy denies precisely this. Cohen, on the other hand, argues that the ethics of law is a baseline for the possibility of justice. Here we can understand the difference between Cohen's term *religion* and Levinas's term *ethics* to refer to the unique responsibility that one person has for another. For Cohen, as for the modern liberal project, the private morality of religion must be in tandem with the public morality of law, which is ethics. Levinas's thought, on the other hand, eclipses the question of the public morality of law by making what liberals would call religion into ethics.[45] Cohen's thought, like modern liberal thought, distinguishes between the public and private realms. Levinas's thought, in contrast, elides any such distinction, but does not replace the public sphere with anything.

All we have left after the destruction of the twentieth century, one might say in the name of Levinas, is the interpersonal realm of ethics. Levinas even understands "law" in this private, interpersonal way. As he puts it in *Otherwise than Being*:

I find the order [of law] in my response itself, which, as a sign given to the neighbor, as a "here I am," brings me out of invisibility, out of the shadow in which my responsibility could have been evaded.... No *structure* is set up with a correlate.... Authority is not somewhere, where a look could go seek it, like an idol, or assume it like a logos. It is not only outside of all intuition, but outside of all thematization, even that of symbolism. It is the pure trace of a 'wandering cause,' inscribed *in me*.[46]

Law is not even a "structure" for Levinas. The task of philosophy and revelation should be, according to Levinas, the making of the outer forms of life – law – more inward. While Cohen attempts to preserve both the inner and outer forms of truth, what he calls respectively religion and ethics, for Levinas, in and of itself, the externality of law is ultimately unredeemable. Law must be made internal. It must be inscribed "in me." We can appreciate here the implications of Levinas's messianic sympathies, explored in Chapter 3, as they play out in his philosophy of law. For Levinas, revelation and ethics, and not some set of external laws, inscribe the truth in me.[47] Levinas secularizes the Christian theological notion of incarnation in claiming that as regards our ethical obligation, we are all incarnate. Theology, philosophy, politics, and law are fused for Levinas *in me*. Cohen's liberal affirmation of the externalities of law that make for free individuality is from Levinas's perspective ultimately "an idol."

My aim in this chapter has been to show that Levinas's project loses what may be best in Cohen's project: an emphasis on the rationality of law as the basis of politics and ethics. Whereas I concluded Chapter 3 by suggesting that Levinas's thought does not take the reality of revelation with regard to philosophy seriously, and therefore cannot be said to be an appropriate model for thinking about Jewish revelation, I conclude this chapter by suggesting that Levinas's thought cannot be said to be an appropriate model for thinking about modern rationalism. These two chapters have aimed to show how Levinas's post-Christian, yet messianic, claims for the fusing of philosophy and revelation leave him unable to speak authoritatively about either Jewish revelation or the moral resources of philosophy.

But the point of comparing Levinas and Cohen has not been to suggest that Cohen's thought is unproblematic. This is a subject at once beyond the scope of this study and immediately relevant to the basic questions of this study. As we will see in Chapter 5, Strauss argues that Cohen's is the best model of modern rationalism, but that it ultimately fails in its aspirations. The reasons for this evaluation are directly relevant to what we have discussed in this chapter. Cohen's great importance for Strauss derives from his equation of law with revelation. But Cohen's messianic aspirations for philosophy destroy his very project, according to Strauss. While Cohen rightly focused on law, his view of law is premised on a faith in philosophy that is *rationally* unjustified.

We have seen in this chapter that Cohen's concept of law is based on a rejection of Kant's notion of sensibility. Kant's idealism is premised on his notion of a rational will. Cohen's philosophy of law, we have seen, takes Kant's notion of the rational will to its logical conclusion by filtering out the remnants of Kantian sensible experience. From the perspective of Strauss's thought, then, Levinas's focus on the sensible is the logical outcome of Cohen's focus on reason. Here we might aptly apply the analysis of Stanley Rosen, a student of Strauss's, to the relation between Cohen's and Levinas's philosophies. Rosen points out that Kant's concept of the rational will is fraught with ambiguity, which accounts for, among other things, the ways in which Nietzsche and Heidegger after him can be said to be heirs of Kant. Rosen writes:

The transcendental ego [for Kant] possesses two intellectual faculties, which he calls *Vernunft* and *Verstand*. Both faculties are 'spontaneous' and 'autonomous,' albeit in different sense of the terms. *Verstand* produces concepts spontaneously; these unify sensations into objects of experience, which are also possible objects of scientific knowledge. *Vernunft* produces the idea of a spontaneous, extraworldly cause of a series of conditions within the spatiotemporal world, namely of itself as initiating moral action within the world. . . . There is no empirical confirmation of Kant's hypothesis, however, since what counts as experience, and also as confirmation, is created by our acceptance of the hypothesis. Freedom in the third sense means that we are free to accept or to reject the worlds of knowledge and morality as 'defined' by Kant. As a consequence, these worlds are radically contingent. We are free to posit chaos as the primeval condition.[48]

While, from an ethical point of view, Levinas wants to fight against the notion that chaos is the primeval condition, his post-Heideggerian philosophical starting point, which posits affectivity and not reason as the basis of subjectivity, at the same time affirms this chaos. As Rosen points out, this tension is inherent in Kant's transcendental idealist project. Cohen and Levinas are two sides of the same coin. It remains to be seen whether Strauss can offer a rational alternative to what he claims is this failed form of modern rationalism. This will be the subject of Part 3 of this book. But before turning to Strauss's alternative, we turn now, in Chapter 5, to a detailed consideration of Strauss's engagement with the philosophy of Hermann Cohen.

The Possibility of Premodern Rationalism: Strauss's Transformation of Hermann Cohen

*L*EO STRAUSS CONCLUDED BOTH HIS FIRST AND LAST MAJOR WORKS with reference to Hermann Cohen.[1] The argument of Strauss's first published book – *Spinoza's Critique of Religion* – is rooted in Strauss's initial work on Cohen's interpretation of Spinoza. Strauss's second book – *Philosophy and Law* – begins and ends by declaring that Cohen is right that the philosophy of Maimonides represents "true rationalism" and more particularly that Maimonides is better understood as a Platonist than as an Aristotelian. Strauss's last published work, *Studies in Platonic Political Philosophy*, published posthumously, ends with an essay on Cohen, which was also the introduction to the English translation of *Religion of Reason Out of the Sources of Judaism*. Interestingly, though this essay on Cohen is the final essay in *Studies in Platonic Political Philosophy*, it doesn't have much to say about Plato. Although Strauss claims in this essay not to have read *Religion of Reason* for forty years, those familiar with Strauss's project will recognize that it is from an engagement with Cohen that Strauss forms his basic reading of Maimonides and then Plato. These readings changed in emphasis throughout Strauss's career, but they remained fundamental to his philosophical program.

In this chapter, I explore Strauss's philosophical relation to Cohen. It is not an overstatement to suggest that Cohen is responsible for Leo Strauss's turn to medieval Jewish philosophy. The focus of this chapter, however, is not primarily on the details of Cohen and Strauss's respective readings of Maimonides.[2] Instead, I explore the broader hermeneutical questions involved in Strauss's reading of Cohen. I suggest that Cohen's readings of Maimonides and Spinoza before him shape the hermeneutical issues that are at the very heart of Strauss's own hermeneutical approach both in their content and in their methodological presuppositions. In a theme that connects Strauss's concerns about Plato, Maimonides, and contemporary politics and ethics with Cohen's concerns about these same issues, Strauss argues that Cohen's thought provides profound insight into a number of fundamental issues. Yet Strauss argues that Cohen is right for the wrong reasons – and almost despite himself. I suggest that in his reading of Cohen, Strauss performs his own prescription for how to read classical Jewish texts and in so doing reverses the parameters of Cohen's philosophical program.

In this connection, the argument of this chapter is threefold. First, Leo Strauss couldn't have been Leo Strauss without Hermann Cohen. Second, in becoming Leo Strauss, Strauss has reshaped, if not possibly destroyed, the possibility of Hermann Cohen's very project, thus bearing witness to Strauss's claim, which he quotes from and then turns against Cohen, that "it is a question of whether such reshaping is not the best form of annihilation."[3] And third, in reshaping Cohen's project, Strauss questions the relation that Cohen posits between history and truth, on the one hand, and philosophy and revelation, on the other. We begin by turning to Cohen and Strauss's shared attempt to save philosophy from historicism.

5.1. HISTORY AND TRUTH, OUTSIDE AND IN

Strauss shares with Cohen the task of preserving an autonomous realm for philosophy, which means primarily a realm that is beyond and not constructed by history. In *Natural Right and History* Strauss defines "historicism" as the notion that "all human thoughts or beliefs are historical."[4] Strauss famously argues there that historicism is incoherent on its own terms, for it brings with it its own demise. Strauss agrees with Cohen that the view that truth is constituted by history destroys not only the possibility of philosophy, or reason, but also of religion, or revelation.

Where Strauss and Cohen disagree perhaps most fundamentally is on the relation between philosophy and revelation. Strauss maintains that philosophy and revelation exist in a complementary but necessary and irresolvable tension. Cohen maintains that there is no such tension, once we understand philosophy and revelation properly. Cohen is also a greater fan of historical progress than Strauss is. These very fundamental differences between Strauss and Cohen on the relation between philosophy and religion as well as historical progress are connected to, if not rooted in, their respective hermeneutical approaches to what each regards as the problem of historicism. As Cohen expressed it perhaps most succinctly in his introduction to his *Religion of Reason*, a methodological approach for him is always and of necessity connected to its philosophical theme. Cohen argues that we cannot distinguish between philosophical methodology and philosophical content. Strauss very much agrees with Cohen on this point and is a pupil of Cohen's in this regard.

Where Strauss disagrees with Cohen is on the very methodological approach for accomplishing the goal he shares with him: again, the preservation of an autonomous realm for philosophy that is beyond historical construction. Strauss insists that historicism can be averted only by working through the historicist position, and not, as Strauss claims Cohen does, by simply ignoring the historical context of philosophy.

In a little-cited essay of 1931, titled "Cohen and Maimonides," Strauss criticizes Cohen's approach to the relationship between philosophy and history. While deeply flawed as an end in itself, Strauss argues that a historicist approach to the texts of the past is fundamentally superior to Cohen's idealist one. In fact, Strauss suggests, a historicist approach to texts has something profoundly in common with traditionally religious approaches to texts (which the former would of course deny). Strauss writes:

To understand the author as he understood himself, that is precisely the ambi-tion of the historian. . . . Cohen, on the other hand, proceeds from the Kantian insight, that it is possible to understand an author better than he understood himself. Cohen names this [attempt at] 'understanding an author better than he understood himself,' 'idealizing interpretation.'[5] This idealizing interpretation differentiates itself from allegorical interpretation through the consciousness of the interpreter's distance from the author, in fact by his superiority to the author.[6]

The modern historian would be surprised to find himself compared to the reli-gious allegorical reader. But the difference between them concerns not, as the historian might believe, their respective goals. Rather, the difference concerns the different tools they bring to their shared goal of understanding the author as he understood himself. In contrast, Cohen's interpretive goal, and Levinas's after him, is to understand an author better than he understood himself. For Cohen, the author's intentions are not relevant to interpretation. What are relevant are the philosophical and ethical assumptions that the author brings to the text. Strauss suggests that while the historian and the allegorical reader approach the text with humility as they try to understand what the author intended, idealizing interpretation is premised on the interpreter's superiority to the author.

Strauss maintains that Cohen's "idealizing" approach to interpretation is an apologetic reaction to the Enlightenment critique of religion, which, despite its good intentions, is premised on the view that the Enlightenment has won its battle against any claims for revelation. In this context, Strauss pinpoints Cohen's "internalist" approach to Jewish revelation. In the introduction to his 1935 *Philosophy and Law*, Strauss points out that:

the later thinkers, who recognized that any compromise between orthodoxy and the Enlightenment is untenable, accomplished the move from the level on which the Enlightenment and orthodoxy had done battle, and on which the moderate Enlightenment had striven for a compromise, to another, a 'higher' level, which as such made possible a synthesis of Enlightenment and orthodoxy. Thus it was on this newly won level that the later thinkers re-established the foundation of the tradition – of course, as cannot be otherwise in synthesis, in a modified 'internalized' form . . . all 'internalizations' of the basic tenets of the tradition rest at bottom on this: from the 'reflexive' premise, from the 'higher' level of the post-Enlightenment synthesis, the relation of God to nature is no longer intelligible and thus is no longer even interesting.[7]

As we can see from our discussion in Chapter 4, in using the term *internalization* (*Verinnerlichung*), Strauss aptly and succinctly describes not only Cohen's theological concepts, his particular neo-Kantian methodology, but also his approach to history. I suggest in what follows not only that Strauss rightly understood the methodological basis that sustains Cohen's entire philosophy, but that he also molded his own approach to philosophy, theology, and history by reversing Cohen's methodology.

Let us turn first to Cohen's theological categories and Strauss's criticisms of them. In *Religion of Reason*, Cohen describes creation and revelation as follows:

[Creation] is no longer a question of a mythical interest in a unique primeval act. . . . [T]he problem of creation transfers its meaning from the realm of causality to the realm of teleology. Consequently the share of reason in religion takes cognizance of the problem of ethics, whereas creation, insofar as it is seen from the point of view of causality, requires only a coming to terms with logic. . . . [R]evelation is the continuation of creation insofar as it sets as its problem the creation of man as a rational being.[8]

Strauss points out that while Cohen believes that he is rejecting the Enlightenment criticism of religion, Cohen's position is premised on the assumption that there can be no true disagreement between philosophy and revelation, an assumption that represents the victory of Enlightenment claims about religion.[9]

While well intentioned, Strauss maintains that Cohen's approach to creation and revelation only digs the grave of revelation deeper. Strauss notes that Cohen's internalist approach to creation and revelation is ironic in that Cohen was interested in a return to tradition.[10] Rosenzweig, Cohen's student, recognized more than anyone else had that revelation must be understood on its own terms, but even his "new thinking," Strauss claims, is premised on Enlightenment prejudice.[11] Even Rosenzweig, who argued in the *Star of Redemption* that the weakness of modern theology is captured in its denial of the possibility of miracles, could not accept the traditional concept of creation on its own terms.[12]

To take revelation seriously, argues Strauss, means simply this: to accept the idea that it is possible that God created the world and has given the world his divine law. The inability to accept this possibility and the attempt to describe the "true meaning" of creation and revelation otherwise, lies in a fundamental misconception about traditional religious claims about creation and revelation. This misconception was perpetuated by Enlightenment philosophers (and Spinoza before them) precisely so that there could be no real argument about revelation. Strauss argues that medieval Jewish philosophers never argued that creation or revelation was a proven philosophical fact. Instead, the traditional claim is much more limited: that it is possible that God created the world and revealed himself to humanity. This is a claim that simply cannot be refuted, argues Strauss. Only an overblown view of the capacities of philosophy could defeat such a view. The so-called Enlightenment quarrel with revelation combined such an overblown view of philosophy with a caricatured conception of beliefs about revelation. The seeming victory of the Enlightenment is based on the success of a strategy that essentially makes a conversation about the relation between philosophy and revelation impossible. While he means to defend the possibility of revelation, and even return to the tradition, Cohen, Strauss maintains, shares in a post-Enlightenment assumption that revelation simply cannot trump philosophy. As we saw in Chapter 4, Cohen (and Levinas), despite his scathing criticisms of Spinoza, shares this very assumption that Spinoza helped to initiate.

Strauss contends that historical study is the beginning (though certainly not the end) of the way to move beyond the prejudices that so deeply define the modern age.[13] We can only begin to grasp the truths of the past by recognizing and moving beyond these prejudices. In his 1930 book on Spinoza, Strauss did not believe that it was possible to return to assessing the truth of premodern rationalism. But, as he notes in his introduction to *Philosophy and Law*, this too was a prejudice defined by the Enlightenment. Strauss's work on and criticism of Cohen's interpretation first of Spinoza and then of Maimonides helped him move beyond this prejudice. In a book review of 1931, the same year that he published his essay on Cohen and Maimonides, Strauss describes the necessity of moving from the outer form of *historisch* truth to the inner form of philosophical truth. He writes:

Bearing in mind the classic representation of the natural difficulties in philosophizing, in other words, the Platonic allegory of the cave, one can say that today we are in a second, much deeper cave, than the fortunate ignorant persons with which Socrates was concerned. We need history first of all to reach the cave from which Socrates can lead us to the light. We need preparatory instruction – that is, precisely learning by reading.[14]

Strauss elaborates on the movement from this second cave in *Philosophy and Law*, in which he suggests that taking seriously the historical context of philosophizing is the starting point for reaching the truths of philosophy, which are beyond historical context. Strauss, like Cohen, aims to reach the timeless truths of the philosophic tradition, but unlike Cohen, Strauss maintains that to do so we must begin by first historicizing philosophy:

To that end and only to that end is the 'historicizing' of philosophy justified and necessary: only the history of philosophy makes possible the ascent from the second, 'unnatural' cave, into which we have fallen less because of the tradition itself than because of the tradition of polemics against the tradition, into that first, 'natural' cave which Plato's image depicts, to emerge from which into the light is the original meaning of philosophizing.[15]

Strauss reads Cohen by putting him into his philosophical context, which is one saturated by post-Enlightenment prejudice. The possibility of philosophy begins for Strauss with the possibility of reading sensitively, which means first reading with sensitivity to historical context and thereby gaining the possibility of coming to philosophical truth, which is beyond history.

In the next two sections, we explore Strauss's twofold claim that the historicizing of philosophy is the necessary prerequisite for grasping the true and eternal quarrel between philosophy and revelation, a quarrel that modern philosophy simply and destructively eclipses. To appreciate the first part of this claim, we turn in Section 5.2 to Strauss's criticism of Cohen's reading of Spinoza. We then turn in Section 5.3 to Strauss's criticism of Cohen's reading of Maimonides to appreciate the second part of Strauss's claim.

5.2. READING SPINOZA OR ON THE NECESSITY OF HISTORICIZING PHILOSOPHY

Strauss begins his 1924 essay "Cohen's Analysis of Spinoza's Bible Science," which analyzes Cohen's 1915 essay "Spinoza on State and Religion, Judaism and Christianity," by stating that

It is typical of Hermann Cohen's style that he couches the critique of an idea in the critique of the possibly accidental expression of that idea. This is the way of our intensive and penetrating *traditional* art of interpretation, which takes each word seriously and weighs it carefully. Thus, Cohen already objects to the title 'Theologico-Political Treatise,' where he misses 'a reference to philosophy, which may be assumed to contribute to theology as well as to politics.'[16]

Strauss is, of course, absolutely right about Cohen's style. In Chapter 4, we have mentioned Cohen's elucidation of his title "religion of reason out of the sources of Judaism" as his introduction to this book. Cohen, like traditional Jewish interpretation, "takes every word seriously and weighs it carefully." With this in mind, Strauss sums up Cohen's criticism of Spinoza, which for Cohen is captured in the perhaps seemingly incidental title of Spinoza's book, "Theologico-Political Treatise":

> [Cohen's] criticism of the title contains in a nutshell the criticism of the book. Philosophy is missing [in the title], and without the link of philosophy the joining together of theology and politics must appear arbitrary. Thus the examination of the title alone arouses the suspicion that the book may have nonobjective presuppositions.[17]

Strauss proposes in effect to reverse Cohen's method by showing, by way of a historical-critical approach, that Spinoza was justified in not referring to philosophy in his title. As we discussed in Chapter 4, for Cohen, there is an "unnatural connection" between the literary critique of the Bible (the "Theologico" in the title) and the "publicist task" (the "Political" in the title). Again, based on what he calls the "unnaturalness" of this lack of connection in the title, Cohen argues that Spinoza titled his book as such, and made the arguments he made, based not on "objective," true considerations, but on his subjective, negative feelings about Judaism. Strauss argues in contrast that there were historical reasons why Spinoza titled his book as such, and that once we appreciate this, we can understand contra Cohen that Spinoza came to his conclusions about Judaism and Christianity on the basis of objective, philosophical considerations.[18] Whereas Cohen begins by considering the inner form of Spinoza's argument (the logical meaning of the title) and then moves to what he regards as the outer form of his argument (the question of Spinoza's personal character), Strauss begins with what he argues is the outer form of Spinoza's arguments (Spinoza's historical context) and moves to the inner form of his argument (the question of whether Spinoza's arguments are philosophically justifiable).[19]

Strauss's argument against Cohen is simple. According to Strauss, because Spinoza sought to protect the freedom of inquiry "from the public powers – and there were two public powers, the secular and the spiritual.... [I]n Spinoza's historical context, the connection between a theory of the state [*Staatstheorie*] and the critique of the Bible is sufficiently motivated."[20] Once he has shown that the title makes sense given its historical circumstances, Strauss proceeds to argue that the *Treatise* is not incompatible with the *Ethics.*[21] While Spinoza put himself outside of historical Judaism as he knew it, his rejection of the law is philosophically possible (though not necessarily philosophically defensible). Strauss thus begins and ends in opposite places in which Cohen begins and ends. For Strauss, Spinoza's approach is historically conceivable and therefore can be made sense of philosophically. For Cohen, Spinoza's approach is philosophically impossible and therefore can only be made sense of historically, which means for Cohen by way of Spinoza's personal life.

Let us recall again Cohen's distinction between empirical (*historisch*) and *a priori* (*geschichtlich*) views of history. Again, for Cohen, history's ideal end, its inner form, its *geschichtlich* character, determines the pure will and action to transform the outer form of history, its *historisch* character. When Strauss rejects Cohen's method of "internalization" in his 1935 *Philosophy and Law*, his rejection is in keeping with his earlier criticism of Cohen's historical method. Indeed, in "Cohen's Analysis of Spinoza's Bible Science," Strauss connects Cohen's philosophical method with his antihistoricist argument. Strauss writes:

> Is it necessary to point out to Hermann Cohen the idea with which the *Critique of Pure Reason* begins? It is doubtful that Spinoza's critique of the Bible begins with the ban; assuming, however, that it begins with the ban, it need not therefore arise from it alone. The essential thing, i.e. the contents, would have arisen from Spinoza's own context of thought [*Denkzusammenhang*], while the sense impression of the ban merely provided the occasion: 'Thus we see that the ostensibly psychological interest makes a critical substitution [*Unterschleif*] that is *fatal* and *typical*.' Thus concludes Hermann Cohen his exposition of the previously mentioned idea . . . [in] the third edition of his famous work, *Kant's Theory of Experience.*[22]

As Michael Zank points out, the context for Cohen's remark in *Kant's Theory of Experience* is his discussion of English sensualism, which Cohen claims is "a common psychological misunderstanding of Cartesian philosophy." In Zank's words, "[b]y referring to this passage, Strauss portrays Cohen as falling short of his own methodological postulate when he looked for extraneous psychological motivations to explain why Spinoza combined political philosophy with criticism of the Bible."[23]

But Strauss's comment goes beyond claiming that Cohen should have heeded his own warnings about mixing philosophy with psychology. Strauss also raises the question of whether Cohen, in his critique of Spinoza, has not exposed the flaw at the heart of his neo-Kantianim. Let us recall the beginning of *The Critique of Pure Reason*, to which Strauss refers. Kant writes:

> There can be no doubt that all our knowledge begins with experience. For how should our faculty of knowledge be awakened into action did not objects affecting

our senses partly of themselves produce representations, partly arouse the activity of our understanding to compare these representations, and, by combining and separating them, work up the raw material of the sensible impressions into that knowledge of objects which is entitled experience?

But though all our knowledge begins with experience it does not follow that it arises out experience. For it may well be that even our empirical knowledge is made up of what we receive through impressions and of what our own faculty of knowledge . . . supplies from itself.[24]

Strauss evokes Kant's famous beginning not only to question Cohen's psychologism but also to question Cohen's especially internalist or internalizing interpretation of Kant, in which Cohen, from Strauss's perspective, does not take seriously enough what Kant calls "the raw material of sensible impression."

Recall again Cohen's criticism of Kant's view of sensation, a criticism that forms the basis of Cohen's neo-Kantianism. As we saw in Chapter 4, Cohen criticizes Kant for making thought too dependent on sensation. Cohen bases his neo-Kantianism on the postulate that thought grounds sensibility. Strauss, I suggest, wants to call this very methodological basis into question by referring to the opening of *The Critique of Pure Reason*. Strauss's criticism of Cohen then is not only that Cohen gives too much weight to sensation or synthetic knowledge (in psychologizing Spinoza) but that he gives *too little* weight to sensation or synthetic knowledge (in ignoring the importance of the *historisch* context of Spinoza's work). Strauss suggests, to use the term he applied eleven years later to Cohen, that Cohen's method is internalist not only when it comes to Cohen's theological categories but also when it comes to Cohen's approach to history and finally also when it comes to the methodological basis of Cohen's transcendental method.[25]

Strauss criticizes Cohen's method of moving from the *geschichtlich* form of history to the *historisch* form of history, or from the inner form to the outer form, while simultaneously justifying his own opposite movement, which we might describe as moving from the *historisch* to the *geschichtlich*, or from the outer to the inner. In "Cohen's Analysis of Spinoza's Bible Science," Strauss is a defender of what he calls the "historical-critical" interpretation. But even in this early essay, before Strauss became "Strauss," he uses the "historical-critical" method to arrive at what he describes as true, philosophical considerations that are beyond history, that is, whether Spinoza's arguments make *philosophical* sense, what Strauss describes as "objectively justified." As he is in this early essay, Strauss would remain a life-long opponent of a wholly *historisch* approach to history, which would either reduce truth to historical progress or historical context. In this sense, although highly critical of

Cohen, Strauss, while defending a "historical-critical" method, remains in a broad sense closer to Cohen's own goal of arriving at philosophical truth beyond history, than he does to any truly historicist methodology. As he developed his esoteric/exoteric approach to reading texts, Strauss became even closer to Cohen in this antihistoricist goal, while still suggesting, as he does in his Cohen-Spinoza essay and in *Philosophy and Law*, that it is only possible to come to transhistorical truth by working through (and not by bypassing as Cohen does) the historicist method.

In this context, we should discuss briefly Strauss's own description of his transformation in the preface to the English translation of *Spinoza's Critique of Religion*. Strauss writes:

The change of orientation . . . compelled me to engage in a number of studies in the course of which I became ever more attentive to the manner in which heterodox thinkers of earlier ages wrote their books. As a consequence of this, I now read the *Theologico-Political Treatise* differently than I read it when I was young. I understood Spinoza too literally because I did not read him literally enough.[26]

Strauss came to emphasize the necessity of a kind of literal reading that is less historicist than the reading he offers in his initial reading of Spinoza. That Strauss understood Spinoza too literally because he did not read him literally enough means for Strauss that he literally had not paid sufficient attention to Spinoza's literal style. Yet Strauss's more literal attention to Spinoza does not lead him to read Spinoza as Cohen does (i.e., as starting with a literal rendition of the title). Rather, from a methodological point of view, Strauss continues along the path that he outlines in his Spinoza-Cohen essay in beginning first with a historicist point and then working through this point to come to a transhistorical truth. This transhistorical truth for Strauss is the eternal tension between philosophy and revelation (a tension that Strauss argues Spinoza misleadingly denies by asserting that philosophy has the final say in regard to *truth* claims made by revelation). Substantively also, Strauss's claims about Spinoza intensify rather than change. Strauss's early and later readings of Spinoza are united by the argument that Spinoza's goal is to free philosophy from the shackles of religion and politics. That Strauss did not read Spinoza literally enough means for Strauss that he did not notice, in his early work on Spinoza, the ways in which Spinoza's criticism of Judaism is really a foil for his devastating critique of Christianity and revealed religion more generally. The focus on the double-layered meanings of Spinoza's work, of course, marks Strauss's change of orientation.

The sensitivity to history that marks Strauss's change in orientation concerns his attention, as he says, "to the manner in which heterodox thinkers of earlier ages wrote their books." As Strauss puts it in his essay "Persecution and the Art of Writing," "[p]ersecution . . . gives rise to a peculiar technique of writing, and therewith to a peculiar type of literature, in which the truth about all crucial things is presented exclusively between the lines. That literature is addressed, not to all readers, but to trustworthy and intelligent readers only."[27] Strauss's esoteric reading of Spinoza begins with this sensitivity to historical context and concludes with an antihistoricist axiom that concerns the eternal nature of humanity and the special provenance of philosophy for recognizing this eternal nature:

Thoughtless men are careless readers, and only thoughtful men are careful readers. Therefore an author who wishes to address only thoughtful men has but to write in such a way that only a very careful reader can detect the meaning of his book. But, it will be objected, there may be clever men, careful readers, who are not trustworthy, and who, after having found the author out, would denounce him to the authorities. As a matter of fact, this literature would be impossible if the Socratic dictum that virtue is knowledge, and therefore that thoughtful men as such are trustworthy and not cruel, were entirely wrong.[28]

We see here not only the substantive but also the methodological continuity between Strauss's early work on Spinoza and his reorientation toward esoteric writing that would dominate his mature work. Both move from the outer form of empirical history to the inner form of rational truth.[29] I have suggested that this movement is rooted in Strauss's initial engagement with Cohen's reading of Spinoza and more particularly in Strauss's reversal of what he aptly calls "Cohen's method of internalization."

5.3. MAIMONIDES AND THE POSSIBILITY OF PREMODERN RATIONALISM

For Strauss, the quarrel between philosophy and revelation is the basis for the possibility of rationalism. Historical study (though not historicism) is necessary if the modern reader is to access this philosophical possibility. In what follows, I continue to explore the development of Strauss's methodological position on the relation between history and truth and his substantive position on the relation between philosophy and revelation. I suggest that Strauss developed the seeds of his mature views on both these matters through his engagement with, and further reversal of, Cohen.

Strauss shares with Cohen the position that Maimonides's philosophy represents "true rationalism." However, what they actually mean by this is quite different. In his 1931 essay on Cohen and Maimonides, Strauss criticizes the details of Cohen's attempt to elucidate the true rationalism of Maimonides, but Strauss also shapes his own project by arguing that Cohen is right in his conclusions about Maimonides; however, he is right for the wrong reasons. As he does in his essay on Cohen and Spinoza, Strauss argues that Cohen is wrong even on his own terms. Whereas Strauss locates in Spinoza's philosophy the roots of modern rationalism and thereby the roots of the self-destruction of philosophy, he finds in Maimonides the possibility of rethinking the possibility of rationalism.

Strauss begins by proposing to exhibit no tolerance for what he argues is Cohen's misreading of Plato and Aristotle, as well as Maimonides, Hegel, and Kant. Quoting Cohen's *Religion of Reason* – "Monotheism cannot have any tolerance with regard to polytheism. Idolatry has to be destroyed absolutely. This decision is the precondition of true monotheism, the monotheism of love for God, of worship grounded in love"[30] – Strauss evokes Cohen's own charge with regard to the articulation of true monotheism. In assigning himself this (from a Cohenian point of view) "prophetic" task, Strauss notes that he is also in keeping with Cohen's notion of philosophy, which is the duty to root out all error.[31] For all the detail and complexity of argument, Strauss's general point is fairly straightforward. He argues that Cohen misunderstands Maimonides because of his (Cohen's) methodological misconceptions. Nonetheless, Strauss argues that Cohen, perhaps inadvertently, comes to the correct conclusions: Maimonides represents true rationalism and Maimonides is truly a Platonist. The details of why Strauss thinks Cohen is wrong go to the heart of Strauss's own project, which concerns the possibility of a return to premodern rationalism. But to appreciate Strauss's claims about the possibility of premodern rationalism we must understand in greater detail Strauss's own approach to Cohen.

In a general characterization of what he calls Cohen's idealizing approach to Maimonides, Strauss writes:

[Cohen's] new interpretation is not a mutilation but a 'transformation,' a transformation from the mythic dawn to later on. [and now Strauss quotes Cohen:] 'And it is a question whether such transformation is not the best kind of annihilation.' [*Religion der Vernunft*, p. 204; *Religion of Reason*, p. 174] Whoever knows Cohen knows that this question is only rhetorical: [Strauss quotes Cohen again:] 'Against every routine approach the insight must prevail that progress in religious understanding has been accomplished through the revision and reinterpretation of the sources, while these themselves remain preserved in their individual layers and have been rearranged or given different emphasis.' [*Religion der Vernunft*, p. 44; *Religion of Reason*, p. 58][32]

Significantly, Strauss quotes this same line of Cohen's – "And it is a question whether such transformation is not the best kind of annihilation" – thirty-four years later in the 1965 preface to the English translation of *Spinoza's Critique of Religion*. With both citations, the reference is off by a page. We might immediately want to call this insignificant, yet, in the case of the 1931 essay, the philosophical content of the disclaimer with which Strauss follows this quotation – which comes from the introduction to *Religion of Reason* – can also be found on the page that Strauss actually quotes. In the comments preceding the ones that Strauss quotes, Cohen attests to the rhetorical nature of his question about whether transformation is "not the best kind of annihilation." Cohen writes:

In the very mind which brings forth the new motive, the aftereffect of the institution which is to be fought lingers on. In this development the old motive preserves its right in the new one; it retains its share in the development toward the new one. Thus the new idea remains connected with the old one even then, when it does not entirely eliminate the old institution, but only transforms it.[33]

Cohen maintains that change in a tradition (and the context here is prophetic change) is in keeping with the original idea and is *not* in this sense "annihilation."

It is curious then that Strauss, who certainly considers himself a careful reader and writer, not once but twice (in 1931 and 1965) gives an inaccurate reference for Cohen's comment and that, in the case of the 1931 reference, he does not follow this reference with what Cohen actually writes on the page that he cites. This is especially curious because in Strauss's 1965 reference to Cohen's question about whether transformation is not the best form of annihilation, he does *not* follow this quotation, as he does in 1931, with the correct disclaimer that the question for Cohen is only rhetorical. In his preface to *Spinoza's Critique of Religion*, Strauss implies by way of omission that the view that transformation is the best form of annihilation *is* actually Cohen's view. The context of Strauss's quotation of Cohen (who is not referred to in the text) is not Cohen's thought, but the hermeneutics of tradition more broadly. Strauss writes:

Within a living tradition, the new is not the opposite of the old but its deepening: one does not understand the old in its depth unless one understands it in the light of such deepening; the new does not emerge through the rejection or annihilation of the old but through its metamorphosis or reshaping. 'And it is a question of whether such reshaping is not the best form of annihilation.'[34]

What are we to make then of Strauss's comments about Cohen's hermeneutical approach in both this early and then this mature essay? This is especially interesting in the case of the preface to the Spinoza book, whose purpose is Strauss's attempt to account for his change of orientation and also for the roots of his own intellectual development; roots that he maintains in this essay are still relevant for understanding his later thought.

My suggestion is that Strauss's quotation of Cohen's question of "whether such reshaping is not the best form of annihilation" relates not only to his criticism of what is wrong with Cohen's approach to Maimonides, and therefore to the formation of Strauss's mature project, but also to Strauss's own relation to Cohen. Strauss's relation to Cohen is one of transformation and thus annihilation. In his work on and comments about Cohen, Strauss thus affirms the question that for Cohen is only rhetorical (and hence can't be answered in the affirmative). For Strauss, transformation *is* the best form of annihilation. Strauss does not reject but transforms Cohen's own contentions about Maimonides, Plato, Judaism, philosophy, as well as "contemporary" ethics and politics to annihilate Cohen's very project.[35]

Strauss argues not that Cohen is wrong about Maimonides but that Cohen is exactly right that Maimonides is the true model of rationalism and that Maimonides is truly a Platonist and not an Aristotelian. Yet Strauss argues that Cohen's reasons for arguing as he does – and hence Cohen's very project – needs to be transformed. This transformation, of course, is the heart of Strauss's project, which is to rethink the modern prejudice that a return to premodern philosophy is impossible. To appreciate this transformation and hence annihilation, let us turn then to Strauss's arguments about Cohen and Maimonides.

As he does in the case of Cohen's interpretation of Spinoza, Strauss begins his criticism of Cohen's interpretation of Maimonides with a historical-critical point. He argues that the dichotomies that Cohen presents between Hegel and Kant on the one hand and between Aristotle and Plato on the other hand are historically inaccurate, for Hegel was a Kantian and Aristotle was a Platonist. This appreciation for the historical placement of a philosopher is in keeping with what I have suggested is Strauss's affirmative response to Cohen's rhetorical question, that transformation might be the best form of annihilation. Yes, Hegel and Aristotle are different from Kant and Plato respectively, but they are only truly different because of their reliance on their predecessors. Hegel and Aristotle respectively transform Kant and Plato's respective philosophies and if one is convinced by either of their arguments (which, of course, Cohen is not) then their success will be based upon this transformation, which amounts to an annihilation of his predecessor.

Strauss acknowledges that there is a difference between Plato and Aristotle, but he argues that the difference isn't what Cohen maintains it is. Cohen argues in his 1908 essay on Maimonides that Maimonides is a Platonist and not an Aristotelian because Maimonides has ethics at the heart of his system. For Cohen, Plato, ethics, and true rationalism go together. In short, Plato's great insight is his recognition of the good that is beyond being (a view that we have seen Levinas unwittingly repeats). Cohen argues that Plato's notion of the good is not only the height of ethics but of rationalism also because Plato, as opposed to Aristotle, puts ethics on par with science.[36]

Strauss maintains that Aristotle is a Platonist precisely in the sense in which Cohen argues he is not.[37] Cohen agrees that Aristotle does make a distinction between ethics and science, or more broadly, between ethics and speculation (what Cohen calls *cognition*). Yet Strauss argues that Plato makes this very distinction and that Aristotle is only following Plato in doing so. Strauss claims further that Maimonides is in keeping with both Plato and Aristotle in adhering to such a distinction. Cohen's entire interpretation of Maimonides and the Cohenian program become questionable in this light. Strauss argues that ethics is not Maimonides's primary philosophical motivation and by implication that true rationalism is not marked by what Cohen maintains is the confluence between ethics and cognition, as well as between pure and practical reason.[38] Strauss implies that if this confluence is not founded in Plato and Maimonides, as Cohen claims it is, then the Cohenian program and Cohen's ethics in particular fall apart.

In the final part of his essay on Cohen and Maimonides, Strauss criticizes Cohen's interpretation of Maimonides's doctrine of negative attributes. Cohen claims that Maimonides's attributes of action determine God as the model of ethics. For Strauss, Cohen's interpretation denies the metaphysical dimension of Maimonides's doctrine in favor of ethics.[39] Cohen, of course, would respond that metaphysics *is* ethics. Indeed, this is the crux of Cohen's claim about Plato's notion of the good: that it is both metaphysical *and* ethical, that its metaphysical reality is its ethical meaning. Strauss's response to this claim is that for Maimonides the world does not exist because of ethics. Rather the world exists because God created the world.[40] According to Strauss, the highest good for Maimonides is not ethical behavior but pure understanding. But even though pure understanding is a higher good than ethical behavior, for Maimonides the philosopher is not the highest possibility for the human being. Rather, the prophet, who combines the rational with the imaginative faculties, is the highest possibility for the human being. Here again Strauss is in agreement with Cohen's conclusion that prophecy is the peak of humanity, but once again he transforms the content of Cohen's argument. Whereas for Cohen, following Steinthal, prophecy represents the inner form of reason, for Strauss, prophecy represents the attempt to secure the divine law. In his early essay on Cohen and Maimonides, Strauss begins to develop the arguments he will make a bit later in *Philosophy and Law* concerning the centrality of law for Maimonides.

In *Philosophy and Law*, Strauss criticizes not Cohen directly but Cohen's student, Julius Guttmann, for being blind to the relation between philosophy and law in medieval Jewish philosophy.[41] From Strauss's perspective, Guttmann's blindness in this regard is predicated on a modern and indeed a Cohenian prejudice: the belief that modern philosophy is superior to medieval philosophy. Interestingly, the reason for this blindness is also blindness to what Strauss contends is the real difference between Aristotle and Plato. Strauss holds that their true difference concerns not the relation between ethics and cognition but the status of philosophy. Drawing on Avicenna in his 1931 essay, and then also on Alfarabi in *Philosophy and Law*, Strauss argues that the medieval Islamic philosophers whom Maimonides followed aligned themselves with Plato rather than with Aristotle. According to these Islamic philosophers, Plato understood philosophy to be both constrained and made possible by the law. For the medieval Islamic philosophers, the relation between philosophy and law in Plato (and the Plato of the *Laws* in particular) philosophically anticipates the proper relation between philosophy and revelation.

What then is, according to Strauss, the proper relation between philosophy and revelation from the Maimonidean perspective? In answering this question we come full circle in Strauss's transformation of Cohen's interpretation of Maimonides, and indeed of the Cohenian project more broadly. Let us recall Strauss's comments in the introductory essay to the translation of Cohen's *Religion of Reason* about Cohen's view of law. Strauss writes:

[Cohen] has the courage to say that Revelation and Law are identical. According to him, the Law is either the moral law or is meant to contribute to man's moral education. More precisely, all particular commandments concern means; their suitability is therefore subject to examination. In the last analysis the Law [for Cohen] is symbol.[42]

Strauss agrees with Cohen that revelation and law are identical, but once again he contends that Cohen has come to the right conclusion for the wrong reasons. That revelation and law are identical for Cohen means that there is a fundamental confluence between philosophy and revelation (as Strauss notes the law for Cohen is the moral law). In contrast, that revelation and law are identical for Strauss means that there is a fundamental tension between philosophy and revelation. Strauss argues that Maimonides, in following the medieval Islamic interpretation of Plato, recognizes this tension and thereby recognizes the limitation imposed on philosophy by law. According to Strauss, Maimonides is more Platonic than Aristotelian because Aristotle, in contrast to Plato, understands philosophy as unrestrained in regard to the law. Strauss also ironically brings Cohen closer to Aristotle in this interpretation, for he notes correctly that the suitability of the commandments for Cohen is "subject to examination." Where Cohen's notions of revelation and law bolster modern philosophy, Strauss's arguments about revelation and law are meant to show the limitations of philosophy as it has been classically conceived.[43]

The possibility of a modern rationalism rests for Strauss on the recognition that philosophy is necessarily limited when it comes to making claims about universal laws. This isn't to say that philosophy does not have a critical function to play in directing society. On the contrary. Strauss's claim is that philosophy can only play a role in guiding society by acknowledging its limited function. In contrast, the modern rationalism inaugurated by Spinoza among others is premised not only on a denial of such limitation but also more specifically on an attempt to refute any skepticism about our ability to reason. As Richard Popkin has pointed out, skepticism was used in early modern European thought not to criticize but *to defend* religion.[44] Spinoza argues against a skeptical defense of religion. As he put it:

Surely I cannot marvel enough that people should want to make reason, the divine light, [God's] greatest gift, subordinate to dead letters, which could have been distorted by the wicked conduct of men.... They think it pious to trust nothing to reason and to their own judgment, but impious to doubt the reliability of those who handed down the Sacred Books to us.[45]

Along with this "skeptical" position, Spinoza also attacks "dogmatism," and specifically Maimonides whom he claims was "the first person among the Pharisees who frankly maintained that Scripture should be accommodated to reason."[46] For Strauss, these characterizations of skepticism and dogmatism both miss the mark when it comes to Maimonides and pave the way toward what is considered modern rationalism and its demise.

For Strauss, Maimonides is neither the skeptic nor dogmatist described by Spinoza. Maimonides is the paradigm of rationalism for Strauss because he recognizes that while philosophy is weak in regard to grounding a universal law, revelation still does *not* have the status of philosophical truth. It is for this reason that from a Maimonidian point of view, religious dogmatism as a claim to truth beyond faith is impossible. Religious and philosophical rationalism depend upon appreciating the incommensurability between philosophy and revelation, *from both sides*. Here Strauss's criticism of Rosenzweig is relevant. While Strauss contends that Rosenzweig had the right impulse to consider the limitations of philosophy in the context of revelation, he also suggests that Rosenzweig's debt to the historicism of his time prevented him from fully restoring the separate tasks of philosophy and revelation. Because these separate tasks were not fully restored, Rosenzweig's thought, Strauss claims, did not ultimately make it possible to move toward a modern rationalism. As Strauss puts it in his preface to *Spinoza's Critique of Religion*, Rosenzweig could provide no *reasons* for choosing one orthodoxy over another. Strauss's reading of Rosenzweig contrasts with his reading of Judah Halevi, usually taken to be a mystic. According to Strauss's readings, Halevi was actually more of a rationalist than Rosenzweig. While Rosenzweig and Halevi both recognized *philosophically* the limitation of philosophy with respect to revelation, Halevi,[47] as opposed to Rosenzweig, offers *reasons* for rationally choosing Jewish orthodoxy over Christian and Moslem orthodoxy.[48] Rosenzweig, in contrast, does not offer *reasons* for choosing Jewish orthodoxy over any other kind.

Spinoza's twin attacks on "skepticism" and "dogmatism" are shared by both Cohen and Levinas. Again, Cohen's critical idealism is an attempt to secure the priority of thought over sensation. We might say that in his criticism of Kant's notion of sensible experience, Cohen finds Kant too skeptical. At the same time, Cohen's "internalist" interpretations of creation and revelation stem from, as Strauss shows, his premise, inherited from the Enlightenment, that traditional theological claims are fundamentally dogmatic. Levinas, as the flip side of Cohen, privileges sensibility over reason, but in doing so also attempts to get beyond what he considers to be traditional dogmatism and skepticism. Like Cohen, Levinas has an "internalist" reading of creation and revelation. Creation is not God's act in producing the world, but rather my sense of my self as a creature (which I know by way of sensibility).[49] But Levinas's disavowal of dogma and emphasis on sensibility do not allow skepticism the final word. Indeed, the second to last chapter of *Otherwise than Being* is an attempt to show that skepticism is predicated on the fundamental truth and certainty of ethics. Here too we might say that Levinas finds Kant too skeptical. While Kant's critique of pure reason leaves room for faith, Levinas's seemingly even more devastating critique of pure reason ends by suggesting that reason is grounded by the certainty of the ethical relation (which also destabilizes reason and thereby accounts for skepticism).[50]

Different as they are from each other, Cohen's and Levinas's arguments share with Spinoza a caricatured view of both premodern skepticism and "dogmaticism." For Strauss, the legacy of Spinoza and Enlightenment philosophy is the attempt to build a modern view of reason on these caricatures. The problem, Strauss claims, is not just that these are caricatures but that these caricatures lead to modern reason's own demise. In Chapter 4 I suggested that Levinas's position amounts to an ethical voluntarism and that it is difficult, on philosophical and political grounds, to call such a voluntarism "rational." Philosophically, Levinas's position is the result of the tension inherent in Kant's transcendental idealism. Levinas, Cohen, and Heidegger all follow different trajectories of this tension. The only way out of this tension, if not contradiction, Strauss maintains, is the rethinking of another Enlightenment prejudice: that today's thinking is superior to yesterday's thinking and its hermeneutical extension, which is that it is possible to understand an author better than he understood himself.

5.4. BEYOND COHEN?

Cohen's project fails for Strauss not only for philosophical and methodological reasons but for existential ones. As Strauss puts it in his introductory essay to *Religion of Reason*, "Cohen seems almost to face the possibility actualized not long after his death by national socialism. But his 'optimism' was too strong."[51] The most basic question that must be asked of Hermann Cohen today is Cohen's own question. Has history made questionable not just Cohen's optimism but Cohen's belief in the superiority of modern philosophy? We have seen in this chapter that it is in answering this question in the affirmative that Leo Strauss became Leo Strauss.

Levinas's philosophy is uncomfortably situated between Cohen's and Strauss's philosophies. I have suggested that Levinas's philosophy falls short of Cohen's philosophy in putting forward a rationalist defense of ethics. On the other hand, if one of the central impetuses of Levinas's thought is to take seriously the reality of evil and its implications for rethinking the notion of natural equality as the first principle of ethics and politics, then Strauss's project, based on Levinas's own premises, is the more consistent and compelling version of what Levinas purports to be doing.

I have also suggested throughout these last three chapters that the legacy of post-Kantian philosophy is ramified in the twin positions of Cohen and Levinas, with Cohen's position leading to Levinas's position once the faith in the powers of reason breaks down. This isn't to say, however, that a post-Kantian defense of a religious or philosophical rationalism isn't possible. I am suggesting more minimally that Strauss raises some serious questions about such a possibility. But in raising these questions we should not forget Strauss's great admiration for Cohen, for all of his criticism of him. First and foremost, Strauss appreciates Cohen's attempt to put law at the center of his view of both revelation and modern society. We turn now, in the final part of this book, to the implications of Strauss's effort to rethink modern rationalism for contemporary conceptions of secular and religious law. There too we will consider for this same enterprise the implications of Levinas's thought.

PART THREE

POLITICS

6

Against Utopia: Law and Its Limits

*D*ESPITE THE CONTROVERSY THE NAME LEO STRAUSS CONTINUES TO generate in current discussions of and about American politics, Strauss never drew out the implications of his thought for any practical political program. In part, we may attribute this controversy to general ignorance, willful or otherwise, of Strauss's work. Given all the talk about Strauss, not many people, outside of those called "Straussians" and a few of their severest critics actually read Strauss's work. Yet even among, or especially among, Straussians, the implications of Strauss's thought for understanding the nature of politics remains hotly contested.[1] It would not be an overstatement to suggest that the appropriation of Strauss (by fans, critics, and the uninformed alike) in current debates about politics would be worthy of a book-length study.[2]

The task of the third and final part of this book is at once narrower and broader than the attempt to sort out Strauss's reception in contemporary politics. Focusing only on Strauss's published work,[3] I attempt in this chapter to draw out the contours of Strauss's notion of a rational politics, from a theoretical point of view. To this end, I maintain that it is essential to focus on the conceptual links between Strauss's work in medieval Jewish philosophy and his American work in the history of political philosophy. While the contradictory claims about Strauss among Straussians (a discussion of which I reserve mainly for the notes to this chapter) are not the main focus of what follows, the connection between Strauss's Jewish and American work may clear up certain misconceptions about Strauss's view of politics, specifically in connection with his notions of natural right and religion.[4] Strauss, I argue, does not present a defense of natural right compatible with Christian views of natural law, as one set of Straussians argues, nor, as a different set of Straussians maintains, does Strauss's philosophical skepticism ultimately undermine the *intellectual* (and not merely instrumental) importance of religion in politics. Instead, I contend, the central element of Strauss's conception of politics revolves around the *philosophical skepticism* that arises from the irreconcilable tension between philosophy and law. But far from making religion secondary to politics, Strauss's philosophical skepticism only bolsters religion's intellectual and moral importance in political life. In making these arguments, two themes from Part 2 of this book, and from Chapter 5 particularly, are especially relevant: the first is that the possibility of rationalism rests for Strauss on the recognition that philosophy is necessarily limited when it comes to *constituting or grounding* universal laws and the second is Strauss's emphasis on the important role of philosophical skepticism in premodern defenses of religion.

Stressing Strauss's continuing concern with the relation between philosophy and law, Sections 6.1 and 6.2 of this chapter explore the continuity between Strauss's work in medieval Jewish philosophy and the history of political philosophy and bring to light Strauss's continued ambivalence about Christianity and its relation to modern philosophy. Section 6.3 of the chapter elaborates on Strauss's philosophical skepticism and antiutopianism, which are intrinsic to his insistence on an irreconcilable tension between philosophy and law and to his positive conception of a rational politics. In this context, I suggest that, Levinas's fear and rejection of skepticism, like certain contemporary affirmations of natural law in Strauss's name, exemplify what Strauss criticizes in modern philosophy and its conception of politics. Section 6.4 of the chapter turns to the relation between religion and politics in the context of Strauss's philosophical skepticism and suggests why religion, understood for Strauss in the framework of diasporic Judaism, rather than Christianity, may have a positive and mutually beneficial relation to liberal democracy. Finally, the conclusion, Section 6.5, briefly considers the implication of this analysis for understanding, from Strauss's perspective, the role of religion in contemporary American society – a subject of great contemporary interest and controversy among Strauss's self-professed followers.

6.1. PHILOSOPHY, LAW, AND THE DIFFERENCE BETWEEN JUDAISM AND CHRISTIANITY

To understand Strauss's continuing concern with the relation between philosophy and law, religious and civil, it is necessary to consider briefly his early interest in medieval Jewish and Islamic philosophy. Looking back on Strauss's work in the 1930s and the 1940s in Germany, France, England, and then the United States, one can easily get the distinct impression that there were at least two very different scholarly personas, the one concerned with medieval

Jewish philosophy and the one concerned with the history of western political thought. Indeed, Strauss's interpreters have, for the most part, adhered to this two-person view, with most of the interest in Strauss focusing on the latter persona and relegating the former persona to Strauss's seemingly quaint if not provincial origins as a German Jew.[5] But Strauss's early "German" concern with medieval Jewish philosophy and his mature "American" contention that secular[6] modernity is symptomatic of a rational, moral, and political decay are of a piece and they are connected by the political implications of Strauss's interest in the status of law in medieval Jewish and Islamic philosophy. We can begin to appreciate this connection by turning to one of the first lectures Strauss gave as a new German-Jewish émigré to the United States.

At the New School for Social Research, Strauss began his American career by trying to account for the intellectual roots of the rise of National Socialism. In a 1941 lecture, titled "German Nihilism," delivered to his New School colleagues, Strauss describes this intellectual root as a "depreciation and contempt of reason." Strauss's perhaps surprising claim is that this "contempt of reason" stems from the *atheism* intrinsic to modern society. Far from being the pinnacle of reason, atheism for Strauss fractures the critical function of reason. Not too subtly, Strauss's description of "German Nihilism" is also a criticism of the alternative theories about National Socialism proposed by his German-Jewish émigré colleagues at the New School. Strauss contends that leftist and liberal critics of National Socialism assume that they can refute something without completely understanding it. As he puts it, "one cannot refute what one has not thoroughly understood."[7] What needs to be understood about National Socialism and the strand of thought that Strauss calls "German Nihilism" is its *moral* motive. Here Strauss repeats a claim that he made in his 1932 review of Carl Schmitt's *The Concept of the Political.* Strauss claimed that Schmitt hadn't understood the *moral* motive of his own work and for this reason Strauss finds Schmitt too much of a liberal – a claim that Strauss's subsequent liberal critics continue to find particularly audacious.[8]

Despite the rhetoric that continues to accompany discussions of Strauss because of his comments about and presumed intellectual relation to Schmitt, one cannot fully understand Strauss's *moral* criticism of those he calls "German nihilists" without reference to what he proposes as an alternative theoretical notion of politics and morality. This alternative is based on Strauss's particular reading of medieval Islamic philosophy. In the lecture "German Nihilism" Strauss does not mention Islamic philosophy, but his interpretation of medieval Islamic philosophy, which he developed while living in Weimar,

Germany, corresponds directly to his definition of *civilization* in this lecture
(which he claims German nihilism rejects) as "the conscious culture of human
reason, i.e. science *and* morals."[9] For Strauss, the relation between science and
morals concerns the relation between *philosophy and law*, the subject of his
second major book, published in 1935 in Germany, which goes by that very
title.

As mentioned briefly in Chapter 5, in *Philosophy and Law* Strauss began
to make his argument for the importance of Islamic philosophy for *recovering* medieval Jewish philosophy. Strauss's specific contemporary target in
the first of the three essays of *Philosophy and Law* is Julius Guttmann's *The
Philosophy of Judaism*. The first and third essays of *Philosophy and Law* implicitly link Guttmann's account of medieval Jewish philosophy and nineteenth-
century Jewish interpretations of Islam.[10] Drawing on the unpublished work
of his brother-in-law Paul Kraus, Strauss claims that the study of Alfarabi and
Averroes makes possible a different and truer reading of medieval Jewish
philosophy than Guttmann presents.[11] Strauss equates Guttmann's liberal
assumptions about "culture" with his philosophical assumption that philosophy and revelation at bottom reflect that same "field of culture."

In Chapter 9 we will have occasion to explore in greater detail the
theological-political connection that Strauss insists on in his understanding of
Jewish revelation and Guttmann's subsequent criticism of Strauss's position.
Here, however, we must focus on the interconnection between Strauss's claims
about Jewish and Islamic law and his concern, in 1941, with German nihilism.
While Strauss's focus in *Philosophy and Law* is on the status of Jewish, or religious, law, we should not forget that he looks back from medieval Jewish and
Islamic philosophy to Plato and, emphasizing the significance of Plato's *Laws*,
claims that the classical conception of law concerns and also anticipates the
tense yet necessary relation between philosophy and law in medieval Jewish
philosophy. Strauss not only projects the tension between philosophy and law
back onto the classical past, but he also stresses this tension in contemplating
the central issues at stake in modern, liberal democracy. It is important to
note once again Strauss's 1941 definition of *civilization*. Civilization, defined
as the "the conscious culture of human reason, i.e. science *and* morals," is
for Strauss the conscious culture of the relation between philosophy *and* law.
German nihilism, and the inability of the philosophical left to respond to it,
results for Strauss from "the depreciation and the contempt of reason."[12] As
we saw in the first two parts of this book, Strauss suggests that the twentieth-
century depreciation of reason follows from the overblown political and social
status of philosophy in the modern period.[13]

In the same year, 1941, that Strauss lectured on German nihilism he also published his seminal essay, "Persecution and the Art of Writing." While Strauss's essay on esoteric writing may seem an archaic topic when compared to his lecture on the roots of National Socialism, they are intellectually related. The common theme of both is a criticism of atheistic society animated by Strauss's claims about the differences between Judaism and Islam, on the one hand, and Christianity, on the other hand. As discussed briefly in Chapter 1, Strauss sets out in "Persecution and the Art of Writing" to describe what he calls "sociology of philosophy."[14] Against prevailing notions of the sociology of knowledge, Strauss attempts to rethink what he contends is *the* basic philosophical question, from Plato forward. This question is: what is the relationship between thought and society? In answering this question, Strauss distinguishes between Judaism and Islam on the one hand, and Christianity on the other, maintaining that the former understands revelation as divine law, while the latter understands it as revealed theology. Strauss suggests that "[t]his difference explains partly the eventual collapse of philosophic inquiry in the Islamic and in the Jewish world, a collapse which has no parallel in the Western Christian world."[15]

Read out of context, one might think that because of his claim about the eventual collapse of philosophical inquiry in the Islamic and Jewish worlds, that Strauss is complimenting Christianity and criticizing Judaism and Islam. But the opposite is the case. Strauss insists in this essay and in all of the essays that would accompany this one in the 1952 book titled *Persecution and the Art of Writing* that the profundity of the Islamic and Jewish medieval philosophical traditions lies in their claim that philosophy and revelation are fundamentally irreconcilable. For both these traditions of thought, philosophy as a way of life is in fundamental opposition to revelation as a way of life. Acknowledging the fundamental incommensurability of philosophy and revelation, medieval Islamic and Jewish philosophy both recognize the need to coordinate them politically. For Strauss, the eventual demise of philosophical inquiry in the Islamic and Jewish world, while regrettable, is not nearly as troubling as the fusion of revelation and philosophy in medieval Christian theology. The demise of philosophy leaves Islamic and Jewish revelation intact. But as importantly, this demise also leaves the possibility of philosophy intact. As Strauss puts it:

The precarious state of philosophy in Judaism as well as in Islam was not in every respect a misfortune for philosophy. The official recognition of philosophy in the Christian world made philosophy subject to ecclesiastical supervision. The precarious position of philosophy in the Islamic-Jewish world guaranteed its private character and therewith its inner-freedom from supervision. The status of philosophy in the Islamic-Jewish world resembled in this respect its status in classical Greece.[16]

In contrast to the Islamic-Jewish world, Strauss claims, the melding of revelation and philosophy in medieval Christendom destroyed the meanings of both revelation and philosophy.

In a very important sense, Strauss seems to locate the invention of the possibility of an atheistic, secular society with Thomas Aquinas.[17] To be sure, this is an odd claim at first glance, both as a general contention and as an interpretation of Strauss. In terms of the latter, Strauss is most often taken to consider Machiavelli's "anti-theological ire" as the intellectual source of modernity.[18] Yet while Strauss strongly criticizes Machiavelli's thought, he at the same time suggests that Machiavelli was correct in understanding the *political weakness* of Christianity and of Christian scholasticism in particular. As one recent interpreter puts it, Strauss "quietly agreed with Machiavelli's criticism of Christian scholasticism for having openly promulgated a teaching . . . that led men to aspire to transcend their need for *law*."[19] And, according to Strauss, it is Aquinas and Christian scholasticism that attempt to transcend the need for law.

Simply put, Strauss's contention is that because Christian scholasticism made philosophy the handmaiden of theology in its understanding of natural law, the Enlightenment, following Machiavelli's instrumentalization of philosophy, was eventually able to make theology the handmaiden of philosophy. Strauss maintains that in contrast to the medieval Christian scholastics, the profundity of the Jewish and Islamic medieval philosophers lies in their recognition that revelation and philosophy can neither be synthesized (as in the Christian scholastic view of natural law) nor can they refute one another. Revelation and philosophy are therefore incommensurable. Revelation simply cannot be proven philosophically (and hence revelation cannot trump philosophy on its own terms), but revelation can also not be disproved philosophically (and hence philosophy cannot trump revelation on its own terms). By claiming that philosophy can and does lend *philosophical* support to revelation, medieval Christian scholasticism opened up the door for the Enlightenment conception of a far too overreaching "philosophy." As Strauss puts it rather succinctly, "I do not deny, but assert, that modern philosophy has much that is essential in common with Christian medieval philosophy."[20] Or, as he puts it elsewhere, "modern philosophy emerged by way of transformation of, if in opposition to, Latin or Christian scholasticism."[21]

Let us leave aside the questions of generalization in Strauss's historical account (to which I have not done justice in this extremely brief and reductive rendering of his position) to turn to the *philosophical* point that Strauss attempts to make. Strauss's central point is that medieval Christian theology replaced the Jewish understanding of revelation as divine law with a synthesis of revelation and philosophy. In this sense, Christian scholasticism made revelation a matter of *knowledge* and not legislation.[22] The overblown political and social status of philosophy in the modern period was made conceptually possible, Strauss contends, by the initial Christian synthesis of philosophy and revelation, which amounted to a disregard for the precarious relation between philosophy and law. This disregard led ultimately to the decline of philosophy in twentieth-century historicism, which is the result of the inability of reason to live up to the unrealistic standards set by Enlightenment thinkers. Again leaving aside Strauss's historical account of this development, let us notice that philosophically Strauss accepts what he calls "radical historicism" as the logical outcome of modern philosophy.

In the context of his claim that modern philosophy has imploded upon itself, Strauss attempts to rethink the possibility of a philosophical rationalism. At the basis of Strauss's criticism of modern rationalism and what he contends are its historicist aftereffects is his contention that a fully *philosophically* justified law is unavailable. The perhaps negative insight that philosophy is necessarily *limited* when it comes to founding, by itself and on its own terms, *universal* laws is the basis of a true philosophical rationalism, argues Strauss.[23] Philosophy plays a critical and necessary role in guiding society, but it can only do so by acknowledging its limited function when it comes to providing a *universal ground* for law. Against both Christian scholasticism *and* modern Kantian claims, Strauss maintains that it is not possible to discover a *universal* morality and law for whose *foundations* we can *rationally* account.

6.2. THE QUESTION OF NATURAL RIGHT

This argument is consistent with a number of themes in *Natural Right and History*, which is considered Strauss's most American book and, oddly, especially in light of the title of the book, is often read as a defense of natural law.[24] While I certainly do not intend to provide a full account of this work, I'd like to point out that in *Natural Right and History*, Strauss affirms the very themes about philosophy, revelation, and the impossibility of natural law that he emphasizes in his early work. Interestingly, Strauss does so in the context of his criticism of trends in American social and political science and in his discussion of Max Weber more particularly. Weber's problem, for Strauss, is that his atheism is too comprehensive, thus robbing it of critical force. This false comprehensiveness originates in Weber's inability to take the possibility of revelation seriously. As Strauss puts it:

Philosophy has to grant that revelation is possible. But to grant that revelation is possible means to grant that the philosophic life is not necessarily, not evidently, *the* right life. Philosophy, the life devoted to the quest for evident knowledge available to man as man, would rest on an unevident, arbitrary, or blind decision. This would merely confirm the thesis of faith, that there is no possibility of consistency, of a consistent and thoroughly sincere life, without belief in revelation. The mere fact that philosophy and revelation cannot refute each other would constitute the refutation of philosophy by revelation.

It was the conflict between revelation and philosophy or science in the full sense of the term and the implications of that conflict that led Weber to assert that the idea of science or philosophy suffers from a fatal weakness. He tried to remain faithful to the cause of autonomous insight, but he despaired when he felt that the sacrifice of the intellect, which is abhorred by science and philosophy, is at the bottom of science or philosophy.[25]

From Strauss's perspective, Weber's atheistic disenchantment with atheism is fundamentally flawed because of the post-Christian philosophical assumption upon which it is built. As Strauss puts it, "Weber overestimated the importance of the revolution that had taken place on the plane of theology, and he underestimated the importance of the revolution that had taken place on the plane of rational thought."[26] In claiming a universal, rational status for itself, modern atheism is, for Strauss, symptomatic of the demise of reason. Paradoxically, Strauss suggests, for atheism to be an intellectually rigorous and critical position, the atheist must acknowledge the *possible* truth of theism. Modern atheism does not acknowledge the limitations of philosophy when it comes to founding (though not explicating) universal truths for all people. Philosophical atheism rests on, to use Strauss's words, "an unevident, arbitrary, or blind decision,"[27] one that Strauss in his personal life may have been happy to affirm. However, because of this "blind decision," the atheist cannot philosophically claim a universalizable, rational ground for atheism and must therefore grant the possibility, if not for herself than surely for others, of divine revelation (and one may understand this as Strauss's intellectual, as opposed to personal, position).

Strauss illustrates what he claims is the pitfall of modern atheism in his analysis of Weber. Weber's response to his despair at the possibility of autonomous insight was to develop his neo-Kantian methodology. Strauss maintains that, ironically, however, this methodology was unable to offer an account of the "social world," the goal of Weber's analysis. This fundamental weakness of

Weber's thought, for Strauss, stems from his inheritance of a modern school of thought that denies precisely the *philosophical* relevance of prephilosophical forms of life: "In the spirit of a tradition of three centuries, Weber would have rejected the suggestion that social science must be based on an analysis of social reality as it is experienced in social life or known to 'common sense.'"[28]

Perhaps surprisingly, Strauss's early attempt to revalue the anti-Semitic rhetoric of Paul de Lagarde, to be discussed in greater detail in Chapter 7, illuminates this later criticism of Weber. As Strauss put it in a 1924 essay, "What Lagarde understands as Jewish materialism is the putting of the law before spirit, of the finished matter before process, and of culturedness [*Gebildetheit*] before the acquisition of culture [*Bildung*]."[29] In the United States, twenty-eight years later, it is precisely the putting of the law before the spirit, the putting of common sense before philosophy, *which involves acknowledging the possibility of theism*, that Strauss recommends as an antidote to a Weberian view of social science.[30]

Yet the affinity between *Natural Right and History* and Strauss's consideration of the centrality of law in medieval Jewish and Islamic philosophy (as opposed to Christian theology) runs deeper. In the chapter on classical natural right in *Natural Right and History*, Strauss indicates this affinity with a footnote to "The Law of Reason in the Kuzari," one of the essays included in *Persecution and the Art of Writing*. The note to this essay is appended to the following sentence: "There exists an alternative medieval interpretation of Aristotle's doctrine, namely, the Averroistic view or, more adequately stated, the view characteristic of the falāsia, as well as of the Jewish Aristotelians."[31] The context of this comment is Strauss's distinction between the Aristotelian view of natural right and the Socratic-Platonic view. For Aristotle, Strauss writes, "there is no fundamental disproportion between natural right and the requirements of political society."[32] In contrast, Strauss maintains, the Platonic-Socratic view of natural right recognizes a fundamental discrepancy between the justice of natural right, which is independent of law, and the justice of the city, which is of necessity dependent on law. Strauss illustrates this point by describing the difference between "just ownership" and "legal ownership." The former concerns what belongs to someone by nature, while the latter concerns what belongs to someone by law. Strauss uses an analogy that we mentioned in Chapter 2. He suggests that a small person may own a big coat, while a big person may own a small coat. Legal ownership stipulates the justice of private ownership, but from the perspective of natural right, the small person should have the small coat and the big person should have the big coat.

We see that Strauss reiterates his view of the difference between Plato and Aristotle that he articulated in his 1931 essay, discussed in Chapter 5, on "Cohen and Maimonides." In his American discussion of classical natural right, Strauss repeats his early, German claim that Plato differs from Aristotle in insisting on a fundamental gap between philosophy and law.[33] The title of Strauss's Halevi essay concerns what Halevi could have meant by "law of reason." Through a detailed analysis of Halevi's *Kuzari*, Strauss concludes, "the *iura naturalia* are really not more than the indispensable and unchangeable minimum of morality required for the bare existence of any society." But as Strauss points out, the unchangeable minimum of morality is, from a moral point of view, not very much after all:

he [the philosopher in Halevi's *Kuzari*] mentions among the governmental laws of the Divine code the prohibition against murder, e.g. while he does not mention it among the governmental and rational nomoi which are known independently of revelation; this again is easily understandable considering that the Bible prohibits murder absolutely, whereas a gang of robbers, e.g., would merely have to prohibit the murder of other members of the gang.[34]

In explicating Halevi's position, Strauss elaborates on Halevi's comment in the *Kuzari* that "[e]ven a gang of robbers must have a kind of justice among them if their confederacy is to last," (the analogy that refers to, without mentioning, Plato's parable of the robbers in *Republic*, Book 1, 342b–d).[35] Significantly, Strauss, in *Natural Right and History*, uses Halevi's analogy of a gang of robbers when he writes in his chapter on the "Origin of the Idea of Natural Right":

But it is unfortunate for the defenders of justice that it is also required for the preservation of a gang of robbers: the gang could not last a single day if its members did not refrain from hurting one another, if they did not help one another, or if each member did not subordinate his own good to the good of the gang.[36]

Halevi's Averroism, or "Jewish Aristotelianism," finds its most profound expression in what Strauss claims is Halevi's ultimate analysis of the "Law of Reason." As Strauss sums up:

By calling both the Law of Reason and the Natural Law rational *nomoi*, by thus, as matters stand, identifying that part of the Law of Reason which is relevant to men who are not philosophers, with the Natural Law, the scholar [in Halevi's *Kuzari*] tacitly asserts that the Natural Law is not obligatory and does not command, or presuppose, an inner attachment to society.[37]

Here we see that when Strauss refers in *Natural Right and History* to "the Averroistic view" as "an alternative medieval interpretation of Aristotle's doctrine" that he means by this that the Averroistic view is Platonic in a way that the Christian reading of Aristotle is not.[38] Once again Plato's *Laws*, and its medieval Islamic interpretation, is central for Strauss. As we have seen especially in Chapters 1 and 5, Plato and the "Jewish Aristotelians," Strauss insists, recognize a fundamental tension between philosophy and law, which is also the tension between philosophy and "the city." It is the Christian interpretation of Aristotle, and particularly Thomas Aquinas's notion of natural law, that denies this tension.[39]

In *Natural Right and History* Strauss makes this very argument about Aquinas, who represents a third version of classical natural right. Here it is necessary to quote Strauss at length:

> The Thomistic doctrine of natural right or, more generally expressed, of natural law is free from the hesitations and ambiguities which are characteristic of the teachings, not only of Plato and Cicero, but of Aristotle as well. . . . *No doubt is left*, not only regarding the basic harmony between natural right and civil society, but likewise regarding the immutable character of the fundamental propositions of natural law; the principles of the moral law, especially as formulated in the Second Table of the Decalogue, suffer no exception, unless possibly by divine intervention. The doctrine of *synderesis* or of the conscience explains why the natural law can always be duly promulgated to all men and hence to be universally obligatory. It is reasonable to assume that these profound changes were due to the influence of the belief in biblical revelation. If this assumption should prove to be correct, one would be forced to wonder, however, whether the natural law as Thomas Aquinas understands it is natural law strictly speaking, i.e. a law knowable to the unassisted human mind, to the human mind which is not illuminated by divine revelation. . . . According to Thomas . . . natural reason creates a presupposition in favor of the divine law, which completes or perfects the natural law . . . the ultimate consequence . . . is that natural law is practically inseparable from natural theology. . . . Modern law was partly a reaction to this absorption of natural law by theology.[40]

We have now come full circle from Strauss's early interest in the relation between philosophy and law to his mature writings on classical conceptions of natural right. A central theme emerging from Strauss's early and late work is the inextricable tension between philosophy and law – which is the inextricable tension between philosophy and society. When Strauss states that the philosopher speaking in the *Kuzari* does not have an "inner attachment" to the city, he is arguing, as he also does in *Natural Right and History*, that the only kind of morality that the philosopher qua philosopher recognizes is the morality of a gang of robbers, that is, a morality that makes the function of any *closed* society possible. Strauss's claim in his early and late work is that only divine revelation can guarantee a *universal* morality that can extend beyond the bounds of particular, closed societies.

We will have occasion in the conclusion of this book to discuss the merits of Strauss's arguments. My goal here, however, has been to emphasize Strauss's insistence in his early and late work that revelation and philosophy cannot be synthesized into a unified whole. The problem with Aquinas, Strauss argues, is that he relies on theology to make his claims about natural law. For Strauss, the issue is not only philosophical (what philosophy can know on its own) but also political and historical. As he states, in *Natural Right and History*, modern versions of natural law and right reacted to the theological assumptions of medieval scholasticism. While Hobbes is problematic for Strauss, more troubling is the philosophical conclusion that Heidegger and others draw from modern accounts of natural right, which is to deny that we can speak of nature, and human nature more particularly, at all.

In his early and late work, Strauss connects Christian scholasticism with what he claims is the ultimate demise of philosophy and revelation in the modern world. Far from being a conservative defender of Christian civilization, as some Straussians claim, Strauss raises issues that make us consider the role of Christianity in the making of modernity. So too, far from defending a Christian scholastic reading of Aristotle, again as some Straussians claim, Strauss favors the Islamic reading of Aristotle that, he argues, is fundamentally Platonic in its emphasis on the insurmountable tension between philosophy and the city.[41]

We have seen that for Strauss the tension between philosophy and the city is also the tension between philosophy and law. Strauss maintains that Aquinas implicitly denies this tension in his conception of natural law. Strauss's notion of classical natural right does not conform to Aquinas's Aristotelianism. But, perhaps more importantly, Strauss's emphasis on the insurmountable tension between philosophy and law points to the way in which he finds the Socratic-Platonic notion of classical political right *politically* (though not philosophically) problematic.[42] As Strauss states explicitly in *Natural Right and History*, the Socratic-Platonic notion of natural right is ultimately utopian in that its feasibility is based on the assumption that the wise will rule. As Strauss emphasizes, in *Natural Right and History* and beyond, this kind of political utopianism is extremely dangerous in reality. While an analysis of Strauss's reading of Plato's *Republic* is beyond the scope of this book, it is important to note that Strauss's antiutopianism conforms to his reading of the *Republic*, which Strauss understands as fundamentally antiutopian in its insistence that philosophers are not and cannot be compelled to rule. This reading of the *Republic*, of course, clashes with most modern readings, which find Plato utopian, for better or for worse, precisely because of what is taken as the *Republic*'s insistence on the rule of the wise. But here again it is important to note that Strauss reads the *Republic*, as his medieval Jewish and Islamic predecessors did, in the context of the *Laws*, which again emphasizes the ultimate tension between philosophy and law (or philosophy and society) – a tension that reflects a profoundly antiutopian perspective.

Strauss's antiutopianism coheres with his reading of Aquinas. Again, according to Strauss, on Aquinas's account of natural law "no doubt is left, not only regarding the basic harmony between natural right and civil society, but likewise regarding the immutable character of the fundamental propositions of natural law; the principles of the moral law. . . ." Strauss's criticism of the philosophical implications of the medieval scholastic view of natural law and the political implications of the Platonic-Socratic view of natural right are profoundly linked: in different ways, each, for Strauss, is fundamentally utopian in its refusal of the full implications of philosophical skepticism, the former because it doesn't recognize that law cannot be fully grounded *philosophically*, the latter because it doesn't recognize the ultimate tension between philosophy and society from a *political* perspective.[43]

6.3. SKEPTICISM AND ANTIUTOPIANISM

For Strauss, rationalism – philosophical, religious, and political – is intimately connected to recognizing the fundamental and irresolvable tension between philosophy and law, or between philosophy and society. Acknowledgement of this tension entails an affirmation of philosophical skepticism. But Strauss's philosophical skepticism differs profoundly from modern skepticism precisely because Strauss's kind of skepticism also is skeptical of itself.[44] Politics as the formal coordination of philosophy and revelation or of philosophy and law imposes a limitation on both. I suggested in Sections 6.1 and 6.2 that the reading of Strauss as a defender of Christian civilization does not emphasize enough Strauss's skeptical bent. Although they are in many ways extremely different from one another, Levinas's philosophy shares an important philosophical presupposition with the Christian conservative reading of Strauss's philosophy . Both Levinas and the Christian conservative reading of Strauss's philosophy fear and subsequently deny philosophical skepticism. Their shared denial of skepticism, I contend in what follows, weakens, if not defeats, the respective goals of each of their projects and in doing so illuminates further, for the purposes of this chapter, the parameters of Strauss's skepticism and antiutopianism.

To appreciate these points, let us turn briefly to Drucilla Cornell's sustained attempt to bring Levinas, by way of Derrida, into contemporary conversations about the interpretation of American law. Significantly, in the context of our discussion of Strauss's view that the formal relation between philosophy and law is one of mutual limitation, Cornell titles her important work on this subject *The Philosophy of the Limit*. Confining my remarks to Cornell's discussion of Levinas, though I think they could be equally applied to Derrida, I suggest that Levinas's rejection of skepticism marks his thought not as a philosophy of the limit but one that does not recognize the limits of both law and philosophy when they are, by necessity, faced with one another. This mutual limitation, and the necessary tensions and conversations that emerge from it, is for Strauss the basis of rationalism.

Contrary to my suggestion in Chapter 4 that Levinas ultimately attempts to present a rationalism on irrationalist terms, the premise of Cornell's *The Philosophy of the Limit* is a rejection of the often dominant view of Derrida's, and by implication Levinas's, thought as irrationalist. As Cornell puts it, "the identification of deconstruction with ethical skepticism is a serious misinterpretation."[45] As support for this claim, Cornell cites Levinas's words in *Otherwise than Being*:

The limits of the present in which infinity betrays itself breaks up. Infinity is beyond the scope of the unity of transcendental apperception, cannot be assembled into a present, and refuses being recollected. This negation of the present and of representation finds its positive form in proximity, responsibility and substitution. This makes it different from the presuppositions of negative theology. The refusal of presence is converted into my presence as present, that is, as a hostage delivered over as a gift to the other.[46]

Cornell rightly understands Levinas to be rejecting what he calls skepticism when he claims that "The refusal of presence is converted into my presence as present." In Chapter 4, I described Levinas's rejection of skepticism as the claim that beneath skepticism, almost as a transcendental condition, is the ethical relation. Skepticism, for Levinas, signifies a kind of infinite regress that can be described, to use Cornell's terms, as the "irrationalist" view that meaning is ultimately "indeterminate." Affirming the view that skepticism is the indeterminacy of meaning, Levinas claims that the very instability of knowledge points to the ethical relation (in Levinas's terms, "my presence as present . . . delivered over as a gift to the other").

The extremely telling point of Levinas's and Cornell's arguments is their association of "skepticism," and of "negative theology," with a kind of infinite regress that suggests that truth is ultimately indeterminate. Cornell is right that Levinas wants to reject skepticism. But Levinas's and Cornell's views of and responses to skepticism are ultimately parasitic on a very modern notion of reason that Levinas and Cornell seek to reject but inadvertently affirm.

The kind of skepticism that results in an infinite regress is a child of modern reason; it is the flip side of the claim that reason is self-sufficient. Again, Levinas has more in common with Spinoza than he may want to admit. From different sides, both understand reason as claiming self-sufficiency for itself and for this reason both can only understand skepticism as an ultimate denial of reason.

Strauss's skepticism is quite different. In Strauss's view, classical philosophy is fundamentally skeptical, but in its skepticism it is also skeptical of itself; it recognizes its dependence on society or on law by way of its self-reflective skepticism. Bringing Strauss into conversation with Levinas and Cornell we might say, in Strauss's name, that a true philosophy of the limit recognizes the limits of everything, including skeptical reason. Once again, the terms Cornell uses to describe Levinas are both accurate and telling. Cornell claims an "unerasable moment of utopianism" as "inherent in 'deconstruction' and in the writing of Emmanuel Levinas on the ethical relation."[47] Cornell finds Levinas attractive and affirms his view that "thoroughgoing social and legal transformation" is both desirable and possible. As will be discussed in greater detail in Chapters 7 and 9, Levinas, in a number of seminal essays, actually claims to reject utopian thinking. I suggest here, however, and will argue further in Chapters 7 and 9, that Cornell is right that Levinas's utopianism is perhaps captured best in his claim that law and ethics must be one and the same.

For Strauss, in contrast, a true philosophy of the limit is antiutopian. For all of its importance, law, divine and positive, cannot by definition claim the final good for itself, but instead remains in tension with other competing claims for the good. Levinas gives too little *and* too much credit to law. On the one hand, philosophy, which is at the same time morality for Levinas, recognizes no limitation in the regard to the law. This is where Levinas, from Strauss's perspective, gives too little credit to law. On the other hand, when the law is made ethical (which is for Levinas the true definition of law), law, as ethics, knows no limitation because it is the one and only ultimate good. In this sense, from Strauss's perspective, Levinas gives too much credit to law. Significantly, the Straussian position that presents Strauss as a defender of a Christian conception of natural law, like Levinas's philosophy, collapses competing goods into the good of law.[48] The view that the American Founding is confluent with a classical notion of natural right overvalues law in assuming that law – and in this case the Declaration of Independence – can encapsulate one universal good for all humanity.[49]

By not recognizing that their fear of skepticism is itself the child of modern reason Levinas's thought and the Christian conservative reading of Strauss remain embedded in the political, philosophical, and theological frameworks that each seeks to overcome.[50] Most simply, Levinas's philosophy and the Christian conservative reading of Strauss deny what is perhaps the central tenet of Strauss's thought, which is that "human beings will never create a society which is free from contradictions."[51] For Strauss, there are multiple human goods, the two most profound of which are those represented by Jerusalem and Athens, or revelation and philosophy. These goods cannot cancel each other out and they must, therefore, exist side by side, though they can never be synthesized. Politics is the formal coordination of these competing goods. And a proper political coordination is rational when it continually delimits the scope of each competing good while at the same time recognizing the need for a continual conversation between them. The possibility of modern rationalism for Strauss depends on this healthy skepticism about the possibility of positing only one human good. This is a skepticism that invites rather than dismisses competing conversations about the good life.

6.4. SKEPTICISM AND RELIGION

Those who read Strauss as a skeptic tend to suggest either that religion is ultimately philosophically irrelevant to Strauss's thought or that religion, at best, only has a politically instrumental significance for Strauss.[52] In contrast to these positions, I argue in this section that Strauss's skepticism not only bolsters the role of religion in his thought but also the *philosophical and intellectual* importance of religion, and Judaism more particularly, for politics.[53] As I argued in Chapter 5, Strauss's criticism of Spinoza hinges on what he suggests is Spinoza's dogmatic rejection of philosophical skepticism. The medieval Jewish and Islamic philosophers, Strauss maintains, provide a model of rationalism because they coordinate their commitment to philosophical skepticism – which, for Strauss, is the true meaning of philosophy – with their commitment to divine law. But in the absence of a society predicated on divine law (the return to which Strauss never advocated or even intimated was possible), are we not left only with skepticism? And if we are only left with skepticism, how, intellectually, can religion be anything else, in a modern democratic society, than an accommodation to current political structures?

Of those influenced by Strauss's thought, Walter Berns has expressed perhaps most clearly the view that while religion is important for American democracy it must of necessity take a back seat to politics. In an aptly titled chapter "The Religious Problem" in his now classic study *Taking the*

Constitution Seriously, Berns concludes that religious tolerance as conceived by the American Constitution

does not, then, depend on an open and official declaration of disbelief; certainly no such declaration has ever been issued in this country. But if our experience can be generalized, it does properly depend on a way of life from which at least weakened belief follows as a consequence. That, surely, is one of the consequences of a life devoted to commerce. Rather than being a whole way of life, religion, in the commercial republic, becomes merely a part of life, in most cases, a part consigned or relegated to one day (or one morning) a week. Commerce – business, if you will – leads men, perhaps imperceptibly, away from the continuous concern with those issues characteristic of life in a preconstitutional age.[54]

Berns's position is predicated on a dichotomy between a theocracy and a secular, if religiously tolerant, government. This dichotomy reflects an assumption that "religion" means "Christianity" and points to the obvious, yet highly significant, difference between the role of religion in a liberal democracy and the role of religion, to mention only the most extreme yet also the most historically relevant example, in the Holy Roman Empire.

Berns, of course, never claims that his position is Strauss's position. But it is worth noting that while other aspects of Berns's arguments about the American Constitution, and particularly his claims about formalism, may be strongly confluent with the basic presuppositions of Strauss's thought, his conclusion about the relation between religion and liberal democracy is at odds with the position that I will suggest would actually follow from Strauss's analysis.[55] My contention is that Berns's conclusion is only possible on the basis of viewing religion as Christian, which Berns clearly does. My suggestion is that inclusion of the significance, if not centrality, of Judaism in Strauss's thought makes his conception of the relation between religion and politics in American political life not less but more relevant.

It is once again important to recognize that Maimonides is the paradigm of true rationalism for Strauss. And the particular political context of Maimonides's philosophical and religious rationalism is highly relevant to what Strauss regards as Maimonides's philosophical, theological, and political success. Maimonides, living in Moslem Spain, lived in a theocracy, but the religious laws of this theocracy were not his community's religious laws. Maimonides's discussion of divine law is predicated on the fact that Jewish civilization, since the advent or rise of rabbinic Judaism after the destruction of the second Temple in the first century, was not and did not purport to be theocratic. While Jewish communal leaders certainly exercised political authority within the Jewish community, this authority only came in the context of the political authority of an external community. The relevant point here is that this political fact in no way diminished the religious significance or meaning of Jewish religious law or of the Jewish religion. It is also interesting to note in the context of Berns's consideration of the relation between religious tolerance and commerce that, unlike other communities in the medieval period, the medieval Jewish community in particular was deeply involved in and developed economic and commercial life. Berns's view that "[c]ommerce – business, if you will – leads men, perhaps imperceptibly, away from the continuous concern with those issues characteristic of life in a pre-constitutional age" applies only in the context of defining religion as a matter of faith, and not law. From a Jewish perspective, rabbinic, medieval, and modern, commerce is incorporated into religious life,[56] which is not "relegated to one day (or one morning) a week" precisely because religious life, understood first and foremost (though, of course, not exclusively) in the framework of religious law encompasses commerce and all aspects of daily and profane living.

These points are historical and no doubt far more complicated than I have indicated. But my point for the purposes of this chapter is philosophical. My contention is that from Strauss's perspective, religion, defined as Judaism and not Christianity, need not inevitably suffer but may well prosper within a constitutional democracy. Having a nonreligious set of laws (from the perspective of a particular religious community) to which a religious community's religious laws need accommodate themselves need not, by definition, lead to weakened belief. From Strauss's perspective, medieval Jewish rationalism is in no way weakened but is strengthened from having to respond to such a situation.

Maimonides's political situation may allow us a deeper appreciation of Strauss's skepticism. Once again it is helpful to recall Strauss's description of Aquinas's synthesis of revelation and philosophy in his notion of natural law as "free from the hesitations and ambiguities which are characteristic of the teachings, not only of Plato and Cicero, but of Aristotle as well." The classical philosophical, Jewish, and Islamic traditions all share for Strauss a profound sense of hesitation and ambiguity that he suggests the medieval scholastic reading of Aristotle attempts to overcome. Rationalism for Strauss is defined by this ambiguity, which is most profoundly expressed in the tension between philosophy and law. The Jewish medieval political situation institutionalizes the ambiguity between philosophy and law in that religious law for the Jews is doubly ambiguous in its political reality. It's not just that a Jewish thinker, such as Maimonides, may consider the relation between philosophy and Judaism but also that Judaism, defined for both Strauss and Maimonides as adherence to the divine law, must consider its divine law within the framework of a legal context external to it.

Strauss never offers a full account of the differences between medieval Islamic and Jewish thought, but we may speculate here that this double ambiguity is what separates Islamic and Jewish rationalism from each other. This may be the reason that Strauss uses the terms *Islamic philosophy* and *Jewish thought* to describe the medieval rationalists. For the former, there are only two positions, which amount to an either/or: philosopher or believer. For the latter, however, there are three positions: philosopher, believer, or "thinker." This third option, I suggest, is the position held by Maimonides, from Strauss's perspective. This may be one reason that Strauss famously describes *The Guide of the Perplexed* not as a philosophical book but as a Jewish one.[57] Jewish thought remains caught between the either/or position, but does not, like Christian scholasticism, synthesize the two positions. Rather, Jewish thought amounts to the formal relation between philosophy and revelation. It is a relation fraught with an ambiguity that does not resolve itself. Maimonides for Strauss is the model of religious, philosophical, and political rationalism because of his refusal to resolve philosophical, theological, and political ambiguities. The refusal to provide an ultimate solution to fundamental ambiguity is the mark of the philosopher, and of Socrates in particular, for Strauss. But it is Plato – the father of political philosophy – who anticipates the necessity of formalizing ambiguity on a political level, an anticipation that, Strauss claims, is only borne out in Maimonides's thought.

Once again, I suggest that it is the Jewish political situation of Maimonides that uniquely shapes Strauss's notion of rationalism, which may have particular application in a liberal democracy. Structurally, religion in a liberal democracy resembles the medieval Jewish political situation. All religions in the United States, for instance, must operate within the framework of the American Constitution and American law. In this way, all religious communities are required to come face to face with the ambiguities of political and religious life, whether they accept or deny these ambiguities. Berns is right that for some religious communities this may lead to weakened belief. On the other hand, however, for a number of contemporary American Christian communities, for instance, the ambiguity created by living in a liberal democracy serves as an impetus for generating a more profound sense of Christian faith that, some contemporary Christian theologians argue, a theocratic Christianity decimated. It is not a coincidence in this context that a number of American Christian theologians who affirm the positive potential for faith created by living in a non-Christian society (even if some of these thinkers are critical of such a society from a Christian point of view) describe themselves as "Israel-like" and as "exilic."[58]

By creating the political conditions for religious exile, a liberal democratic order may strengthen religious belief rather than weaken it. The challenge on a theological level, from the perspective of Strauss's thought, would be to remain open to the philosophical, political, and indeed religious ambiguity created by this political situation. For Strauss, this is precisely what Maimonides is able to do. In Chapter 9, I turn to the question of whether, from Strauss's point of view, such a religious rationalism is possible in the modern period. My point here, however, is that the difficulty of such a religious rationalism or of religious faith does not, as Berns's view might suggest, stem from the *political structure* of liberal democracy, that is, from the fact that religious communities must define their faith within a nonreligious framework.

6.5. RELIGION AND SOCIETY, OR RELIGION IN AMERICA

One might reasonably wonder how Strauss can claim, at least on the reading I have offered in this chapter, that religion in particular, and not the customs and beliefs of the people in general, can provide the possible moral basis of a society. After all, there seems to be ample evidence in Strauss's reading of Plato to suggest that the philosopher recognizes, on moral and not merely utilitarian grounds, the necessity of the *doxa*, or opinions, of the city. As Strauss puts it in his commentary on the *Crito*: "however profound the difference, or the antagonism, between Socrates and the non-philosophical citizens may be, in grave situations he identifies himself completely, as far as his body is concerned, with the city, with the people."[59] Or, as Thomas Pangle, elaborating on Strauss's position, puts it: "though Socrates remained in his deepest thinking essentially solitary . . . he nevertheless 'originated a new kind of study of the natural things – a kind of study in which, for example, the nature or idea of justice or natural right, and surely the nature of the human soul or man, is more important than, for example, the nature of the sun.'"[60] In the context of explicating the philosopher's moral relation to the city, Pangle concludes that the tension between philosophy and revelation for Strauss is best understood as a subset of the tension between philosophy and poetry.[61]

Pangle's reading of Strauss gives us good reason to question the centrality of Judaism in Strauss's thought, which I have argued for throughout this chapter. But in this connection, I follow Kenneth Hart Green who has argued, against Pangle, that the tension between philosophy and revelation, especially as understood by Maimonides, holds a particular if not central place in Strauss's thought. Green suggests, and I would concur, that biblical revelation differs for Strauss from poetry in its claim for a *universal*, and not a particular or closed, society.[62] As Strauss puts it, "Only by surrendering to God's experienced call which calls for one's loving him with all one's heart, with all one's soul, and with all one's might can one come to see the other human being as one's brother and love him as oneself."[63]

Although Strauss does not apply these comments to a discussion of the American Founding, they may well be relevant in reflecting on the American experiment, which consists in the possibility of citizenship for all peoples, regardless of their traditions and customs. We may describe the American experiment, to borrow a phrase from one recent interpreter of Levinas, as a "community of those who have nothing in common."[64] This certainly is not to imply that American democracy is empty of content, but it is to claim that in theory there are no prerequisites (beyond being a human being) for the rights of citizenship. These rights are made possible by the belief that "all men are created equal." For Strauss, such a belief *is* rooted in biblical revelation, which he understands as having a particular Jewish content. Indeed, Strauss's comment that "Only by surrendering to God's experienced call which calls for one's loving him with all one's heart, with all one's soul, and with all one's might can one come to see the other human being as one's brother and love him as oneself" paraphrases, but does not cite the Jewish creed "Hear O Israel, the Lord is our God, the Lord is One" from Deuteronomy 6:4–9, "You shall love the Lord your God with your heart, with all your soul, with all your might." These verses continue with an instruction to teach one's children that the Lord is the God of Israel and the prayer continues with Deuteronomy 11:13–21, which describe the rewards and punishments that will follow from obeying, or not, God's laws. The universal morality of what I will call (with some reservation) Judeo-Christian revelation, described for Strauss by the central prayer of Judaism, provides the moral foundations for society.

However, contrary to the way Strauss has been interpreted by some of his followers, the possibility of biblical morality is not, on Strauss's own terms, an established principle of reason because reason cannot establish such a principle. In this context, Harry Jaffa's descriptions of the Declaration of Independence and the American Founding are particularly curious in light of Strauss's thought. Concisely summarizing his own thought, Jaffa writes:

> the Declaration addressed a problem peculiarly that the Christian West, arising from the conflicting claims of reason and revelation [addressed]. The idea of human equality, independent of sectarian identity, led to the idea of the enlightened consent of the governed on the ground of law. It enfranchised Aristotle's idea of law as 'reason unaffected by desire' by removing from the jurisdiction of theology and theologians the judgment of rationality. It was no less pious for doing so, because

it incorporated into the idea of enlightened consent respect for the rights with which all mankind had been endowed by their creator. . . . In the Declaration (and more generally in the American Founding), we find a principled ground for law that we cannot find in Aristotle. What we do find, however, is fully in accordance with Aristotle's intention, within a framework consistent with biblical religion.[65]

We have explored throughout this chapter some of the fundamental difficulties of reading Strauss, as Jaffa does, as valorizing the Christian West and its concepts of morality and law. More specifically, it is important to reconsider the opening lines of *Natural Right and History* of which Jaffa has made much. After quoting the Declaration of Independence, "all men are created equal," Strauss asks: "Does this nation in its maturity still cherish the faith in which it was conceived and raised? Does it still hold those 'truths to be self-evident'?"[66] The key word, I want to suggest, in Strauss's question is *faith.* From Strauss's point of view, the question is whether Americans still have *faith* in the principles of the Declaration, but this is because the Declaration does not present, to use Jaffa's phrase, "a principled ground for law." Strauss's use of quotation marks for "truths to be self evident" emphasizes, moreover, his notion that these "self-evident truths" are a matter of faith and not rational fact. From the point of view of Strauss's thought, universal law for all peoples cannot be *grounded* rationally. Only revelation can provide this ground, but this ground remains a matter of faith, and not reasoned fact. Strauss's question then is whether Americans still *believe* in these articles of faith, which are always precarious for they are defined by the people's will to believe.

Strauss's skepticism about the self-sufficiency of reason, especially as it relates to law, finds expression in the room he leaves for faith. But Strauss's philosophical skepticism more generally denies faith (as well as philosophy) a rational ground. It is the tension between these points that accounts for what Strauss elsewhere calls "the mutual influence of philosophy and theology." If we understand "rationalism" simply as an insistence on providing *reasons* for embracing one view (philosophical, theological, or political) over another, the mutual influence of philosophy and theology, which is one of tension and not fundamental confluence, creates the possibility of a rational politics. For Strauss the tension and *hence conversation* between philosophy and theology creates the possibility of a rational ground for politics because politics demands rational justification.

To explore some of the dimensions of Strauss's conception of a rational politics, and what I will continue to argue is Levinas's ultimately and politically dangerous utopian politics, Chapter 7 turns to the meanings of Zionism and the establishment of the State of Israel as understood by both Strauss and

Levinas. Chapter 8 will continue to draw out the implications of Strauss's and Levinas's conceptions of politics in connection with their shared attempts at a hermeneutics of retrieval in their respective readings of classical Jewish texts. After exploring the importance of Judaism for understanding Strauss's and Levinas's view of politics in Chapters 7 and 8, Chapter 9 turns to their respective contributions to modern Jewish thought generally and to conceptions of Jewish law particularly. Finally, Chapter 10, the conclusion of this book, considers the relevance of Strauss's and Levinas's philosophies in current debates about politics.

Zionism and the Discovery of Prophetic Politics

$\mathcal{B}$OTH LEVINAS AND STRAUSS HAD AN AMBIGUOUS RELATIONSHIP TO Zionism. Much to the consternation of various critics, particularly in Levinas's case, they both loyally defended the establishment of the State of Israel and its continued right to existence. Yet at the same time, and perhaps more importantly, both were deeply ambivalent about the Jewish nature of the state and its potential to affect future Jewish identity positively. As I suggest in greater detail in this chapter, this shared ambivalence is rooted in a deeper ambivalence for both Levinas and Strauss about the possibility of political solutions in general. In Strauss's case, this characterization might seem odd, given Strauss's American reception especially in recent years as a, if not *the*, political dogmatist. Part of the goal of the third and final portion of this book is to complicate contemporary political views of Strauss by looking more deeply at the relatively few instances of concrete political reflection on his part. At the same time, while Levinas has been faulted by some (including myself in the last section of this book) for his lack of engagement with politics, it is on the question of Zionism that his potential political theory is ramified most fully. By examining Strauss's and Levinas's respective relations to Zionism, we can simultaneously recognize Strauss's often unappreciated ambivalence about politics qua politics and Levinas's underappreciated attempt to think through concrete political realities.

This chapter focuses on Strauss's growing ambivalence about Zionism on the one hand and Levinas's increasingly religious understanding of Zionism on the other. Section 7.1 of the chapter considers Strauss's early commitment to political Zionism and his increasing doubt about Zionism's potential to provide a solution to the Jewish problem. Emphasizing the conceptual relationship between Strauss's early affirmation of what he considered the materiality of Zionism and his developing notion of the materiality of Jewish law, Section 7.2 turns to the evolution of Strauss's interest in a "forgotten type of writing," and its connection to Strauss's conception of the role of the prophet or statesman in politics. Section 7.3 turns to the development of Levinas's conception of Zionism and his growing attribution of religious meaning to the Jewish state that he understood as, what I will call, a non-political politics. The conclusion, Section 7.4, of the chapter reconsiders the relation between religion and politics in Strauss's and Levinas's conceptions of Zionism, arguing that Levinas's concrete politics in relation to the Israeli state are incoherent at best, and fanatical at worst. This incoherence, I suggest, stems from Levinas's conflation of philosophy, religion, and politics, a conflation that Strauss criticizes in Heidegger's thought, which can be applied to Levinas's as well.

7.1. THE EARLY STRAUSS: ZIONISM AND LAW

Strauss opens the preface to the English translation of *Spinoza's Critique of Religion* describing, among other things, his commitment to political Zionism when he wrote the book in the Weimar republic, in the years 1925–8.[1] As Strauss put it in a public conversation with his old friend Jacob Klein in 1970, "When I was seventeen, I was converted to Zionism – to simple, straightforward political Zionism."[2] Yet the mature Strauss had a more ambivalent relation to Zionism. In the preface, he criticizes cultural Zionism in strong terms. Strauss contends that while proponents of cultural Zionism claimed to be concerned with Jewish matters they are not, because cultural Zionism, as its founding ideologue, Ahad Ha'am, would admit, is predicated on an affirmation of the Jewish people divorced from the Jewish God. While Strauss remained a lifelong defender of political Zionism, maintaining that the creation of the Jewish state is a fact of which all Jews ought to be proud, he also proclaims in the 1965 preface that political Zionism before and after the creation of the State of Israel, "was in no way employed . . . in matters Jewish."[3]

Strauss's early writings in the 1920s in defense of political Zionism do not differ from these later remarks in terms of the analysis of what Zionism *is*, but only in his evaluation of the *desirability* of a Zionist solution. The early Strauss believed political Zionism could offer a solution to the Jewish problem and that conterminously the solution it would offer would be a rejection of core aspects of the Jewish past. The mature Strauss would deny the first part of this proposition in large part because he questioned strongly the desirability of the second. Let us turn first to Strauss's early analysis of and insistence on the break with the Jewish past that political Zionism brings.

Affirming the connection between political Zionism and the rejection of the Jewish God, Strauss wrote in a 1928 review of Sigmund Freud's *The Future of an Illusion* that:

in the age of atheism, the Jewish people can no longer base its existence on god but only on itself alone, on its labor, its land, and on its state. It must even as a people break with traditions that so many individuals have already long since broken with; better the hones narrowness and barrenness of civilization than the breadth and plenty that the atheist would be able to purchase only at the price of a lie. . . . Political Zionism, wishing to radically ground itself, must ground itself in unbelief.[4]

Because of its more self-conscious recognition of what Strauss calls in this review of Freud "the age of atheism," Strauss strongly preferred political Zionism to cultural Zionism, which he described as having a "spiritually pious attitude toward life" (*Lebensfrömmigkeit*) that got in its way of concrete political judgment. Strauss's goal in his early Zionist essays was to force contemporary Zionists to be more aware of and honest about the implications of their own positions, a disposition and desire on Strauss's part that, I would suggest, marks all of his work, from this early period forward.

Already in the early 1920s Strauss was committed to upsetting commonly held views to the point of offense.[5] As he put it a 1923 newspaper article that emphasized the intellectual affinity between Zionism and anti-Semitism, "Any naïve politicizing on his [the German Jew's] part drives him easily to confuse the Jewish with the German interest, as well as the Jewish – specifically the *galut*-Jewish – idea of political life with the corresponding German one."[6] Naïve politicizing meant first and foremost for Strauss the refusal of German Jewry to recognize both the reality and the *truth* of anti-Semitism. In a 1924 essay on the infamous anti-Semite Paul de Lagarde (1827–91), published in Martin Buber's journal *Der Jude*, Strauss went so far as to praise Lagarde for his "probity and sobriety" in regard to the Jewish problem.[7] The early Strauss implicitly agreed with the cultural Zionist Ahad Ha'am that Herzl's political Zionism was the child of anti-Semitism.[8] But for Strauss, as opposed to Ahad Ha'am, this was not a vice but political Zionism's great virtue.[9]

Nevertheless, even in his strong defense of political Zionism, Strauss differed from Herzl in his deep interest in and commitment to an understanding of Judaism, and not just the Jewish people. Whereas "Judaism" held no positive content for Herzl, and whereas Herzl was happily ignorant of all aspects of positive Jewish life, history, and culture, Strauss, even in this early stage, was concerned with repudiating apologetic forms of liberal Judaism in the name of Jewish sources. Like the cultural Zionists, whom he criticized so strongly,[10]

Strauss sought a biblical referent for his embrace of Zionism. But in sharp contrast to the liberal Jewish reading of the prophets as concerned with a kind of universal social justice, Strauss began his essay on Zionism and anti-Semitism by quoting Joshua 9:7: "And the men of Israel replied to the Hivites, 'Peradventure ye dwell among us; and how shall we make a covenant with you?'" For Strauss, this statement expressed the political realist position that political Zionism and by implication modern anti-Semitism exposed and espoused, especially when one considers Deuteronomy's statement "and when the Lord thy God shall deliver them up before thee, and thou shalt smite them [i.e., the Hivites among them]; then thou shalt make no covenant with them, nor show mercy unto them."[11]

Curiously, Strauss's early Zionist writings laid the ground for a kind of hermeneutics of retrieval that, I suggest in Chapter 8, is at a very minimum *non-Zionist* in its emphasis on exile as the highest Jewish and philosophical modality. Strauss's early consideration of Jewish law in the context of his analysis of the truth contained in certain forms of anti-Semitism provides the link between these two very different, though not entirely uncomplementary, political sensibilities in his early work. In his short 1924 piece on Lagarde, Strauss anticipates the *philosophical* argument he would make, first in *Philosophy and Law*, and then in *Persecution and the Art of Writing*, about the importance of medieval Islamic conceptions of law. Strauss begins his reflection on Lagarde by agreeing with his criticism of liberal Jewish apologetics. Strauss summarizes Lagarde's position, with which he agrees and affirms:

And then there is the attitude of these people [the Jews] toward their own history; what they do not like, they deny. 'Modern Judaism always sails under false colors.' They have but one tendency, which is the political-apologetic tendency. Liberal Judaism praises as the virtues of Judaism: 1. monotheism – but that has as little to do with religion as knowing the number of German residents has to do with patriotism; and it is by no means specifically Jewish; 2. absence of dogmas – but it is no virtue to have no consistent view of God and divine matters; it is a downright moral deficiency; 3. tolerance – but that is a sign of a lack of seriousness; every religion is exclusive.[12]

As he would in his criticism of Schmitt in 1932, Strauss agrees in 1924 with Lagarde's criticism of the *neutrality* of liberalism and "secularism," as expressed especially in its principle of tolerance. And as is the case with his criticism of Schmitt, Strauss may seem to be agreeing a bit too much with the anti-Semitic views of Lagarde. But Strauss does differentiate himself at the end of this article from Lagarde, by stating that: "No sooner do they almost touch than they move apart – the radical moralism of the German hailing from Fichte, and the radical moralism of the Zionist writers and politicians who stand under entirely different influences."[13] As he would suggest even further and in more detail in his 1941 lecture to his colleagues at the New School, "German Nihilism," discussed in Chapter 6, Strauss believes that the moralism of German nationalists is superior to what he claims is the weakness of the secular notion of tolerance. Moralism must be met with moralism. And it is when these moralisms meet that Strauss believes the moral underpinning of Zionism would have the upper hand.

Why is Zionism morally superior to German nationalism, according to Strauss? In answering this question, Strauss once again takes a clue from Lagarde, whose position he summarizes as follows:

The characteristic features of Judaism are its being devoid of reality [*Entwirk-lichtheit*] and its 'materialism.' What Lagarde understands as Jewish materialism is the putting of the law before spirit, of the finished matter before process, and of culturedness [*Gebildetheit*] before the acquisition of culture [*Bildung*]. In the community that is materialistic and devoid of reality, and as its antithesis, there arises in the line of the prophets Jesus; he contrasts the election of Israel with the divine sonship of all human beings, the synagogue-state with the kingdom of God, descent from Abraham with spiritual rebirth. There is no reconciliation between Judaism and Christianity; Judaism is the anti-Christian principle pure and simple.[14]

For Lagarde, inwardness (*Innerlichkeit*) was the gift of Jesus to the world. This gift had, according to Lagarde, been bastardized by Paul, who made Christianity worldly (*Verweltlichung*) and hence more outward, material, and Jewish.[15] Strauss accepts the dichotomy between Judaism and Christianity suggested by Lagarde. But his view is that in its very "materialism" *and commitment to the priority of law* Judaism is superior to Christianity.

In the context of Lagarde's emphasis on *Innerlichkeit*, the timing of Strauss's essay on Lagarde is also quite relevant. It was in 1924 that Strauss published his essay criticizing Hermann Cohen's reading of Spinoza. As I argued in Chapter 5, Strauss reverses the trajectory of Cohen's attempt at understanding the outer form of history (its *historisch* character) by way of its inner form (its *geschichtlich* character). Not insignificantly, Strauss criticizes liberal German-Jewish thought, and Cohen in particular, in the introduction to *Philosophy of Law* for its method of internalization (*Verinnerlichung*). As Strauss put it: "all 'internalizations' of the basic tenets of the tradition rest at bottom on this: from the 'reflexive' premise, from the 'higher' level of the post-Enlightenment synthesis, the relation of God to nature is no longer intelligible and thus is no longer even interesting."[16]

In *Philosophy and Law*, Strauss begins to identify law with the materialism and outwardness that the method of internalization and its spiritual ideal, *Innerlichkeit*, deny. In this context Strauss makes reference to another Lagarde – Georges de Lagarde, scholar of medieval and reformation thought who argued for the continuity, and not antithesis, between clerical thinking and what he called the "spirit of the laity" (*l'esprit laïque*).[17] Drawing on Georges de Lagarde's claims about the continuity between Christianity and the conception of the modern state, Strauss maintains in the first chapter of *Philosophy and Law*, entitled "The Quarrel of the Ancients and the Moderns," that "the Islamic and Jewish philosophers of the Middle Ages are 'more primitive' than the modern philosophers because they are guided not, like them, by the derived idea of natural right, but by the *primary, ancient* idea of *law*, as a unified, total regime of human life: in other words, because they are pupils of *Plato* and not pupils of Christians."[18] To this statement Strauss appends the following reference to Lagarde: "A confirmation of this is furnished by the way Averroism was received in the Christian world. One may with a certain right describe Christian Averroism as the forerunner of the modern conception of the state, but the original Averroism's conception of the state is ancient throughout."[19]

Whereas in his early Zionist writings, Strauss sees Zionism as an affirmation of Jewish materiality, and hence in Paul de Lagarde's view, "primitiveness," in *Philosophy and Law* Strauss begins to see Jewish law as this very affirmation of materiality. In this context he begins to link the premises underlying the notion of the modern nation-state – an idea upon which political Zionism is predicated – to the corrosive inwardness that has come to define Christian civilization and its child: so-called secular modernity. Strauss's affirmation of the "material" and "primitive" nature of political Zionism becomes his affirmation of the materiality and "primitiveness" of Jewish law. At the same time, Strauss's early commitment to atheism in the name of Zionism begins to erode as he considers more fully the meanings of Jewish law.

In this connection, and despite some of the ways in which Strauss continues to be received, Strauss begins in *Philosophy and Law* to *reject* the dichotomy between "orthodoxy" and "atheism."[20] As he puts it in the introduction to the book:

the present situation, appears to be insoluble for the Jew who cannot be orthodox and who must consider purely political Zionism, the only 'solution of the Jewish problem' possible on the basis of atheism, as a resolution that is indeed highly honorable but not, in earnest and in the long run, adequate. This situation not only appears insoluble but actually is so, as long as one clings to the modern premises. If finally there is in the modern world only the alternative 'orthodoxy or atheism,' and if on the other hand the need for an enlightened Judaism is urgent, then one sees oneself compelled to ask whether enlightenment is necessarily modern enlightenment. Thus one sees oneself induced . . . to apply for aid to the medieval Enlightenment, the Enlightenment of Maimonides. . . . [W]e shall attempt in what follows to point out the leading idea of the medieval Enlightenment that has become lost to the modern Enlightenment and its heirs . . . : *the idea of Law*.[21]

In *Philosophy and Law*, Strauss begins his attempt at retrieving the wisdom of the past. While a number of scholars have noted the transitional character of *Philosophy and Law* in Strauss's corpus, the importance of this book for and its continuity with the later Strauss has not been acknowledged enough. It is true that Strauss had not yet developed his conception of esoteric writing. But an essential basis for this conception – the idea that contemporary thinkers overlook the political context of the history of philosophy and its *philosophical* implications – is already at work in *Philosophy and Law*.

One of the important differences between *Philosophy and Law* and the later essays of *Persecution and the Art of Writing* concerns Strauss's different interpretations of the meaning of prophecy for Maimonides. The third chapter of *Philosophy and Law* focuses on the Maimonidean view that prophecy is an overflow of the rational and imaginative faculties. The details of Strauss's claims about Maimonides are less important for our purposes than is the more basic point that in the last chapter of *Philosophy and Law* Strauss still views prophecy in *epistemological* terms, while in *Persecution and the Art of Writing*, Strauss understands Maimonidean prophecy in *political* terms.[22] Yet it is worth recalling that *Philosophy and Law* was not written as a coherent book but rather that, in the hopes of securing a position at The Hebrew University of Jerusalem in 1935, Strauss had put together what are actually three very different essays to produce this book. In this context, it is important to notice that within *Philosophy and Law*, Strauss anticipates his mature view of prophecy when he writes in a footnote: "We do not deny . . . that the problem of 'belief and knowledge' is the central problem of medieval rationalism. Our quarrel with Guttmann is only about the meaning of 'belief' here, and it seems to us more precise to say 'law and philosophy' rather than 'belief and knowledge.'"[23]

In his later work, Strauss denies his earlier contention at the end of *Philosophy and Law* that "Plato . . . does not permit the philosophers 'what is now permitted them,' namely the life of philosophizing as an abiding in the contemplation of the truth. He 'compels' them to care for others and to guard them, in order that the state may really be a state, a true state. . . ."[24] Whereas this statement could be taken to support the idea of a philosopher-king, the mature Strauss's claim is that the philosopher never could nor ought to be compelled to rule.[25] The premise of Strauss's sociology of philosophy, as defined in "Persecution and the Art of Writing," is that there is a fundamental tension between philosophy and society, a tension that, I would argue, is the same tension for Strauss between philosophy and law. The impetus for esoteric writing is this very tension.

The transition between Strauss's early and mature work is marked by Strauss's increased ambivalence about both philosophical and political certainty. Whereas the early Strauss affirmed political Zionism because he perceived it as offering both political and philosophical certainty – that is, security for Jews in a land of their own and a kind of philosophical atheism – the mature Strauss denied the certainty of both of these propositions. Most basically, Strauss's turn to a forgotten type of writing centered on his increasing sense that politics cannot provide philosophical answers and that philosophy cannot provide political answers. Many have interpreted Strauss's views of esoteric and exoteric writing as representative of both philosophical and political dogmas, that is, atheism and elitism. But the trajectory of Strauss's thought shows that the opposite is the case as his conceptions of political and philosophical certainty loosen, if not dissolve. As I argue in Chapter 8, Strauss's conception of esoteric writing is antidogmatic at its core. For Strauss, there are real human tensions that cannot be fully worked out, either philosophically or politically, just as there are competing and incommensurable human goods. Esoteric writing, on Strauss's reading, is an attempt to acknowledge these tensions without falsely dissolving them. And it is precisely the figure of the prophet who is able to balance the often contradictory needs of competing, incommensurable, and multiple goods in society.

Viewing Zionism as a solution to the Jewish problem for Strauss is of a piece with the modern assumption that philosophy can provide answers to fundamental questions. For Strauss, political Zionism can offer a practical response to the needs of modern Jews, but it cannot be a solution to what it means to be a Jew in the modern world. This position may explain Strauss's mildly ambivalent stance toward the State of Israel in his one public defense of it. This defense took the form of a letter to the editor of the conservative journal, *The National Review*, in 1957. Strauss wrote this letter in response to the journal's opposition to Israel. In Strauss's words, "It is incomprehensible to me that the authors who touch on that subject are so unqualifiedly opposed to the state of Israel."[26] In characteristic fashion, Strauss attempts to refute what he takes to be the *National Review*'s criticisms of Israel on its own terms. Sympathizing with the *National Review*'s generally conservative position, Strauss maintains that a conservative ought not to be unqualifiedly opposed to the State of Israel. Drawing on his experience living in Israel during the academic year 1954–5, Strauss rejects a number of charges against the state, and, most specifically, the claim that it is run by labor unions.[27] But, writes Strauss, even if these charges were true: "a conservative is a man who knows that the same arrangements may have very different meanings in different circumstances." He also praises Herzl as a "fundamentally a conservative man, guided in his Zionism by conservative considerations." Significantly, however, he concludes his letter by stating that "Political Zionism is problematic for obvious reasons," but does not elaborate on these reasons in the letter.[28] It seems fair to suggest that these problems for Strauss consist in the fact that Zionism cannot provide a solution to the Jewish problem because Zionism is a rejection of the Jewish past, and hence of Judaism.

7.2. STRAUSS'S PROPHETIC POLITICS OUT OF THE SOURCES OF ZIONISM

Strauss extends his rejection of Zionism as a solution to the Jewish problem to his analysis of modern politics generally. The retrieval of a forgotten type of writing, to be discussed in more detail in Chapter 8, is the retrieval of the necessary tension between the unanswerablitiy of what Strauss claims are the permanent problems of humanity and the practical need for providing solutions. In "The Literary Character of the Guide for the Perplexed," Strauss writes: "Maimonides asserts that the prophet's ascent to the highest knowledge is followed by his descent to the 'people of the earth,' i.e. to their government and instruction. The prophet is, then, a man who not only has attained the greatest knowledge, indeed a degree of knowledge that is not attained by mere philosophers, but who is able to perform the highest political functions."[29] In distinction to his earlier formation in *Philosophy and Law*, here Strauss defines the prophet's superiority to the philosopher not in terms of epistemology, that is, not by the earlier view that the prophet combines an overflow of both the rational and imaginative faculties as opposed to the philosopher who only possess the former, but by the prophet's "descent to the 'people of the earth'" and ability "to perform the highest political functions."[30] To use the terms Strauss applies to the philosopher at the end of *Philosophy and Law*, the prophet, or the statesman, is compelled "to care for others and to guard them."

While Strauss often blatantly affirms and distinguishes between the categories of "philosophers, statesman and the masses," these categories are perhaps best understood as formal or ideal ones. As Timothy Fuller has described Strauss's use of categories in another context I would suggest that these categories are "a strategic doctrine, arguable but indemonstrable, a protective measure against modern excesses."[31] Strauss does state in his essay on Halevi that to be a Jew and philosopher is impossible. Yet he also argues there that Halevi had been a philosopher, and had returned to Judaism.[32] The status of Maimonides is also ambiguous for Strauss. On the one hand, he maintains that Maimonides is not a philosopher but a prophet, and on the other, he maintains that Maimonides is a philosopher, disguised as a prophet. Much has been written on these apparent contradictions, and while there may be something of significance in these slippages, intentional or otherwise, it is also possible to express Strauss's position on this matter, at least very minimally, in fairly straightforward terms. A prophet or a statesman is someone who has an appreciation for philosophy, but whose loyalty to his or her community outweighs the commitment to the absolute search for truth beyond opinion. In this sense, Strauss's views the prophet not as an iconoclast but as an "immanent critic" who takes his bearing from his fundamental commitment to his community.[33] Philosophy and politics are both necessary, but philosophy alone cannot provide political solutions and politics alone cannot provide philosophical answers. The true prophet, or statesman, for Strauss, balances and preserves the goodness of both philosophy and politics not by synthesizing the two but by recognizing and maintaining the tension between them.

From Strauss's point of view, it is the confusing of this matter that explains some of what he regards as the great errors of modern philosophy and politics. As he puts it in his study of Machiavelli:

if it is proper to call the prophet the founder of a new social order which is all-comprehensive and not merely political or military, then Machiavelli is a prophet... What is immanent Machiavelli suggests then, is not the conquest of a new promised land, but a new revelation, the revelation of a new code, a new Decalogue.... The bringer of the new code is none other than Machiavelli himself; he brings the true code, the code which is in accordance with the truth, with the nature of things.[34]

The possibility of Machiavelli's new code, Strauss maintains, stems from his dismissal of the Bible in favor of ancient political practice alone and his subsequent dismissal of the distinction between theory and practice in ancient political philosophy.[35] Where Machiavelli differs from, for instance, Maimonides is in seeing himself as the revealer of a new code. A true prophet, for Strauss, as for Maimonides, is one who honors and hones not his own wisdom but the received wisdom of the past. The prophet or statesman is answerable "for the law, and before the law." Machiavelli reduced politics to power, while also reducing theory, or philosophy, to propaganda: "Machiavelli is the first philosopher who attempted to force change, to control the future by embarking on a campaign, a campaign of propaganda."[36]

As is well known, Strauss's claims about the errors of modern philosophy are linked to his political criticism of the horrors of the twentieth century and to the Nazi genocide in particular.[37] As we saw in Chapter 6, the focus of Strauss's criticism is on intellectuals who lacked the moral and political resources to resist fascism. Of particular note, of course, is Martin Heidegger, whose philosophy Strauss greatly respected from a philosophical point of view. Strauss's criticism of Heidegger is an extension of his criticism of Nietzsche, to be discussed briefly in Chapter 8. For Strauss, Heidegger, like Nietzsche, lacked the proper care for society that a wise philosopher possesses. This care for society, I have argued, is not merely instrumental for Strauss but also philosophical because, contra Nietzsche and Heidegger, the philosopher is *not* a prophet or a lawgiver. In Strauss's words, for Heidegger "the question of the best, or the just, political order has been superseded by the question of the probable or desirable future."[38]

The complexities of Heidegger's philosophy and political involvement with Nazism are, of course, beyond the scope of this study. Nevertheless, following Robb McDaniel, I would suggest that Strauss's point about Heidegger is compelling and useful for appreciating Strauss's broader conception of the relation between philosophy, religion, and politics, especially as this conception relates to Levinas's view of this relation. As McDaniel has put it

While Heidegger's turn against Plato and Aristotle to the pre-Socratic philosophers is well-documented, it must be noted that this is largely a later phenomenon in Heidegger's thought. In the rectoral address, Heidegger sees his turn toward politics as essentially Platonic. Not only does Heidegger finish his address with a quote from Plato – the only historical Greek who Heidegger actually cites – but his description of politics and the three 'forms of service' to the state are clearly derived from the three classes in Plato's Republic. . . . This makes the Heidegger-Strauss relationship on Plato and the philosopher-king particularly interesting.[39]

And as Michael Zimmerman has noted, "Long after 1934, Heidegger continued to believe that the philosopher should play a leading role in shaping an alternative to Bolshevism and Americanism."[40] In Heidegger's words, "A historical Volk without philosophy is like an eagle without the high expanse of the glowing ether, wherein its soaring [*Schwingen*] attains its purest flight [*Schwung*]."[41]

Despite Heidegger's criticisms of the western philosophical tradition, and of modern philosophy and the Platonic legacy in particular, the early Heidegger nonetheless ascribes to himself the role of philosopher-king. In contrast, Strauss's retrieval of Plato is precisely an attempt to dismantle the long-held interpretation of Plato, and the *Republic* particularly, as advocating a philosopher-king. Because the quest for truth beyond opinion easily becomes immoderate when it is not coupled with an appreciation for the common sense of the opinions of society, the notion of a philosopher-king is not only both politically and philosophically unfeasible, but also profoundly undesirable. On Strauss's reading, Heidegger ascribes a religious meaning to philosophy at the expense of the social context upon which philosophy is politically and philosophically parasitic. Heidegger places himself in the role of prophet without recognizing that the prophet is answerable "for the law, and before the law."

Turning the philosopher into a lawgiver, Heidegger, like Machiavelli, conflates theory with practice. As Strauss put it to Voeglin in a letter of 1950: "the root of all modern darkness from the seventeenth century on is the obscuring of the difference between theory and praxis, an obscuring that first leads to a reduction of praxis to theory (this is the meaning of so-called rationalism) and then, in retaliation, to the rejection of theory in the name of praxis that is no longer intelligible as praxis."[42] There is truth to both and wisdom consists in the ability to recognize and embrace these two different, yet necessary, truths. As Strauss elaborates elsewhere

the Aristotelian distinction between theoretical and practical sciences implies that human action has principles of its own which are known independently of theoretical science (physics and metaphysics) and therefore that the practical sciences do not depend on the theoretical sciences or are not derivative from them. The principles of action are the natural ends toward which man is by nature inclined and of which he has by nature some awareness. This awareness is the necessary condition for his seeking and finding appropriate means for his ends, or for his becoming practically wise or prudent.[43]

Heidegger, from Strauss's point of view, in making himself a philosopher-king, obscures this very difference. While Heidegger claimed to be overcoming what he called *modern philosophy*, he merely turned the modern reduction of praxis to theory into a reduction of theory to praxis. And in doing so he fashioned himself a modern prophet with no recourse to the question of the best, or just, political order.

7.3. LEVINAS'S ZIONISM: FROM POLITICS TO RELIGION

Like Strauss's, the development of Levinas's thought took place within the context of debates about Zionism, and particularly within debates about political

Zionism. It is worth recalling that Theodor Herzl became a Zionist while reporting on the Dreyfus affair in France.[44] In Herzl's words

The Dreyfus Affair is more than a judicial error: it is a clear manifestation of the desire of most Frenchmen to condemn a Jew and – through him – all Jews. "Death to the Jews!" cried the crowd as the Captain's symbols of rank were ripped from his uniform. And where? In France. In modern, civilized, Republican France one hundred years after the Declaration of the Rights of Man for Jews.[45]

From a historical perspective, the question of Zion would have been an important part of Levinas's formative years within at least two contexts of his early life. Herzl returned to Austria to found the Zionist movement, but he did not succeed with persuading much of German-speaking Jewry of the importance of Zionism. After the sixth Zionist Congress in 1904, he took his message to Russian Jewry, which became the backbone of the Zionist movement. It would be hard to imagine that, in his early years in Lithuania, Levinas could have been unaware of the Zionist movement. And when Levinas went to study in France in 1930, discussion of the Dreyfus affair was particularly prevalent. For instance, as Marie-Ann Lescourret, Levinas's biographer, has noted, Levinas recalled the discussion of Dreyfus in Maurice Pradines's course on ethics and politics that he took at the time.[46]

In his impressive study, *Levinas and the Political*, Howard Caygill has recently called attention to the ways in which debates about Zionism prompted Levinas from early on to rethink the trinity of the Declaration of the Rights of Man: freedom, equality, and fraternity.[47] As we saw in Chapter 1, Levinas redescribes the notion of fraternity, maintaining that fraternity is made possible not by equality but by a fundamental inequality. As he puts it in *Otherwise than Being*, "The equality of all is borne by my inequality, the surplus of my duties over my rights."[48] At the same time, as we saw in Chapter 3, Levinas maintains that freedom arises from my bondage to the other. From his early work forward, Levinas thought that Zionism and the eventual establishment of the State of Israel could offer a model of such a reconceptualization. But somewhat paradoxically, Levinas also claimed that the significance of Zionism, and political Zionism in particular, was fundamentally apolitical. Unlike the political Zionists, Levinas's focus was not primarily on the survival of the Jewish people and nationhood. And unlike the cultural Zionists, Levinas's interest was not primarily on the renewal of Jewish culture and peoplehood. Instead, Levinas's positive interest in Zionism was on the significance of Zion for all of humanity. Strikingly, for all his frequent references in his early and later writings on Zionism to the significance of the Dreyfus affair for western modernity, Zionism became for Levinas not a political solution but a *religious* enterprise. Yet according to Levinas, this is not a dismissal of politics but a movement toward an ethical politics or, as he puts it elsewhere, a "monotheistic politics."[49]

Because he is a philosopher of "the other," critics continue to be perplexed if not outraged by what was Levinas's relative silence about the suffering of the Palestinian people. In particular, Levinas's public comments about the massacre of Palestinian refugees at Sabra and Shetila, while under the watch of Israeli soldiers, by Phalangist Militias in 1982 has particularly disturbed his critics. Asked by Shlomo Malka in a radio broadcast following this massacre, "Isn't history, isn't politics the very site of the encounter with the 'other,' and for the Israeli, isn't the 'other' above all the Palestinian?" Levinas replied,

My definition of the other is completely different. The other is the neighbor, who is not necessarily kin, but who can be. And in that sense, if you're for the other, you're for the neighbor. But if your neighbor attacks another neighbor or treats him unjustly, what can you do? Then alterity takes on another character, in alterity we find an enemy, or at least then we are faced with the problem of knowing who is right and who is wrong, who is just and who is unjust. There are people who are wrong.[50]

Some have suggested that Levinas's comments are simply at odds with what should have been his political views. But Howard Caygill, mentioned at the beginning of this section, has recently presented the most sophisticated and persuasive argument on this subject, suggesting that Levinas's comments about the Israelis and the Palestinians are consistent with his philosophy, and disturbingly so from Caygill's point of view.

Caygill rightly focuses on Levinas's distinction between "the third" and "the other." Simply put, Levinas insists that the centrality of the ethical demand of the other person does not obviate the need and demand for justice and thereby law. Levinas calls this demand for justice "the third," by which he refers to the structure of an ethical relationship in which more than two people are involved. "The third" is the realm of politics and law because, Levinas rightly notes, the coordination of multiple relations beyond the face-to-face relation requires rules and regulations. While making a clear distinction between what he calls ethics (or interpersonal relations) and politics (or law), Levinas nevertheless continues to insist increasingly in his later writings that his philosophy of the other profoundly concerns itself with and values justice. In Levinas words:

It is not that the entry of a third party would be an empirical fact, and that my responsibility for the other finds itself constrained to a calculus by the 'force of things.' In the proximity of the other, all the others than the other obsess me, and already this obsession cries out for justice, demands measure and knowing, is conscious.[51]

But while asserting the connection between what he calls "the proximity of the other" and the demand of justice for all, Levinas nevertheless still maintains a fundamental distinction between "the other" and "the third": "This 'thirdness' is different from that of the third man, it is the third party that interrupts the face to face of a welcome of the other man, interrupts the proximity of approach to the neighbor, it is the third man with which justice begins."[52] Emphasizing that violence is intrinsic to Levinas's understanding of ethics – in Levinas's words "Only beings capable of war can rise to peace"[53] – Caygill points out that within Levinas's thought the "other" can be, *ethically*, against the "third." Therefore, according to Caygill, in the context of the technicalities of Levinas's philosophy, it is *not* inconsistent for Levinas to stand ethically with his Israeli "other" against the Palestinians.

While Caygill's analysis is useful and persuasive, I contend that, bracketing what seem to be Levinas's concrete political judgments, the problem with Levinas's consideration of the State of Israel is both deeper and simpler than the relation between "the other" and "the third." Caygill's analysis of Levinas's concrete, political statements about the State of Israel in terms of his philosophy reinstates Levinas's fundamental merging of philosophy, religion, and politics. But far from presenting a concrete political program or even judgment, Levinas's views of the State of Israel are incoherent. Whereas the trajectory of Strauss's thoughts about Zionism leads to the need to separate and consider the different yet complex relation between practice and theory, or between politics and philosophy, the trajectory of Levinas's thought suggests the opposite. Levinas's comments about Zionism are a concrete instance of his conflation of philosophy and politics. This conflation is intensified and made possible by a more fundamental conflation in Levinas's thought: the conflation between philosophy and religion, which becomes, in concrete political judgment, the conflation between religion and politics.

To call Levinas's comments about the State of Israel incoherent is, of course, not to deny their potential political implications. But it is to suggest that his claims about Zionism, despite Caygill's very coherent argument to the contrary, do conflict with aspects of his thought. In this sense, my claim is at once weaker and stronger than Caygill's. It is weaker in that I do not believe that Levinas's philosophy can be fully captured in his statements about Zionism. But it is stronger in that I do not believe that Levinas's philosophy can produce a coherent political theory at all. In the conclusion of this chapter, I draw out this argument in greater detail. But to do so, I turn first to the development of Levinas's views of Zionism and the State of Israel, the following synopsis of which is very much indebted to Caygill's fine study.

In his early writings about Israel after the state's establishment, Levinas emphasized the importance of diaspora Jewish existence, while also downplaying the significance of the political dimensions of Zionism in favor of Jewish ethics. In 1949, the year after Israel's establishment, Levinas encouraged his readers not to forget "two thousand years of participation in the European world"[54] in the face of growing awareness of the Nazi genocide. In 1950, Levinas explicitly divorced ethics from politics in representing Judaism as apolitical in what he described as its antiutopian bent:

If Judaism is attached to the here below, it is not because it does not have the imagination to conceive of a supernatural order, or because matter represents some sort of absolute for it; but because the first light of conscience is lit for it on the path that leads from man to his neighbor.... To be without being a murderer. One can uproot oneself from this responsibility, deny the place where it is incumbent on me to something, to look for an anchorite's salvation. One can choose utopia. On the other hand, in the name of spirit, one can choose not to flee the conditions from which one's work draws its meaning, and remain here below. And that means choosing ethical action.[55]

As Samuel Moyn has remarked, "Levinas's presentation of Judaism in this period as the source of a moral realism that provided a safeguard against the wishful and treacherous desire for a revolutionary alternative to the burden of responsibility not only followed from his creative interpretation of Jewish tradition but also from the Cold War and transconfessional imperative of thinking 'after utopia.'"[56] Levinas's presentation of Judaism in terms of an antiutopian morality coheres with the view of politics that Levinas would develop in *Totality and Infinity* in 1961. Common to both is the simultaneous insistences first on a separation between ethics and politics, and then on the possibility of nonpolitical/ethical political order.

In the period immediately prior to and including *Totality and Infinity*, Levinas's interpersonal ethic implied a kind of political realism in that it is premised on the fundamental claim that politics qua politics cannot be ethical. Still, Levinas does insist in *Totality and Infinity* that ethics informs politics, that transcendence informs ontology, and that infinity informs totality, not just from a transcendental perspective but also from the normative point of view that ethics ought to inform politics. Put more simply, while Levinas in *Totality and Infinity* insists on a distinction between ethics and politics, he nevertheless claims that it is an ethical imperative that ethics ought to inform and transform political institutions. The moral mistake, which he equates with mistaken utopian views, is to believe that this transformation can ever be complete or lasting, except in what Levinas calls "eschatological" time, that is in a time that is not yet, but also in the realm of what it means to be human will never be.

Within this conception of the relation between ethics and politics, Levinas attempts to deny the strictly political importance of the State of Israel and its religious importance divorced from ethics. As he put it in 1951, "What genuinely matters about the State of Israel is not that it fulfills an ancient promise, or heralds a new age of material security . . . but that it finally offers the opportunity to carry out Judaism's social law."[57] Yet even in the context of describing the meaning of the State of Israel in philosophical/ethical terms, Levinas veers toward describing it in religious terms. In the same essay of 1951 he writes: "an Israeli experiences the famous touch of God in his social dealings" or a bit farther on: "Justice as the *raison d'être* of the State, that is religion. It presupposes the high science of justice. The State of Israel will be religious because of the intelligence of its great books which it is not free to forget. It will be religious through the very action that establishes it as a State. It will be religious or it will not be at all."[58]

The rhetoric of these comments shouldn't be surprising given Levinas's messianic aspirations for philosophy. What is more striking perhaps is the degree to which, after *Totality and Infinity*, and especially after 1967, Levinas's religious claims about the State of Israel intensify as he describes, after the Six-Day War, the *religious* meaning of Zionism:

The Nazi persecution and, following the exterminations, the extraordinary fulfill-ment of the Zionist dreams of a State in which to live in peace is to live dangerously, gradually became history. The passion in which it was finished and this bold new beginning, in spite of conflicting signs affecting them, were felt, even yesterday, to be signs of the same notion of being chosen or damned – that is to say, of the same exceptional fate.[59]

The allusion to Christ's passion is unmistakable, as is Levinas's emphasis, in another essay of 1968, to holy martyrdom: "It is not because the Holy Land takes the form of a State that brings the Reign of the Messiah any closer, but because the men who inhabit it try to resist the temptation of politics; because this State proclaimed in the aftermath of Auschwitz, embraces the teaching of the prophets; because it produces abnegation and self-sacrifice."[60] "The Holy Land," for Levinas, is prophetic in its resistance to politics and thereby in what I called its nonpolitical/ethical politics. In *Otherwise than Being*, especially in the fifth chapter entitled "Witness and Prophecy," Levinas explores in greater philosophical detail the category of "prophecy," which expresses the possibility of this nonpolitical politics: "It is in prophesy that the infinite escapes the objectification of thematisation and dialogue, and signifies as *illeity*, in the third person."[61] Prophecy for Levinas is the interruption of politics and the subsequent return to politics after this interruption.

The themes of prophecy, witness, and the meaning of Zionism all come together in Levinas's 1975 essay "God and Philosophy." In many ways a summary of his mature thought, this essay ends with an interpretation of prophecy: "Prophesying is pure testimony, pure because prior to all disclosure; it is subjection to an order before understanding the order."[62] But the beginning of the essay is as significant as its end is for the way that Levinas frames his argument about philosophy's need of God. In the preliminary note to the essay Levinas describes his understanding of the practical, we might even say political, meaning of the argument he presents:

The text we are publishing here is based on the core content of each of these lectures [given in France, Belgium, and Israel]. This itinerary of lectures has given it an ecumenical character. We mention this especially in order to render homage to the life and work of Professor Hugo Bergmann who, having very early settled in Jerusalem, was always faithful to Israel's universal vocation which the state of Zion ought to serve only, to make possible a discourse addressed to all men in their human dignity, so as then to be able to answer for all men, our neighbors.[63]

At the end of the essay, Levinas concisely summarizes the definition of responsibility that emerges from philosophy's encounter with God, which he describes in this essay as "trauma": "Responsibility for the neighbor is precisely what goes beyond the legal and obliges beyond contracts: it comes to me from what is prior to my freedom, for a non-present an immemorial."[64] Whereas the mature Strauss defines prophecy as responsibility "for the law, and before the law," the mature Levinas suggests that prophecy is responsibility "beyond the legal." And whereas Strauss understands prophecy's roles as the compulsion "to care for others and to guard them," the meaning of prophecy for Levinas is ultimately one of, what he calls "trauma."

I leave for now a discussion of the concrete political implications of Levinas's position with regard to the State of Israel, a subject to which we will return soon, to point out perhaps an even more basic formal similarity underlying Levinas's and Strauss's mature conceptions of prophecy, which as we will see in greater detail in Chapter 8, is its intimate connection to the theme of "persecution." In Levinas's case, the central chapter of *Otherwise than Being*, "substitution," is rooted in the notion of persecution as *the* ethical modality: "In the trauma of persecution it is [in substitution] to pass from the outrage undergone to the responsibility for the persecutor, and, in this sense from suffering to expiation for the other. Persecution is not something added to the subjectivity of the subject and his vulnerability; it is the very movement of recurrence."[65] Persecution, for Levinas, is the vulnerability of the self before the other. It is also the infinite responsibility that no political system based on the rule of law could bear, if, as Levinas maintains, I am responsible even for the persecution of my persecutor.

But Levinas's attempt to upset contemporary liberal conceptions of politics and law goes deeper. Ethics, as the substitution of the self for the other, means that the other's physical needs become my needs or better, my needs are the other's physical needs.[66] In a further description of the meaning of persecution as the substitution of the self for the other, Levinas also suggests that the ethical relation is the "self's gnawing away at itself." Even the seemingly inaliable right to one's own body becomes highly questionable in the ethical relation. Indeed, it is helpful to recall Levinas's use of the term *maternity* to describe the ethical relation.

Is not the restlessness of someone persecuted but a modification of maternity, the groaning of the wounded entrails by those it will bear or has borne? In maternity what signifies is a responsibility for others, to the point of substitution for others and suffering both from the effect of persecution and from the persecuting itself in which the persecutor sinks. Maternity, which is bearing par excellence, bears even responsibility for the persecuting by the persecutor.[67]

But perhaps the most provocative term Levinas uses to describe what it is to be disembodied by the other for the sake of the other is *incarnation*, which is the flesh made other – indeed made divine – in the ethical relation: "Incarnation is not a transcendental operation of a subject that is situated in the midst of the world it represents to itself; the sensible experience of the body is already and from the start incarnate. The sensible – maternity, vulnerability, apprehension – binds the node of incarnation into a plot larger than the apperception of self. In this plot I am bound to others before being tied to my body."[68] Levinas's ambivalence about politics as constituted by institutions and law is also present in his description of the self's "gnawing away at itself," "maternity," and "incarnation." Again, in his own words, the State of Israel's greatness is found in the "resistance to politics." The meaning of the existence of the State of Israel, for Levinas, does not concern home and security for Jewish people but rather the risk the Jewish people are willing to take in potentially martyring themselves for the sake of all others. By living in the land of Israel Jews gnaw away at themselves in their ethical substitution for others.[69]

In Strauss's case, the notion of persecution, we will see in greater detail in Chapter 8, goes hand in hand with the view of the Jew and the philosopher as exilic. While Strauss affirms exile as perhaps the most profound human modality, he in no way suggests that this difficult way of being should be everyone's. The prophet's, statesman's, and wise philosopher's nobility arises from the recognition that it is perhaps cruel to impose the homelessness of philosophical truth on everyone.[70] We can also understand Strauss's support for the actual State of Israel in this context. While Zionism cannot offer a solution to the Jewish problem, from Strauss's point of view it is cruel to deny actual Jewish people the right to a homeland, especially given the suffering of the Jewish people in the twentieth century.

Ironically, it is perhaps the recognition that such an ethic of risk cannot be universalized especially when it comes to affirming such risk for one's family and immediate neighbors that accounts for Levinas's response to the massacres at Sabra and Shetila. Recall Levinas's comment that "if your neighbor attacks another neighbor or treats him unjustly, what can you do? Then alterity takes on another character, in alterity we find an enemy, or at least then we are faced with the problem of knowing who is right and who is wrong, who is just and who is unjust. There are people who are wrong." For Levinas, an enemy is someone who attacks one's immediate other. And in viewing an enemy as such, one must, in Levinas's view, make a judgment, perhaps even a violent one, about who is and is not just. Caygill is certainly right that Levinas's political contention in this case parallels his distinction between "the third" and "the other." But more basically, Levinas's contention taken in the context of his philosophy as a whole reflects his very fundamental conflation of philosophy, religion, and politics.

7.4. RELIGION AND POLITICS

In conclusion, I suggest that Levinas's conflation of philosophy, religion, and politics renders all three categories in his thought incoherent. To make this argument, I turn to the implicit premise of Caygill's study of Levinas's political thought, which is that it is possible and useful to understand Levinas's philosophy by way of his comments or lack thereof about the Israeli-Palestinian conflict. While, as I have noted several times already in this chapter, Caygill's analysis of the technicalities of Levinas's thought is persuasive in many ways, his framing of the issue may beg the very question that should be put to Levinas, which is Strauss's basic question about the relation between philosophy and politics. The idea that we can find in philosophy philosophical assumptions that lead to particular political solutions is one of the very fundamental issues that Strauss's thought seeks to put into question. While rightfully acknowledging the historical and political contexts of Levinas's work, Caygill seems to buy into Levinas's assumption that there is a direct and uncomplicated relationship between philosophy divorced from historical and political concerns (i.e., Levinas's particular brand of phenomenology, discussed in Chapters 3 and 5) and politics. It is on the basis of this assumption that Caygill can find a direct link between these philosophically technical assumptions (the relation between the "third" and the "other") and Levinas's public comments about the State of Israel and its neighbors. My suggestion, in contrast to Caygill's, is that Levinas's very understanding of philosophy as providing a messianic and universal cure for the ills of concrete political life and realities renders Levinas's political thought meaningless.

We can appreciate what I am suggesting is the incoherence of Levinas's political thought by taking the political implications of his statements about the State of Israel to their logical political conclusions. As we have seen in this chapter, Levinas increasingly attributes a religious meaning to the State of Israel after 1967, describing its existence in terms of risk and passion. In the context of these comments, it would not be difficult to interpret Levinas as a religious Zionist. After all, as a historical and political movement, religious Zionism only really gains force after 1967.[71] And as Levinas's comments seem to suggest, religious Zionism does not understand itself in the context of the political framework that defines the Israeli State. Rather, the mission of religious Zionists from their own perspective is not constrained by the mandates of the Israeli democratic system but by divine mandate. In Strauss's words,

when religious Zionism understands itself, it is in the first place Jewish faith and only secondarily Zionism. It must regard as blasphemous the notion of a human solution to the Jewish problem. It may go so far as to regard the establishment of the state of Israel as the most important event in Jewish history since the completion of the Talmud, but it cannot regard it [the state] as the arrival of the messianic age, of the redemption of Israel and of all men.[72]

Levinas's "monotheistic politics," which I characterize in this chapter as a nonpolitical politics, could well describe the religious Zionist vision of its nonpolitical (in the sense of the normative politics of the Israeli state) politics (in the sense of the actual political actions of political Zionists, such as the settlement and defense of what they consider divinely mandated occupation of land). In Levinas's words, "It is not because the Holy Land takes the form of a State that brings the Reign of the Messiah any closer, but because the men who inhabit it try to resist the temptation of politics; because this State proclaimed in the aftermath of Auschwitz, embraces the teaching of the prophets; because it produces abnegation and self-sacrifice."[73] From their own perspective, religious Zionists sacrifice themselves and their children not for the actual State of Israel but for the reign of the messiah.

Anyone vaguely familiar with Levinas's thought, however, would not recognize the preceding description of his thought. In fact, in a footnote to his lectures "Messianic Texts" Levinas would seem to distance himself from any such ideas. After mentioning Gershom Scholem's distinction between apocalyptic messianism and the rationalist messianism of the rabbis, Levinas writes, "Not everything has been said, however, as Scholem sometimes seems to think, on the subject of the rationalist nature of this messianism"[74] and adds that his commentary is meant to explicate further this rationalist messianism. Not only does Levinas distinguish his view of messianism from any apocalyptic view, but his notion of God is one of an absence whose presence is only manifested in the face of the other.

Levinas's God is not godly, his religion is not religious, and his politics is not political. While Levinas and some of his interpreters maintain that these positions must be understood in the context of Levinas's radical ethics of alterity, the concrete example of Zionism and the State of Israel shows, I believe, the incoherence of Levinas's view of politics. The incoherence, I maintain, is rooted in his conception of philosophy, which the comparison with Strauss helps us to consider. As was the case for Strauss, Levinas self-consciously approaches politics and reading in the context of his political criticism of the horrors of the twentieth century and the Nazi genocide in particular. Some have suggested that Levinas's silence on the Palestinian issue is not unlike Heidegger's silence during and after the Holocaust.[75] In my view, this comparison is overstated and ignores the obvious facts about Levinas's and Heidegger's respective political involvements, while also conflating the Israeli occupation with the Nazi genocide. Nevertheless, philosophically speaking, Levinas shares with Heidegger an overinflated view of the political potentials and immediate relevance of philosophy and philosophers. As is the case for Heidegger, for Levinas (to use Strauss's words) "the question of the best, or the just, political order has been superseded by the question of the probable or desirable future."

From the point of view of Strauss's thought, for Levinas, as for Heidegger, the inability to reflect critically on politics is linked to the conflation of theory and practice. Let us again recall Strauss's claim to Voeglin that "the root of all modern darkness from the seventeenth century on is the obscuring of the difference between theory and praxis, an obscuring that first leads to a reduction of praxis to theory (this is the meaning of so-called rationalism) and then, in retaliation, to the rejection of theory in the name of praxis that is no longer intelligible as praxis." Levinas understands himself to be responding to the very crisis described by Strauss. As he puts it toward the beginning of *Totality and Infinity:* "Hitherto the relation between theory and practice was not conceivable other than as a solidarity or a hierarchy: activity rests on cognitions that illuminate it; knowledge requires from acts the master of matter, mind and societies – a technique, a morality, a politics – that produces the peace necessary for its pure existence."[76] As Caygill has remarked, Levinas's claim about theory and practice "immediately and deliberately puts into question the context of his notion of the political, which is neither a theoretical ideal guiding action nor the routine acts of societal mastery exposed by sociological and empirical political science."[77] In an important sense, Strauss too is a critic of both a one-sided theoretical approach to politics and a one-sided practical reduction of politics. As we saw in Chapter 6, the prophet or the statesman for Strauss mediates between theory and practice, allowing each its proper place, but allowing neither to dominate. As we will see in Chapter 8, the tension between theory and practice is at the core of Strauss's conception of esoteric writing.

We have seen in this chapter that despite his attempt to get beyond a hierarchal conception of theory and practice, Levinas's notion of politics ends in incoherence, as does his conception of the State of Israel, whose increasingly tortured history in relation to Levinas's pronouncements can only make clearer. Levinas would do well to heed his own claim in the name of biblical morality that "Utopia seems not just vain in itself, it is also dangerous in its consequences," for it is only as utopian that one can make sense of Levinas's nonpolitical politics.[78] Looked at from a political point of view Strauss's thought, taken on its own terms, would offer a far more moderate view of contemporary Israeli politics than Levinas's would. Ironically, Strauss's moderate politics, which seeks the common good and practices moderation, may have greater potential to recognize "the other" than does Levinas's. We turn now in Chapter 8 to explore the intimate relations between Strauss's and Levinas's politics, on the one hand, and their respective claims to have retrieved the true meaning of classical Jewish texts on the other hand. As is the case with his politics, I suggest in Chapter 8 that Strauss's hermeneutics may respect the otherness of the text far more than Levinas's does.

Politics and Hermeneutics: Strauss's and Levinas's Retrieval of Classical Jewish Sources

*W*E SAW IN CHAPTER 7 THE INTIMATE CONNECTION BETWEEN Strauss's and Levinas's respective views of Zionism and the development of their mature conceptions of politics. In this chapter, we turn to the deep-seated connection between their respective conceptions of politics and their shared attempt to retrieve the true meaning of classical Jewish texts (albeit different ones). Among readers of Strauss, no issue is as hotly contested as his contentions about esotericism. Strauss's contentions about authorial meaning are often taken, for better or for worse, as elitist if not authoritarian and dogmatic claims. In contrast, Levinas's hermeneutic claim for an originary ethical moment is often taken as, to use Levinas's own terminology, an opening to the "other." Far from being considered authoritarian, Levinas's hermeneutic presupposition is often considered a lone moral stance in a sea of violent appropriations of "the other."

I argue in this chapter that the opposite is the case. Rather than presenting an authoritarian impulse, Strauss's view of esotericism is profoundly anti-dogmatic and open to other voices – and certainly far more so than Levinas's so-called ethical hermeneutic is. To begin to appreciate this claim, it is helpful to recall Strauss's comment to Voeglin, quoted in Chapter 7, that "the root of all modern darkness from the seventeenth century on is the obscuring of the difference between theory and praxis, an obscuring that first leads to a reduction of praxis to theory (this is the meaning of so-called rationalism) and then, in retaliation, to the rejection of theory in the name of praxis that is no longer intelligible as praxis." Esoteric writing as Strauss describes it is not a substitution of theory for practice or of practice for theory. Instead, esoteric writing reflects for Strauss the necessary tension between the two. Put another way, as Strauss reiterates often, esotericism cannot be understood apart from exotericism.[1] I maintain that while Strauss's hermeneutic is inherently dialogical, Levinas's is one-dimensional. While Strauss's insistence on separating philosophy, religion, and politics leads to an appreciation – philosophical, religious, and political – of multiple human voices and goods, Levinas's merging of philosophy, religion, and politics reduces all difference to what he contends is the command of ethics. Ironically in terms of their respective receptions, Strauss's claims about esoteric writing convey a far greater concern for "otherness" than Levinas's seemingly ethical hermeneutics does.

Section 8.1 of the chapter elucidates the basic parameters of Strauss's claims about esotericism in the context of what I will suggest are philosophical meanings of exile for Strauss.[2] In Section 8.2, I turn to the deep confluence between Levinas's nonpolitical politics and his hermeneutic retrieval of what he claims is the original ethical meaning of Jewish law. Finally, in Section 8.3 I consider the relation between politics and reading for Strauss as it relates to his commitment to liberal education.

8.1. STRAUSS'S HERMENEUTICS: ESOTERICISM, EXILE, AND ELITISM

A crucial, if usually overlooked, presupposition of Strauss's view of esotericism is that Strauss's concern is with *written* texts. This basic point should immediately qualify some of the debates about the esotericism of Strauss's own work and what may have been his own views. From the perspective of his own claims about esotericism, what may or may not have been Strauss's own views are irrelevant to interpreting his work. Despite some of the rhetoric surrounding the arguments between former students of Strauss, purported oral communications between teacher and student simply cannot, on Strauss's own terms, have any bearing on how to understand his thought. Moreover, Strauss's contentions about and readings of various authors whose works he claims have an esoteric dimension are not based on private access to anyone's thought. Strauss did not know any of the authors to whom he applied his esoteric method. Implicit to Strauss's contentions about esotericism is the view that the texts he describes as esoteric are public documents: they are available to all readers. If these texts were only available to the intellectual elite, there would be no reason for esotericism in the first place. But precisely because these texts are universally available, this also means that any careful reader can have access not just to the texts but also to the esoteric meaning of the text. It should be emphasized then that the esoteric meaning of a text for Strauss is decipherable to a, and in fact *any*, careful reader. Otherwise, Strauss would not be able to discover them because he, after all, concerned himself for the most part with thinkers who had long been deceased. The availability of esoteric knowledge is not limited to secret clubs of the elite. Instead, the esotericism that Strauss writes about is available to anyone who can read carefully.

One of Strauss's most trenchant critics has understood this point well. Shadia Drury has rightly noted that the question of Strauss's own esotericism is misplaced. Interpreters who approach Strauss as if it is necessary to do so with secretly communicated knowledge miss the simple fact that one need but read Strauss's work carefully.[3] While Drury's point is helpful, this is not to say that her conclusions about Strauss are correct.[4] What we can glean from Drury, without descending into the thorny battlefield of Strauss's critics and defenders, is her recognition that one need not have known Strauss personally, just as Strauss didn't know personally any one of the authors about whom he wrote, to understand what she calls "the ideas of Leo Strauss." Understanding these ideas, as Strauss contends in his claims about writing and reading, begins and ends with carefully reading the published record, which does not require initiation into any kind of secret club.

Strauss's instructions for how to read carefully are fairly straightforward. An interpretation of a given text must begin "from an exact consideration of the explicit statements of an author." However, "The context in which a statement occurs, and the literary character of the whole work of its plan must be perfectly understood before an interpretation of the statement can reasonably claim to be adequate or even correct."[5] Strauss's hermeneutic approach is in an important sense without content. As Paul Cantor has put it, "interpretation [for Strauss] cannot hope to proceed according to universal and unequivocal rules, which will always yield unambiguous and unassailable results. . . . One can offer principles of interpretation, but not rules, unless one means rules in the sense of rules of thumb."[6] Methodologically, Strauss's claims about esotericism ought to be judged according to detailed, textual argument about his readings of particular texts.[7] My concern in this study, however, is not with Strauss's reading of particular texts but with the philosophical impetus for and religious and political implications of Strauss's claims about reading and esotericism. As Stanley Rosen has put it, "The serious question is not *whether* philosophers practiced esotericism – every thoughtful human being does so to one degree or another – but *why*."[8]

Despite the way Strauss is so often perceived, the question of concern for others is at the heart of his view of esotericism. As Steven Lenzner has remarked, Strauss only uses the term *esotericism* in *Persecution and the Art of Writing*[9] and hence only in connection with his discussions of Halevi and Maimonides, who, though quite different from each other, follow the model of the prophet because their interest is in preserving the law, while leaving room for philosophy.[10] As Strauss reiterates in the context of Maimonides's

claims to this effect, esotericism is a pedagogic device used by religious leaders to properly educate their students. As Strauss puts it, "Education is the
highest sense of philosophy. Philosophy is [a] quest for wisdom or quest for
knowledge regarding the most important, the highest, or the most comprehensive things; such knowledge, he suggested, is virtue and is happiness. But
wisdom is inaccessible to man, and hence virtue and happiness will always be
imperfect. In spite of this, the philosopher, who, as such, is not simply wise, is
declared to be the only true king; he is declared to possess all the excellences
of which man's mind is capable, to the highest degree."[11]

As a number of Strauss's interpreters have noted, Strauss's own interest in
esotericism was pedagogical in that the notion of esotericism is bound up with
the possibility – that Strauss claims modern readers deny – of reading ancient
texts on their own terms.[12] We will return to this point soon but before we do
so it is necessary to recognize that on Strauss's own terms, the conception of
esotericism as mass deception is not only a caricature of Strauss, but misses the
underlying impetus for his claims. An aspect of the often-reactionary response
to Strauss's claims about esotericism is a repetition of the very assumption
that Strauss seeks to call into question. Richard Rorty, for example, expresses
this assumption concisely when he writes:

This idea [esotericism], familiar from the work of Leo Strauss and his followers, is
one for which I have no sympathy. It presupposes that the masses are still unable
to kick their metaphysical habit, and that we ironical types must therefore be
prudently sneaky in our dealings with them. My hunch is that if the masses could
learn . . . that the powers that be are not ordained by God, then they can learn to
get along without metaphysical backup for their deep attachment to democratic
institutions.[13]

Ironically, given his own political and moral commitments, Rorty's comments about Strauss are instructive because they reveal, I would argue, a far
deeper intolerance and elitism than Strauss's claims about esotericism do.
Rorty is convinced that "ironical types" such as he simply know the truth
that there is neither a God nor a metaphysical backdrop. Based on an at least
questionable and certainly a narrow reading of the histories of philosophy
and theology, Rorty's pragmatism dogmatically rejects any possible claims
about God or metaphysics. Leaving aside questions about metaphysics and
its history, however, the political implications of Rorty's comments are more
telling. From Rorty's perspective, there is simply no room within a democratic order for religion, save within what he calls the private sphere, or,
for that matter, for people with truly differing opinions about things that
matter to them. Rorty can only see esotericism as "sneakiness," because he

implicitly denies the possibility of truly competing claims about the good life.[14]

Yet, one may still wonder whether esoteric writing, as described by Strauss, implies a condescending attitude toward other people or the masses? In attempting to answer these questions, it is important to recall that philosophy, classically understood, is for Strauss a fundamentally private or individual endeavor. Nevertheless, the care for society is an essential aspect of not only political but also philosophical wisdom, Strauss maintains. In writing about esotericism, Strauss explicitly links the wisdom of philosophers with trustworthiness and the concern for avoiding cruelty. In Strauss's words:

Thoughtless men are careless readers, and only thoughtful men are careful readers. Therefore an author who wishes to address only thoughtful men has but to write in such a way that only a very careful reader can detect the meaning of his book. But, it will be objected, there may be clever men, careful readers, who are not trustworthy, and who, after having found the author out, would denounce him to the authorities. As a matter of fact, this literature would be impossible if the Socratic dictum that virtue is knowledge, and therefore that thoughtful men as such are trustworthy and not cruel, were entirely wrong.[15]

This passage alerts us again to the context in which Strauss makes his claims about double-layered writing. The question is whether within a repressive political society a careful reader will, cruelly perhaps, report an author to the authorities for expressing unorthodox opinions. Strauss maintains that esoteric writing is premised on the Socratic notion that knowledge requires virtue and that therefore a philosophically wise person, by definition, is trustworthy and seeks to avoid cruelty.

Strauss criticizes Nietzsche precisely for lacking the virtues of trustworthiness and avoidance of cruelty.[16] While in many ways Strauss agrees philosophically with Nietzsche, he is critical of him because he did not sufficiently care for the society in which he lived. Some critics, of course, interpret this to mean that Strauss merely suggests that Nietzsche should have been, to use Rorty's word, more "sneaky" about his beliefs.[17] But this is to miss Strauss's point. As I have argued throughout this book, the wise philosopher for Strauss is dependent on society not only for purely instrumental reasons but philosophically and morally as well. While Nietzsche proclaimed that the philosopher is the giver of the law – "Genuine philosophers . . . are commanders and legislators . . . , e.g. Plato"[18] – the mature Strauss denies precisely this. Though the philosopher's way of life begins and ends with his own sense of wonder, the philosopher as a human being always begins and remains in society. The philosopher thus affirms when he can the customs of his society (i.e., when they are not morally or politically problematic). He does so not only because he recognizes that his own activity is parasitic on these customs but also because, though still distinct from it, philosophical truth is parasitic on common sense:

Socrates implied that disregarding the opinions about the nature of things would amount to abandoning the most important access to reality which we have, or the most important vestiges of truth which are within our reach. He implied that 'the universal doubt' of all opinions would lead us, not into the heart of the truth, but into a void. Philosophy consists, therefore, in the ascent from opinions to knowledge or to the truth, in an ascent that may be said to be guided by opinions. It is this ascent which Socrates had primarily in mind when he called philosophy 'dialectics.' Dialectics is the art of conversation or of friendly dispute. The friendly dispute which leads toward the truth is made possible or necessary by the fact that opinions about what things are, or what some very important group of things are, contradict one another. Recognizing the contradiction, one is forced to go beyond opinions toward the consistent view of the nature of the things concerned. . . . The opinions are thus seen to be fragments of the truth, soiled fragments of the pure truth.[19]

As we saw in Chapter 7, the philosopher who recognizes the need to descend back to the masses is perhaps, on Strauss's account, no longer a "pure" philosopher because he now philosophizes, as did Halevi and Maimonides, in the context of the law as a given. He becomes then the prophet or the statesman, who is the immanent critic of his community.

To put this in Rorty's own terms, irony is only possible within a social context, that is, there must be something to be ironic about. But whereas Rorty leaves and advances a profound split between the private and public realms, Strauss maintains that the philosopher become statesman, or as Rorty might have it, "the social critic," has a responsibility toward society or toward, what Strauss calls following Aristotle, "the common good." From Strauss's perspective, the philosopher cannot live by irony alone. It is this philosophical insight, I have argued, that propels the skeptical philosopher to recognize the limits, political, moral, and philosophical, of his own skepticism. The esotericism about which Strauss writes is not "sneaky" because it represents a kind of care with which the philosopher become statesman approaches society. Unlike Rorty, the truly wise philosopher does not need everyone to believe the philosopher's account of philosophical truth. Seen in the context of Strauss's view of the wise philosopher as an immanent critic, Rorty's ironist is committed to a "'revolutionary' quest for the other city." Convinced that there is only one truth – the truth of the ironist – Rorty's philosopher will not and cannot recognize or tolerate that there are multiple and incommensurable human goods, even while he embraces philosophy as the ultimate good. As Strauss puts it in the context of his reading of Plato:

The individual dialogue is not a chapter from an encyclopedia of the philosophic sciences..., still less a relic of a state of Plato's development. Each dialogue... reveals the truth about that part. But the truth about a part is a partial truth, a half truth. Each dialogue, we venture to say, abstracts from something that is most important to the subject matter of the dialogue.[20]

Yet surely, Rorty might answer, Strauss is condescending in suggesting that the masses cannot handle the truth. It is true that Strauss believes that people will suffer if philosophers disabuse them of all of their beliefs. For this reason, it is cruel of the philosopher to do so in an unthinking manner. Esotericism is for Strauss a method by which the prophet takes care to propel his interlocutor toward a greater critical stance without imprudently destroying the interlocutor's worldview. Very profoundly, esotericism is an educational tool. Linked to Strauss's claims about esotericism is his view that philosophy is a matter for mature minds. To again return to Rorty's terms, from Strauss's perspective, one cannot raise a child on irony. To employ the educational method a bit further, not all students have the same capacity or, as importantly, disposition for philosophical learning. Some, if not most, people, Strauss implies, will find philosophical truth profoundly disturbing. Strauss's claim here has as much to do with what he regards as the nature of philosophy as it has to do with his judgment of "the masses." Philosophical truth, Strauss contends, is difficult and unstable. The wise philosopher, for Strauss, does not do away with this difficulty or instability, but instead lives it. Esotericism for Strauss reflects a psychological mood of tension and anxiety, perhaps less because the philosopher is worried about his personal safety and more because wisdom is the recognition that there are philosophical, theological, and political problems that cannot be resolved.[21] In a statement that could be applied to Rorty, Strauss writes "no man needs to be ashamed to admit that he does not possess a solution to the fundamental riddle. Surely, no man ought to let himself be bullied into the acceptance of an alleged solution – for the denial of the existence of the riddle is a kind of solution to the riddle – by the threat that if he fails to do so he is a 'metaphysician.'"[22] For Strauss, philosophical wisdom embodies these tensions, while living constructively within the world and as part of human society.

It is, of course, not a coincidence that Strauss develops his view of esotericism while in exile. As a number of critics have noted, in his readings of Plato, Strauss often emphasizes that the philosopher is a stranger to the city.[23] As Eugene Sheppard has argued, the notion of exile is central to Strauss's thought and is

an especially useful heuristic device for recognizing, from the perspective of
Strauss's intellectual biography, the significance of the fact that Strauss wrote
"Persecution and the Art of Writing" and the essays that would accompany
the later book of this title, while he was in exile.[24] I would add to Sheppard's
thesis that the philosopher, for Strauss, is in a permanent state of exile because
he of necessity lives in two places at once and for this reason is never entirely
at home. While the philosopher lives in society, his ultimate dwelling lies in
the homelessness of his philosophical quest. But this cuts both ways. To live
in exile is still to live somewhere. And most people, save philosophers, do not
want to live in exile. They want to live at home. From Strauss's perspective, the
wise philosopher's humanity allows him to understand and even appreciate
this human desire, even if he rejects it.[25]

As I have argued throughout this book, the wise philosopher, for Strauss,
is able to recognize philosophy's own limitation qua philosophy. Catherine
Zuckert's elaboration of Strauss's position on Socrates and Aristophanes is
particularly helpful in making this point:

When Aristophanes accuses Socrates in *The Clouds* of lacking prudence and self-
knowledge, because he lacks eros, the comic poet accuses the philosopher of not
recognizing the inescapable limitations of the human condition and the frustra-
tion of human desire that necessarily results. Ridiculously perching himself in a
basket hanging above the earth, Socrates thinks he has more in common with the
expansive, light element than with the 'ephemerals' below. Failing to recognize the
limitations of his own existence, Socrates does not feel and so does not understand
the desire of others to overcome them. . . . [T]he philosopher's moral failings are
ultimately a product of intellectual error. Socrates does not understand the way
in which human nature, although part of nature, is distinctive. Any account of
the whole which does not recognize the tensions among the different parts is
patently inadequate. . . . Because the poet begins with the human and examines
it in relation to both what is higher and what is lower, he provides a more accurate picture of the whole. Whereas philosophy is reductive and hence destructive,
Aristophanes' poetry not only provides a salutary teaching but also reveals the
truth, if in a 'cloudy' form, to those able to understand.[26]

On Zuckert's reading, Strauss, as he says, recognizes that poetry is a formidable
opponent for philosophy. This point is of philosophical significance because
the philosopher understands the philosophical life as the good life, not as
one good life among others. The wise philosopher is able to recognize this
error, which leads to compassion. While from the philosopher's perspective,
happiness may only be in reach of the philosopher, the wise philosopher, that
is, the compassionate philosopher, recognizes that the philosopher's happiness
would not be happiness for others.[27] To return to the theme of exile, the wise
philosopher recognizes that exile is the philosopher's mode of being precisely

because the philosopher is, by definition, not at home. Nevertheless, justice requires that the philosopher show compassion for others, that is, it would be unjust to require nonphilosophers to be philosophers.[28] As Strauss puts it, "philosophy is repulsive to the people because philosophy requires freedom from attachment to 'our world.'"[29]

We can appreciate further Strauss's conception of philosophy as exilic by looking briefly at his description of the parameters of Maimonides's project in the *Guide of the Perplexed*. In his first published suggestion that Maimonides is an esoteric writer, Strauss self-consciously examines what it means to *write about* an esoteric text. Clearly referring to himself, Strauss writes:

No historian who has a sense of decency and therefore a sense of respect for a superior man such as Maimonides will disregard light-heartedly the latter's emphatic entreaty not to explain the secret teaching of the Guide. It may fairly be said that an interpreter who does not feel pangs of conscience when attempting to explain that secret teaching and perhaps when perceiving for the first time its existence and bearing lacks that closeness to the subject which is indispensable for the true understanding of any book. Thus the question of adequate interpretation of the *Guide* is primarily a moral one.[30]

Strauss aligns his dilemma with Maimonides's own and by doing so points to the basic motivation that directs Strauss's claim about esotericism. The question is: given the prohibition against publicly revealing the secrets of the Torah, why did Maimonides *write* the *Guide* in the first place? Maimonides tells his readers that he will offer an account of the relation between metaphysics and the two secrets of the Torah: the secret of creation (*ma'aseh bereshit*) and the secret of the vision of God in Ezekiel's chariot (*ma'aseh merkavah*). From at least the rabbinic period forward, these two secrets were not to be written about explicitly. The understanding of these secrets was confined to oral instruction for only select students. Strauss's question is why would Maimonides even offer to reveal these secrets in writing, given the traditional prohibition against doing so? The centrality of this question in Strauss's reading of the *Guide* reveals the clear distinction that Strauss makes between the esotericism of oral communication and esoteric writing. The latter is Strauss's concern.

In offering an answer to why Maimonides committed the secrets of the Torah to writing, Strauss reflects, as the title of this essay, "The Literary Character of the *Guide of the Perplexed*," indicates, on the *Guide*'s literary form, which is that of a letter from Maimonides to a gifted student of his, Joseph. This letter, Maimonides tells his readers in the *Guide*, is made necessary by the fact that Joseph was, like many Jews of Maimonides's time, traveling in far and distant lands.[31] The letter (i.e., the *Guide*) is Maimonides's attempt to continue to provide instruction to his student because personal communication is not possible. Considering the literary form of the *Guide* in light of Maimonides's transgression of committing to writing what should have remained an esoteric, oral tradition, Strauss surmises that

Joseph's departure was a consequence of his being a Jew in the Diaspora. Not a private need but only an urgent necessity of nation-wide bearing can have driven Maimonides to transgress an explicit prohibition. Only the necessity of saving the law can have caused him to break the law.[32]

Strauss's identification of his own problem with Maimonides's thus becomes all the more apparent. Strauss's response to the historian's moral dilemma of how to write about an esoteric text follows from his appreciation of Maimonides's decision to break the law to save it. Strauss is willing to make the seemingly immoral and indecent move of revealing the secrets of an esoteric text to save those secrets. The secret that Strauss seeks to save is insight into the political, philosophical, and theological meaning of what Strauss calls "a forgotten type of writing."[33] This insight concerns both the necessity and limits of politics as it relates to philosophy and the necessity and limits of philosophy as it relates to politics. More broadly, just as Strauss maintains that Maimonides broke the law to save the law, so too Strauss offers a seemingly subversive reading of Maimonides to save the very possibility of reading.

Strauss's own attempt at deciphering the great texts of the past is rooted in his dedication to liberal education. As he put it: "We cannot be philosophers... but we can love philosophy; we can try to philosophize. This philosophizing consists... primarily and in a way chiefly in listening to the conversation between the great philosophers or... the greatest minds, and therefore in studying the great books."[34] Strauss's hermeneutic is dialogical in at least two ways: first, as we have seen, in the emphasis on the multiple speakers in the great texts of the past and, second, in the emphasis on the present's conversation with the past. In the conclusion of this chapter we will turn to the question of whether Strauss can sustain this dialogicism without succumbing to historicism, which is, of course, one of his fundamental philosophical goals. First, however, we must turn to Levinas's own hermeneutic of retrieval in his attempt to offer a nonhistoricist reading of Jewish texts.

8.2. LEVINAS'S HERMENEUTIC: FROM LAW TO ETHICS

As we saw in Strauss's case, Levinas's approach to the reading of classical Jewish texts is organically connected to his perspectives on politics more generally. But more particularly than this, Levinas maintains that classical Jewish texts reflect the permanent, philosophical problems of humanity to which modern people have lost access, in no small part due to the historicist assumptions that saturate twentieth-century intellectual life. Along with his philosophical works, Levinas also gave lectures and published on Jewish texts, contending that the Talmud in particular "refers to philosophical problems" and also "proceeds from a mediation radical enough also to satisfy the demands of philosophy."[35]

In his first Talmudic reading, on messianic themes in *Sanhedrin* 99a, Levinas maintains that the Talmud's discussions of the different views of Rabbi Jochanan and Shmuel on the messianic era "reflect two positions between which thought somehow oscillates eternally."[36] Levinas is specifically interested in the following statement: "R. Hiyya b. Abba said in R. Jochanan's name: All the prophets prophesied [all the good things] only in respect of the messianic era; but as for the world to come, 'the eye hath not seen, O Lord, beside thee, what he hath prepared for him that waiteth for him'."[37] Levinas maintains that the positions of R. Jochanan and Shmuel taken together anticipate the philosophical problem of how to respond to Hegel's *Phenomenology of Spirit.* As Levinas describes this tension: "Does spirit indicate a quasi-divine life that is free of the limitations of the human condition, or does the human condition, with its limits and its drama, express the very life of the spirit?"[38] Levinas favors the latter position, implying not too subtly that Shmuel's is a Jewish response to Hegel. As we saw in Chapter 7, Levinas equates what he claims is this Jewish, ethical, and antiutopian position with biblical morality. Again, as he puts, "One can choose utopia. On the other hand, in the name of spirit, one can choose not to flee the conditions from which one's work draws its meaning, and remain here below. And that means choosing ethical action."[39]

As we can already see from our brief discussion of Levinas's Talmudic readings, his hermeneutic corresponds with his claim about the philosophical meaning of the text. Levinas's hermeneutical supposition is antihistoricist: "Our approach assumes that the different periods of history can communicate around thinkable meanings, whatever the variations in the signifying material which suggests them."[40] And the meaning of the discussion between R. Jochanan and R. Shmuel is also antihistoricist, that is, the human condition is permanent and eternal. In a broad sense, the relation between Levinas's hermeneutical approach and the philosophical content of his reading of Jewish texts parallels this relation in Strauss's thought. Yet their antihistoricist hermeneutics are quite different as are their respective politics. Let us turn then to what is arguably Levinas's most politically revealing Talmudic reading in which he considers the meaning of the reception of Jewish law by the Israelites.

As part of a colloquium in December of 1964, Levinas presented a reading of the tractate *Shabbat* 88a and 88b, titled "The Temptation of Temptation."[41] *Shabbat* 88a–b is a commentary on Exodus 19:17 "And they stopped at the foot of the mountain. . . ." The context is precisely the receiving of the law by the Israelites. Perhaps no other reading of Jewish sources offered by Levinas reflects as clearly what would be his mature stance on a nonpolitical/ethical politics. Just as we saw that Strauss's retrieval of a forgotten kind of writing is profoundly tied to his claim for an eternal tension between philosophy and politics, so too we will see that Levinas's retrieval of the wisdom of the Talmud is tied strongly to his attempt to elucidate a nonpolitical politics.

The Talmudic text that Levinas reads in "The Temptation of Temptation" begins with Rav Abdimi bar Hama bar Hasa's explanation of this verse: "This teaches us that the Holy One, Blessed be He, inclined the mountain over them like a tilted tub and that He said: If you accept the Torah, all is well, if not here will be your grave." In his commentary on the text, Levinas seeks to understand what, if any, kind of coercion is involved in the acceptance of the Torah. The Talmud's (and Bible's) description of the experience of the Israelites is that they did before they heard, they responded to God with "*na'aseh v'nishma*," "we will do and (then) we will hear." But what does it mean to act before hearing? Levinas claims that the Torah derives its authority from its fundamental recognition of the existential meaning of what it is to be human. Human subjectivity, for Levinas, *is* being in the position of the Israelites standing at the foot of the mountain with the mountain lifted over them. The Israelites can choose the Torah or they can choose death. What choice do they have? Their choice then is, in terms of how we ordinarily understand choice, a choiceless choice. Levinas maintains that this choiceless choice and the affirmation of it – "we shall do and then we shall hear" – describes what it means to be a human being, which is to be in the throes of obligation prior to having the ability to make free choices.

For Levinas, moral, religious, and even epistemological authority derives from this human condition. As he puts it in his commentary on *Shabbat* 88a–b:

Wouldn't Revelation be precisely a reminder of this consent prior to freedom and non-freedom? Therefore it would not simply be a source of knowledge parallel to those which come from natural insight. Adherence to it [revelation] would not coexist *side* by *side* with the internal adherence which works through evidence. The first, Revelation, would condition the second, Reason.[42]

In the last paragraph, I mentioned Levinas's broad claim that epistemologically responsibility for another person makes knowledge and truth possible. This is what he means by revelation conditioning reason. His claim in regard to the

Israelites is that this initial choiceless choice made human freedom possible, that is, that we do make choices. "*Na'aseh v'nishma*" is a moment before time, for Levinas. It is what makes temporality possible. Moral, religious, and epistemological authority rest upon acknowledgment of this moment before time, a moment for which we cannot account in historical terms, a timeless moment that Levinas calls "revelation." Responsibility is always prior to freedom and ethics is the modality of this prior responsibility. Levinas's interpretation of "*Na'aseh v'nishma*" is identical to his conception in *Otherwise than Being* of prophesy as infinity: "the obedience prior to all representation, this allegiance before any oath, this responsibility prior to commitment, is precisely the other in the same, inspiration and prophesy, the *passing itself* of the Infinite."[43]

What's important to notice immediately about Levinas's claims about revelation is that even in a discussion of a specific talmudic text that refers for all intents and purposes to a very specific moment in Jewish history and to a set of very particular commandments, Levinas wants to deny that this moment is in any way historical or even ultimately specific. As Levinas concludes, "Thus, the Torah would play a role of the first importance in the theory of knowledge itself." Doing before hearing expresses for Levinas not adherence to a specific set of legal prescriptions but rather the timeless, existential state of humanity. The ethical condition of humanity, as Levinas describes it especially in *Otherwise than Being or Beyond Essence*, is that of being a hostage to another person. Just as the Torah is born from an act of violence – the holding of the tub over the heads of the Israelites – so my responsibility as a human being derives from the hold that another person (any person, by virtue of his or her humanity) has over me.

In his Talmudic readings, Levinas directs the contemporary reader to the timeless authority of the Talmud and Torah, which are embodied in the elucidation of this moral truth. Defending his hermeneutic, Levinas quotes from the end of his selected text: "A Sadducee saw Raba buried in study, holding his fingers beneath his foot so tightly that blood spurted from it."[44] Levinas contends that Raba's action supports the hermeneutic that *he and Raba* are demonstrating. Levinas argues:

As if by chance, to rub in such a way that blood spurts out is perhaps the way one must 'rub' the text to arrive at the life it conceals. Many of you are undoubtedly thinking, with good reason, that at this very moment, I am in the process of rubbing the text to make it spurt blood – I rise to the challenge! Has anyone ever seen a reading that was something besides this effort carried out on a text? To the degree that it rests on the trust granted the author, it can only consist in this violence done to words to tear from them the secret that time and conventions have covered over with their sedimentations, a process begun as soon as these words appear in the open air of history. One must, by rubbing, remove this layer which corrodes them.[45]

The first thing that Levinas and Raba have in common is that they are readers. But a reader, for Levinas, is also someone who must take risks. He must be someone who is willing to bloody not only the text but also himself. Notice that Levinas's reading of this text is made possible by first offering a different rendition of the text than he offers when he begins his lecture. In the beginning of the lecture, Levinas quotes the Talmud as stating that Rabba was "holding his fingers beneath his foot so tightly. . . ."[46] When Levinas quotes this verse he already offers an interpretation of it. Now he reads the verse as stating that Raba was *rubbing* his foot: "holding his fingers beneath his foot *and rubbing it so hard* that blood spurted from it."[47] Levinas's own rendition of the text is thus a further bloodying of the text.

But the meaning of the blood and the violence of the blood go further. The blood of Raba's foot is ambiguous. It represents both life and death, which Levinas suggests are inextricably intertwined. Blood, of course, gives life, but to bleed is to risk death. The past – the sedimentations of time and conventions – must die in order that the eternal truth may live. Levinas's reading of the blood of Raba's foot suggests that in order for ethics to live, the tradition must die because if the tradition, which is the result of time and conventions, is not rubbed away, the truth will be corroded. Note the formal similarity between what Levinas regards as the relation between trust and violence that produces timeless truth and the image of God holding the tub over the Israelites in order that they may have true freedom. Again, he states that if the text "rests on the trust granted the author, it can only consist in this violence done to words." The reader, like Levinas and Raba, violently approaches the text and invests his own blood in the violent struggle between reader and author so that the text may live. For Levinas, there is symmetry between the reading of the text, which implicitly brings violence with it, and God's threatening the Israelites with the upside-down mountain. This seeming violence on the part of God and the reader produces the timeless truth of revelation.

Despite his claim that his is a philosophy of the "other," Levinas's interpretative framework denies precisely the possible "otherness" of views different from his own. While Levinas, drawing on Raba, wants to make much of the violence done to the reader – what he might call, in the terms of *Otherwise than Being*, the self's gnawing away at itself in its relation to the other – Levinas's hermeneutic in the end violates the text's own voice. Indeed, Levinas claims that the text as a living document requires this shedding of blood. But if, as Levinas maintains, the reader must bring the text to life so that its original meaning may live, it is hard to understand in what way the text may speak. In the context of this particular text, the tension between the text and Levinas's reading is quite blatant. The text describes God's giving of the ritual law to the people of Israel at a particular point in time. Levinas claims that this text concerns neither a supernatural or personal God, nor the particularity of the people of Israel or the law it receives, nor a particular moment in sacred history. Rather, Levinas suggests, the text is about the timeless ethical situation intrinsic to the existential situation of all of humanity. I do not wish to deny that multiple claims for the meanings of a text are possible. But what I would like to point out is the striking discord between what Levinas says the text is about and the text itself, a discord for which Levinas does not even attempt to account.

Common to Levinas's philosophical arguments and his Talmudic readings is the contention that the ethics of the face of the other is neither predicated upon nor subject to rational or textual *argument*. Whatever may be said of Levinas's claims from a philosophical point of view, imagining the *interpretive* value of Levinas's hermeneutic is difficult. Levinas's hermeneutic implicitly denies the otherness of a text and for this reason one may reasonably wonder why Levinas bothers to read at all if he knows the meaning of a text in advance. Ironically, perhaps, Strauss's hermeneutic approach is more "Levinasian" in spirit than is Levinas's own hermeneutic approach. It is only through careful philological and historical analysis, Strauss might claim, were he speaking to Levinas that the "otherness" of a text can be ascertained and that the reader can enter into a truly dialogical relation with a text and truly be transformed.

8.3. POLITICS AND READING

I have argued in this chapter that Strauss's notion of esotericism is not dogmatic but dialogical, as is his conception of politics as the coordination of competing conversations about the good life. Yet leaving the matter at this point would leave Strauss open to the charge of historicism, which he clearly wants to avoid. The question is: if Strauss is not a dogmatist, as I have argued, doesn't the dialogical emphasis of Strauss's hermeneutic suggest that a text's meaning is always produced only in relation to the reader? If meaning is fundamentally relational, that is, dialogical, how can we ever speak of "understanding an author as he understood himself"? For these reasons, isn't Strauss's contention that "[t]he task of the historian of thought is to understand the thinkers of the past *exactly* as they understood themselves, or to revitalize their thought according to their *own* interpretation of it"[48] self-contradictory?

To consider these questions, it is necessary to elucidate a bit further Strauss's debt to Heidegger. I concluded Chapter 7 by emphasizing Levinas's affinity with Heidegger, and differentiating Strauss from them both. I suggested that, on Strauss's reading, Heidegger's and Levinas's error lies in a shared overinflated sense of philosophy, which denies the distinction between theory and practice. But now, in the context of our consideration of Strauss's hermeneutics, it is necessary to point out not only his affinity with Heidegger but also that the possibility of his criticism of Heidegger is made possible in an important way by Heidegger. That is, Strauss's attempt to reinstate the difference between theory and practice is made possible by Strauss's notion that it is possible to retrieve wisdom by attempting to remember the wisdom of the past. But if this is the case, can Strauss truly claim, as he does, to retrieve permanent, and not just historical, human problems? And if Strauss cannot lay claim to such a possibility, how can he defend the coherence of his view of esotericism?

To answer this question, it is helpful to turn to Strauss's correspondence with Hans-Georg Gadamer, Heidegger's protégé, on this matter. Viewing his philosophy as a more consistent version of Heidegger's conception of historicity, Gadamer criticizes Strauss for what he regards as an indefensible lack of historical consciousness. Gadamer responds to Strauss by explicitly distancing himself from Heidegger and drawing the parallel between Heidegger's position and Strauss's. Gadamer writes: "My point of departure is not the complete forgetfulness of being, the 'night of being,' rather on the contrary – I say this against Heidegger as well as against Buber – the unreality of such an assertion."[49] What Gadamer objects to perhaps most fundamentally in Strauss's hermeneutics of retrieval is Strauss's contention that we can understand an author as an author understood his or herself. Gadamer insists not that "true understanding" is impossible but that the very concept is premised on a category error that posits a false dichotomy between absolute and relative understanding. In Gadamer's words to Strauss, "We have been pressed by Schleiermacher and the romantic hermeneutics into the false radicality of a 'universal' understanding (as the avoidance of 'misunderstanding'). I see in that a false theory for a better reality."[50]

While Strauss's reply to Gadamer is not comprehensive, it does offer us an opportunity to reflect on the relation between Strauss's conception of politics and his hermeneutics of retrieval. Strauss writes to Gadamer:

I have always seen that there remained in the text something of the utmost importance which I did not understand, i.e. that my understanding of my interpretation is very incomplete; I would hesitate to say however that no one can complete it or that the finiteness of man as man necessitates the impossibility of adequate or complete or 'the true understanding.'[51]

Strauss does not claim, here or elsewhere, to have provided the final truth as to the meaning of a particular text. The meaning of a text, from Strauss's perspective, must be found in its details, which are debatable and always subject to discussion. With this, Gadamer would agree. Where they disagree is in Strauss's instance that this conclusion does not imply, as Gadamer and others would have it, that "true understanding" is not possible. From Strauss's perspective, historicism of Gadamer's sort has thrown the baby out with the bathwater. Strauss's response to Gadamer is simply to ask: why does the reality of incomplete interpretation imply in theory that true understanding is impossible? Strauss does not refute Gadamer's position but instead shifts the burden of proof to the historicist who must now answer the question of why true understanding has been ruled out as a possibility.[52]

Strauss's intellectual enterprise can be summed up as the attempt to shift the burden of proof to contemporary thinkers who take for granted what he claims are ultimately unthinking dogmas. Despite some claims of Strauss's admirers and detractors alike, Strauss does not provide definitive answers to the meanings of nature or authorial intention. He is instead interested in these issues as formal questions that ought to be considered despite the fact that, or perhaps because, these notions seem to be so out of favor.

Strauss's claims about esoteric writing are best understood in the context of his commitment to liberal education, which he sees as an ongoing dialogue with and about great literary texts. Of course, some find the enterprise of revitalizing the thought of the great thinkers of the past inherently elitist. Yet Strauss's conceptions of both esotericism and liberal education are inherently egalitarian in that everyone has the *opportunity* to enter into this dialogue. At the same time, the canon of great texts of the past is not fixed for Strauss. Indeed, much of Strauss's scholarly life was spent devoted to expanding the canon of accepted texts. As he put it, "The greatest minds to whom we ought to listen are by no means exclusively the greatest minds of the West."[53] Despite the continued controversy over Strauss's political legacy, Strauss's interest in and focus on esotericism is tied intimately to his commitment to liberal education, which at its core is fundamentally transnational as well as transpolitical. Nevertheless, liberal education, like philosophy, does not and cannot exist in a vacuum. The teacher, for Strauss, is like a prophet or statesman in that he or she must negotiate through moderation the proper balance between theory and practice. While liberal education cannot provide political solutions, it can and should provide a clear-sighted view of the world and its problems that may, outside of the university, lead to practical solutions. But liberal education's contribution to practical solutions may be more negative than constructive. What the university offers is an opportunity to think through problems in their complexity rather than to provide their solutions. I turn now, in Chapter 9, to Strauss's consideration of the riddles of what he calls "the theologico-political predicament." While Strauss offers no clear solutions to this predicament, I argue that his elucidation of the predicament is precisely his perhaps invaluable contribution to contemporary Jewish thought.

Revelation and Commandment: Strauss, Levinas, and the Theologico-Political Predicament

𝒜 S IS WELL KNOWN, IN PRESENTING THE BEGINNINGS OF HIS intellectual journey Strauss characterized himself as "a young Jew . . . in the grips of the theologico-political predicament." By "theologico-political predicament," Strauss refers to the structure of liberal democracy in which "the bond of society is universal human morality, whereas religion (positive religion) is a private affair."[1] As he describes it in the preface to the English translation of *Spinoza's Critique of Religion*, the particular theologico-political predicament he found himself in as a young German-Jew was due to a twofold phenomenon: first, the privatization of prejudice (what Strauss calls "discrimination" in "Why We Remain Jews," written the same year as the preface) caused by the relegating of religion to the private sphere and second, Jewish responses not to just this new form of political discrimination, but also to the opportunities of full citizenship. Strauss's analysis of the relation between the privatization of prejudice and the rise of National Socialism has rightly received some attention, but for the purposes of constructive Jewish thought, it is also in the context of describing Jewish theological responses to the theologico-political predicament that Strauss offers a strong criticism of twentieth-century Jewish thinking about law.

I argue in this chapter that Strauss's discussion of modern Jewish conceptions of law should be considered more seriously for two reasons. First, Strauss's claims about modern Jewish conceptions of law help to elucidate the meaning of his term *theologico-political predicament*. Second, Strauss's view of Jewish law is *theologically* coherent and offers an important challenge to some of the basic presuppositions of twentieth-century Jewish thought. To flesh out these points, the chapter proceeds as follows. Focusing on Strauss's early criticism of Julius Guttmann, and Guttmann's eventual response, Section 9.1 considers potential objections to Strauss's constructive inclusion in debates about modern Jewish thought. Section 9.2 examines Strauss's criticism of post-Kantian conceptions of law and specifically his *theological* criticism of German-Jewish conceptions of Jewish law. Turning in Section 9.3 to American jurisprudence and to the work of Robert Cover in particular, I argue that Strauss's analysis of modern assumptions about Jewish law aptly describes the role of Jewish law in contemporary American legal theory. It is in this context that the chapter analyzes Levinas's claims about Jewish law, which exhibit an affinity not only with the Weimar model but perhaps even more so with recent appropriations of Jewish law in American legal discussions. Finally, the conclusion, Section 9.4, turns again to consider briefly what Strauss's contribution to contemporary Jewish thought might be.

9.1. STRAUSS AND MODERN JEWISH THOUGHT: THE GUTTMANN DEBATE

We can begin to understand some of the fundamental issues that a consideration of Strauss's view of Jewish law raises by turning first to objections to even including Strauss as a contributor to discussions of modern Jewish thought. Sometimes underlying the objection that Strauss chose not to concern himself primarily with Jewish thought in his mature work, and therefore was not ultimately concerned with the problems of Jewish thought, is the suspicion that because Strauss wasn't a believer he can't be a resource for constructing the parameters and content of a contemporary Jewish thought. Oddly, this suspicion often comes from those who are involved in the academic study of Judaism or Jewish thought, and not from religious Jews who have no ties to academia (who, as far as I know, have no interest in or even knowledge of Strauss). The charge that Strauss's personal beliefs disqualify him as an interlocutor in discussions of Jewish thought is one that has plagued not only the intellectual reception of Strauss but also his personal fate early on. In the early thirties, Gershom Scholem encouraged Strauss to publish his work in medieval Jewish philosophy in the hopes of securing a position for Strauss at The Hebrew University of Jerusalem. After reading *Philosophy and Law*, however, Scholem's hopes for a position for Strauss were dashed. Writing to Walter Benjamin in 1935, Scholem, who remained a lifelong admirer of Strauss, wrote that he did not think that the faculty of The Hebrew University would "vote for an appointment of an atheist to a teaching position that serves to endorse the philosophy of religion."[2] As Scholem predicted to Benjamin, Strauss did not get the job.

The implication of the view that Strauss, by definition, is not and cannot be a player in debates in contemporary Jewish thought because he was not a believer raises an issue far beyond how to understand Strauss's personal beliefs, which is whether one needs to believe something to understand it. Critics of Strauss who equate him with Nazi thinkers such as Carl Schmitt, merely because Strauss sought to understand Schmitt's thought before criticizing it, share the unspoken view that understanding implies belief with those who would reject Strauss as an interlocutor in current debates about Jewish thought. But implicit and explicit in Strauss's commitment to liberal education is his contention that understanding does not require belief. In fact, Strauss maintains, understanding is necessary so that we may decide both what we do believe and, just as importantly, how we will defend that which we believe to be true and criticize that which we believe false. The question then to be asked in the context of Strauss's relation to contemporary Jewish thought is not whether he was a believer or not, but whether he has adequately understood the nature and problems of Jewish thought. As we have seen throughout this study, Strauss contends that the central problem for Jewish thought, medieval and modern, concerns the fundamental status of the law. Most of modern Jewish thinking ultimately denies this status, argues Strauss, even, or perhaps especially, when the law's centrality is acknowledged. It is Strauss's criticism of those modern Jewish thinkers who affirm the centrality of law that is our concern in this chapter.

Before turning to this criticism it is necessary to acknowledge the obvious objection to Strauss's claim about law, which is: why should the law be definitive in defining Judaism, when a whole variety of candidates for definition might be available? On what basis could Strauss make this claim? If it is on the basis of history, that is, on the view (which is certainly correct) that prior to emancipation the Jewish religion and Jewish life had been at least minimally defined by the sociopolitical structure of Jewish law, hasn't he simply defeated his own purpose? That is, if Strauss's claim about Jewish law is historical, it is all too easy to reply that if history defines the one enduring feature of Judaism, one cannot speak about Judaism in a transhistorical fashion, as Strauss does or seems to want to do. But this is not Strauss's position on the centrality of Jewish law. As Strauss begins the first chapter of *Philosophy and Law*, "There is no inquiry into the history of philosophy that is not at the same time a *philosophical* inquiry."[3] Strauss's claim about the centrality of Jewish law is a philosophical claim.[4]

In his belated reply to Strauss's criticism of him in *Philosophy and Law*, Julius Guttmann appreciated Strauss's philosophical inquiry into the history of medieval Jewish thought.[5] But just as Strauss argues in *Philosophy and Law* that Guttmann imposes his own philosophical views onto medieval Jewish rationalism, so Guttmann, in his reply to Strauss, argues that Strauss imposes his own philosophical views onto medieval Jewish philosophy. Guttmann insists that Strauss has imposed what is ultimately his own pessimistic dispo-sition onto his study of Maimonides and his predecessors.[6] To avoid such a subjective approach, Guttmann maintains, it is necessary to derive philosoph-ical categories *scientifically*. According to Guttmann, the modern categories of "religion" and "religious consciousness" are first necessary to provide the possibility of scientific, historical access to medieval Jewish philosophy.[7]

When he criticizes Strauss, Guttmann repeats the basic premises and form of Hermann Cohen's criticism of Spinoza. As we saw in Chapter 4, beginning with the premise that Spinoza's position on Judaism is *by definition* philosoph-ically indefensible, Cohen suggests that Spinoza's criticism of Judaism can only be explained through his personal motives, that is, in connection with his personal historical circumstances, which, Cohen claims, were less than honorable. Because he finds Strauss's philosophical conclusions philosophi-cally unconvincing *from the start*, Guttmann understands Strauss's philoso-phy (as Cohen understands Spinoza's) as issuing from his personal biases. Yet, as we saw in Chapter 5, Strauss, in his early work, consciously reverses the trajectory of this kind of criticism by arguing that historical contextual-ization of an author should precede philosophical judgment. In the case of Spinoza, the question for Strauss is first what are the historical circumstances of Spinoza's writings and then second are they philosophically defensible? Strauss's approach to Maimonides in *Philosophy and Law* is consistent with this trajectory. His claim is that within the historical context of medieval Jewish philosophy, the law simply preceded existentially the possibility of phi-losophizing. It is this basic historical point *and its philosophical implications* that Guttmann misses, according to Strauss, in suggesting that "'philosophy of religion' is actually the original achievement of medieval philosophy."[8]

While Strauss's ultimate stake in his position is, as he states, philosoph-ical and not only historical, it seems hard to dispute the fact that Strauss's position is actually more historically accurate than Guttmann's.[9] From a historical perspective, Strauss's claim is simply that for Maimonides, adher-ence to the law, however that adherence might be defined, was a given and at a very minimum a sociopolitical reality from within which the possibility of philosophizing could take place. Understanding the historical context of phi-losophy is philosophically necessary, argues Strauss, precisely so that modern categories are not projected back onto medieval philosophical texts. Again, in Strauss's words, "We need history first of all to reach the cave from which Socrates can lead us to the light. We need preparatory instruction – that is, precisely learning by reading."[10]

Significantly, perhaps, in his response to Strauss Guttmann makes no mention of, and therefore provides no response to, Strauss's explicit

methodological claims in *Philosophy and Law*, a point that is especially curious given that Guttmann does emphasize that he self-consciously focuses
exclusively on Strauss's early methodological approach. This omission may
give some credence to what seems to be Strauss's wholly dismissive view
of Guttmann's response[11] for it helps to explain Guttmann's basic misunderstanding of Strauss's philosophical position in *Philosophy and Law*. Guttmann
maintains that Strauss argues that for the medieval philosophers philosophy
determines the truth of the law, while the law determines the parameters of
what philosophy can know. In keeping with his own neo-Kantian assumptions, Guttmann understands Strauss's position in *epistemological* terms yet,
as Strauss states, his point about the law is *political*. While, as discussed in
Chapter 7, in *Philosophy and Law* Strauss does understand Maimonidean
prophecy in epistemological terms, it is also worth recalling that it is in connection with his direct criticism of *Guttmann* that Strauss anticipates his
mature thought in claiming that *the law* is not an epistemological matter but
a political one. As Strauss puts it, "We do not deny...that the problem of
'belief and knowledge' is the central problem of medieval rationalism. Our
quarrel with Guttmann is only about the meaning of 'belief' here, and it
seems to us more precise to say 'law and philosophy' rather than 'belief and
knowledge.' "[12]

Just as we have seen throughout this book that the argument between
Strauss and Levinas concerns the status of modern philosophy, so too the
debate between Strauss and Guttmann revolves around this very question.
The difference between Strauss and Guttmann is surely about the meaning
of revelation for Maimonides and his predecessors. But, according to Strauss,
once revelation is understood primarily as revealed law, and not as philosophical knowledge, it is necessary also to rethink, from a modern perspective, the
medieval Jewish and Islamic (and Strauss argues classical Greek) conception
of philosophy. For Strauss, the law is the prephilosophical context for philosophy. But the law is not derived through philosophical activity, although
philosophy can clarify its meaning.[13] On Strauss's reading of medieval Jewish
and Islamic philosophy, it is philosophy's relation to law that determines the
scope of philosophical activity, not from an epistemological point of view but
from a social and political one. According to Strauss, Guttmann imposes his
conception of *modern philosophy*, with its Christian conception of revelation
as knowledge, onto the study of medieval Jewish rationalism. This means for
Strauss that Guttmann does not understand the scope and meaning of revelation but also of philosophy. The philosophical inquiry of Strauss's historical
study of Maimonides and his predecessors concerns a philosophical consideration of the very scope of philosophical activity as it relates to revealed law

and not, as Guttmann believes, an epistomological investigation into the truth status of "religious consciousness."

Beyond the particular debate between Strauss and Guttmann, appreciating their different methodological approaches to the relation between history and philosophy is telling for understanding Strauss's most basic criticism of Guttmann and just about all of modern Jewish thought. From Strauss's point of view, it is only because Guttmann dismisses the historical and, hence the philosophical, centrality of law for medieval Jewish philosophy that he can and does claim that his reading of medieval Jewish philosophy is in fundamental continuity with medieval Jewish philosophy. As Strauss sums up Guttmann's position, "'philosophy of religion' is actually the original achievement of medieval philosophy." One of Strauss's main criticisms of modern Jewish thought and, as we will see in Section 9.2, modern Jewish philosophical conceptions of law especially, is its refusal to acknowledge the fundamental break with the Jewish past that emancipation brings. This refusal, from Strauss's point of view, is not merely of historical significance (for one thing, this is perhaps the most obvious fact of modern European Jewish history) but of *theological and philosophical* significance. The refusal to acknowledge this difference, Strauss maintains, is ultimately a philosophical and theological rejection of the veracity of revelation that differs only in intention from the seemingly devastating modern critiques of religion.

9.2. ON NOT ACKNOWLEDGING THE MODERN BREAK WITH THE JEWISH PAST

Before turning to the details of Strauss's understanding of (to borrow a title from Levinas) revelation in the Jewish tradition, it is helpful to note that in distinguishing between the Jewish past and present and admonishing other Jewish thinkers for not doing so, Strauss would find an unlikely ally in the thought of an American contemporary of his, Mordecai Kaplan (1881–1983). Kaplan begins his most theological work, *The Meaning of God in Modern Jewish Religion*, by chastising contemporary Jewish thinkers for their lack of intellectual probity. As he puts it, "Sentimentally attached to the old and distrustful of the new, they try to persuade themselves and others that no radical change has taken place in human thinking, and that none is necessary in the Jewish religion."[14] In terms of the content of their thoughts, it would perhaps be difficult to find a more dissimilar pair of thinkers than Strauss and Kaplan. But the impetus for their respective philosophies begins with the same underlying premise: that modernity constitutes a fundamental break with the Jewish past and that modern Jewish thinkers have refused to acknowledge this break with disastrous consequences for the possibility of contemporary Jewish life.[15] Whereas the targets of Kaplan's criticism are the ideologues of the reform and conservative movements in America, Strauss's targets are the German-Jewish thinkers who influenced these practical ideologies.

The real disagreement between Kaplan and Strauss lies is in what is lost in and gained by modernity. It is Strauss the nonbeliever who emerges as the defender of the ultimate value of Jewish revelation as it has been classically understood. As he puts it in what could seem a direct criticism of Kaplan's position:

I believe, by simply replacing God by the creative genius of the Jewish people, one gives away, one deprives oneself – even if one does not believe – of a source of human understanding. . . . Now I do not wish to minimize folk dances, Hebrew speaking, and many other things – I do not want to minimize them. But I believe that they cannot possibly take the place of what is most profound in our tradition.[16]

What is most profound for Strauss in the Jewish tradition is a belief in a transcendent God who has revealed, and continues to reveal, himself to the Jewish people by way of the Torah.[17]

These comments would seem to put Strauss squarely in the company of those modern Jewish thinkers who have often been acclaimed in contemporary Jewish thought circles for insisting on the possibility of, to apply Strauss's apt description of Rosenzweig's position, revelation as "the experience of an unequivocal command addressed to me here and now as distinguished from general laws or ideas."[18] Yet despite what seems to be Strauss's explicit endorsement of the enduring theological profundity of Jewish revelation, along with his equally explicit statements about the ultimate moral, political, and even epistemological shortcomings of philosophy, many have and remain skeptical of his motives. The main objection is that Strauss has simply and falsely set the bar too high: his distinction between the "tradition" and the present is too stark as is, perhaps even more basically, his distinction between philosophy and revelation.[19] I suspect that these claims are based less on a reading of what Strauss actually has to say about Judaism, philosophy, and revelation than on what appears to be the increasingly emotional climate that the name "Leo Strauss" seems to elicit. Leaving the reasons for this climate aside, let us turn briefly to Strauss's own statement about how the nonbeliever may approach the Jewish religion. These comments, I suggest, will allow us to begin to appreciate the *theological* significance that Strauss attributes to the theologico-political predicament.

In a lecture originally delivered in 1957 in the "Works of the Mind" series at the University of Chicago,[20] Strauss considers how a contemporary person might read the opening chapters of Genesis. At the beginning of the lecture, Strauss reiterates his claim that atheism is a philosophically incoherent position. As he puts it, "Experience can show at most that the contention of biblical faith is improbable, but the improbable character of biblical belief is admitted and even proclaimed by the biblical faith itself."[21] Strauss's suggestion, then, is that the contemporary reader (who does not from the start approach the Bible from the perspective of the believer) may approach the Bible from neither a religious nor an atheistic perspective, but from an agnostic one.

The agnostic position, that is, the position that honestly admits ignorance about the possible truth of the Bible, can approach the Bible openly. Strauss notes that when the book of Genesis begins, we do not know who is speaking. According to the Bible's own account, it cannot be a human speaking because humanity has not yet been created, it must be God speaking. Strauss makes much of the fact that there is no argument whatsoever for God's existence. This doesn't mean, for Strauss, that the Bible is irrational or even mythological. On the contrary. Strauss claims that the Bible elucidates a conception of authority *and rationality* that is just as accessible to human beings as is a philosophical conception of authority.[22] But God's authority cannot be recognized by a human initiative. The theme of Genesis, according to Strauss, is that only God can proclaim his own authority. This is the meaning of revelation. In Strauss's words:

The Bible rejects the principle of autonomous knowledge and everything that goes with it. . . . The mysterious God is the last theme and highest theme of the Bible. Man is not master of how to begin; before he begins to write he is already confronted with writings, with holy writings, which impose their law on him.[23]

In his detailed reading of the first two chapters of Genesis, Strauss attempts to elucidate the difference in biblical and philosophical conceptions of authority. He reads the first chapter of Genesis as proclaiming that cosmology, or wondering at the way things essentially *are*, is not a theme of the Bible as it is of philosophy. The first chapter of Genesis suggests that the creation of the world is subordinate to God the creator. While God has created the earth to run by its own laws, the earth and the heavens are not subjects in and of themselves. What we learn from the first chapter of Genesis is that God has created the world. Chapter 2 of Genesis, Strauss maintains, continues and reinforces this theme. The intention of philosophical contemplation, on the other hand, is to consider the nature of the good life, a quest that, as mentioned, is always ongoing. The second chapter of Genesis stands in marked contrast to this point of view. For the Bible, knowledge of good and evil is not based on contemplation of the nature of things but on God's law.[24] In the preface to *Spinoza's Critique of Religion*, Strauss sums up his argument about the nature of authority in Judaism: "the foundation, the authoritative layer, of the Jewish heritage presents itself, not as a product of the human mind, but as a divine gift, as divine revelation."[25]

Strauss's brief reading of Genesis helps to give philosophical content to Strauss's description of the medieval Jewish philosophers who begin philosophizing within the preexisting reality of the law. To quote Strauss's reading of Genesis once again, "Man is not master of how to begin; before he begins to write he is already confronted with writings, with holy writings, which impose their law on him." The law imposes a sociopolitical reality, but it does so for *theological* reasons. The relationship between God and the people of Israel is mediated by the law. The political reality of Jewish law, for Strauss, cannot be divorced from its theological impetus. As one recent interpreter of Maimonides describes what, I suggest, aptly captures Strauss's position:

> defining *dat* [religion] in terms of law is not a reductive position, identifying religion with politics at the expense of its spiritual movement. Maimonides is not accounting for the phenomenology of religious experience but rather for the fact that in the Jewish conception, the human relationship with God is mediated by, and institutionalized through, a law, the Torah. Maimonides sees the institutional organization of religion around the law as rooted in political reality and as making possible the achievement of a political and religious ideal – a community devoted to attaining human perfection.[26]

Despite the persistent caricature of Strauss as presenting a crude dichotomy between reason and revelation,[27] Strauss in no way denies the potential rationality of a belief in revelation; in fact, he consistently maintains, in both his early and late work, that a commitment to revelation is just as rational as a commitment to philosophy. At the same time, as emphasized in Chapter 1, Strauss maintains that biblical revelation and philosophy both begin with nonrational criteria yet both subsequently move toward rationality. Strauss's point in insisting on a distinction between the two is fairly minimal and also wholly consistent with, again, Franz Rosenzweig's attempt to take the givenness of revelation seriously from a philosophical perspective. As Rosenzweig put it in his now famous essay "Apologetic Thinking":

> No one became a Jewish thinker within the private domain of Judaism. Thinking was not thinking about Judaism (which was simply taken for granted, and was more of an existence than an 'ism'); it was thinking within Judaism, learning – ultimately ornamental, rather than fundamental, thinking. Anyone who was to think about Judaism, somehow had to be drawn to the border of Judaism, if not psychologically then intellectually. His thinking was thus determined by the power

that had brought him to the border and the horizon of his gaze was defined by the degree to which he had been carried to, near, or across it.

Apologetics is the legitimate strength of this thinking, but also an inherent danger.[28]

Translated into Strauss's framework, thinking within Judaism means that Judaism is a given; it is not something that needs or can be established through the use of philosophical reason. Philosophy, in contrast, for Strauss, seeks to move beyond any givens.

It is in connection with Rosenzweig that we can appreciate more deeply Strauss's *theological* challenge to modern Jewish thought. Rosenzweig has increasingly come to be considered and praised as the paradigm of the assimilated Jew returning to Judaism. Contra Rosenzweig, a cursory glance of Strauss's claims about Jewish law could lead one to conclude that Strauss understands Judaism as a dry legalism. But, as we have seen, in his understanding of Jewish revelation Strauss, like Rosenzweig, emphasizes the centrality of the belief in and relationship to a God who reveals himself to the human.

Strikingly, Strauss criticizes Rosenzweig's view of the law not on legalistic grounds, but on *theological* ones. Strauss suggests that Rosenzweig's understandings of revelation and law, despite his intentions to the contrary, are predicated on not taking the *theological* presuppositions of Jewish law seriously enough. As Strauss puts it:

absolute experience will not lead back to Judaism – for instance, to the details of what the Christians call the ceremonial law – if it does not recognize itself in the Bible and clarify itself through the Bible, and if it is not linked up with the considerations of how traditional Judaism understands itself and with meditations about the mysterious fate of the Jewish people.[29]

Rosenzweig, of course, was profoundly aware of the tension between the "unequivocal command addressed to me here and now," and the positive, or ceremonial, laws of Judaism. In his famous debate with Martin Buber on the law, Rosenzweig attempted to balance the tension between individual experience and the demands of the law by suggesting that Jewish ceremonial law was binding for the individual Jew, but nonetheless the experience of God's revelation (what he called *Gebot*) remains the primary and necessary force behind the positive law (what he called *Gesetz*).[30]

Rosenzweig's commitment was to reinvigorate what he regarded as the true meaning of Jewish law, which had been spoiled not by the rabbinic tradition (as Buber would have it) but by its modern interpreters who had presented Jewish law (for better or for worse) as a yoke to be borne. Contrary to the view that the law is intrinsically prohibitive, Rosenzweig maintained that Jewish law allows its adherents to experience a new kind of freedom:

One refrains from working on the Sabbath because of the positive commandment concerning rest; when refraining from eating forbidden food one experiences the joy of being able to be Jewish even in the every-day and generally human aspect of one's material existence. Even an act of refraining becomes a positive act.[31]

By understanding the law's positive possibilities, rather than its negative prohibitions, Rosenzweig suggested that the relation between the command of the revealing God and particular laws coming from this command could be brought again to life. It is on Rosenzweig's description of the meaning of the law that Strauss criticizes him:

[H]e [Rosenzweig] opposed their [Rosenzweig's orthodox Jewish contemporaries] inclination to understand the Law in terms of prohibition, denial, refusal, and rejection, rather than in terms of command, liberation, granting and transformation, the opposite of inclination. It is not immediately clear, however, whether the orthodox austerity or sternness does not rest on a deeper understanding of the power of evil in man than Rosenzweig's at first glance more attractive view. . . .[32]

While Rosenzweig's thought is predicated on a break with the rationalist tradition of German-Jewish thought, Strauss points out that his view of law, and therefore of Judaism more generally, shares with this rationalist, and particularly neo-Kantian, tradition a fundamentally utopian view of human nature.[33] From a biblical and then rabbinic point of view, Strauss maintains, moral knowledge begins not with the human being but with the mysterious God. Appropriately, Strauss makes this point with reference to Hermann Cohen:

Cohen too cannot well deny that the state must use coercion, but, opposing the Kantian distinction between morality and legality, he denies that coercion is the principle of law. . . . He is as uneasy about coercion as he is about power: the state is law, for the state is essentially rational, and coercion begins where reason ends. All this follows from the premise that morality is self-legislation and that it can be actual only in and through the state. . . . Since he [Cohen] attacks Spinoza in the name of Judaism, it may suffice here to quote a Jewish saying: 'But for the fear of the government, men would swallow each other alive.'[34]   [Pirkei Avot 3:2]

Strauss does not explicate his contention about Cohen's view of law further, but as is the case with much of the highly condensed argument of the preface to *Spinoza's Critique of Religion*, Strauss's concise and understated formulations reveal a deep knowledge of the arguments of modern Jewish thought and an analytic depth that is often lacking in these discussions. For this reason, it is helpful to draw out the meaning of Strauss's statement about Cohen.

As discussed briefly in Chapter 4, in both his writings on ethics generally and Judaism particularly, Cohen seeks to vindicate from Kant's harsh critique a concept of law. Again, according to Cohen, a "Pauline prejudice" is responsible for the Kantian split between public law as the mark of coercion and private, or individual law, as the mark of freedom. Kant had made this distinction perhaps most succinctly in division one of book three of his *Religion within the Limits of Reason Alone*: "A *juridico-civil* (political) *condition* [*Zustand*] is the relation of men to each other in which they all alike stand socially under *public juridical laws* (which are, as a class, laws of coercion). An *ethico-civil* condition is that in which they are united under non-coercive laws, *i.e., laws of virtue* alone."[35] It is also in this work that Kant famously claimed that Jewish law epitomizes clericism and the coercion intrinsic to public juridical law. While Cohen rightly recognizes that Kant's concepts of law and freedom are based on a "Pauline prejudice" against legality, Cohen nonetheless maintains this very prejudice in his redescription of law.[36] Cohen argues against Kant and "Paul" that law is intrinsic to morality, but he goes further and argues that law has no relation to coercion. In this sense, Cohen accepts what had become the traditional Protestant reading of Paul's equation between law and coercion by inverting it.[37] Having corrected Kant's error, Cohen's argument that the law is the scientific foundation of ethics also dissolves the problem of coercion.[38] Because the norms of right speak to every person, and hence produce what we might call modern individuality, the problem of coercion disappears. The norms of right create the possibility of ethics because they create the possibility of the free individual. Simply put, every person is the same under the law. Hence the law – public, juridical law – produces (to use Cohen's neo-Kantian vocabulary) free individuality. Cohen augments his philosophy of law in his posthumous *Religion of Reason*, but his argument that law produces free individuality without coercion remains unchanged.

Strauss's claim that Rosenzweig, in his defense of the obligatory nature of Jewish law, did not understand the "deeper understanding of the power of evil in man" intrinsic to the Jewish theological understanding of law should be understood in the context of Strauss's broader point that Jewish law is predicated not only on the theological presupposition that God has revealed himself to humanity but also on a particular view of human nature that suggests that the coercive power of law is necessary because not all people will always do the right thing without it. As Strauss put it to Scholem in the context of Maimonides, "Surely Rambam [Maimonides] was no 'optimist.' I don't wish to say that he was sure that meanness and vulgarity will be coeval with man but he certainly believed that inequality will be coeval with man."[39] This is not to suggest, however, that the law's ultimate end is coercive power, but it is to suggest that coercion is an aspect of Jewish law that should not be denied.[40] As Strauss points out in the context of his comment about Cohen, the denial of the law's coercive power is tied to a particularly optimistic view of human nature in the belief that human beings left to their own devices are capable of legislating and instituting a universal morality for themselves.[41]

Remarkably, just about all of modern Jewish thought especially in the German-Jewish tradition is predicated on a denial of the coercive aspect of Jewish law and by implication of the political nature of Judaism.[42] While Strauss does not mention Moses Mendelssohn's view of law in the preface to *Spinoza's Critique of Religion*, it should be noted that Mendelssohn, the father of German-Jewish thought, defines Judaism – which he defines as adherence to the ceremonial law – precisely as noncoercive.[43] Arguing against Spinoza's reduction of Jewish law to politics, Mendelssohn denies the political nature of Judaism by reading a utopian peace into Jewish religion and law.[44] Mendelssohn goes further in this attempt at inversion and argues that it is Christianity that is truly coercive, for Christianity demands and coerces faith.

Exempting various Zionisms, much of modern Jewish thought, nonorthodox and orthodox alike, can be understood as an attempt to understand Judaism in nonpolitical terms.[45] What is highly significant for our discussion of Strauss is that his criticism of modern claims that Judaism is not political in nature is made not from a political perspective but from a *theological* one.[46] As we saw in Chapter 7, Strauss remained a lifelong defender of political Zionism. Although a strong critic of cultural Zionism, he also argued that political Zionism, before and after the creation of the State of Israel, "was in no way employed . . . in matters Jewish." In short, Strauss argued that Judaism has a political dimension, but he made this claim *with reference to Jewish theology*.

9.3. JEWISH LAW IN AMERICA

Far from being a relic of what some would surely consider the outdated debates of Weimar Jewry, Strauss's basic insight, again made from a *theological* point of view, that modern Jewish thinking is plagued by the denial of the political dimension of Jewish law continues to play itself out in the contemporary American context. As Suzanne Last Stone has shown, discussion of Jewish law has surprisingly come to play an important role in contemporary American legal theory in which the Jewish legal model is taken as a productive countermodel to the American one.[47] This trend parallels a popular trend in literary theory in which a number of philosophers and literary theorists have argued that the rabbinic tradition is a countermodel to the totalizing and violent presuppositions of western notions of reason.[48] Not coincidently, Levinas is increasingly used as a resource in these arguments.[49] For some American legal and literary theorists, Judaism, as instantiated by rabbinic discourses on law, is a model of true democracy because it is, they claim, pluralistic, egalitarian, and antihierarchical. At the basis of all of these claims are two shared assumptions: first that rabbinic discourse and by implication Jewish law does not involve any form of political coercion and second that the theological suppositions of rabbinic discourse, if there are any, are not relevant to the contemporary appropriation, for literary or political purposes, of this model. From Strauss's perspective, these twin claims would be evidence of the theologico-political crisis and incoherence of modern times. More particularly, in the context of a theory of law, these claims reflect a particularly utopian hope for human society that, Strauss claims, Jewish theological views of law by definition reject.

Let us turn first to the well-known American legal philosopher Robert Cover, whose main body of work centers on insisting on acknowledging the violence and coercion intrinsic to the law – a violence and coercion that Cover rightly maintains is implicitly denied by most of modern legal theory. In a now famous essay, Cover argued that "Legal interpretation takes place in a field of pain and death."[50] Cover's main target in these remarks is the hermeneutical jurisprudence of Ronald Dworkin, but this argument could be and should be extended to much of twentieth-century Anglo-American legal theory. Cover's point is simply that Anglo-American legal theory denies the obvious fact that law is coercive and violent. While law makes free individuality a legal reality, it at the same time is premised on the possibility of violence toward the individual who does not conform to the law.

It is helpful to consider a comment Strauss makes about Cohen to appreciate Cover's simple yet absolutely fundamental point. In *Religion of Reason* Cohen describes what he calls "religion's share in reason" as the need of an individual to take his guilt upon himself.[51] Cohen maintains that religion is the internalization of a judge's imposition of punishment onto a criminal. What is striking, however, is that in his *Ethics*, when describing a judge's imposition of punishment onto a criminal, Cohen does so within the context of his broader claim that law has nothing to do with coercion. Cohen follows Mendelssohn in claiming that "religion of reason," that is, Judaism, does not involve coercion yet he goes further in making the remarkable claim that punishment is not coercive but rather for the criminal's own sake. As Strauss puts it,

"A further consequence [of Cohen's denial that coercion is a principle of law] is that Cohen must understand punishment, not in terms of the protection of society or other considerations which may be thought to regard the criminal not as 'an end in himself' and only as a means, but in terms of the self-betterment of the criminal alone."[52] Put back into Cover's terms, Anglo-American legal theory's basic presuppositions are in keeping with the neo-Kantian denial that coercion is a principle of law.

Broadly speaking, Cover would seem to share with Strauss not only the basic contention that it is necessary to acknowledge that coercion is an undeniable aspect of law but also the conclusion that this doesn't mean that law is reducible to power. As Cover argues, all legal systems must be understood in the context of a broader narrative story:

No set of legal institutions or prescriptions exists apart from narratives that locate it and give it meaning. For every constitution there is an epic, for each decalogue a scripture. Once understood in the context of the narratives that give it meaning, law becomes not merely a system of rules to be observed, but a world in which we live.[53]

Although Strauss does not, as Cover does, speak of law as "narrative," Strauss's notion of Jewish law, it should be clear, is intimately tied to the theological narrative that the Jewish tradition tells about the one God who has revealed himself to humanity by way of the people of Israel. Furthermore, law, for Strauss, is not a mere set of rules but it is the prephilosophic life world in which individuals find themselves.[54]

Based on their two basic shared claims about law – that much of modern legal theory is predicated on a denial of the coercive element of law and that law cannot be understood outside of broader interpretive frameworks – Cover's thought might seem from the perspective of Strauss's thought an important antidote to much of modern legal theory. But the opposite is the case. Remarkably, for all his emphasis on the necessity of acknowledging the coercive possibilities of law and the broader interpretive frameworks intrinsic to any legal system, Cover denies precisely both of these when it come to his discussion of Jewish law. While there are a growing number of American legal theorists (and literary theorists) who understand Jewish law as neither theological nor political, Cover may be unique in making such a claim in the context of his attempt otherwise to show the intimate connections between narrative, nomos, and violence.

In his posthumously published "Obligation: A Jewish Jurisprudence of the Social Order," Cover contrasts what he calls a jurisprudence of obligation, which he claims the Jewish tradition exemplifies, with a jurisprudence of rights, which he claims modern political liberalism exemplifies.[55] In Stone's succinct summary of Cover's position:

Rights theory, Cover asserted, has exhibited a marked propensity for violence throughout its long history. Rooted in the 'myth' of the social contract, rights theory begins with the premise that individuals are free, autonomous, and discrete subjects, who surrender some of their rights to achieve collective goals, such as security. When linked with Hobbesian political theories of liberalism, this radical 'myth of individualism' sets in motion a 'monstrous and powerful collective engine,' the national state, 'with its almost unique mastery of violence.' By contrast, Cover asserted, the Jewish jurisprudence of duty has evolved for nearly two millennia independent of an autonomous state or other hierarchical authority. In the absence of external institutions compelling obedience to the law, the internal structure of law itself must promote adherence. The 'common, mutual, reciprocal obligation' at the center of law makes possible continued adherence to the law without resort to violence.[56]

There is much to be said about Cover's analysis, both in terms of his perception of modern political theory and rabbinic hermeneutics, but for the purposes of this chapter I focus broadly on Cover's assumptions about the rabbinic political and theological realities. In so doing, I follow Stone's general analysis, which I consider within the parameters of Strauss's thought.

Stone offers her criticism of Cover from two perspectives, one which she calls an external analysis, and the other which she calls an internal analysis. The former refers to the historical and literary context of rabbinic texts, while the latter refers to the internal, self-understanding of the rabbinic tradition. This dual approach, I would suggest, is consistent with Strauss's claim about Jewish law, which, I have argued, operates both as, in Stone's terms, an external historical and political analysis and as an internal theological analysis. In the conclusion of this chapter, I turn briefly to methodological implications of this approach for contemporary Jewish thought.

Returning to Stone's analysis of Cover, Stone shows that on both counts (external and internal) Cover's claims are highly problematic. To begin with, the notion that premodern Jewish society, governing itself according to halakhah while adhering to the laws of an external host society, was not political or coercive is simply inaccurate. Rabbinic authorities authorized not only corporeal punishment but more importantly and more dominantly social sanctions against those members of the community who did not conform to the law.[57] At the same time, "the ever-present coercive shadow of divine accountability" is intrinsic to the halakhic framework. This is the reason, for instance, that Maimonides includes belief in reward and punishment as one of his thirteen principles of faith.[58]

I would add to Stone's basic yet incisive points that while Jewish orthodoxy in the modern era may not have the authority to extend physical punishments to its members, and while the power of social sanctions within a society in which religious affiliation is a matter of voluntary association is by definition lessened, we should not underestimate the social coercion intrinsic to Jewish orthodoxy, or to any communal orthodoxy predicated on adherence to laws. Because adherence to the law is largely, though not entirely, a public matter, coercion in the form of shame and the possibility of social ostracization is a matter of fact in the most liberal of Jewish orthodoxies. So too, social pressure is intrinsic to *any* sort of communal and moral life. As Strauss quotes Nietzsche to make this point, the human being "is 'the beast with red cheeks,' the only being possessing a sense of shame."[59] For Strauss, self-respect, which is tied to the uniquely human quality of shame, cannot be separated from law: "Since there is a necessary connection between morality (how a man should live) and law, there is a necessary connection between the dignity of man and the dignity of the political order: the political is *sui generic* and cannot be understood as derivative from the subpolitical."[60] That Cover, in his analysis of Jewish jurisprudence, doesn't recognize this bespeaks the depth of his utopian vision of not just Jewish society, but of human society more generally.

But more damaging to Cover's claims is Stone's penetrating analysis of the internal point of view of rabbinic culture. It has become commonplace among academics to argue that rabbinic culture recognizes a plurality of voices and is egalitarian in so doing.[61] But this is a fundamental misreading of rabbinic texts – understood on their own terms – and at the same time indicative of attempts by modern scholars to understand Jewish law and legal discussions as devoid of not just political but also theological reality. Once again Strauss's comment in *Philosophy and Law* that "The necessary connection between politics and theology (metaphysics) . . . does not have to lose sight of the metaphysical problems that stand in the foreground. . . . If, on the other hand, one begins from the metaphysical problems, one misses, as the history of the inquiry to date clearly shows, the political problem" is particularly apt. Appreciating the political context of rabbinic discussion allows us to recognize the theological presuppositions of this discourse.

Notably, Stone points out, contemporary authors arguing for the pluralistic, egalitarian view of rabbinic culture often choose the same text to make their point.[62] This is the now famous *Oven of Akhnai* story from the Babylonian Talmud, Baba Metzia 59b. The story concerns a rabbinic discussion about the ritual status of an oven. A first-century rabbi, Rabbi Eliezer ben Hyrkanos, claimed that the oven was not unclean, while the sages claimed that it was. To prove his point, Rabbi Eliezar, after presenting a series of signs to support his view, invoked heaven by stating "If the halakhah agrees with me, let heaven be the proof" to which a heavenly voice responded "How dare you oppose Rabbi Eliezer, whose views are everywhere halakhah?" Yet despite this irrefutable proof, Rabbi Joshua responded, quoting Deuteronomy 30:13, "It is not in Heaven." The story concludes with Rabbi Jeremiah, a fourth-century sage, stating "we pay no attention to a heavenly voice for God already wrote in the Torah at Mount Sinai (Exodus 23:2): 'You must follow the majority.'" Stone points out that the literary context and reception of this story in rabbinic culture is far more complex than contemporary readers appreciate. Yet more telling, for the purposes of our discussion in this chapter, is Stone's reversal of the basic assumption shared by contemporary legal and literary scholars that this story, and rabbinic culture more generally, is antiauthoritarian. Drawing on a wide range of sources, Stone points out that the rejection of Rabbi Eliezar's opinion (an action that is treated with a great deal of ambivalence by the Talmud) reflects a first-century attempt of a group of rabbis, gathered at *Yavneh* after the destruction of the second Temple to assert their authority against older authorities, one of which Rabbi Eliezar represented. Rather than reflecting a fluid, pluralistic, nonhierarchical notion of authority, legal meaning in rabbinic culture "is upheld ... solely through the institutional hierarchy of a professional community of interpreters, which exercises the authority to decide and whose consensus determines both meaning and behavior. Correctness in interpretation is thus a product of the authority of the interpreters."[63]

Cover, or a range of scholars who share the pluralistic, egalitarian view of rabbinic culture, might object to this argument by claiming that it is wholly historicist and does not reflect the ethical underpinnings of rabbinic discourse. Such, for instance, might be Levinas's view, which would suggest that the meaning of rabbinic texts comes from the contemporary reader's ethical engagement with these texts, an engagement that mirrors the true and original meaning of the text. From Levinas's perspective, situating rabbinic texts within their historical context would confirm a Hobbesian view of society that, he might claim, rabbinic discourse seeks to overcome. The argument between what I am describing as Levinas and Cover's position against the historical and textual analysis provided by Stone would seem to be at a standstill. Recourse to historical and literary analysis would, at least for Levinas if not for Cover, conform to the notion that historicism and, to use Cover's categories, a rights-based morality go together. Both articulate a violent view of human relations that a truly Jewish jurisprudence seeks to overcome.

The objection that I am ascribing to Levinas and Cover reflects the way in which both of their thoughts cohere philosophically with the paradigm of modern Jewish thought described in Section 9.2 that, following Kant's division between a "*juridico-civil* condition" and an "ethico-civil" condition, can only understand coercion and law in terms of an either/or situation. In Cover's case this is particularly ironic in that he seeks to overcome neo-Kantian notions of law. In Levinas's case this is ironic because he claims that his philosophy is profoundly antiutopian and he describes his antiutopian vision not only with reference to the Bible but to a biblical (and hence rabbinic[64]) conception of law. Let us recall again Levinas's comments that:

The Bible does not begin the building of an ideal city in a void.... To recognize the necessity of a law is to recognize that humanity cannot be served by at once magically denying its condition. The faith that moves mountains and conceives of a world without slaves immediately transports itself to utopia.... The man of utopia wishes unjustly. Instead of the difficult task of living an equitable life, he prefers the joy of solitary salvation.[65]

Levinas seems to share Strauss's view that "[t]he clean solutions of which people dream and dreamt have led either to nothing, or to a much greater bestiality than the uneasy solutions with which sensible people will always be satisfied."[66]

Yet Levinas's philosophy, at its most basic, is predicated on nothing other than a desire to bracket out from coercion and violence a sphere of morality that remains pure, if even for a moment. Does not Levinas's philosophical scheme merely restate, in different terms, Kant's fundamental distinction between a "*juridico-civil* (political) condition" and an "*ethico-civil* condition"? Is not the face-to-face relation a desire for "the joy of solitary salvation"? Levinas, of course, claims that it is not the case because the ethical relation is always concerned with what he calls "the third," or "with justice." It is questionable whether Levinas, on his own philosophical terms, can sustain notions of justice and law. What is less questionable, however, is the utopianism that imbues Levinas's description of *Jewish* law. As Levinas puts it "Judaism is humanity on the brink of morality without institutions."[67] Jewish law, far from reflecting the outer structure of communal and political life, is for Levinas the inner meaning not only of Judaism but of civilization and humanity as well:

But that condition, in which human morality returns after so many centuries as to its womb, attests, with a very old testament, its origin on the hither side of civilizations. Civilizations made possible, called for, brought about, hailed and blessed by that morality – which can, however, for its part, only know and justify itself in the fragility of the conscience, in the 'four cubits of the *Halakhah*," in that precarious, divine abode.[68]

Before proceeding, it is important to consider a potential objection from Cover and Levinas to the preceding descriptions of their positions. Were Cover and Levinas to concede all the preceding points, including their share in perpetuating the neo-Kantian thought they both seek to overcome, might they not justly reply that given the alternatives of reading the rabbis historically or ethically, that they simply prefer the latter. Their shared effort, then, is in developing a contemporary model of ethical and legal discourse. This objection may seem compelling, but to respond to it, it is first necessary to note another implication of the fact that the position Cover and Levinas may want to defend is based on the Kantian dichotomy between violence and coercion on the one hand and, on the other hand, a peaceable ethical moment that is predicated on not being this sphere of violence. Beginning with Kant, such a dichotomy is possible only on the basis of rejecting the notion that theology properly understood concerns God and that only within the presupposition of divine reality does theology concern morality. The Kantian legacy, which both Levinas and Cover share in this respect, refuses to acknowledge the possibility of any kind of theological reality that is not directly translatable into ethics. Yet Stone's analysis of rabbinic authority shows not only that it is other than pluralistic and nonhierarchical from an historical point of view, but as importantly, nonpluralist or nonhierarchical from a *theological* point of view. The criterion for rabbinic authority *understood on its own terms* does not concern a power struggle but rather religious knowledge and *piety*. As Stone notes, the Talmud often characterizes the rabbinic sage as "a living Torah."[69] While Thomas Hobbes or Michel Foucault may refuse this interpretation, Levinas and Cover do not have this luxury precisely because their philosophies are premised on an attempt to overcome the reduction of human relations to power.

The implication of a more internally coherent notion of rabbinic authority for contemporary legal, literary, and in the case of Levinas, ethical appropriations of rabbinic texts is telling. In Stone's analysis:

Rabbinic interpretation is thus the very opposite of positing God's absence and substituting the discursive community. God is always present through his Torah. In turn, the authority of the discursive community to proclaim the law ultimately is rooted in the purity of intent of those who perceive their task as a continuing pursuit of God's will. Thus, it may be precisely the *religious* mindset that accounts for the particular way of looking at the normative world that contemporary theorists have found so attractive.[70]

Stone's question for Cover is whether American constitutional theory can or should provide "an adequate substitute for God's partnership."[71] Within the context of American legal theory, Stone offers good reason to be wary of such an aspiration. Our question for Levinas in the context of our discussion of Jewish law is whether ethics can provide an adequate substitute for God's partnership? Levinas, of course, thinks it can and does. But, as Levinas would acknowledge, this comes at the cost of denying the possibility of a theological reality that directs ethical life. But as I have argued especially in the last three chapters, Levinas's denial of the possibility of a theological reality coupled with his simultaneous employment of theological categories in making his claims about ethics results in a rationally untenable ethics and politics. While the implications of Cover's vision of politics may be described as naively utopian, the implications of Levinas's politics are equally utopian, but also more disturbing because Levinas does not even recognize communal norms, or nomos, as a criterion for rational judgment.

At the same time, because his ethical philosophy is predicated on a denial of a theological reality, Levinas's thought in no way offers a modern Jewish justification for the observance of Jewish law. While Levinas's thought has increasingly been taken as a viable articulation of Jewish thought, his denial of a theological reality that defines Judaism is in marked contrast to Strauss's claim that, if we understand the (rabbinic) tradition as it understands itself, law and faith, or politics and theology, cannot be separated.[72] Levinas not only separates politics and theology in his articulation of a contemporary Jewish thought but he denies the political and the theological dimensions of Judaism in his ethical interpretations and readings of rabbinic texts. In contrast, while Strauss honestly confesses his inability to believe in the God of Judaism, he nevertheless respects the integrity of the tradition by insisting on the continual and complex interplay between theology and politics in Judaism.[73]

9.4. THE CHALLENGE OF CONTEMPORARY JEWISH THOUGHT

The challenge that Stone's analysis brings to Cover parallels in important ways the challenge that Strauss brings to Guttmann and to modern Jewish thought (including Levinas) more generally. Levinas, Cover, and Guttmann may, of course, describe the Jewish tradition in any way they like (as may anyone). Yet they defeat their own purposes, on their own terms, in claiming continuity between their constructions of Judaism and the tradition itself. Remaining heir to *Wissenschaft des Judentums*, Guttmann, in his criticism of Strauss, values historical truth, but in doing so weakens his own claims for philosophical continuity with the tradition by not recognizing the ways in which the valorization of history as a final source of truth may ultimately undermine his, or any, claim for the continuity between past and present. Fully recognizing the dangers of valorizing history as a source of truth for the timeless claims of philosophy, Levinas disavows a historical interest in Judaism and yet he claims at the same time that his interpretation of Judaism is the true and even originary one.[74] Levinas's twin and irreconcilable claims in this regard are particularly ironic and telling. In the context of a philosophy and ethics of the "other," Levinas does not recognize the "otherness" of the Jewish tradition. From an ethical perspective, rather than remaking the other or the tradition in one's own image (and in Levinas's case in the image of his ethical philosophy), is it not better to admit honestly that an impasse may exist?

As is the case with Mordecai Kaplan, mentioned in Section 9.2, there have been and are many Jewish theological affirmations of the perceived impasse that modernity brings to Jewish thought and life. Strauss would affirm such positions for their honesty, even if Strauss would find these theological responses significantly wanting. But such evaluation is, of course, a matter for debate.

Yet the position Strauss stakes out, I would suggest, may not only offer important challenges to modern Jewish thought but also may point a way (not chosen by Strauss) for constructive Jewish thought. As I argued in Section 9.2, Strauss in many ways extends arguments made by Franz Rosenzweig. While some will no doubt continue to find Strauss's formulations and criticism of modern Jewish thought overly formalistic, his appreciation and criticism of Rosenzweig may have important and indeed surprising resonances with a current trend in American Jewish thought, which represents itself with the label "postcritical."[75] Here it is helpful to quote Strauss's own clarification of what he might mean by Jewish orthodoxy:

When I say 'the Jewish faith as our ancestors held it,' I do not mean that every particular belief (even if entertained by the majority of Jews, or the large majority of Jews, for centuries) must necessarily be binding. I happen to know a bit of the Jewish medieval thinkers, and I know that quite a few very powerful and important changes were made by them. I believe – and I say this without any disrespect for any orthodox Jew – that it is hard for people, for most Jews today, to believe in verbal inspiration (I mean in verbal inspiration of the Torah), and in the miracles – or most of the miracles – and other things. I know that. My friend Rabbi Harris is not here, but I am in deep sympathy with what he means by a 'postcritical Judaism.' I think that it offers a perfectly legitimate and sensible goal, namely, to restate the essence of Jewish faith in a way which is by no means literally identical with, say, Rambam's 'Creator of the world,' or with something of this kind – I mean, with any traditional statement or principles. That is not the point. But a Judaism which is not belief in the 'Creator of the word,' that has problems running through it.[76]

Like Rosenzweig, Strauss emphasizes the vibrant prephilosophical life world of Jewish life and texts, one that is subject to historical change, but whose essential theological cohesiveness is found in the living relationship with the divine.[77] Where Strauss departs from Rosenzweig and some of his contemporary followers is in insisting that Jewish texts and not the Jewish people are the prime locus of revelation and create the standard for theological reflection. (Or better, perhaps, that the Jewish people are only a locus of revelation in connection with the Torah.[78])

Finally, Strauss's contribution to current debates in modern Jewish thought may also be important from a methodological point of view. For good reason, much has been made of the ambiguous status of history and historiography in modern Jewish Studies. Yet after the waning of the neo-Kantian models of Guttmann and Cohen, less attention has been paid to the role of history in Jewish philosophical analysis, with the prevailing assumption being that an acknowledgement of the historicity of the tradition by definition undercuts any attempt to articulate its true meaning.[79] Strauss's value as a constructive thinker of modern Judaism may be in placing the burden of proof onto a wholly historicist account of Judaism. Simply put, can history not be used as a tool to move, in Strauss's words, out of the second cave of modernity into the possibility of appreciating traditional Jewish texts on their own terms? Just as Strauss argues that the philosophical possibility of divine revelation only requires that it not be absolutely refuted, so too the possibility of transhistorical truth only requires that history not necessarily be the final truth. And how, on its own terms, that is on the premise that modern historiography like everything else is a historical phenomenon, can the study of history lay claim to such a status?[80]

10

◌

Concluding Thoughts: Progress or Return?

*T*HE PORTRAIT OF STRAUSS PAINTED IN THE PAGES OF THIS BOOK
is not likely to be one that will be satisfying to many of those who
call themselves "Straussians" nor to many of those who have great antipathy
for Straussians. If this is the case, this study will have been in some sense
successful. This isn't to suggest that the preceding pages and arguments are
not open to challenge. I am sure that they are and I hope that they will be
challenged for the sake of further argument not only about Strauss but about
the kinds of questions that he poses to contemporary thinkers. But beyond
particular disagreements, Strauss's thought should be dissatisfying to those
who seek definitive answers to large philosophical and political questions.
And what Strauss's many admirers and enemies have in common is precisely
the belief that definitive answers are available. The enduring importance of
Strauss's thought, however, lies in the questions he poses, and not in any of
the answers he might seem to provide.

Strauss's intellectual aim was to question contemporary dogmas, including
first and foremost the commonplace views that all truth is a matter of historical
circumstance and that we cannot talk about human nature. On neither issue,
however, does Strauss provide a definitive counterargument, that is, that there
is transhistorical truth or that there *is* a human nature. Instead, his contention
is that the cases against transhistorical truth and human nature have not
been made definitively. Perhaps most profoundly in the context of this study,
Strauss maintains that one of the deepest intellectual prejudices of modern
western life, and particularly modern academic life, is the belief that biblical
revelation has been refuted for once and for all. While we have no reason to
believe that Strauss was a believer in biblical revelation, I have argued that his
claims provide a far more compelling starting point for anyone interested in
defending a rational belief in revelation than most contemporary religiously
motivated defenses of revelation do.

None of this is to argue, however, that Strauss's positions are the correct ones, or even fully adequate by the criteria he posits. As we have seen throughout these pages the basis of Strauss's thought is a questioning of "the notion of a guaranteed parallelism between intellectual and social progress."[1] Even with, or perhaps because of, his emphasis on the comedic aspects of Plato's dialogues, Strauss's view of this human predicament, that is, the lack of parallelism between intellectual and social progress, is in an important sense tragic.[2] As Robert Pippin has described it, for Strauss the implications of the human predicament mean that "the chief political virtue is moderation, the chief vice, idealism; the central modern folly: the promise that philosophy can play a public role, that by understanding ourselves as we truly are ... we will also be able to establish peace, conquer *fortuna*, rationally coordinate the pursuit of private ends in a public realm, achieve a social order and rule of law held together, defended, and reproduced by appeal to reason."[3] This characterization is helpful, I suggest, first for appreciating what I maintain is Strauss's enduring value as a thinker (as well as, therefore, for pinpointing the key issue upon which critics of Strauss ought to focus) and second for recognizing some of the strangeness, if not absurdity, of contemporary claims about Strauss's role in current American political policy. Let us turn first to what I argue is and is not Strauss's enduring legacy and then to current claims about Strauss and American foreign policy. After considering these two points, I turn finally to the question of Strauss's relation to political modernity beyond current, partisan debates.

10.1. STRAUSS'S PHILOSOPHICAL LEGACY

It is not difficult, though it remains important, to raise objections to the particularities of Strauss's historical and analytic framework, from the perspectives of both "modernity" and "Judaism." In terms of the former, Pippin has argued perhaps most persuasively that Strauss's view of the development of modernity does not sufficiently account for "potential safe stops" on the road to modernity generally, and for Rousseau's conception of positive freedom more particularly.[4] Philosophically this means, Pippin maintains, that Strauss can only beg the question of "the natural order of things," or the question of the human as human. As Pippin puts it, Strauss's "solution involves denying that a teleological understanding of ourselves and of nature is a direct competitor with non-teleological accounts, that they are not answers to the same question, and that each question, understood properly in its own domain, is a legitimate one. Strauss himself suggests this solution in language that seems to reflect his debt to Husserl and Heidegger. . . . However, unless we are willing to accept something like Husserl's methodology, with its suspensions, bracketing, and reductions, such a strategy will still not uncover, and would make much more dubious, any notion of a distinctive, 'natural' point of view."[5]

I agree with Pippin's analysis and would suggest that a similar analysis can be made with respect to Strauss's positive contribution to modern Jewish thought. Nevertheless, in my view the practical and theoretical shortcomings of his thought are something of which Strauss is not only aware but emphasizes. Strauss does beg the question of nature, just as he begs the question of historicism, and just as I suggest now, he begs the question of "Jewish rationalism." As he puts it, "the evidence of all solutions is necessarily smaller than the evidence of the problems."[6] Strauss's thought is limited not only from a practical point of view, but also from the point of view of theoretical solutions. But, I suggest, this is essentially its value. To appreciate this, let us adumbrate more fully the practical limitations of his thought (by which I mean Strauss's conscious inability to provide solutions, including theoretical ones) for contemporary Judaism.

Just as Strauss ultimately begs the question of a "distinctive, natural point of view," so too he ultimately begs the question of the framework of the Jewish rationalism to which he seems to point. I have argued that Strauss's claim is that only biblical revelation can provide the possibility of a universal morality. Yet from the point of view of Jewish thought and indeed from the point of view of what Strauss maintains are the proper parameters of Jewish thought, this is a very thin definition, that is, biblical morality is at once too particular and too universal. It is too particular because there is nothing essentially "Jewish" about it, as opposed to "Christian" or even, perhaps, "Islamic," so why call it "Jewish"? At the same time, and for the same reason, from the point of view of Jewish thought, it is too universal. In other words, what is the positive and unique content of Judaism for Strauss?

Just as Pippin points to Strauss's debt to Husserl particularly in formulating his conception of nature, it is also possible to point to Strauss's debt to Hermann Cohen in formulating his conception of a Jewish rationalism. And while Strauss's refusal to accept Husserl's methodology accounts for the formalism and perhaps emptiness of his conception of nature, so too Strauss's refusal to accept Cohen's methodology accounts for the formalism and perhaps emptiness of his conception of Jewish rationalism. Put another way, while both Husserl and Cohen would have recourse, on their own terms, to a more positive content of "nature" and "Jewish rationalism," Strauss loses precisely such recourse in rejecting these two forms of neo-Kantianism precisely because of their, in Strauss's view, overinflated conceptions of the possibilities of philosophy.

Yet in the context of Judaism, perhaps the most important question for Strauss would be to ask which contemporary Jewish people would be convinced by his construction of Jewish rationalism. As we have seen throughout this book, for Strauss the tension between philosophy and law is a productive one. Jewish law provides a prephilosophical context for philosophy, while philosophy provides critical judgment for considerations of law (but not the grounding of law). In the context of contemporary Jewish life the question is twofold. First, Strauss's brand of Jewish thought offers no reasons for nonbelievers to believe and thus to adhere to the law. Exempting those who already follow Jewish law, Strauss provides no theoretical impetus for anyone to do so. This is, of course, definitional for Strauss in that philosophy simply *cannot* provide *ultimate reasons* for belief and action (and even for belief in philosophy, which is the living of the philosophical life). What Strauss's model does provide is the possibility of inducing nonbelievers to respect Jewish law and religion as worthy conversation partners for people. In this important sense it is not a coincidence that this is precisely the position that many followers of Strauss take: they are not religiously observant but they have a genuine respect for Judaism qua Judaism.[7] This in itself is not a problem, and perhaps it is even admirable, but it does point to the practical limitations of Strauss's religious thought. But again this is a point well acknowledged and defended by Strauss.

We can see the practical limitation of Strauss's religious thought from the other side as well. With a couple of notable exceptions Jewish orthodoxy over the last century has not engaged with philosophy. While the reasons for this are no doubt complicated, it seems fair to say that there is not, for the most part, a popular Jewish orthodox interest in philosophical activity, while there is no shortage of intellectual interest, for instance, in the sciences. From the point of view of Strauss's thought, this is an unfortunate situation that deprives orthodox Jewry a critical rationalism that is its proper inheritance. But it is bad for Judaism as well because it too, like any belief system, quickly becomes immoderate without self-critical intervention. On this point Strauss is once again heir to Hermann Cohen who attempted, perhaps more than any other modern Jewish thinker, to move away from an ethno-cultural view of Judaism – even in orthodox circles – by way of philosophical thinking.

From the point of view of Strauss's own well-known question "Progress or Return?" it would seem that the answer for him is "neither." Whereas Cohen favored the former and Rosenzweig the latter, Strauss chooses neither. Strauss plainly states that "[o]nly we living today can possibly find a solution to the problems of today. But an adequate understanding of the principles as elaborated by the classics may be the indispensable starting point for an adequate analysis, to be achieved by us, of present-day society in its peculiar character, and for the wise application, to be achieved by us, of these principles to our tasks."[8] But the relation between today and the past – progress and return – remains, in the final analysis, unresolved. Some, friends and enemies of Strauss alike, may see this as an indictment of Strauss, but I would suggest that his strength as a thinker, indeed as a philosopher, is found here. For Strauss, the question of progress or return is a question that cannot be answered fully, at least in theoretical terms. But there are practical solutions and there is always the need for human action. Yet any solution comes with a cost.[9] Strauss's contribution to contemporary Jewish thought, in my view, is his ability to point out the costs of various solutions, an awareness or acknowledgment of which is largely absent in contemporary Jewish life. And Strauss's enduring importance as a thinker more generally is precisely his insistence on considering fully the implications and meanings of different practical solutions.

Strauss's achievement as a thinker is his insistence that there are real human problems that perhaps cannot be answered definitively. I say "achievement" because the only way to refute Strauss in a definitive sense would be to deny that there may be permanent human problems. And as he suggests, this denial is a solution of sorts. It may well be possible to dispute many of Strauss's readings of particular philosophical texts or many of the details of his history of modernity, but it is more difficult to evade his questions. The same goes for those interested in or committed to Judaism or Christianity in the modern world. There is no doubt that it is possible to argue with aspects of Strauss's descriptions of both. Yet in both cases, Strauss raises a fundamental challenge. In the case of Judaism, the question is whether the modern dissolution of the theological-political dimension of Jewish life brings a fundamental break with the Jewish past. The implications of such a break remain open to question, of course.[10] In the case of Christianity, the question is whether, for Christians critical of modernity, aspects of Christianity's historic theological rejection of the law contributed to the very modernity that they would like to transcend.[11] Christians may, of course, challenge Strauss's very understanding of Christianity. Yet whatever one's final judgment as to Strauss's view of Judaism or Christianity, or both, Strauss's analysis of the conundrums faced by modern Jews and Christians remains, I would contend, relevant. And engaging these conundrums, whatever the outcome, is an opportunity for those who care deeply about these issues not only to reflect critically on what may be their unthinking assumptions but also to strengthen their own views by recognizing, and addressing the weaknesses in their positions.[12]

Pippin's engagement with Strauss is exemplary because he considers Strauss on his own terms. But even Pippin, as he would surely admit, has not dispensed with the very questions that Strauss asks about modernity, which, among other things, includes the desirability of the modern conceptions of freedom, a question that restates what Strauss claims is *the* philosophical question, which is: what is the best life?[13] This is not a question with an easy answer or, better, this is a question with many answers. As one perhaps unlikely student of Strauss has put it in an essay aptly titled "A Student of Leo Strauss in the Clinton Administration": "From a legal/political point, thought enjoys unprecedented freedom in liberal democracies. But liberal democratic society tends to deprive philosophy (and culture in general) of depth and significance. . . . It is all too easy to see speech – philosophy, literature, cultural criticism – as a right without responsibilities, or a play without consequences."[14] It should go without saying that recognizing or even considering this criticism of liberal democracy is in no way an endorsement of a "brutal and repressive political order."[15]

Before turning briefly to the contemporary political controversy that encircles Strauss, it is important to point out that many if not most of the participants in the academic disputes that surround Strauss do not provide arguments for their dislike of what they take to be Strauss's ideas. Instead, many simply object to Strauss on the basis of what they take to be democratic or liberal concerns. For example, Shadia Drury, perhaps Strauss's most devoted critic, offers almost no argument against Strauss but seems to believe instead that by showing that Strauss was at best highly suspicious of liberal democracy that he ought to be discredited. The question of Strauss's stance on liberal democracy is obviously an important topic, but one beyond the scope of this book. Nevertheless, two points ought to be noted. First, at a very minimum there is a debate to be had about Strauss's relation to liberal democracy, as a number of scholars have argued.[16] Second, and perhaps more importantly, definitions of liberal democracy are fluid and up for grabs. Even if Strauss were shown to be a critic of various aspects of liberal democracy, this would in no way automatically remove him from the parameters of debates about and defenses of liberal democracy.[17]

Yet more basically than these two points, the lack of engagement and argument with Strauss's contentions reflects the very prejudice that Strauss seeks to expose in modern intellectual life, which is the dogmatic view that the important questions about human life have been settled once and for all or, what amounts to the same thing, are irrelevant. Strauss's interest in and respect for premodern thought revolves around his contention that despite contemporary academic prejudice, premodern thought is fundamentally antidogmatic, while contemporary thought is dogmatic. On the one hand, Strauss did view the human predicament as tragic in that there will never be, according to him, the "full reconciliation among fellow citizens."[18] Yet Strauss was not an advocate of tragic resignation but rather of dispelling what he took to be human fantasy. At the same time, he did not see his view as the only one but affirmed that there were formidable opponents to the Platonic philosophical position, including first and foremost religion and poetry.

As Strauss saw, these points are not only of academic or intellectual interest. They are also politically relevant. Perhaps one of the more important features of Strauss's thought for contemporary purposes is that we fool ourselves, to our own detriment, by blindly believing our own pieties rather than asking ourselves whether we can rationally defend our beliefs or not. The relevance of Levinas's thought to contemporary political concerns lies here as well. While Levinas and many of his followers believe that his thought advocates a respect and claim for the necessity of justice, I have argued in this book that these claims simply cannot be sustained on Levinas's own terms. I have no doubt that Levinas and many of his sympathizers make a claim for justice only with the best of intentions. But good intentions are not enough and in the end, as Strauss shows especially in the case of modern defenses of religion, only weaken our capacity for critical judgment.

10.2. AGAINST CONTEMPORARY APPROPRIATIONS OF STRAUSS

None of this is to deny that Strauss's thought can be used for political purposes or that people have used Strauss's thought for political purposes. But it is difficult if not profoundly dubious to posit a direct link between Strauss's thought and contemporary public policy, including first and foremost the war with Iraq. I do not know what Strauss would have said about Iraq (and neither does anyone else), but far more importantly from the perspective of Strauss's thought, this would not have mattered. Strauss's theory of reading is precisely that: it concerns written texts, not private communications. It is true that these written texts are concerned with the question of the best regime, as William Kristol and Steven Lenzner have recently noted, and a point upon which their critics have quickly picked up, but this seems a rather general claim that anyone impressed with Aristotle might make. It hardly seems to imply an endorsement of George W. Bush's actions in Iraq.[19] At the same time, it is highly questionable whether Strauss, for whom, as Pippin puts it, "the chief political virtue is moderation, the chief vice, idealism," can be said to be the intellectual godfather of the war with Iraq. Perhaps most telling in this context of George W. Bush's particular political views and policies, Strauss also maintained strongly that one cannot love a country, including the United

States of America, as one loves God. The love of God for Strauss cannot in any way be equated with love of country. In his words:

It is very far from me to minimize the difference between a nation conceived in liberty and dedicated to the proposition that all men are created equal, and the nations of the old world, which certainly were not conceived in liberty. I share the hope for America and faith in America, but I am compelled to add that the faith and that hope cannot be of the same character as that faith and that hope which a Jew has in regard to Judaism and which the Christian has in regard to Christianity. No one claims that the faith in America and the hope for America is based on explicit divine promises.[20]

Finally, in the context of contemporary debates about the Bush administration's policies on Iraq and the Middle East more generally, it is important to underscore the irony that Strauss was devoted to revitalizing Islamic philosophy, in direct opposition to Christian thought, for the very sake of the future of western civilization.

Still, this doesn't mean that neo-conservatives have no right or reason to admire Strauss as they do, but only that from this very brief discussion the blatant and immediate conceptual link, not even to speak of a policy link, is in no way obvious. It should be noted that for the most part it is not the neo-conservatives who posit a direct policy link between their views and Strauss but their enemies who do so. Nevertheless, if neo-conservatives find Strauss inspirational, there is nothing wrong with this in and of itself. As Jonathan Lear put it in a letter to the New York Times, there is no difference between liberal politicians in Washington relying on John Rawls and conservative politicians in Washington relying on Leo Strauss.[21] I would add that in both cases if one were interested in the question of whether politicians get Rawls or Strauss right, one ought to read Rawls or Strauss and then decide.

It is here that the importance of Strauss for both current political and academic discussions converges. In Strauss's words, "one cannot refute what one has not thoroughly understood."[22] But the point here, I would argue, goes far beyond, and is far more important, than an endorsement or criticism of Rawls or Strauss. Strauss's constructive contribution to current political debates may well be to remind us that we cannot defeat our enemies without understanding them on their own terms. Just as Strauss in 1941 bravely considered that what he called German nihilism might have a moral motivation, so too it might behoove us to consider the intellectual motivations of Islamic fundamentalism, taken on its own terms. Understanding does *not* require belief. To consider Islamic fundamentalism on its own terms is not to defend it but to understand it precisely so we may defeat it. Practically and philosophically, we do ourselves and humanity a great disservice by not taking seriously views that we may hold repulsive. To draw on Levinas's terminology, though perhaps not on his intentions, our own humanity is at stake in recognizing the other not on our own terms, but on the other's.

10.3. IS MODERNITY WORTH DEFENDING?

All of this said, there still remain a number of important objections to the picture of Strauss that I have described in this book. One question that still must be raised, especially in the contemporary context of what only seems to be the global rise of religious fundamentalism and calls for theocratic politics (both abroad and in the United States), is whether the picture of Strauss that I have presented in this book does not, ironically enough, make Strauss into a kind of theocrat? I have argued that Strauss maintains strongly that politics requires religion precisely for the moral grounding that it uniquely brings. And I have also argued that Strauss considers any conception of politics without religion to be morally debased and ultimately nihilistic. Have I perhaps unwittingly turned Strauss into a friend of the Ayatollahs? Are "the politics of revelation" then merely a vehicle for all sorts of authoritarianism? Put into less alarmist terms, while I stated before that Strauss teaches us today that we must understand Islamic fundamentalism to defeat it, on what grounds should Islamic fundamentalism – on Strauss's view – be not simply understood but defeated? Why is modernity worth defending, if it is?

To respond to these important and serious objections, it is necessary to turn one last time to Strauss's understanding of the interconnection between rationalism and skepticism. As I have argued throughout this book, Strauss's skepticism is one that is also skeptical of itself. It is precisely here that we find Strauss's intellectual defense of religion. But Strauss also maintains that people with religious convictions and certainly theologians ought to be skeptical about their own abilities to make absolute claims about God's revelation. Indeed, according to Strauss, the modern critique of religion is premised on the denial of skeptical arguments within traditional theological discourse. In other words, belief is belief because it can never, by definition, attain epistemological certainty. The tension between philosophy and revealed religion, for Strauss, is double-sided. Philosophy cannot attain epistemological certainty especially as it pertains to matters of universal morality, but *equally so* revealed religion cannot attain epistemological certainty in regard to its belief system. However, this doesn't mean, for Strauss, that neither philosophy nor revealed religion can make reasonable or rational claims. His point is that philosophy and revealed religion become reasonable or rational precisely when they recognize their inherent limitations vis-à-vis one another. The dialogue and continued tension between philosophy and revealed religion (but not their ultimate synthesis) provides both with the demand to *justify rationally* their own positions.

In this study, I have highlighted the implications of this skeptical framework in Strauss's thought for what I have argued are the resources for a rational defense of religion over and against the implications of this framework for limiting the fanatical claims made by religion for the simple reason that the former has been particularly unrecognized in most of the extensive (if contradictory) literature on Strauss. Yet the latter is certainly important and follows from the former. Strauss's strength as a contemporary thinker remains, I would argue, that he speaks to both sides of the equation.[23] Yet more than this, Strauss's thought perhaps uniquely accounts for the inability and weakness of modern intellectuals (and twentieth-century intellectuals in particular) to conceive of the enduring power of religious belief, an enduring power that no one could deny today (even if they find it incomprehensible). In this sense, Strauss's thought may well offer nonbelievers a framework for criticizing fanatical religious claims on their own terms.

The bigger problem for Strauss's thought is not then that he may be a friend of the Ayatollahs or of religious fundamentalists (he clearly is not) but whether he can or even wants to defend the intrinsic superiority of *political* modernity (in contradistinction to philosophical modernity) over and against premodern authoritative political systems. Does Strauss on his own terms offer us any resources for making or even supporting such a claim? In an important sense, he has given us good reason to think he does and cannot. Some of Strauss's critics believe that Strauss was so antiliberal as to be in favor of fascist coercion. One such critic has recently quoted the following 1933 letter of Strauss to Löwith:

Just because Germany has turned to the right and has expelled us, it simply does not follow that the principles of the right are therefore to be rejected. To the contrary, only on the basis of principles of the right – fascist, authoritarian, *imperial* – is it possible in a dignified manner, without the ridiculous and pitiful appeal to 'the inalienable rights of man' to protest against the mean nonentity. I read Ceasar's commentary with deep understanding, and I think of Virgil, 'under imperial rule the subjected are spared and the proud are subdued.' There is no reason to crawl to the cross, even to the cross of liberalism, as long as anywhere in the world the spark glimmers of Roman thinking. And moreover, the ghetto is better than any cross.[24]

While there can be no doubt that after the Nazi genocide Strauss's comments are chilling, it is also important to recognize that these comments are written beforehand. Strauss's later thinking attacks the view that authority – and state authority in particular – is defined and legitimated by coercion. In many respects, this is the heart and upshot of his criticism of Weber in *Natural Right and History*. At the same time, even in the context of these remarks Strauss's interest is not in coercion but in what he takes to be the moral consequence of Virgil's comment: the subjected are spared and the proud are subdued, a political and moral value that he maintains modern political philosophy and indeed modern politics have discarded.[25]

Nevertheless, despite these disclaimers, we cannot doubt Strauss's preference for premodern philosophical and political thought and we must therefore press harder for his view of political modernity. Another letter to Löwith may clarify Strauss's position somewhat:

I myself might actually agree with everything Plato and Aristotle demand (but this I tell only you). . . . I assert that the polis – as it has been interpreted by Plato and Aristotle, a surveyable, urban, morally serious (übersichtliche städtische, moralisch-ernste) society, based on an agricultural economy, in which the gentry rule – is morally politically the most pleasing: which still does not mean that I would want to live under such a polis (one must not judge everything according to one's private wishes) – do no forget that Plato and Aristotle preferred democratic Athens as a place to well ordered polises: for philosophy's moral-political considerations are necessarily secondary.[26]

That "philosophy's moral-political considerations are necessarily secondary," according to Strauss's thought, has been one of the central themes of this book. But here, in the conclusion of this book, we must ask whether Strauss's very position that separates philosophy from politics by definition implies that it is philosophically impossible (or dishonest in the sense of what philosophy is) to endorse political modernity from a philosophical point of view? As I argued especially in Chapter 6, the attempt to *justify rationally* American democracy (and by implication any form of democracy, as the quotation from Strauss's letter to Löwith makes clear) on either philosophical or religious grounds is untenable from the point of view of Strauss's thought.

Yet this doesn't mean that there are no political implications that follow from Strauss's decidedly apolitical conception of philosophy. To appreciate the political implications of Strauss's conception of philosophy we must turn one last time to the contours of Strauss's philosophical skepticism. Aryeh Botwinick has articulated perhaps most clearly the implications and parameters of Strauss's conception of skepticism as it pertains to politics. According to Botwinick, a strong case can be made "for reading Strauss as a mitigated skeptic who embraces liberalism precisely for its affinities with mitigated skepticism."[27] Botwinick aims to show the conceptual overlap between Strauss's skepticism and the problems James Madison addresses in *Federalist Number Ten*. I leave aside the more detailed debate about potential philosophical affinities between Strauss's skepticism and the American Founding to focus on Botwinick's more general point:

Strauss aims for what he has called a "rational liberalism" which is to say a liberalism that is completely institutionally aware of the limitations of reason.... The case for democracy in Strauss rests upon the skeptical limitations of philosophical reason. The case for liberalism in Strauss rests upon the implications of reflexivity. Skepticism itself cannot be fully trusted. Liberal brakes on democratic rules are therefore required to ensure that not even a democratic reading of the common good is translated into public policy in its entirety. Ultimately, for Strauss – politics – like knowledge and understanding – represents movement toward a continually receding shore.[28]

We are now able to provide an answer, albeit a limited one, to the question I posed earlier as to the grounds by which, in Strauss's view, Islamic fundamentalism ought to be defeated and not merely understood. Just as I argued that Strauss cannot be said to be an ideological or philosophical friend of the Ayatollahs because he demands skepticism on the part of the believer and on the part of the unbeliever, Strauss's philosophical skepticism does lead to a positive view of liberal democracy for the reasons outlined by Botwinick. In this sense, Strauss does offer the potential for the defense of political modernity, but not of philosophical modernity. Yet notice that what Strauss does not offer, and I submit cannot offer on his own terms, is an argument for democratic or liberal politics based on a philosophical affirmation of the equality of all peoples. The individual rights and liberty endorsed by Strauss result not from a philosophical proclamation of the intrinsic worth of each individual (again, for Strauss only revealed religion can make such a proclamation on the basis of faith) but from the recognition that no individual (or group) alone (including philosophers) has access to the final truth.

One important objection to this claim is that Strauss does not seem to be concerned with individuals for the most part, save individual philosophers. Indeed, in many ways Strauss's concern is not with regulating the relations between individuals but with moral regulation over *collective* matters. Yet Strauss's engagement with modernity does recognize both the reality of modern, individual identity as well as the undesirability of appeals to tradition qua tradition as authoritative because these appeals equate the conventional with the good.[29] Strauss's strong criticism of "tradition" as an authoritative category differentiates him from other important twentieth-century conservatives and, while he has much in common with their emphasis on the priority of duties over rights, from communitarians also.[30] Strauss's rejection of "tradition" may allow the possibility of considering his engagement, and even possible endorsement, of liberal democracy on the grounds of its recognition of the complex and irreducible relation between individuals and respective communities.[31]

While Strauss is unable, or perhaps refuses, to affirm philosophically, in advance of all other considerations, the superiority of political modernity's stance on the intrinsic equality of all people, his thought does not preclude the political choice for modernity. In the end, the challenge he leaves us is precisely the one with which he is centrally concerned: is there a permanent tension between thought and society, between philosophy and politics, which even liberal democracy cannot overcome?

Notes

1. In 2003–4, articles alleging Strauss's direct influence on the war with Iraq appeared in *The New York Times*, the *Boston Globe*, the *International Herald Tribune*, *The New Yorker*, and *Harpers*, among others. See the conclusion of this book for a discussion of these allegations.

2. For instance, Shlomo Malka's question to Levinas in the name of Levinas's philosophy: "Isn't history, isn't politics the very site of the encounter with the 'other,' and for the Israeli, isn't the 'other' above all the Palestinian?" (LR, p. 294). I discuss this in greater detail in Chapter 8.

3. For instance, Levinas writes, "Surely the rise of the countless masses of Asiatic and underdeveloped peoples threatens this new-found authenticity [of Israeli Judaism]? On the world stage comes peoples and civilizations who no longer refer to our Sacred History, for whom Abraham, Isaac and Jacob no longer mean anything. As at the beginning of Exodus, a new king arises who does not know Joseph" (DF, p. 165) or "I often say, although it's a dangerous thing to say publicly, that humanity consists of the Bible and the Greeks. All the rest can be translated: all the rest – all the exotic – is dance" (*French Philosophers in Conversation: Levinas, Schneider, Serres, Irigaray, Le Doeuff, Derrida, Raoul, Mortley*, London and New York: Routledge, 1991, p. 18). Compare these comments to Strauss: "The greatest minds to whom we ought to listen are by no means exclusively the greatest minds of the West" (RCPR, pp. 42–4).

4. For a recent consideration of the complexities and unrelenting influence of historicism in modern Judaism, see David N. Myers, *Resisting History: Historicism and Its Discontents in German-Jewish Thought* (Princeton: Princeton University Press, 2003).

5. PAW, p. 19.

6. I thus disagree with Susan Orr's interesting study *Jerusalem and Athens: Reason and Revelation in the Works of Leo Strauss* (Lanham, MD: Rowman and Littlefield, 1995), in which she argues that Strauss actually favors Jerusalem. In my view, he favors neither philosophically. Nevertheless, I strongly agree with what I take to be the proper implication of Orr's argument, that Strauss's position on revelation actually offers a profound starting point for those interested in defending a belief in biblical revelation.

7. *The Philosophy of the Limit* (New York: Routledge, 1992), to be discussed in Chapter 7.

8. I would add to this that Levinas, despite his difficult rhetoric, is also a thinker who, with some work, can be understood and discussed in straightforward terms. Some of Levinas's defenders maintain that one can only write or speak about Levinas using his terminology and by implication that it is a distortion to try to figure out what Levinas is saying in more straightforward terms. I would suggest that Levinas's own self-understanding as, at very least, a thinker concerned with philosophical themes precludes such a position. See Chapter 3 for further discussion.

CHAPTER 1. STRAUSS AND LEVINAS BETWEEN ATHENS AND JERUSALEM

1. "Jerusalem and Athens," JPCM, p. 379–80.
2. MITP, p. 111.
3. PAW, p. 19.
4. EI, p. 24.
5. DU, p. 156.
6. TeI, p. 70; TI, p. 73.
7. TeI, p. 339; TI, p. 303.
8. PG, p. 74; PL, p. 88, emphasis in the original.
9. NRH, pp. 75–6.
10. SCR, p. 12.
11. TM, p. 13.
12. "Jerusalem and Athens," JPCM, p. 400.
13. PG, p. 64; PL, p. 76; as Strauss put it later "*The Laws* opens with the word 'god'; there is no other Platonic dialogue that opens in this manner. *The Laws* is Plato's most pious work. In the *Apology of Socrates* Socrates defends himself against the charge of impiety, of not believing in the gods in whom the city believes. In *The Laws* the Athenian stranger devises a law against impiety which would have been more favorable to Socrates than the corresponding Athenian law" (AAPL, p. 2).
14. PG, p. 67; PL, p. 81.
15. AUP, p. 386.
16. As Thomas Pangle puts it in the context of Strauss's reading of Plato, "Justice in the fullest sense comes to sight, in what men say about it, as an object of aspiration: as the 'common good' which binds men together in the mutual dedication in a political community" (introduction to SPPP, p. 6).
17. For a historical account of Salanter see Immanuel Etkes, *Rabbi Israel Salanter and the Mussar Movement*, Jonathan Chipman, trans. (Philadelphia: The Jewish Publication Society, 1993). While some attention has been given to Levinas's use of Salanter, a point that ought to be noted, but which has not, is that the Mussar movement was elitist, and not a mass movement as Levinas's claims would suggest.
18. *Guide of the Perplexed*, Shlomo Pines, trans. (Chicago: University of Chicago Press, 1963, 3: 28).
19. Ibid.
20. Levinas also differs from Maimonides in this regard, see *Guide* 3: 28.
21. "Jerusalem and Athens," JPCM, p. 403.
22. Martin Heidegger, *Nietzsche*, David F. Krell, ed. (San Francisco: Harper Collins, 1991, 4: 164).
23. NP, pp. 57–8.

24. AM, April 1935.

25. DF, pp. 14–15. For a recent discussion of Levinas's use of Maimonides see Henri Bacry, "La Bible, le Talmud, la connaissance et la théorie du visage de Levinas" in *Emmanuel Levinas Philosophie et judaïsme*, Danielle Cohen-Levinas and Shmuel Trigano, eds. (Paris: In Press Éditions, 1999, pp. 13–19).

26. TN, p. 172, emphasis added.

27. Sylvain Zac, *Spinoza et l'interprétation de l'écriture* (Paris: Presses Universitaires de France, 1965).

28. DF, p. 111.

29. Originally published in *Proceedings of the American Academy of Jewish Research*, XIII, 1943, pp. 47–96 and in *Essays on Maimonides*, S.W. Baron, ed. (New York: Columbia University Press, 1941, pp. 37–91). Both reprinted in PAW, 1952.

30. Strauss's self-proclaimed change of orientation came with a programmatic essay also of 1941: "Persecution and the Art of Writing." His 1941 Maimonides essay is contemporaneous with this change in orientation, by which Strauss meant his attention was turned to the ways in which greater writers of the past dealt in their literary style with the problem of political persecution.

31. Thus Gillian Rose is wrong when she scathingly remarks that Strauss denies the question of divinity in Greek philosophy (*Judaism and Modernity: Philosophical Essays* [Oxford and Cambridge: Blackwell, 1993], p. 17–18). As Strauss puts it: "The notion, the divine law, it seems to me is the common ground between the Bible and Greek philosophy. And here I use a term which is certainly easily translatable into Greek as well as into biblical Hebrew. But I must be more precise. The common ground between the Bible and Greek philosophy is the problem of divine law" ("Progress or Return," JPCM, p. 107). Rose also writes "Strauss misrepresents Greek rationalism by presenting classical philosophy as if it were simply skeptical or silent regarding Greek gods." This characterization is also entirely wrong. See, for instance, Strauss's statement "the divine law, it seems to me is the common ground between the Bible and Greek philosophy" ("Progress or Return?," JPCM, p. 107). Rose's characterization is particularly odd because she quotes "Progress or Return?" elsewhere in her essay. Ironically, Rose's own proposal mirrors what I will suggest in the following pages is actually Strauss's position: "I discern and propose a different *tritium quid*: that the relation between philosophy and Judaism be explored neither in terms which presuppose self-identity nor in terms of mutual opposition but in terms of their evident loss of self-identity" (*Judaism and Modernity*, p. 18).

32. JPCM, p. 106.

33. "Progress or Return?," JPCM, p. 122.

34. JPCM, pp. 122–3.

35. "Jerusalem and Athens," JPCM, p. 380.

36. For a recent close textual reading of Strauss on Maimonides, and the shifts in Strauss's interpretations, see Steven Lenzner, "A Literary Exercise in Self-knowledge: Strauss's Twofold Interpretation of Maimonides," *Perspectives on Political Science* 31 (4) (fall 2002), pp. 225–34.

37. The enormity of the scholarship on Maimonides is, of course, beyond the scope of this book. It is worth noting, however, that Strauss's interpretation is more in keeping with the Jewish historical reception of Maimonides, while Levinas's interpretation is very much akin to nineteenth-century liberal Jewish readings of Maimonides, and

Hermann Cohen's in particular. For more on the latter, see Almut Sh. Bruckstein's translation of and commentary on Cohen's *Ethics of Maimonides* (Madison: University of Wisconsin Press, 2003). For a compelling and controversial *theological* analysis of the historical Jewish reception of Maimonides, an analysis that I believe accords with the theological and philosophical impetus of Strauss's reading of Maimonides, see Marc B. Shapiro *The Limits of Orthodox Theology: Maimonides' Thirteen Principles Reappraised* (Oxford and Portland, OR: The Littman Library of Jewish Civilization, 2004).

38. PG, p. 66; PL, pp. 78–9.

39. PG, p. 62; PL, p. 75. In Chapter 9 I discuss Julius Guttmann's response to this argument of Strauss.

40. The important philosophical and historical issue concerns the respective association between the public realm and religion, on the one hand, and the private realm and philosophy, on the other. Unfortunately, arguments about the relation between individual experience and public experience often degenerate too quickly into reductive judgments about mass-elite distinctions. Certainly a consideration of such distinctions is politically important, but we miss an opportunity for critical reflection by jumping too quickly into political judgment on these matters. We need to ask first about the philosophical descriptions they provide of "philosophy" and "religion" respectively, and then about the political implications of these suggestions.

More recent Heidegger scholarship has complicated this issue in terms of Heidegger's thought, as much of the secondary literature has moved toward recognition of the philosophical importance of sociality for Heidegger. (Though on the other hand, this recognition has always been present in that Heidegger's students, Arendt and Löwith, pursued exactly this issue in Heidegger's philosophy.) Where the early "existentialist" reading of Heidegger insisted on a dichotomy between sociality and authentic being in the world, many recent interpreters have questioned this sharp dichotomy. As Thomas Sheehan puts it, for Heidegger "Our sociality – co-extensive with finitude, and its first gift – is what makes it possible and necessary to take-as and to understand 'is.' Our sociality is *die Sache selbst*," ("A Paradigm Shift in Heidegger Research," *Continental Philosophy Review* 34 [2001], pp. 183–202). Indeed, Levinas agrees with Sheehan's description and, interestingly, he does so in the context of a criticism of Martin Buber, see "Martin Buber's Theory of Knowledge," PN, p. 19. It is beyond the scope of this chapter to provide a full account of sociality in Heidegger, but from our very brief discussion a helpful point can be made, which is relevant for our consideration of Strauss.

41. Significantly, Strauss anticipates recent discussions in anthropology that make this very argument with regard to the definition of religion as it relates specifically to Islam. Interestingly, most of these current arguments make no mention of Judaism and suggest both implicitly and explicitly that the tension is between Islam and Christianity. See for instance Talal Asad, *Formations of the Secular: Christianity, Islam, Modernity* (Stanford: Stanford University Press, 2003) and his earlier *Genealogies of Religion: Discipline and Reasons of Power in Islam and Christianity* (Baltimore: Johns Hopkins University Press, 1993).

42. EI, p. 114.

43. EI, p. 118.

44. Ibid.

45. "The Law of Reason in the *Kuzari*," PAW, p. 141.
46. "The Law of Reason in the *Kuzari*," PAW, p. 140. As Strauss puts it elsewhere: "To quote the medieval thinker, Yehuda Halevi, 'The wisdom of the Greeks has the most beautiful blossoms, but no fruits,' with 'fruits' here meaning actions. That asocial perfection that is contemplation normally presupposes a political community, the city, which accordingly is considered by the philosophers as fundamentally good, and the same is true of the arts, without whose services, and even model, political life and philosophic life are not possible. According to the Bible, however, the first founder of a city was the first murderer and his descendents were the first inventors of the arts. Not the city, not civilization, but the desert, is the place in which the biblical God reveals Himself. Not the farmer Cain, but the shepherd Abel, finds favor in the eyes of the biblical God" ("Progress or Return?," JPCM, p. 109). I discuss Strauss's view of Cain in greater detail at the end of this chapter. In Chapters 3, 6, and 9, I further discuss the significance of Halevi for Strauss.
47. EI, p. 24.
48. In Strauss's words, "the philosopher cannot give this law either to himself or to others; for while he can indeed *qua* philosopher, *know* the principles of a law in general and the principles of the rational law in particular, he can never *divine* the concrete individual ordinances of the ideal law, whose precise stipulation is the only way the law can become effectual, or simply, can become–law" (PG, p. 59; PL, p. 71).
49. EI, p. 117.
50. PAW, pp. 18–19.
51. As Levinas puts it, "The phenomenological epoche does not destroy the truths proper to the natural attitude but wants only to clarify their sense" (TIHP, p. 147).
52. See in particular the end of Husserl's *Cartesian Meditations*, Dorion Cairns, trans. (The Hague: Kluwer Academic Publishers, 1977).
53. ITN, pp. 181–2.
54. As I will argue in Chapter 7, Strauss faults Heidegger for not following through on his own conclusion when it came to politics.
55. See Chapter 6 for a broader discussion of this matter.
56. More broadly, the problem of nature represents for Strauss the *possibility* of recovering the *possibility* of both philosophy and revelation. As he put it to Karl Löwith in 1935, "We are natural beings who live and think under unnatural conditions . . . that unbelieving science and belief no longer have, as in the Middle Ages, the common ground of natural knowledge, on which a meaningful quarrel between belief and unbelief is possible" (CLS, pp. 183–4). But as I will argue in greater detail in Chapter 6, this common ground is in no way for Strauss natural law. As importantly, rethinking nature is the central issue for rethinking politics. As Strauss put it later to Löwith: "the fact that [the polis] is institutional is still no proof that it is *contra naturam* . . . some institutions *assist* natural tendencies" (CCM, p. 113, emphasis in the original).
57. NRH, p. 94.
58. FPP, December 19, 1950, p. 74. See Chapter 6 for a more extensive discussion of the problem of natural right.
59. "God and Philosophy," CPP, pp. 167–8.

60. Levinas writes: "The *despite oneself* marks this life in its very living. Life is life despite life – in its patience and its aging. . . . The passivity of the 'for-another' expresses a sense in it in which no reference, positive or negative, to a prior will enters. . . . The loss of time is not the work of a subject" (AQ, p. 86; OTB, p. 51).

61. AQ, p. 90; OTB, p. 53.

62. See Chapters 2 and 7 for more on the relation between TI and OTB.

63. When Levinas actually uses the term *nature* he has in mind either Hobbes's view of human nature or a scientific view of a fixed natural, cosmological order. In an important sense, Levinas does not reject either of these views of nature. The first view he ascribes to politics, the second to science. Neither is wrong and in their proper spheres both are necessary and true. But neither view of nature, Levinas argues, is ethical. It is in this sense that ethics supersedes nature for Levinas. Levinas articulates this position perhaps most clearly in DI. See also Adriaan Peperzak's brief discussion of Levinas on nature in relation to Heidegger on nature in *To the Other: An Introduction to the Philosophy of Emmanuel Levinas* (West Lafayette, IN: Purdue University Press, 1993, p. 89, n. 4).

64. TeI, pp. 312–13; TI, pp. 279–80.

65. TeI, p. 312; TI, p. 279.

66. I leave aside in this context Levinas's view of gender. For more on this issue see Leora Batnitzky, "Dependency and Vulnerability: Jewish and Feminist Existentialist Constructions of the Human," in *Women and Gender in Jewish Philosophy*, Hava Tirosh-Samuelson, ed. (Bloomington: Indiana University Press, 2004, pp. 127–52) as well as Claire Katz, *Levinas, Judaism, and the Feminine: The Silent Footsteps of Rebecca* (Bloomington: Indiana University Press, 2003).

67. "The Prohibition against Representation and 'The Rights of Man,'" AT, p. 127. See also "The Rights of the Other Man," AT, pp. 145–9.

68. As, for instance, John Locke put it in his *Second Treatise of Government*, "there [is] . . . nothing more evident, than that creatures of the same specifics and rank, promiscuously born to all the same advantages of nature . . . should also be equal amongst another without subordination or subjection," (Indianapolis: Hackett Publishing, 1980, ch. 2). The debate among Straussians concerning Locke's legacy is, of course, a subject in and of itself. See in particular, Thomas Pangle, *The Spirit of Modern Republicanism: The Moral Vision of the American Founders and the Philosophy of Locke* (Chicago: University of Chicago Press, 1990).

69. NCP, p. 109.

70. TeI, p. 86; TI, p. 87.

71. NRH, p. 124.

72. NRH, p. 123.

73. Again, the parallel between Talal Asad's recent work and Strauss's work over half a century ago is particularly ironic on this point. In Asad's words, "the modern idea of secular society included a distinctive relation between state law and personal morality, such that religion became essentially a matter of (private) belief – a society presupposing a range of personal sensibilities and public discourses that emerged in Western Europe at different points in time together with the formation of the modern state" (*Formations of the Secular: Christianity, Islam, Modernity*, p. 206). In Chapter 6, I discuss Strauss's claims about the interrelation between Christianity and the modern state in greater detail.

74. *Philosophy and the Turn to Religion* (Baltimore: Johns Hopkins University Press, 1999, p. 38).
75. *Philosophy and the Turn to Religion*, p. 42.
76. "Violence and Metaphysics: An Essay on the Thought of Emmanuel Levinas," in *Writing and Difference*, Alan Bass, trans. and intro. (Chicago: The University of Chicago Press, 1978, pp. 79–153).
77. "Faith and Knowledge," in *Religion*, Jacques Derrida and Gianni Vattimo, eds. (Stanford: Stanford University Press, 1998, pp. 65–6).
78. In Chapter 8, I discuss the relation between Levinas's "Jewish" and "philosophical" writings more extensively.
79. DF, p. 10; DL, p. 23.
80. See for instance *Midrash Rabbah*, vol. 1, H. Freedman, trans. (London: Soncino Press, 1961, Genesis, XXII. 7).
81. See especially DF, pp. 8–9.
82. DF, p. 20.
83. NRH, pp. 31–2.
84. NRH, p. 105.
85. As he puts it in "Jerusalem and Athens": "the messianic age will be the age of universal peace: all nations shall come to the mountain of the Lord, to the house of the God of Jacob, 'and they shall beat their swords into plowshares, and their spears into pruning hooks: nation shall not lift up sword against nation, neither shall they learn war anymore' (Isaiah 2:2–4). The best regime, however Socrates envisages it, will animate a single city which as a matter of course will become embroiled in wars with other cities. The cessation of evils that Socrates expects from the establishment of the best regime will not include the cessation of war" (JPCM, p. 403).
86. PAW, p. 140.
87. NRH, pp. 106–7; PAW, pp. 140–1. See Chapters 6 and 9 for further discussion of this matter.

CHAPTER 2. LEVINAS'S DEFENSE OF MODERN PHILOSOPHY: HOW STRAUSS MIGHT RESPOND

1. Of particular interest is Robert Bernasconi's, "The Silent Anarchic World of the Evil Genius," *The Collegium Phaenomenologicum: The First Ten Years*, G. Moneta, J. Sallis, and J. Taminiaux, eds. (Dordrecht: Kluwer, 1988, pp. 257–72).
2. Whereas in *Time and the Other* [originally lectures given in 1946–7] Levinas criticizes Heidegger's "being-toward-death" by describing "being-toward-another," in *Totality and Infinity* Levinas attempts to ground his phenomenological account of "being-toward-another" by making an argument that posits a separable, independent subject who is thereby capable of being for another.
3. Edmund Husserl, *Cartesian Meditations*, Dorion Cairns, trans. (The Hague: Martinus Nijhoff, 1960), p. 26.
4. See, for instance, the discussion in Jill Robbins, "Facing Figures: Levinas and the Claims of Figural Interpretation," in *Transitions in Continental Philosophy*, A. Dallery, S. Watson, and E. M. Bower, eds. (Albany: State University of New York Press, 1994, pp. 283–91).

5. Levinas describes the erotic relation and the parent-child relation in particularly gendered terms. The erotic relation is the relation with "the feminine" while the ethical relation is between father and son. Again, I leave aside in this context Levinas's view of gender. See note 66 of Chapter 1.

6. *Cartesian Meditations*, p. 26. See also p. 69.

7. René Descartes, *Meditations on First Philosophy*, in *Descartes: Philosophical Writings*, Elizabeth Anscombe and Peter Thomas Geach, trans. (Indianapolis: Bobbs-Merrill, 1971, p. 71).

8. See especially Husserl's second meditation.

9. *Cartesian Meditations*, p. 25, translation altered.

10. See especially the fifth meditation.

11. Martin Heidegger, *Being and Time*, John Macquarrie and Edward Robinson, trans. (San Francisco: Harper Collins, 1962, p. 68).

12. Jean-Luc Marion, *Cartesian Questions*, Daniel Garber, trans. (Chicago: University of Chicago Press, 1999, pp. 99–100).

13. From *Seventh Responses*; quoted in Marion, p. 104.

14. For the characterization of Husserl, see the first paragraph of 2B, "enjoyment and representation." For the contrast with Heidegger, see the opening lines of 2A.

15. "It is not that at the beginning there was hunger; the simultaneity of hunger and food constitutes the paradisal initial condition of enjoyment" (TeI, p. 144; TI, p. 136).

16. TeI, pp. 141–2; TI, p. 134.

17. TeI, p. 143; TI, p. 135.

18. TeI, p. 143; TI, p. 135.

19. TeI, p. 146; TI, p. 138.

20. TeI, p. 135; TI, pp. 128–9.

21. TeI, pp. 133–4; TI, p. 127.

22. TeI, p. 94; TI, p. 93.

23. TeI, p. 11; TI, p. 26.

24. AQ, p. 52, n. 2. For some reason this appears as a different note in the English translation, see OTB, ch. 2, n. 4, p. 188.

25. *Being and Time*, p. 165.

26. This formulation is my own.

27. SCR, p. 184.

28. SCR, p. 183. See also Strauss's comments to Löwith about Descartes and the invention of modern philosophy in CCM, p. 112.

29. SCR, p. 185.

30. See especially meditation five in Descartes's *Meditations on First Philosophy*.

31. Marion, *Sur l'ontologie grise de Descartes: Questions cartésiennes* II (Paris: J. Vrin, 1975, pp. 31, 61, 177, 282–5, and § 17).

32. "Does Thought Dream?," in *Cartesian Questions*, pp. 18–19.

33. Again, Levinas would find it very disturbing to be equated with Spinoza. In Chapter 4, I examine Levinas's relation to Spinoza in greater detail.

34. SCR, p. 31.

35. "Midway between the critique of Spinoza the renegade and that of Maimonides the believing Jew, there stands the new founding of science by Descartes the Catholic. In other words, from Descartes's assumptions, Spinoza's radical critique of religion

does not inevitably and immediately follow. Nevertheless it must be stated that once Maimonides's position is adopted, once the union of faith and knowledge peculiar to his position is accepted as the point of departure, adoption of Cartesianism cannot but lead to critique of religion. . . . Maimonides, by not accepting, as do the Christian theologians, an essential difference between the natural dream, and the dream that is bestowed upon them by grace, but by understanding prophecy as potentially only from what is essential to man as man, binds up his theory of prophecy so closely with his own conception of man, and in particular with the Aristotelian conception of sensory perception and imagination, that his theory stands or falls according to acceptance or rejection of that Aristotelian conception. Spinoza could therefore all the more easily start from Jewish theology rather than from Christian theology, adopt Maimonides's view rather than the view advanced by Descartes, in order to demolish with Cartesian means the unity which Maimonides had attempted to establish between knowledge and faith" (SCR, p. 185).

36. See especially "Pour un humanisme hebraique" in *Les Cahiers de l'Alliance Israelite Universelle*, 1956–61, pp. 1–3; reprinted in DL, pp. 380–4. "Antihumanisme et education," *Bulletin interiur du Consistoire Central des Israelites de France*, 1973–2, pp. 17–28.; "La vocation de l'humain," *Art Press*, 1986, pp. 44–7 (interview by F. Poirie).

37. David Novak, *The Election of Israel* (New York: Cambridge University Press, 1995).

38. *Cartesian Questions*, pp. 129–30. In *Sur l'ontologie grise de Descartes: Questions cartésiennes II* Marion revises this thesis and suggests that the place of human otherness in Descartes is not wholly negative. But even if we accept Marion's later claims about Descartes, his general thesis that Descartes's view of infinity does not apply first and foremost to human relations still stands.

39. PAW, p. 17, n. 13.

40. *Discourse on Method*, VI, in *Descartes: Philosophical Writings*.

41. PAW, pp. 182–3.

42. Husserl's relation to this forgetfulness is an important subject beyond the scope of this book. On the one hand, Husserl's conception of philosophy as science remains close to Descartes's asocial conception. On the other hand, Husserl does seem to suggest, especially in *Philosophy as a Rigorous Science*, that philosophy is the only way for Europe to save itself. (See *Phenomenology and the Crisis of Philosophy: Philosophy as a Rigorous Science, and Philosophy and the Crisis of European Man*, Quentin Lauer, trans. [New York: Harper & Row, 1965]). In Chapter 3 I discuss Levinas's relation to the rise of German metaphysics. A fuller account of phenomenology's relation to German metaphysics should, of course, include an in-depth discussion of Husserl, which is beyond the scope of this book.

43. "Niccolo Machiavelli" in SPPP, p. 211.

44. Introduction to SPPP, p. 26.

45. US, p. 159.

46. Among the opening lines of *Totality and Infinity* is: "Politics is opposed to morality, as philosophy to naïveté" (TeI, p. 5; TI, p. 21). While Levinas attempts in his latter work, including in OTB, to develop a more nuanced view of "justice," he does not give up on this basic view. Politics and justice are the subjects of Part 3 of this book.

47. NRH, p. 147.

CHAPTER 3. 'FREEDOM DEPENDS UPON ITS BONDAGE': THE SHARED
DEBT TO FRANZ ROSENZWEIG

1. TeI, p. 14; TI, p. 28.
2. Robert Gibbs, *Correlations in Rosenzweig and Levinas* (Princeton: Princeton University Press, 1992); Richard Cohen, *Elevations: the Height of the Good in Rosenzweig and Levinas* (Chicago: University of Chicago Press, 1994).
3. "F. Rosenzweig's Anecdotes about Hermann Cohen" in *Gegenwart im Ruckblick: Festgabe für die Jüdische Gemeinde zu Berlin 25 Jahre nach dem Neubeginn,* H. A. Strauss and K. Grossman, eds. (Heidelberg: Lothar Stiehm Verlag, 1970, p. 216, n.13).
4. *Die Religionskritik Spinozas als Grundlage seiner Bibelwissenschaft Untersuchungen zu Spinozas Theologisch-Politischem Traktat* (Berlin: Akademie-Verlag, 1930).
5. See SCR, pp. 9–15 and RCPR, pp. 27–46.
6. Originally published as "Entre deux mondes: Biographie spirituelle de Franz Rosenzweig. Suivi de Débats sur la conference de M. Levinas" in *La conscience juive. Données et débats,* Eliane Amane Amado Levy-Valensis and Jean Halpérin, eds. (Paris: Presses Universitaires de France, 1963, pp. 121–49), translated as "'Between Two Worlds' (the Way of Franz Rosenzweig)," in DF, p. 185.
7. However, I will suggest in Section 3.3 of this chapter that Strauss presents the more compelling reading of Rosenzweig.
8. In terms of the *Star,* we might say that the tension is found in the very question of how to read the book. As I have argued elsewhere, Rosenzweig recommends that the book be read backward, that is from Part 3 to Part 2 to Part 1. See Leora Batnitzky, *Idolatry and Representation: The Philosophy of Franz Rosenzweig Reconsidered,* "The Philosophical Import of Carnal Israel: Hermeneutics and the Structure of Rosenzweig's *Star of Redemption*" (Princeton: Princeton University Press, 2000, ch. 3).
9. Stéphane Mosès, *Système et révélation: La philosophie de Franz Rosenzweig* (Paris: Les Editions du Souil, 1982). Translated as *System and Revelation: Philosophy of Franz Rosenzweig,* Catherine Tihanyi, trans. (Detroit: Wayne State University Press, 1992).
10. Franz Rosenzweig, *Der Stern der Erlösung* (The Hague and Boston: Martinus Nijhoff, 1976, p. 174). Translated as *The Star of Redemption,* William W. Hallo, trans. (New York, University of Notre Dame Press, 1985, p. 156). (Hereafter cited as *Stern/Star.*)
11. *Stern,* p. 204; *Star,* p. 183.
12. Ibid.
13. AQ, p. 195; OTB, p. 122.
14. AQ, pp. 172–3; OTB, p. 109.
15. "Judaism against Paganism: Emmanuel Levinas's Response to Heidegger and Nazism in the 1930s," *History and Memory* 10(1) (spring/summer 1998), pp. 25–58.
16. See Strauss's discussion in "Cohen und Maimuni" in GS 2, pp. 393–436. I discuss this essay in greater detail in Chapter 5.
17. GS 2, p. 274.
18. *Stern,* pp. 117–18; *Star,* pp. 105–6.
19. "Das neue Denken" in *Zweistromland. Kleinere Schriften zu Glauben und Denken,* vol. 3 of *Franz Rosenzweig: Der Mensch und sein Werk: Gesammelte Schriften* (Boston and The Hague: Martinus Nijhoff, 1974–84, p. 143). Translated in *Franz Rosenzweig's "The New Thinking,"* Alan Udoff and Barbara Galli, eds. and trans. (Syracuse: Syracuse University Press, 1999, p. 73).

20. For a comprehensive discussion of Rosenzweig's relation to Halevi see Barbara Galli, *Franz Rosenzweig and Jehuda Halevi: Translating, Translations, and Translators* (Montreal: McGill-Queen's University Press, 1995).

21. PAW, p. 140.

22. PAW, p. 105, n. 29. See also Strauss's "A Giving of Accounts (with Jacob Klein)." *The College* (1970) pp. 22 and 1 (April): 1–5.

23. *Franz Rosenzweig's "The New Thinking,"* Alan Udoff and Barbara Galli, eds. and trans., p. 80.

24. *Franz Rosenzweig's "The New Thinking,"* p. 90.

25. See Rosenzweig's letter of February 4, 1923 to Rudolf Hallo regarding the "Jewish" part of *Understanding the Sick and the Healthy* (*Franz Rosenzweig: Der Mensch und sein Werk: Gesammelte Schriften*) (Boston and The Hague: Martinus Nijhoff, 1974–84, vol. 1, pt. 2, pp. 888–90).

26. Ibid., p. 888.

27. For a more detailed account of Rosenzweig's understanding of history as it relates to Strauss's reading of him, see Leora Batnitzky "On the Truth of History or the History of Truth: Rethinking Rosenzweig via Strauss," *Jewish Studies Quarterly* 7 (3) (September 2000), pp. 223–51.

28. Consider also Rosenzweig's comments in his essay "The Secret of Biblical Narrative Form" about why the Bible is the most important of all books:

> The Bible is not the most beautiful book in the world, not the deepest, the truest, the wisest, the most absorbing... But the Bible is the most important book. That can be proven; and even the most fanatical Bible-hater must acknowledge as much, at least for the past – indeed his fanatical hate acknowledges as much for the present as well. What is at issue here is not a question of personal taste or spiritual disposition or intellectual orientation, but a question of transpired history (*Zweistromland*, p. 827; Lawrence Rosenwald and Everett Fox, trans., *Scripture and Translation* [Bloomington, Indiana University Press, 1994, p. 140]).

29. *Stern*, p. 107; *Star*, p. 97.

30. For more on the relation between Rosenzweig and Heidegger, see Peter Eli Gordon, *Rosenzweig and Heidegger: Between Judaism and German Philosophy* (Berkeley: University of California Press, 2003). For more on Rosenzweig's conception of history, see Batnitzky, "On the Truth of History or the History of Truth: Rethinking Rosenzweig via Strauss."

31. SCR, p. 13.

32. Kant says this in the first critique about Plato's theory of ideas (*The Critique of Pure Reason*, Norman Kemp Smith, trans., New York: St. Martin's Press, 1965), A314/B370, p. 310. There Kant claims to recognize that Plato really aimed at a transcendental rather than an empirical idealism.

33. *Rival Enlightenments: Civil and Metaphysical Philosophy in Early Modern Germany,* (Cambridge and New York: Cambridge University Press, 2001). I am indebted to Samuel Moyn for directing me to this extremely helpful text.

34. PAW, pp. 18–19.

35. Julius Guttmann presents this view in his *Die Philosophie des Judentums* (München: E. Reinhardt, 1933) and in his belated response to Strauss's criticism of this book in "Philosophie der Religion oder Philosophie des Gesetzes?" *Proceedings of the Israel*

Academy of Sciences and Humanities 5 (1971–6), pp. 143–76, to be discussed in detail in Chapter 9.

36. Martin Luther, *Disputation Against Scholastic Theology* in *Martin Luther's Basic Theological Writings*, T. F. Lull, ed. (Minneapolis, MN: Fortress Press 1989, p. 16), as quoted in Hunter, p. 34.

37. See, for instance, Lewis White Beck, *Early German Philosophy: Kant and His Predecessors* (Cambridge: Harvard University Press, 1969). Citing Heido Oberman's *The Harvest of Mediaeval Theology* (Cambridge: Harvard University Press, 1963), J. B. Schneewind also describes Luther as an irrationalist. See *The Invention of Autonomy: A History of Modern Moral Philosophy* (New York: Cambridge University Press, 1998, esp. p. 31). In many ways, Schneewind's study captures what Hunter's seeks to criticize, namely the simultaneously ahistorical and teleological claim that moral philosophy culminates in Kant.

38. Hunter, p. 35.

39. Strauss's claim here is in line with historical scholarship on medieval Jewish discussions of Christianity. In a 1961 article, Haim Hillel Ben-Sasson describes the ways in which medieval Jewish debates about the notion of truth in Christianity emphasized the irrationality of grounding philosophy on faith. As far as I know, Strauss did not influence Ben-Sasson nor does Strauss mention Ben-Sasson's discussion. See Ben-Sasson "Dor golei safarad 'al 'atsmo" (Hebrew) in *Zion* 26 (1961), pp. 23-64. Of particular significance is Section 5 in "Images of Christian Truth," pp. 25–30.

40. This is, of course, the main reason for Strauss's *philosophical* preference of Maimonides over Halevi, and in a certain sense, as we will see in Chapter 4, for Hermann Cohen over Rosenzweig.

41. Hunter, pp. 40–51.

42. Christian Thomasius, *Summarischer Entwurf der Grundlehren, die einem Studioso Iuris zu wissen und auf Universitäten zu Lernen nötig sind* (Leipzig, Germany: Aalen, Scientia Verlag, 1979) hereafter cited as SEG, pp. 47–8, as quoted in Hunter, p. 52.

43. Ibid.

44. SEG, pp. 47–8; Hunter, p. 9.

45. This is not true of the early Kant's focus on human temperaments.

46. RPH, p. 62.

47. Walter Sparn, *Wiederkehr der Metaphysik: Die ontologische Frage in der lutherischen Theologie des fruehen 17. Jahrhunderts* (Stuttgart, Germany: Calwer Verlag, 1976).

48. Hunter, p. 26.

49. Ibid., p. 56.

50. Ibid., p. 57.

51. Walter Sparn, "Das Bekenntnis des Philosophen. Gottfried Wilhelm Leibniz als Philosoph und Theologe," *Neue Zeitschrift für Systematische Theologie*, 28 (1986), pp. 139–78.

52. Hunter, p. 47.

53. Cited in Chapter 1.

54. For more on the historical contextualization of Levinas's philosophy, see Samuel Moyn's masterful *Origins of the Other: Emmanuel Levinas Between Revelation and Ethics* (Ithaca, NY: Cornell University Press, 2005).

55. Hunter, p. 43.

CHAPTER 4. AN IRRATIONALIST RATIONALISM: LEVINAS'S
TRANSFORMATION OF HERMANN COHEN

1. Levinas mentions Cohen in TIHP, p. xxxv and in TI, p. 71. The first comment is negative as Levinas criticizes neo-Kantian philosophy generally for identifying philosophy with science. The second comment is positive as Levinas calls Cohen "a Platonist," which in TI is a compliment (see Chapter 1). For more on these two remarks see Edith Wyschogrod "The Moral Self: Emmanuel Levinas and Hermann Cohen" Da'at 4 (winter 1980), pp. 35–58. Levinas also mentions Cohen in his essay "Evil and Transcendence." See note 5.

2. *Religion of Reason Out of the Sources of Judaism*, Simon Kaplan, trans. Leo Strauss, intro. (New York: Frederick Ungar, 1972), see in particular Cohen's introduction.

3. *Ethik des reinen Willen*, reprinted in *Werke*, Vom Hermann-Cohen-Archiv am Philosophischen Seminar Zürich unter der Leitung von Helmut Holzhey, ed. (Hildesheim, Germany: G. Olms, 1977–87, vol. 7).

4. See Chapter 5 for a discussion of Strauss's comments about Cohen's optimism.

5. In Levinas's words, "the relationship with ontology is reestablished in the 'postulates of pure reason,' as though it were expected in the midst of all these daring moves. In their own way the ideas rejoin being in the existence of God, who guarantees either, in the letter of criticism, the concord of virtue and happiness, or, according to Hermann Cohen's reading, the concord of freedom with nature and the efficacy of a practice decide upon without knowledge. The absolute existence of the Ideal of pure reason, the existence of the Supreme Being, finally prevails in an architecture where the keystone was to be the concept of freedom alone.... Can we not show that, far from being limited to a pure refusal of the norms of knowledge, the thought that proceeds God, and proceeds otherwise than to the thematized, involves psychic modalities that are original, beyond those required by a world of laws without play, with its relation of reciprocity and compensation and its identifications of differences? Such would be the modalities of the disturbance of the Same by the Other, original modalities proper to the 'unto-God' in which the ontological adventure of the soul is interrupted . . . " ("Transcendence and Evil" in CPP, p. 176). As Levinas argues in this essay, evil and transcendence interrupt the "ontological adventure of the soul." And, at least in this essay, it is Cohen's thought that epitomizes the denial of both these disruptions.

6. Strauss's affirmation of constitutionalism is, of course, a major subject among his followers. See in particular the recent *Leo Strauss, the Straussians, and the American Regime*, Kenneth L. Deutsch and John A. Murley, eds. (Lanham, MD: Rowman and Littlefield, 1999).

7. *Resisting History: Historicism and its Discontents in German-Jewish Thought*.

8. Steven S. Schwarzschild, "Two Modern Jewish Philosophies of History: Nachman Krochmal and Hermann Cohen," D. H. L. diss., Hebrew Union College, Cincinnati, 1955, pp. 96–7.

9. Cohen's view of the future as a limit concept is rooted in a mathematical model. See *Logik der reinen Erkenntnis* in *Werke*, vol. 6.

10. TeI, p. 276; TI, p. 246.

11. TeI, pp. 276–7; TI, pp. 246–7.

12. Dieter Adelmann, "H. Steinthal und Hermann Cohen" in *Hermann Cohen's Philosophy of Religion*, Stéphane Moses and Hartwig Wiederbach, eds. (Hildesheim,

Zurich, and New York: Georg Olms Verlag, 1997, pp. 1–33). According to Adelmann, Steinthal was attracted to Boeckhs's idea of philology as "knowledge of the detected one" because Steinthal, as would Cohen after him, was in keeping with an earlier psychology for which "the soul is not a law alone, but is regarded as an ideal state of mind from within" (p. 13). For a recent study of Steinthal see *Chajm H. Steinthal: Sprachwissenschaftlicher und Philosoph im 19 Jahrhundert,* Hartwig Wiedebach and Annette Winkelmann, eds. (Leiden, The Netherlands and Köln, Germany: Brill, 2002).

13. *Hermann Cohen's Philosophy of Religion,* p. 16. Adelmann goes further than previous interpreters of Cohen in suggesting that even as Cohen broke away from his earlier commitment to the interconnection between philosophy and psychology (and from the work of Moritz Lazarus in particular), Cohen's methodology does not break with Steinthal's notions of inner and outer form.

14. Ibid., p. 25.

15. *Religion of Reason,* pp. 13–15.

16. See in particular the following uses in *Religion of Reason* of *Innerlichkeit: Religion of Reason,* pp. xxxvi, 203, 218.

17. A very helpful exception is Steven B. Smith, *Spinoza, Liberalism, and the Question of Jewish Identity* (New Haven: Yale University Press, 1997).

18. *Ethics,* Samuel Shirley, trans. Seymour Feldman, ed. (New York: Hacket, 1982, p. 32).

19. *Ethics,* p. 32.

20. As Levinas puts it, "When knowledge takes on an ecstatic signification . . . it issues in Spinozist unity. . . . And the alleged movement of transcendence is reduced to a return from an imaginary exile" (TeI, p. 307; TI, pp. 274–5).

21. And as Cohen puts it in the context of the history of modern philosophy, "Even Spinoza only wrote an ethics including logic or metaphysics. Thus Hegel's logic also had to include ethics. Idea, the name of concept in its utmost fulfillment, develops an absolute. And this absolute means morality in its highest forms . . . Idea is not the same as what ought to be, neither is concept the same as being . . . This is and remains the fundamental error of all pantheism, including that of the philosophy of identity" *Ethik des reinen Willens,* pp. 44–5.

22. Ibid., p. 364.

23. I cite Richard Cohen's reading of Levinas on Spinoza because it is so extreme. In my view, it is true to Levinas's intentions. See Levinas's claim in his essay "The Spinoza Case" that "Spinoza was guilty of betrayal" (DF, p. 108) and also his claims in "Have You Reread Baruch" that Spinoza does not understand the Talmud (DF, p. 116). But Levinas's basic claim (and Richard Cohen's) that Spinoza did not understand the Talmud only highlights Levinas's misunderstanding of Spinoza and perhaps more importantly what I take to be the erroneous premise of many of those who work on Levinas today, which is that Levinas is somehow "authentically Jewish" because he writes about the Talmud. Levinas's Talmudic readings, discussed in Part 3 of the book, are often interesting and creative. But Levinas and those who follow him do not ask a basic question that must be asked about contemporary appropriations of the Talmud. This question, simply is, what is the political context of the Talmud and how does this differ from contemporary contexts. This is obviously an enormous subject, but it is astounding that this question is not even asked, so much so that Richard Cohen

can claim that Levinas (who had comparatively little Jewish education) understands the Talmud better than Spinoza (whose excellent Jewish education was universally acknowledged in his own day). Cohen suggests that Levinas's great strength is that he starts with the Talmud and not the Bible. This is misleading for many reasons. First, the Talmud starts with the Bible. Second, Maimonides's philosophical work, as well as most medieval Jewish philosophy, begins with the Bible. I discuss these subjects at greater length in Part 3 of the book.

24. *In Proximity: Emmanuel Levinas and the Eighteenth Century*, Melvyn New, Robert Bernasconi, and Richard Cohen, eds. (Lubbock: Texas Tech University Press, 2001, p. 39).

25. *In Proximity*, pp. 30–1.

26. In a 1937 book review of H. A. Wolfson's *The Philosophy of Spinoza*, Levinas criticizes Wolfson for proceeding the other way with regard to Spinoza. As Levinas puts it, "Ce qui est éternal dans une vérité philosophique, c'est la possibilité de son retour. Et ce retour n'est complet que lorsque cette vérité redevient notre contemporaine.... Mais il ne faut tout de meme pas oublier que le message d'une philosophie n'est pas dans ses causes; que l'attitude spectaculaire à l'égard d'une pensée la transforme en un jeu curieux mais étranger; que saisir le mécanisme d'une pensée n'est pas encore la prendre au sérieux et, qu'en somme, faire repenser une doctrine, ce n'est pas nécessairement la faire comprende" (RHW, pp. 118–19).

27. DF, p. 116.

28. PN, pp. 121–2.

29. PN, pp. 121–2.

30. PN, p. 123.

31. *Kants Theorie der Erfahrung* (Berlin: Dümmler, 1877) reprinted in *Werke*, vol. 1, Einleitung von Geert Edel, 1987, p. 540.

32. *The Critical Philosophy of Hermann Cohen*, John Denton, trans. (Albany: State University of New York Press, 1997, p. 44).

33. *Ethik des reinen Willen*, *Werke*, vol. 7, pp. 227–8.

34. *Ethik des reinen Willen*, pp. 267–8.

35. AQ, pp. 186–7; OTB, pp. 117–18.

36. TeI, p. 77; TI p. 79.

37. For more on Levinas and Kant, see Catherine Chalier, *What Ought I to Do? Morality in Kant and Levinas*, Jane Marie Todd, trans. (Ithaca, NY: Cornell University Press, 2002). Chalier offers a more generous reading of Levinas's positive affinity with Kant than I do here, but I believe that her pairing of the two actually reinforces my general claim that Levinas ought to be understood within the modern metaphysical tradition and that his arguments are predicated on a Kantian framework. See also the conclusion to this chapter.

38. For a sustained argument that Levinas's is a rationalist philosophy, see Theodore de Boer, *The Rationality of Transcendence: Studies in the Philosophy of Emmanuel Levinas* (Amsterdam: J. C. Gieben, 1997).

39. DL, pp. 163–4; DF, pp. 114–15.

40. "Freedom and Commandment" in CCP, p. 17.

41. *In Proximity*, pp. 345–6.

42. See Chapters 7 and 8 for a more detailed discussion of this point.

43. For a more nuanced discussion of the problem with applying a voluntarist framework to Jewish law, see Avi Sagi and Daniel Statman, "Divine Command Morality and Jewish Tradition" *Journal of Religious Ethics* 23 (1) (spring 1995), pp. 39–67.

44. Ben–Sasson's analysis in "Dor Gaulai Sepharad al Astmo" (Hebrew) in *Zion* 26 (1961) is once again relevant. See Chapter 3.

45. See Chapter 7 for further discussion of this point.

46. AQ, p. 234–5; OTB, p. 150.

47. This point makes clear again Levinas's affinity with the Kantian project and particularly, in keeping with Hunter's analysis, the theological dimensions of this project.

48. *Hermeneutics as Politics*, 2nd ed. (New Haven: Yale University Press, 2003, pp. 25–6).

CHAPTER 5. THE POSSIBILITY OF PREMODERN RATIONALISM: STRAUSS'S TRANSFORMATION OF HERMANN COHEN

1. See Alan Udoff's introductory essay on Strauss's relation to Cohen in *Leo Strauss's Thought: Toward a Critical Engagement*, Alan Udoff, ed. (Boulder, CO: L. Rienner Publishers, 1991).

2. Again, see Almuth Sh. Bruckstein's *Ethics of Maimonides*.

3. I discuss the significance of this quotation in Section 5.3.

4. NRH, p. 25.

5. I've added the second quotation marks for the sake of clarity.

6. "Cohen und Maimuni" in GS 2, pp. 400–1.

7. PG, p. 11; PL, pp. 23–4.

8. *Religion of Reason Out of the Sources of Judaism*, p. 70.

9. As Strauss puts it, "The 'internalizing' of these concepts differs from the disavowal of their meaning only in the well-intentioned, if not good, purposes of its authors," PG, p. 11; PL, p. 24.

10. "Did not the movement whose goal is to return to the tradition, the movement whose exemplary and unforgotten expression was the development, if not the teaching of Hermann Cohen – did not that movement have as its actual, though often hidden, impulse precisely the insight into the questionableness of the 'internalizations' with which the nineteenth century generally contented itself?" PG, p. 15; PL, p. 26.

11. See Chapter 3 for a detailed discussion of Strauss's account of Rosenzweig.

12. *The Star of Redemption*, introduction to Part 2, "On the Possibility of Experiencing Miracle," pp. 93–111. Rosenzweig understands creation not as a historical or metaphysical event but rather as the existential state of being a creature. In many ways, Rosenzweig's "new thinking" is defined by this argument as an understanding of being a creature marks the contribution of post-Nietzschean philosophy to the possibility of theological renewal.

13. As Strauss puts it in "How to Study Spinoza's *Theologico-Political Treatise*, "Historical understanding, the revitalization of earlier ways of thinking, was originally meant as a corrective for the specific shortcomings of the modern mind. This impulse was however vitiated from the outset by the belief which accompanied it, that modern thought (as distinguished from modern life and modern feeling) was superior to the thought of the past. Thus, what was primarily intended as a corrective for the modern mind, was easily perverted into a confirmation of the dogma of the superiority of modern thought to all earlier thought. Historical understanding

lost its liberating force by becoming historicism, which is nothing other than the petrified and self-complacent form of the self-criticism of the modern mind" PAW, p. 158.

14. Leo Strauss, "Review of Julius Ebbinghaus's *Über die Fortschritte der Metaphysik,*" *Deutsche Literaturezeitung,* 52 (December 27, 1931), col. 2453, reprinted in GS 2, as cited and translated in Jürgen Gebhard, "Leo Strauss: The Quest for Truth in Times of Perplexity," in *Hannah Arendt and Leo Strauss: German Emigres and American Political Thought after World War II,* Peter Graf Kielmansegg et al., eds. (Cambridge: Cambridge University Press, 1995, p. 98).

15. This quotation comes from Strauss's second note to his introduction to PG, pp. 13–14; PL, p. 136.

16. "Cohens Analyse der Bible-Wissenschaft Spinozas" in GS 1, p. 363; EW, p. 140, emphasis in the original.

17. Ibid., p. 363; p. 341.

18. Ibid., pp. 366–71; pp. 144–5.

19. Before turning to the hermeneutical issues at stake here, let me just lay out Cohen's and Strauss's arguments briefly. According to Strauss, Cohen applies "a historiographic method which stems perhaps from the theological science of apologetics: should a passage by an uninspired author be incomprehensible to the interpreter, or should it seem to the interpreter objectionable, then the interpreter must raise questions about the author's life." Cohen turns to the events of Spinoza's life to explain Spinoza's arguments. According to Cohen, "the critique of the Bible would not have entered this book had it not been prepared by another moment in Spinoza's life." This moment, of course, is the Amsterdam Synagogue's ban on Spinoza and Spinoza's response to that ban written in his "protest pamphlet" [*Protestschrifft*]. For Strauss, Cohen's argument amounts not only to circular reasoning ("Spinoza would not have written his critique of the Bible if he had not held views critical of the Bible") but also to hints in which "no misunderstanding is possible" about Spinoza's hostility to the Jewish people, which makes him look like "[an] informer, a distinct type characteristic of the history of the persecutions of the Jews" (Ibid., p. 363; p. 142).

20. Ibid., p. 366; p. 143.

21. Ibid., p. 376; p. 152.

22. Ibid., p. 366; p. 143.

23. EW, n. 21 to "Cohen's Bible Analysis."

24. *Critique of Pure Reason,* pp. 41–2.

25. It is not insignificant that Strauss refers to the third edition of Cohen's *Kant's Theory of Experience.* As we saw in Chapter 4, it is in the third edition that Cohen makes his argument against Kant's conception of sensibility.

26. SCR, p. 31.

27. PAW, p. 25.

28. Ibid.

29. As Strauss puts it in "How to Study Spinoza's Theologico-Political Treatise, "the *Treatise* is linked to its time, not because Spinoza's serious or private thought was determined by his 'historical situation' without being aware of it, but because he consciously and deliberately adapted, not his thought, but the public expression of his thought, to what his time demanded or permitted" PAW, p. 192.

30. *Religion der Vernunft aus den Quellen des Judentums*, hg. Von Benzion Keller-
    man (Leipzig, Germany: Fock, 1919, p. 60); *Religion of Reason*, p. 52, translation
    altered.
31. "Cohen und Maimuni" in GS 2, p. 408.
32. Ibid., p. 401.
33. *Religion of Reason*, p. 176.
34. Ibid., pp. 24–5.
35. It is important to note that the term *annihilation* [*Vernichtung*] has a special mean-
    ing in Cohen's logic, a meaning to which Strauss does not refer but with which a
    comparison with Strauss's use of the term is helpful for our purposes. In the sentence
    preceding his quotation of Cohen's rhetorical question "whether such reshaping is
    not the best form of annihilation" Strauss, once again, states that "the new does
    not emerge through the rejection or annihilation of the old but through its meta-
    morphosis or reshaping." Strauss's reading of Cohen's use of the term *annihilation*
    implies that annihilation and, of course, transformation are fundamentally temporal
    matters. But for Cohen, transformation and annihilation are not temporal matters.
    This is part of the reason that the question of whether transformation is not the
    best form of annihilation is by definition only rhetorical for Cohen. Annihilation is
    an important component of Cohen's logical principle of origin and its relation to
    judgment. In his *Logic of Pure Cognition*, Cohen writes, "The most important of the
    rights of judgment is that of rejecting and annihilating false judgement.... Being
    able to posit the *requirement of annihilation* [*Vernichtung*] in itself is the vital ques-
    tion of judgment." Cohen continues: "The 'not' expressed by this requirement is
    different completely from the 'nothing,' which is the source of something.... *There
    is no non-A*, and there cannot be a non-A that, as opposed to the nothing of origin,
    has a fulfilled content. All the doubts that non-A may, however, take on meanings
    that may be suited to the justification of its content, must come to an abrupt halt,
    since, in this way, doubt is cast on identity," (*Logik der reinen Erkenntnis*, pp. 106–7).
    "The requirement of annihilation" means for Cohen that we can judge something
    to *not be* something else. He argues contra Hegel that this possibility of negation is
    necessary in conceiving not just identity but also in making judgment possible. It
    shouldn't come as a surprise then that when Cohen uses the term *annihilation* in his
    question about "whether such reshaping is not the best form of annihilation" that
    Cohen, on his own terms, could *only* ask such a question rhetorically. Simply put,
    judgment about truth and falsehood is not a temporal matter for Cohen. There-
    fore, transformation could not be the best form of annihilation or even a form of
    annihilation at all. For annihilation, for Cohen, is an atemporal capacity of judg-
    ment. Strauss's use of the term *annihilation* to imply a temporal transformation is
    in keeping not only with the plain sense of Cohen's rhetorical question "whether
    such reshaping is not the best form of annihilation" but also with his own reversal
    of what I have described as Cohen's view of the relation between the inner and outer
    forms of reason and history.
36. As Cohen puts it, "This assumption [that Maimonides is 'an epigone of Aristotle']
    seems to have ignored how much it deprecates the religious concept and its inher-
    ent value for Maimonidean ethics. With due respect to the god of Aristotle, he
    is truly not the God of Israel.... Due to his principle opposition to the funda-
    mental doctrine of the Good as idea, Aristotle turns into an opponent of ethics

as science.... [Maimonides's] basic aspiration, that theology should culminate in ethics, attests to his rationalism; likewise every stage of Maimonides' dogmatics tends towards ethics. Maimonides' acceptance of the Aristotelian approach towards ethics would thus undermine his rationalism. The difference between the Aristotelian and Maimonidean approach lies consistently and in every respect in the significance of Maimonides' concept of God for his theology and also, as must be assumed, for his ethics" (Hermann Cohen, *Jüdische Schriften* III, B. Strauss, ed. (Berlin: C. A. Schwetschke and Sohn Verlagsbuchhandlung, 1924, p. 302).

37. Stanley Rosen has suggested to me that in the end Strauss does not have a very coherent notion of the differences between Plato and Aristotle (personal correspondence). It seems to me that this distinction is rhetorically quite significant, however, especially in Strauss's later work. See Chapter 6 for a discussion of this distinction in NRH.

38. As Strauss notes, this confluence marks Cohen's philosophy and is the key to his ethics, in which "Das reine Wollen vollzieht sich, vollen der sich in der reinen Handlung" (Strauss's quotation of Cohen's *Ethik des reinen Willen*, in *Werke*, p. 169, as quoted by Strauss in "Cohen und Maimuni," GS 2, p. 406).

39. "Cohen und Maimuni," GS 2, p. 401.

40. Ibid., p. 421.

41. In Chapter 9 I discuss Guttmann's belated reply to Strauss's criticism.

42. Leo Strauss, introductory essay to the English translation Hermann Cohen's *Religion of Reason*, in Hermann Cohen, *Religion of Reason Out of the Sources of Judaism*, p. xxxvi.

43. It is important to mention that Strauss's reversal here is by no means straightforward. Philosophy for Cohen is limited in an important sense by secular law, which is the starting point for Cohen's transcendental deduction of the self. Yet Strauss's attempt to bring Cohen closer to Aristotle, even if problematic on Cohen's own terms, only underscores Strauss's basic question about the quarrel between the ancients and the moderns. Indeed, Strauss's mature work is oriented around an argument about the inadequacy of modern law; an inadequacy that he argues is sustained and marked by the blindness of modern rationalism.

44. Richard H. Popkin, *The History of Skepticism from Erasmus to Spinoza* (Berkley: University of California Press, 1964).

45. Benedict de Spinoza *A Theologico-Political Treatise*, unabridged Elwes translation, (New York, Dover Publications, 1951, p. 192).

46. Ibid., p. 190.

47. See Chapter 3.

48. *Kuzari*, pts. 2–5.

49. More specifically, in OTB Levinas calls this senescence. See Chapter 1 for a brief discussion of this concept in Levinas.

50. As Levinas puts it, "The periodic rebirth of skepticism ... recalls the breakup of the unity of the transcendental apperception, without which one could not *otherwise than be*" (AQ, pp. 265–6; OTB, p. 171). See Chapter 6 for more discussion of the implications of Levinas's view of skepticism.

51. Leo Strauss, introductory essay to the English translation of Hermann Cohen's *Religion of Reason*, p. xxxvi.

CHAPTER 6. AGAINST UTOPIA: LAW AND ITS LIMITS

1. For a summary of this divide see Erik Root Raleigh, "A Strauss Divided," *Clarion* 5(1) (October/November 2000), p. 26.
2. For a discussion of this subject, see Ann Norton, *Leo Strauss and the Politics of American Empire* (New Haven: Yale University Press, 2004).
3. In Chapter 8, I will suggest that such an approach is the only defensible approach to the meanings of Strauss's work, on Strauss's own terms.
4. Basically, my argument is that the "west coast" Straussians are right about the importance of religion for Strauss, but they are right for the wrong reasons, while the "east coast" Straussians are right about Strauss's skepticism, but they draw the wrong conclusions about religion for Strauss by not understanding the centrality of his argument about Judaism.
5. Recent exceptions to this approach are the edited volumes EW and JPCM and Kenneth Hart Green's seminal 1993 study *Jew and Philosopher: The Return to Maimonides in the Jewish Thought of Leo Strauss* (New York: State University of New York, 1993). Eugene Sheppard's 2001 dissertation, *Leo Strauss and the Politics of Exile* (University of California at Los Angeles) is an extremely illuminating discussion of Strauss's intellectual development from his early years in Germany to his arrival in New York. See also his forthcoming *Leo Strauss and the Politics of Exile: The Making of a Political Philosopher* (University Press New England/Brandeis University Press, forthcoming, fall 2006). There have also been some important studies in France along these lines. See in particular Rémi Brauge, *L. Strauss, Maimonide: Essais rassemblés et traduits de l'all* (Paris: PUF, 1988) and Pierre Bouretz, "Leo Strauss devant la modernité juive" *Raisons politques* 8 (November 2002), pp. 22–50. The most comprehensive intellectual history of Strauss's thought is perhaps Daniel Tanguay's *Léo Strauss: Une biographie intellectuelle Essai* (Paris: Grasset, 2003). In Israel there have also been a number of important recent studies. See also Ehud Luz, "Yahaduto shel Leo Strauss" ("Leo Strauss's Judaism"), *Da'at* 27 (1991), pp. 35–60 (Hebrew) and Jonathan Cohen, *Tevunah ve-temurah: panim be-heker ha-filosofyah ha-Yehudit* (Hebrew) (Jerusalem: Mosad Bialik, 1997) and his earlier "Strauss, Soloveitchik and the Genesis Narrative: Conceptions of the Ideal Jew as Derived from Philosophical and Theological Readings of the Bible," *The Journal of Jewish Thought and Philosophy*, 5(1) (1995), pp. 99–143.
6. It is important to note that Strauss rarely uses the term *secularism* and when he does he is often critical of it as a term. See, for instance, his long footnote in his chapter on Weber in NRH, pp. 60–1, n. 22. I discuss this note in the following text. See also "The Three Waves of Modernity," in IPP, pp. 81–98. While Strauss speaks more loosely about secularism in some of his late lectures on Judaism, the term *secular* for Strauss implies an extinguishing of the possibility of revelation because its use is premised on the notion that the truth claims of religion no longer have validity. In contrast, Strauss's view is that secularism more properly reflects not an end to the possibility of the truth of divine revelation but a "revolution . . . on the plane of rational thought" that denies this *philosophic* possibility. In this context, Strauss challenges secular intellectuals to consider whether the atheism intrinsic to secular society is philosophically coherent not only for religious believers, but also, perhaps paradoxically, for atheists.

7. GN, p. 362.
8. NCP, p. 113.
9. GN, pp. 364–5.
10. See in particular Strauss's comments about Moritz Steinschneider in the notes of the third essay. In his 1936 "Quelques remarques sur la science politique de Maïmonide et de Farabi," Strauss discusses the implications of Munk's translation of Maimonides extensively, as well as the work of Steinschneider and Kraus.
11. PG, p. 58, emphasis in the original; PL, pp. 68, 141.
12. GN, p. 364.
13. Significantly, speaking in 1941 in New York at the New School, Strauss suggests that Anglo-American culture, as opposed to German culture, may be able to recall the proper relation between philosophy and law. With this we can appreciate the transition from the "German Strauss" to the "American Strauss." Strauss's American career and his continuing reception in the United States are marked by considering the possible Anglo-American relation to classical political philosophy, which Strauss defines as the prudent consideration of the proper relation between philosophy and society, or philosophy and law.
14. The term *sociology of knowledge* does not appear in the 1941 essay, but only in the 1952 book *Persecution and the Art of Writing*.
15. PAW, pp. 18–19.
16. PAW, p. 21.
17. See Strauss's curious statement about Aquinas, Aristotle, and Heidegger in this connection, in "An Unspoken Prologue," JPCM, p. 450.
18. WPP, p. 44.
19. Clark A. Merrill, "Leo Strauss's Indictment of Christian Philosophy," *Review of Politics* 62(1) (winter 2000), pp. 77–105, at 98, emphasis added.
20. The broader context of this quotation is: "On the *querelle des anciens et des modernes*: I do not deny, but assert, that modern philosophy has much that is essential in common with Christian medieval philosophy; but that means that the *attack* of the moderns is directed decisively against *ancient* philosophy." CCM, p. 106, emphasis in the original.
21. "Preface to Isaac Husik, *Philosophical Essays*," in JPCM, p. 252.
22. Whether this is an accurate description of Aquinas's position is an open question. Strauss's view, however, does accord with Martin Luther's understanding of scholasticism. See the discussion in Chapter 3 of Luther in the context of the historical development of university metaphysics. Luther, however, did not replace scholasticism with an understanding of law but with his view of Christian theology. Strauss also criticizes the Reformation because the Reformation moves even further from any concept of law. See for example Strauss's comment, "For there is a profound agreement between Jewish and Muslim thought on the one hand and ancient thought on the other: it is not the Bible and the Koran, but perhaps the New Testament, and certainly the Reformation and modern philosophy, which brought about the break with ancient thought" RMF, pp. 4–5.
23. Strauss makes this argument in multiple places, perhaps most significantly in NRH and PAW.
24. As mentioned in note 48 of this chapter, John Finnis, while intimately linking natural law with natural right, claims Strauss as a defender of natural law in his *Natural*

Law and Natural Rights (Oxford: Oxford University Press, 1980). As I show in this chapter, Strauss separates natural right from natural law and criticizes the latter while questioning the former.

25. NRH, pp. 75–6.

26. NRH, p. 61, n. 22. Along these lines, see also Strauss's comments to Gershom Scholem in terms of the latter's use of the term *myth* (GS 3, pp. 734, 743).

27. NRH, p. 75.

28. NRH, p. 78.

29. "Paul de Lagarde" (1924) originally appearing in *Der Jude*; reprinted in GS 2, pp. 323–32; EW, p. 94.

30. See NRH, p. 124 for Strauss's claims about Socrates and common sense. I discuss this in greater detail in Chapter 7.

31. NRH, p. 158.

32. NRH, p. 156.

33. It is interesting, if not ironic, that the discussion among the "west coast Straussians" centers on whether Locke was truly an Aristotelian. This is odd in the context of Strauss's explicit interest in and sympathy with what he maintains is a Platonic, and not Aristotelian, view, which centers on the tension – and not confluence – between philosophy (or natural right) and law (or the city). And here it is worth returning to Strauss's qualification of the Aristotelian view of natural right, in which he refers not only to the "Jewish Aristotelians" but also to his essay on Halevi in particular, whose theme, it turns out, is quite pertinent to thinking about what Strauss could have meant by "natural right." For some of this discussion of Locke's Aristotelianism see Harry V. Jaffa *American Conservatism and the American Founding* (Durham, NC: Carolina Academic Press, 1984) and Michael P. Zuckert's more recent *Launching Liberalism: On Lockean Political Philosophy* (Lawrence: University of Kansas Press, 2002).

34. PAW, p. 132.

35. In Halevi's words, "The Rabbi said: 'These and others like them are the rational laws. They are prerequisites – inherently and sequentially – to the Divine Torah. One cannot maintain any community of people without these laws. Even a community of robbers cannot exist without equity amongst themselves; if not, their association could not continue,'" Judah Halevi, *The Kuzari: In Defense of the Despised Faith*, N. Daniel Korobkin, trans. and annotated (Northvale, NJ and Jerusalem: Jason Aronson Inc., 1998, 2:48, p. 94). The rabbi's comments are in response to the Kuzari's question about why the divine law is necessary to know God.

36. NRH, p. 105.

37. PAW, pp. 132 and 139–40. See also Kenneth Hart Green's "Religion, Philosophy, and Morality: How Leo Strauss Read Judah Halevi's Kuzari," *Journal of the American Academy of Religion* 61 (1993), pp. 225–73.

38. For arguments about the Platonizing of Aristotle among medieval Jewish and Islamic thinkers see Shlomo Pines's "The Philosophical Sources of The Guide of the Perplexed" in Maimonides, *The Guide of the Perplexed*, pp. lvii–cxxxiv as well as Richard Walzer's commentary in *Al-Farabi on the Perfect State*, Richard Walzer, trans. and ed. (Oxford: Oxford University Press, 1985, pp. 8–13 and 425–9).

39. Of course, Strauss's contention that the Catholic tradition of natural law represents this fusing might also be historically inaccurate, as a number of recent interpreters

have argued in the context of Thomas Aquinas. See John A. Bowlin, *Contingency and Fortune in Aquinas's Ethics* (New York and Cambridge: Cambridge University Press, 1999) as well as Victor Preller, *Divine Science and the Science of God: A Reformulation of Thomas Aquinas* (Princeton: Princeton University Press, 1967). The concern of this chapter and of this book more generally, is not with the accuracy of Strauss's claims about Aquinas but with the philosophical implications of these claims for understanding Strauss's thought.

40. NRH, pp. 163–4, emphasis added.

41. It is important to recognize that Harry V. Jaffa's claims to the contrary come *after* he wrote his doctoral dissertation under Strauss's supervision. In the dissertation, Jaffa argues for, in his words, "the incompatibility of Thomistic and Catholic Natural Law and Aristotelian Natural Right." The published form of the dissertation is *Thomism and Aristotelianism* (Chicago: University of Chicago Press, 1952, esp. pp. 182–4). It is also important to note that the dissertation was published the year before Strauss's Walgreen lectures were published as *Natural Right and History*. In my view, this gives further credence to the view that *Natural Right and History* does not resolve the problem of natural right (as Strauss thought). Although Jaffa claims that his more mature position is the implication of Strauss's thought, it seems clear from the timing of these publications that Strauss would not have thought so.

42. This stance may explain Strauss's comments to Karl Löwith, August 20, 1946, CCM, that "Whoever concedes that Horace did not speak nonsense when he said 'Expel nature with a hayfork, but it always returns,' concedes thereby precisely the legitimacy in principle of Platonic-Aristotelian politics. Details can be disputed, although I myself might actually agree with everything Plato and Aristotle demand (but this I tell only you)," p. 113. But significantly Strauss continues: "I assert that the polis – as it has been interpreted by Plato and Aristotle, a surveyable, urban, morally serious (*übersichtliche städtische, moralisch-ernste*) society, based on an agricultural economy, in which the gentry rule – is morally politically the most pleasing: which still does not mean that I would want to live under such a polis (one must not judge everything according to one's private wishes) – do not forget that Plato and Aristotle preferred democratic Athens as a place to well ordered polises: for philosophy's moral-political considerations are necessarily secondary," p. 113. Note also the twin implications of Strauss's affirmation of Plato-Aristotle: first, "there can only be closed societies" (p. 107) and second, "There is only one objection against Plato-Aristotle: and that is the factum brutum of revelation" (p. 108).

43. The "west coast" Straussian interest in the grounding of the American Founding on a classical notion of natural right is therefore misplaced on two counts: first, the notion that Strauss affirms philosophically an Aristotelian concept of natural right and second, that Strauss affirms politically a conception of classical natural right to start. I have suggested that that these twin misunderstandings of Strauss are rooted in not acknowledging Strauss's fundamentally skeptical view of philosophy, theology, and politics. I would like to emphasize that my criticism of the "west coast" Straussian position is not based on an account of Strauss's esotericism, the subject of Chapter 8. Rather, my criticism is based on attention to the centrality of Strauss's skepticism in his thought, which an appreciation of the coherence between his writings on medieval Jewish philosophy and natural right highlights.

44. Among studies of skepticism that support Strauss's position from a philosophical and historical point of view, see Petr Lom, *The Limits of Doubt: The Moral and Political Implications of Skepticism* (Buffalo: State University of New York Press, 2001) and Myles Burnyeat and Michael Frede, eds., *The Original Sceptics: A Controversy* (Indianapolis: Hackett, 1977).

45. *The Philosophy of the Limit* (New York: Routledge, 1992, p. 101).

46. OTB, p. 154, as quoted in Cornell, pp. 102–3.

47. *The Philosophy of the Limit*, p. 8.

48. I would argue that the "new natural law" theory of John Finnis also does this. This theory also shares Levinas's fear of skepticism and faith in philosophy. See John Finnis's *Natural Law and Natural Rights* in which he claims Strauss as a proponent of natural law. As I argue in this chapter, this is incorrect.

49. Again, see note 42 for Strauss's comments to Löwith.

50. From the perspective of Strauss's thought, Levinas unconsciously and Jaffa consciously share with Aquinas the attempt to be rid of ambiguity (I would argue that this is also the case for Finnis's "new natural law theory"). As we have seen in this chapter, for Strauss there is a continuous line beginning with Aquinas going to Spinoza and finally to Nietzsche and Heidegger. Spinoza's claims for the ubiquity of reason, his collapsing of theology into philosophy, are made possible by the medieval scholastic collapse of philosophy into theology. And Nietzsche's and Heidegger's critique of such a view of reason and philosophy inevitably stems from the overreaching, and ultimately impossible, claims of modern philosophy.

51. See preface, SCR and "Why We Remain Jews," JPCM.

52. Harvey Mansfield and Walter Berns, to be discussed in the following text, tend to see religion largely as instrumental. In his recent book *Political Philosophy and the God of Abraham* (Baltimore: John Hopkins University Press, 2003), Thomas Pangle attempts to take revelation seriously from a philosophical perspective. Yet while he rightly emphasizes the challenge philosophy brings to religion, Pangle in the end does not acknowledge the intellectual and indeed philosophical challenge that revelation brings to philosophy. See especially pp. 71–102.

53. In this connection, the "west" and "east" coast readings of Strauss share an assumption about the role of religion in Strauss's thought that I argue is profoundly problematic. For both coasts, "religion" means Christianity and not Judaism as distinct from Christianity.

54. *Taking the Constitution Seriously*, (Lanham, MD: Madison Books, 1991, pp. 179–80).

55. Ibid., pp. 181–91. See also Harvey Mansfield, Jr. on formalism, especially in *America's Constitutional Soul* (Baltimore: Johns Hopkins University Press, reprint 1993).

56. See for instance Jacob Katz, *Tradition and Crisis: Jewish Society at the End of the Middle Ages*, Bernard Dov Cooperman, trans. (New York: New York University Press, 1993).

57. SCR, p. 13.

58. See, for instance, the recent work of George Lindbeck and Stanley Hauerwas on this issue.

59. SPPP, p. 51.

60. Introduction to SPPP, p. 18.

61. Introduction to SPPP.

62. See Green, *Jew and Philosopher: The Return to Maimonides in the Jewish Thought of Leo Strauss*, pp. 131–4.

63. SCR, pp. 8–9.
64. Alphonso Lingis, *A Community of Those Who Have Nothing in Common* (Bloomington: Indiana University Press, 1994).
65. Jaffa, *Original Intent and the Framers of the Constitution: A Disputed Question,* (Washington, DC: Regnery Publishing, 1993, p. 322).
66. NRH, p. 1.

CHAPTER 7. ZIONISM AND THE DISCOVERY OF PROPHETIC POLITICS

1. SCR, pp. 1–5.
2. "A Giving of Accounts," JPCM, p. 460.
3. "Why We Remain Jews," JPCM, p. 319.
4. Leo Strauss, "Die Zukunft einer Illusion," *Der jüdische Student* 25(4) (August 1928), pp. 16–28 republished and translated as "Sigmund Freud, The Future of an Illusion (1928)," EW, pp. 203–4.
5. Strauss's 1921 dissertation on Jacobi's theory of knowledge, which attempted to refute the neo-Kantian presuppositions of his mentor Ernst Cassier, seems to be the first published instance of this tendency (reprinted in GS 2). The argument of *Philosophy and Law* attacked Strauss's supervisor of the time, Julius Guttmann. Strauss continues to be quite forthcoming in his mature work. *Natural Right and History*, after all, attacked the reigning dogmas of his own discipline. And, "German Nihilism," discussed in Chapter 6, attacks Strauss's liberal colleagues at the New School, to whom he presented this talk! As I argue later in this chapter and in Chapter 8, I do not believe that Strauss hides his ideas.
6. "Anmerkung zur Diskussion über 'Zionismus und Antisemitismus,'" *Jüdische Rundschau* 28 (September 1923) p. 501; GS 2, p. 313; EW, p. 81. For an excellent discussion on the relations between Strauss's views of Zionism and anti-Semitism, see Eugene Sheppard's article "Raising Zionism to the Level of Antisemitism: Reflections on Leo Strauss as a Young Zionist," *Jewish Studies Quarterly* (forthcoming).
7. As cited in Chapter 6.
8. For a broad discussion of Ahad Ha'am's relation to Herzl, see Ernst Pawel, *The Labyrinth of Exile: A Life of Theodor Herzl* (New York: Farrar, Straus and Giroux, 1989).
9. As Strauss quotes Herzl in the preface of this essay, "To quote Herzl again, 'We are a nation – the enemy makes us a nation whether we like it or not.'"
10. Though for rhetorical purposes Strauss ends this essay by affirming Ahad Ha'am's view that, in Strauss's words, "Anyone to whom this solution seems narrow and imperfect should be reminded of the saying of Ahad Ha'am to the effect that the perfect solution to this question, as to all questions of the galut, has to be sought beyond the limits of galut."
11. This translation is from the Jewish Publish Society, as quoted in EW.
12. GS 2, p. 329; EW, p. 95.
13. GS 2, p. 331; EW, p. 97.
14. GS 2, pp. 327–8; EW, p. 94.
15. Paul de Lagarde, *Deutsche Schriften* 2nd ed. (Göttingen, Germany: Dieterich, 1891, pp. 39–53).
16. PG, p. 11; PL, p. 24.

17. Georges de Lagarde, *La naissance de l'esprit laïque au déclin du Moyen Age*, vols. 1–5, 3rd ed. (Louvain, Belgium: E. Nauwelaerts, 1956–70).

18. PG, p. 61; PL, p. 73. Here it is worth recalling again Strauss's statement to Löwith, quoted in Chapter 6, "On the *querelle des anciens et des modernes*: I do not deny, but assert, that modern philosophy has much that is essential in common with Christian medieval philosophy; but that means that the *attack* of the moderns is directed decisively against *ancient* philosophy."

19. Strauss cites Georges de Lagarde's earlier work, *Recherches sur l'esprit politique de la Reforme*, (Douai, France, 1927, 52 ff. and 81 ff.; PL, p. 141). I am unaware of this edition of Lagarde's, but there is a 1926 edition published as *Recherches sur l'esprit politique de la Reforme* (Paris: Éditions A. Picard, 1926).

20. In his 1970 conversation with Jacob Klein, Strauss describes his commitment to political Zionism in the context of his affirmation of Nietzsche and his movement, at age seventeen, away from Judaism. "I was brought up in a conservative, even orthodox Jewish home somewhere in a rural district in Germany. The 'ceremonial' laws were rather strictly observed but there was little Jewish knowledge.... Furtively I read Schopenhauer and Nietzsche. When I was sixteen and we read the Laches in school, I formed the plan, or the wish, to spend my life reading Plato and breeding rabbits while earning a livelihood as a rural postmaster. Without being aware of it, I had moved rather far away from my Jewish home, without any rebellion. When I was seventeen, I converted to Zionism – to simple, straightforward political Zionism," JPCM, p. 460.

21. PG, pp. 26–7; PL, pp. 38–9, emphasis added.

22. It may be for this reason that Strauss later characterized *Philosophy and Law*, in a letter to Gershom Scholem, as a "Thomistic detour," by which he means that he had viewed revelation as a matter of knowledge (GS 3, p. 728). See Chapter 6 for more on this point.

23. PG, p. 60; PL, p. 141, n. 24. In fact, when, after reading *Philosophy and Law*, Eric Voeglin wrote to Strauss that "I have the impression that you have retreated from an understanding of the prophetic [religious] foundation of philosophizing," Strauss denied any change, stressing the centrality of his conception of law in and after *Philosophy and Law* (FPP, p. 77).

24. PG, p. 122; PL, p. 132.

25. For the most compelling reading of Strauss's position see G. R. F Ferrari, "Strauss's Plato" *Arion* 5(2) (fall 1997), pp. 36–65.

26. JPCM, pp. 413–14, at 413.

27. Strauss also rejects the view that Israel is a racist state.

28. "But I can never forget what it achieved as a moral force in an era of complete dissolution. It helped to stem the tide of 'progressive' leveling of venerable, ancestral differences; it fulfilled a conservative function."

29. PAW, pp. 90–1.

30. The prophet for Strauss is the statesman, PAW, p. 91.

31. Timothy Fuller, "Philosophy, Faith, and the Question of Progress," in FPP, p. 291.

32. Cf. "The Law of Reason in the *Kuzari*," PAW.

33. Strauss's view of the prophet is quite similar to Michael Walzer's view of the prophet as social critic. See Michael Walzer, *Interpretation and Social Criticism*. (Cambridge: Harvard University Press, 1987, pp. 70–89). As Walzer puts it, the prophet can only

succeed by drawing on "the core values of his audience in a powerful and plausible way" (*Interpretation and Social Criticism*, p. 89). The difference between Walzer and Strauss is that the latter maintains that philosophy is distinct from political philosophy and often in tension with it. On this matter, Stanley Rosen's explanation of the quarrel between the ancients and the moderns is helpful. The difference, Rosen maintains, is that the former do not believe that wisdom has been or can fully be achieved while the latter believes that it has been and can be. Classical philosophy, as opposed to modern philosophy that becomes political philosophy, is the placeholder for this doubt. Stanley Rosen, *The Ancients and the Moderns: Rethinking Modernity* (St. Augustine's Press, 2002) and *G. W. F. Hegel: An Introduction to the Science of Wisdom* (New Haven: Yale University Press, 1974). See Chapter 6 for more on Strauss's view of skepticism. For Rosen, the quarrel comes down to an argument between Hegel and the ancients. See Robert Pippen, *Hegel's Idealism: The Satisfaction of Self-Consciousness* (Cambridge: Cambridge University Press, 1989, pp. 91–4) for a very lucid discussion of Hegel on skepticism.

34. TM, p. 83.
35. OT, pp. 183–4; TM, p. 83–4.
36. WPP, p. 46.
37. For a broad overview of Strauss's criticism of social science as it relates to communism see Nasser Behnegar, *Leo Strauss, Max Weber, and the Scientific Study of Politics* (Chicago: University of Chicago Press, 2003).
38. WWP, p. 59.
39. Robb A. McDaniel, *The Philosopher's Jeremiad: Prophecy and Political Philosophy in Leo Strauss and Emmanuel Levinas*, diss., Vanderbilt University, 1990, p. 26, n. 16.
40. *The Heidegger Case: On Philosophy and Politics*, Thomas Rockmore and Joseph Margolis, eds. (Philadelphia: Temple University Press, 1992, p. 75).
41. Heidegger, *Gesamtausgabe*, vol. 43, *Nietzsche: Der Wille zur Macht als Kunst*, Bernd Heimbüchel, ed., winter semester 1936–7 (Frankfurt: Vittorio Klostermann, 1983, p. 105), as quoted in Zimmerman, *The Heidegger Case: On Philosophy and Politics*, p. 75.
42. FPP p. 66.
43. Strauss continues: "Practical science in contradistinction to practical wisdom itself sets forth coherently the principles of action and the general rules of prudence ('proverbial wisdom'). Practical science raises questions which within practical or political experience, or at any rate on the basis of such experience, reveal themselves to be the most important questions and that are not stated, let alone answered, with sufficient clarity by practical wisdom itself" (LAM, pp. 205–6).
44. This is how Herzl portrayed his turn to Zionism. See Ernst Pawel, *The Labyrinth of Exile: A Life of Theodor Herzl*. For a discussion of the Dreyfus affair see Michael Burns, *France and the Dreyfus Affair* (New York: Bedford Books, 1998). For more recent historical claims that dispute Herzl's account of this turn to Zionism as the result of the Dreyfus affair, see Jacques Kornberg, *Theodor Herzl: From Assimilation to Zionism* (Bloomington: Indiana University Press, 1993).
45. *The Complete Diaries of Theodor Herzl* (vols. 1–5), Harry Zohn, trans. (New York: Thomas Yoseloff, 1960, see p. 1899).
46. Marie-Ann Lescourret, *Emmanuel Levinas* (Paris: Flammarion, 1994, pp. 19–50 and 60–4).

47. See especially "The Prohibition against Representation and 'The Rights of Man" and "The Rights of the Other Man" in AT.
48. AQ, p. 248; OTB, p. 159.
49. See especially "The State of Caesar and the State of David" in BV.
50. LR, p. 294.
51. AQ, p. 246; OTB, p. 158.
52. AQ, p. 234; OTB, p. 150.
53. TeI, p. 245; TI, p. 222.
54. DF, p. 39.
55. DF, p. 100.
56. *Origins of the Other*, p. 226–7.
57. DF, p. 218.
58. DF, 218–19.
59. DF, p. 221.
60. DF, p. 263.
61. AQ, p. 234; OTB, p. 150.
62. CPP, p. 171.
63. CPP, p. 153.
64. CPP, p. 171.
65. AQ, p. 176; OTB, p. 111.
66. See Richard A. Cohen, *Ethics, Exegesis and Philosophy: Interpretation after Levinas* (Cambridge: Cambridge University Press, 2001, pp. 1–24) for more on Levinas's use of philosophical references to Israel Salanter, whom, as mentioned in Chapter 1, Levinas draws on for this notion. Again, for a historical account of Salanter see Immanuel Etkes, *Rabbi Israel Salanter and the Mussar Movement.*
67. AQ, p. 121; OTB, p. 75.
68. AQ, p. 123; OTB, p. 76.
69. As Levinas puts it, Israel is "a State which will have to incarnate the prophetic moral code and the idea of its peace" (BV, p. 194). I am grateful to Martin Kavka for this reference.
70. Ironically, perhaps, Levinas's equation of the prophet and exile is similar to Edward Said's equation of the public intellectual and exile. See Said, *Representations of the Intellectual* (New York: Vintage Books, 1996). While their political views were obviously very different, I would argue that Levinas and Said share the conflation of philosophy and politics, in both cases at worst dangerously so, and at best incoherently so. In my view, Strauss's and Walzer's views of the prophet as an immanent critic is far more moderate and coherent (and, perhaps less importantly, historically accurate). See note 33 of this chapter.
71. For a historical overview of the development of religious Zionism, see Aviezer Ravitzky, *Messianism, Zionism, and Jewish Religious Radicalism*, Michael Swirsky and Jonathan Chipman, trans. (Chicago: University of Chicago Press, 1996).
72. SCR, p. 6.
73. DF, p. 263.
74. DF, pp. 296–7.
75. Caygill, p. 159.
76. TeI, p. 15; TI, p. 29.
77. Caygill, p. 100.

78. See Catherine Chalier, *Lévinas: l'utopie de l'humain* (Paris: A. Michel, 1993) for a positive assessment of Levinas's utopianism.

CHAPTER 8. POLITICS AND HERMENEUTICS: STRAUSS'S AND LEVINAS'S RETRIEVAL OF CLASSICAL JEWISH SOURCES

1. See, for instance, Michael Kochin, "Morality, Nature and Esotericism in Leo Strauss's *Persecution and the Art of Writing*," *The Review of Politics* 64(2) (spring 2002), pp. 261–83.
2. See Eugene Sheppard, *Leo Strauss and the Politics of Exile*, to be discussed in greater detail in the following text.
3. *The Political Ideas of Leo Strauss* (New York: Palgrave Macmillan, 1998).
4. There are, in my view, two main problems with Drury's work on Strauss. First, she conflates Strauss with "Straussians," thereby oversimplifying the issues Strauss was interested in and second she provides no arguments against what she takes to be Strauss's ideas, merely stating her dislike of them.
5. PAW, p. 30. In my view, Strauss's claims about writing are conducive to Antonin Scalia's definition of "objectified intent." As Scalia puts it: "We [judges] look for a sort of 'objectified' intent – the intent that a reasonable person would gather from the text of the law, placed alongside the remainder of the *corpus juris*. As Bishop's old treatise nicely put its, elaborating upon the usual formulation: '[T]he primary object of all rules for interpreting statutes is to ascertain the legislative intent; *or, exactly, the meaning, the meaning which the subject is authorized to understand the legislature intended*'(Joel Prentiss Bishop, *Commentaries on the Written Laws and Their Interpretation* [Boston: Little, Brown, and Co., 1882, pp. 57–8]). . . . It is the law that governs, not the intent of the lawgiver. . . . A government of laws, not men. Men may intend what they will; but it is only the laws that they enact which bind us," *A Matter of Interpretation: Federal Courts and the Law*, Amy Gutmann, ed. (Princeton: Princeton University Press, 2001 p. 17). Strauss's claim that we ought to understand an author as he understood himself does not imply a naïve view of authorial intention, that is, that we can get into an author's mind, but rather a more complex view of the discovery of a reasonable reading of a text based on the text itself. In the conclusion of this chapter, I discuss this claim in more detail as well as some of its inherent limitations, which, I suggest, Strauss recognized.
6. Paul Cantor, "Leo Strauss and Contemporary Hermeneutics," in Alan Udoff, ed. *Leo Strauss's Thought: Toward a Critical Engagement*, p. 270.
7. Scalia, like Strauss, maintains that the text provides the rules for this discovery. As Scalia puts it, "You will find it frequently said in judicial opinions of my court and others that the judge's objective in interpreting a statute is to give effect to 'the intent of the legislature.' . . . Unfortunately, it [this principle] does not square with some of the (few) generally accepted concrete rules of statutory construction. One of them is the rule that when the text of a statute is clear, that is the end of the matter. Why should that be so, if what the legislature *intended*, rather than what it *said*, is the object of our inquiry? In selecting the words of the statute, the legislature might have misspoken. Why not permit that to be demonstrated from floor debates? Or indeed, why not accept, as proper material for the court to consider, later explanations by the legislators – a sworn affidavit signed by the majority of each house, for example,

as to what they *really* meant?" In the context of describing what he understands as the contours of democratic theory, Scalia's formulations aptly describe the basic underpinnings of Strauss's interpretative approach. As we saw in Chapter 5, Strauss criticizes strongly the specifically modern Kantian notion that it is possible to understand an author better than he understood himself. This assumption underlies the notion that the "legislature might have misspoken." The implication of Scalia's caustic response to this claim is that such a claim destroys the import of the text qua text. Why have a constitutional text if we disregard it in assuming that we understand its true meaning better than its authors understood it? Put even more simply from the perspective of the underlying impetus of Strauss's thought, why even bother to read if we assume in advance that our way of understanding things is the only true one?

The subject of constitutional interpretation is, of course, beyond the scope of this book. I mention it here, however, to contrast what I believe is Strauss's formalist position, as rooted in his claims about reading and writing, with Jaffa's claim, made in the name of Strauss, that "we do not look outside of the Constitution but rather within it for the natural law basis of constitutional interpretation" (*Original Intent*, op. cit.). Jaffa rejects Scalia's formalism and claims that the Declaration of Independence is the natural law basis of the Constitution. To make this point in connection with Scalia, Jaffa turns to the Lincoln-Douglas debates, the subject of Jaffa's much-revered *Crisis of the House Divided* (Seattle: University of Washington Press, 1973). Summing up Lincoln's view, Jaffa writes: "Lincoln thought that slavery in the territories should be prohibited by Congress, and that the people of the territories should be denied such a right," *Storm over the Constitution* (Lanham, MD: Lexington Books, 1999, p. 117). The premise of Lincoln's view, Jaffa maintains, is the basic moral truth that "all men are created equal." In Chapter 6, I tried to outline the reasons that though the notion that "all men are created equal" is an essential and indeed a unique element of biblical religion from Strauss's perspective, Jaffa's contentions about the contents of natural right and natural law do not cohere with Strauss's thought.

Jaffa's claim that the Constitution is based on what he calls the natural law doctrine of the Declaration of Independence also does not cohere with what I am suggesting is Strauss's textualist framework. Jaffa's basic point in affirming Lincoln's position in the Lincoln-Douglas debate is that despite Douglas's appeal to majority rule, Lincoln recognized what should have been the moral position on slavery based on the natural law foundations of the Declaration. In his criticism of Scalia, Jaffa suggests that Scalia takes precisely Douglas's position (*Storm over the Constitution*). Douglas erred, according to Jaffa's reading of Lincoln, in favoring a procedural form over moral content. However, in the context of his critique of Scalia, Jaffa does not elaborate on the more generous reading he gives in *Crisis of the House Divided* of Douglas's position. There Jaffa generously makes clear Douglas's moral repugnance toward slavery and also Douglas's view that this moral truth was something that the will of the people, outside of governmental mandate, had to be galvanized toward. In his brief essay on Scalia, Jaffa offers the ungenerous reading of Scalia (again whom he explicitly equates with Douglas) as contending that only might makes right. I am not attempting to argue here for the veracity of Douglas's position but would only like to point out that the textualist view that I am ascribing to Strauss through Scalia need not disregard moral truths. The question instead in the context of Scalia is whether *judges* determine for the people moral truth outside of the written law. In the context of Strauss, the question is whether a moral principle, such as natural law as the fusing of reason and biblical revelation, is philosophically possible or politically desirable. As I argued in Chapter 6, the answer to both of these questions from Strauss's point of view is "no." This isn't to say, of course, that Strauss would support the position Jaffa attributes to Scalia, that of Douglas's. In fact, Strauss rejected legal positivism as discredited by fascism (see the discussion of Hans Kelson in NRH, p. 4, n. 2). These are all complicated subjects, which are again beyond the scope of this book. However, as I argue briefly in the conclusion of the book, these and other reasons make it difficult to pinpoint Strauss's exact position in terms of American politics. The reason for this is that Strauss is concerned mainly with questions, and not with answers. My claim in this long note, therefore, is not that Strauss's position is Scalia's (or vice versa) but rather that Strauss's formalism in his hermeneutic approach (which broadly speaking is conducive to the formalism in politics outlined by Berns, *Taking the Constitution Seriously*, and Mansfield, *America's Constitutional Soul*), makes some, if not most, of the claims by Strauss's followers for the relevance of his thought to concrete politics implausible at best.

8. *Hermeneutics as Politics*, p. 123.
9. Lenzner, "A Literary Exercise in Self-knowledge: Strauss's Twofold Interpretation of Maimonides."
10. In contrast, Spinoza, on Strauss's reading, is no longer committed to the preservation of the law but only to philosophy. Spinoza's mistake, or perhaps better, the internal tension in his work, is in his assumption that the past has nothing of value to teach the present. See Chapter 5.
11. LAM, p. 7.
12. See, for instance, Nathan Tarcov, "Philosophy and History: Tradition and Interpretation in the Work of Leo Strauss," *Polity* 16 (fall 1983), pp. 5–29.
13. *Richard Rorty: Critical Dialogues*, Matthew Festenstein and Simon Thompson, eds. (New York: Blackwell, 2001, p. 92). For an illuminating and more sympathetic reading of Rorty on Strauss see Melvin L. Rogers, "Rorty's Straussianism; or, Irony Against Democracy," *Contemporary Pragmatism* 1(2) (December 2004), pp. 95–121.
14. Rorty has recently retracted some of his remarks on religion, in large part because of the influence of Jeffrey Stout's *Democracy and Tradition* (Princeton: Princeton University Press, 2004). Yet given Rorty's long history of antireligious animus, it is hard to imagine what his views that would include taking religion seriously would look like. Nicholas Wolterstorff has been particularly articulate about Rorty's dogmatism in regard to rejecting religion and his desire for everyone to believe the same thing. See Wolterstorff's "An Engagement with Rorty" and Rorty's response "Religion in the Public Square: A Reconsideration" in *Journal of Religious Ethics* 31(1) (spring 2003), for an exchange between them.
15. *Critical Dialogues*, p. 92.
16. See Strauss's exchange with Löwith on this matter in CLS, pp. 182–4.
17. Laurence Lambert also seems to miss the broader point in his otherwise impressive study *Leo Strauss and Nietzsche* (Chicago: University of Chicago Press, 1996), when he maintains in Nietzsche's name that Strauss has a "lack of boldness on behalf of philosophy at a decisive moment in its history" (p. 184).

18. *Beyond Good and Evil*, R. J. Hollingdale, trans. and commentary (Harmondsworth: Penguin, 1973, #211); *The Will Power*, Walter Kaufmann and R. J. Hollingdale, trans. (New York: Random House, 1967, 1972).
19. NRH, p. 124.
20. CM, pp. 161–2.
21. For an account of the role of persecution in Strauss's view of esotericism, see Paul J. Bagley, "On the Practice of Esotericism," *Journal of the History of Ideas* 53(2) (April–June 1992), pp. 231–47.
22. LAM, p. 211. The context of Strauss's statement is his criticism of social science. What Rorty and, perhaps, some aspects of neopragmaticism generally share with social science is the attempt to solve problems by denying them for the sake of utility. But, as Strauss argues, this amounts to providing a solution. Rorty's comments about metaphysics generally and instantiated by his particular comments about Strauss do, in my view, amount to a kind of intellectual bullying. Again, Wolterstorff's characterization of Rorty in *Journal of Religious Ethics* is particularly apropos.
23. See SA, LAPL; also SCR, p. 11.
24. *Leo Strauss and the Politics of Exile*, diss., University of California at Los Angeles, 2001.
25. For Strauss, there is "no comfort other than that inherent in this activity [of philosophy] ... [that] enables us to accept all evils which befall us and which may well break our hearts in the spirit of good citizens of the city of God" (LAM, p. 8). The point though is also that while philosophy is a comfort for the philosopher, philosophy is not a comfort to those not already committed to the philosophical life, cf. Strauss's remarks in "Memorial Remarks for Jason Aronson," JPCM, p. 475: "Death is terrible, terrifying, but we cannot live as human beings if this terror grips us to the point of corroding our core. Jason Aronson had two experiences which protected him against the corrosives as well as its kin. The one is to come to grips with the corrosives, to face them, to think them through, to understand the ineluctable necessities, and to understand without them no life, no human life, no good life, is possible.... The other experience which gave him strength and depth was his realizing ever more clearly and profoundly what it means to be a son of the Jewish people – of the 'am 'olam [eternal people] – to have one's roots deep in the oldest past and to be committed to a future beyond all futures."
26. Catherine Zuckert, *Postmodern Platos* (Chicago: University of Chicago Press, 1996, pp. 136–7).
27. See note 25 in the preceding text.
28. Again note the contrast with Rorty.
29. NRH, p. 113.
30. PAW, p. 55.
31. See the discussion of Berns in Chapter 6 on the issue of commerce.
32. PAW, p. 49.
33. I agree with Stanley Rosen that Strauss does not present any claims to have discovered any secret (*Politics as Hermeneutics*, p. 115).
34. RCPR, pp. 42–4.
35. DF, p. 68.
36. DF, p. 64. For a very helpful discussion of this Talmudic reading in the context of claims for Levinas's Jewish authenticity, see Samuel Moyn, "Emmanuel Levinas's

Talmudic Readings: Between Tradition and Invention," *Prooftexts* 23(3) (fall 2003), pp. 338–64.

37. DF, 60–1. All translation of *Sanhedrin* 99a are as cited in DF.
38. DF, p. 64.
39. DF, p. 100.
40. NTR, p. 6.
41. NTR, pp. 30–50. All translations from *Shabbat* 88a–b are taken from this translation.
42. NTR, p. 37.
43. AQ, p. 235; OTB, p. 150.
44. The question of who the "Sadducee" is in this text is a source of commentary in the Talmud. Levinas suggests that the "Sadducee" here is a "European" because he is shocked by the intensity of Jewish religious learning.
45. NTR, p. 46.
46. The Aramaic term should probably be translated as "squeezing," which is closer to Levinas's first rendition of "holding." Also, it is unclear why Levinas claims that Raba is holding his foot; it is not clear from the Talmudic text whether Raba is holding his finger or his foot.
47. NTR, p. 46, emphasis added.
48. HSMP, p. 322.
49. Strauss to Gadamer, February 26, 1961, CCWM.
50. Gadamer to Strauss, April 1961, CCWM.
51. Strauss to Gadamer, February 26, 1961, CCWM. Or as Strauss puts it to Löwith, "What then is the point of the talk about 'existential' study of history, if it does not lead one to conduct oneself toward the teaching of those who came before in a way that is not know-it-all-contemplative, but learning, questioning, practical?

   "The conception I sketch has nothing *at all* to do with Heidegger, as Heidegger gives merely a refined interpretation of modern historicism, 'anchors' it 'ontologically.' For with Heidegger, 'historicity' has made nature disappear *completely*, which however has the merit of consistency and compels one to reflect," CCM, p. 107, emphasis in the original.
52. Or, as he puts it in the context of Heidegger, "Among the many things that make Heidegger's thought so appealing to so many contemporaries is his accepting the premise that while human life and thought is radically historical, History is not a rational process. As a consequence, he denies that one can understand a thinker better than he understood himself and even as he understood himself: a great thinker will understand an earlier thinker of rank creatively, i.e. by transforming his thought, and hence by understanding him differently than he understood himself. One could hardly observe this transformation if one could not see the original form" ("Philosophy as Rigorous Science and Political Philosophy," SPPP, p. 30).
53. RCPR, pp. 42–4.

CHAPTER 9. REVELATION AND COMMANDMENT: STRAUSS, LEVINAS, AND THE THEOLOGICO-POLITICAL PREDICAMENT

1. SCR, p. 3.
2. While he admired Strauss's "ethical stance," Scholem regarded Strauss's candidacy as an "obviously conscious and deliberately provoked...suicide of such

a capable mind." *Briefwechsel 1933–1940*, Gershom Scholem, ed. (Suhrkamp: Frankfurt/Main, 1980, pp. 192–7); Garry Smith and Andre Lefevere, trans., *The Correspondence of Walter Benjamin and Gershom Scholem, 1932–1940* (New York: Schocken, 1989, pp. 155–8).

3. PG, p. 29; PL, p. 41.

4. In a recent article that concludes with a reconsideration of the Strauss-Guttmann debate, Abraham Melamed points out that Guttmann "contended that there is no one opinion in medieval thought about the relationship between revelation and philosophy." Melamed concludes that while Strauss's thesis revolutionized the field of the study of medieval Jewish philosophy, "when we examine the great controversy between Strauss and Guttmann from a distance of two generations . . . [t]he culmination of the studies of medieval Jewish political thought so far seems to point in the direction of Guttmann after he had read Strauss" ("Is There a Jewish Political Thought?", *Hebraic Political Studies* 1:1, 2005, pp. 52–6). Melamed's point is valid from a historical point of view, that is, from the point of view of the multiple opinions on the relation between philosophy and revelation in medieval philosophy. Yet this conclusion begs Strauss's *philosophical* question that he derives from his historical study that concerns, as I have argued, the scope of philosophical activity and its philosophical implications. Put another way, Maimonides is important on Strauss's reading not as one of many voices in medieval Jewish philosophy but as the most important philosophical voice. Hence, it is not enough to show that there are competing opinions. To refute Strauss, Guttmann would have to show that another opinion was actually philosophically superior to Maimonides's. My claim is not that Strauss automatically wins such a debate but that Guttmann did not in his reply respond to Strauss's actual challenge.

5. "Philosophie der Religion oder Philosophie des Gesetzes?," pp. 143–76. For a particularly helpful discussions of the debate between Strauss and Guttmann, see Moshe Schwarz, "Enlightenment and Philosophy: On Jewish Philosophy in the Modern Era," *Da'at* 1 (1978), pp. 7–16 (Hebrew) and Ehud Luz's preface to his translation of a number of Strauss's essays in *Jerusalem and Athens: A Selection of Essays*, trans. Ehud Luz (Jerusalem: Mossad Bialik, 2001), pp. 54–6 (Hebrew).

6. "Philosophie der Religion oder Philosophie des Gesetzes?," p. 171.

7. Ibid., p. 150.

8. PG, p. 42; PL, p. 55.

9. This is somewhat ironic, of course, given Guttmann's commitment to scientific, historical truth. Guttmann describes his approach as "*historisch*" and Strauss's as "*sachlich-philosophisch.*"

10. As quoted in Chapter 5.

11. See Strauss's passing comment to Scholem regarding Guttmann's response in GS 3, p. 765.

12. PG, p. 60; PL, p. 141, n. 24, as cited in Chapter 7. It bears repeating also that, when, after reading *Philosophy and Law*, Eric Voeglin wrote to Strauss that "I have the impression that you have retreated from an understanding of the prophetic [religious] foundation of philosophizing," Strauss denied any change, stressing the centrality of his conception of law in and after *Philosophy and Law* (FPP, p. 77).

13. See the discussion of *Philosophy and Law* in Chapter 6.

14. *The Meaning of God in Modern Jewish Religion* (Detroit: Wayne State University Press, 1994, p. 14). The book was first published in 1937.

15. Strauss: "the acceptance of the past or the return to the Jewish tradition is something radically different from a mere continuation of that tradition. It is quite true that Jewish life in the past was almost always more than a continuity of a tradition. Very great changes within that tradition have taken place in the course of centuries. But it is also true that the change which we are witnessing today, and which all of us are participating in, is – in one way or the other – qualitatively different from all previous changes within Judaism" ("Progress or Return," JPCM, p. 93). Kaplan introduces his most explicitly theological work, the 1937 *The Meaning of God in the Jewish Religion*, with a distinction between transvaluation and revaluation. The former he states is the interpretative method employed by premodern Jews to Jewish texts and life. The latter is Kaplan's method. What marks the difference between these two approaches, Kaplan maintains, is the sense of continuity with the past. For the sake of a Jewish future, Kaplan favors progress; Strauss return.

16. "Why We Remain Jews," JPCM, p. 34. As far as I know, Strauss made no reference to Kaplan in his work. I would venture that the reference in this quotation is to Ahad Ha'am and to cultural Zionism generally. Kaplan was, of course, deeply influenced by Ahad Ha'am, hence the connection between Strauss's description and Kaplan's thought.

17. I turn in the conclusion to a fuller (though not complete) analysis of how Strauss understands the parameters of the "tradition."

18. SCR, p. 8.

19. Guttmann makes these claims in "Philosophie der Religion oder Philosophie des Gesetzes?," especially pp. 170–3. More recently, Zachary Braiterman makes similar claims about Strauss in "Against Leo Strauss," *The Journal of the Society for Textual Reasoning* 3 (1) (June 2004).

20. JPMC, pp. 359–76. For more on Strauss's reading of the opening chapters of Genesis, see Jonathan Cohen's "Strauss, Soloveitchik and the Genesis Narrative: Conceptions of the Ideal Jew as Derived from Philosophical and Theological Readings of the Bible."

21. JPCM, p. 360.

22. "These considerations show, it seems to me, how unreasonable it is to speak of the mythical or prelogical character of biblical thought as such. The account of the world given in the first chapter of the Bible is not fundamentally different from philosophic accounts; that account is based on evident distinctions which are accessible to us as they were to the biblical author. Hence we can understand that account; these distinctions are accessible to man as man," JPCM, pp. 367–8. See Chapter 6 for a discussion of NRH, pp. 75–6 in this context.

23. JPCM, p. 374.

24. JPCM, p. 373.

25. SCR, p. 6.

26. Menachem Lorberbaum, *Politics and the Limits of Law: Secularizing the Political in Medieval Jewish Thought* (Stanford: Stanford University Press, 2001, p. 74).

27. Recently, Richard Cohen, *Ethics, Exegesis and Philosophy: Interpretation after Levinas*, p. 233. Guttmann also makes this claim, "Philosophie der Religion oder Philosophie des Gesetzes?," p. 170.

28. "Apologetic Thinking," *Der Jude*, Jahrgang VII (1923), pp. 457–64. Translated in *The Jew: Essays from Buber's Journal Der Jude*, selected, edited, and introduced by Arthur

A. Cohen, translated from the German by Joachim Neugroschel (Tuscaloosa: The University of Alabama Press, 1980, p. 267).

29. SCR, p. 8.

30. See the exchange between Buber and Rosenzweig, known as "the builders," on the status of Jewish law included in *On Jewish Learning*, N. N. Glatzer, ed. (New York: Schocken, 1965, pp. 72–92).

31. Ibid., p. 84.

32. JPCM, p. 153.

33. Kant, of course, has a conception of "radical evil," which is wholly rejected by Cohen. Again, see Guttmann's comments regarding Strauss's pessimism in "Philosophie der Religion oder Philosophie des Gesetzes?," p. 171. On the view that the notion that Judaism does not have a concept of the sinfulness of the human being is a modern prejudice, see David Novak's discussion in *Natural Law in Judaism* (Cambridge: Cambridge University Press, 1998). See also Strauss's discussion with Scholem on the status of Jewish conceptions of evil and sinfulness, GS 3, pp. 740–1.

34. SCR, p. 22.

35. *Religion within the Limits of Reason Alone*, Theodore M. Greene and Hoyt H. Hudson, trans. (New York: Harper and Brothers, 1960, p. 87); translation altered.

36. For recent scholarship questioning the view that Paul actually had an intrinsically negative view of the law see, among others, John Gager, *Reinventing Paul* (Oxford: Oxford University Press, 2000); Stanley Stowers, *A Rereading of Romans: Justice, Jews, and Gentiles* (New Haven: Yale University Press, 1994); and Lloyd Gaston, *Paul and the Torah* (Vancouver: University of British Columbia Press,1987).

37. For a more extended argument on this subject see Leora Batnitzky, "Love and Law: John Milbank and Hermann Cohen on the Ethical Possibilities of Secular Society," *Secular Theology*, Clayton Crockett, ed., Routledge Press (March 2001), pp. 73–91.

38. "Ethics can confidently allow the concept of coercion to fall away for right, as ... the concept of law steps forward: in the norms of right [*Rechtsnormen*] ... are the mathematically original shape [*Urform*] of law, in so far as they form the measure of an angle of the regulations and the guiding principles. In the norms [of right], right is legitimated for the concept of law," *Ethik des reinen Willen*, p. 270.

39. GS 3, p. 740.

40. Some of Strauss's critics believe that Strauss was so antiliberal as to be in favor of fascist coercion. Nicholas Xenos has recently suggested this in "Leo Strauss and the Rhetoric of the War on Terror" *Logos* 3 (2) (spring 2004), special issue on "Confronting Neoconservatism," pp. 63–81. I discuss and reject Xenos's allegation at the end of Chapter 10.

41. This is Guttmann's view against Strauss, see "Philosophie der Religion oder Philosophie des Gesetzes?," pp. 171–2.

42. This goes also for certain modern orthodox articulations of law. For example, the arguments of Joseph Soloveitchik, the foremost twentieth-century spokesperson for American modern orthodoxy, and Yeshayahu Leibowitz, the orthodox, Israeli iconoclast, could easily be described according to this schema.

43. Strauss does mention Mendelssohn in the preface, but not on the issue of law. Of particular interest in this connection is Strauss's defense of Jacobi in his introduction to Mendelssohn's work.

44. "Religious doctrines and propositions . . . are not forced upon the faith of the [Jewish] nation under the threat of eternal or temporal punishments." *Jerusalem*, Allan Arkush, trans. (Hanover and London: University of New England Press, 1983, p. 126). Or, more generally, "Divine religion . . . is a moral person, but its rights imply no coercion," p. 73.

45. One reason, of course, is that much of modern Jewish thought remains a response to Spinoza.

46. Again, along with the caricature of Strauss as suggesting that revelation is irrational and philosophy is rational is the caricature that Strauss's position is Spinoza's. The opposite is the case. For this caricature of both Spinoza and Strauss, see Richard Cohen *Ethics, Exegesis and Philosophy: Interpretation after Levinas*, p. 233.

47. "In Pursuit of the Counter-Text: The Turn to the Jewish Legal Model in Contemporary American Legal Theory," *Harvard Law Review* 106(4) (1993), pp. 813–94.

48. See for instance, Susan Handelman, *The Slayers of Moses: The Emergence of Rabbinic Interpretation in Modern Literary Theory* (Albany: State University of New York, 1982).

49. Handelman, among others, utilizes Levinas for this purpose.

50. "Violence and the Word," *Narrative, Violence, and the Law: The Essays of Robert Cover*, Martha Minow, Michael Ryan, and Austin Sarat, eds. (Ann Arbor: The University of Michigan Press, 1992, p. 203).

51. See especially Cohen's chapter on Ezekiel in *Religion of Reason*.

52. Preface in SCR, p. 22.

53. "Nomos and Narrative," *Narrative, Violence, and the Law*, p. 96.

54. As I have suggested, this is the philosophical claim of Chapters 1 and 2 of *Philosophy and Law*; because philosophers are always individuals they find themselves, in the medieval context, in this preexisting life world. Part of the problem *for philosophy* in the modern period, for Strauss, is that it does not acknowledge such a preexisting world and therefore believes it can produce its own social and political world.

55. "Obligation: A Jewish Jurisprudence of the Social Order," *Journal of Law and Religion* 65(5) (1987), pp. 65–90.

56. Stone, pp. 885–6, quoting Cover pp. 66–9.

57. For a very basic outline of the coercive aspects of premodern Judaism see Jacob Katz, *Tradition and Crisis: Jewish Society at the End of the Middle Ages*.

58. Stone, p. 871; Maimonides Commentary on the Mishanah, *Sanhedrin* principle 11, translated in *Maimonides' Commentary on the Mishnah Tractate Sanhedrin*, Fred Rosen, trans. (New York: Sepher-Hermon Press, 1981), pp. 156–7.

59. LAM, p. 207.

60. LAM, p. 207.

61. See David Stern's criticism of this perspective in "Midrash and Indeterminacy," *Critical Inquiry* (15) (1988), pp. 132–61.

62. For a broad range of legal and literary theorists as well as historians who use this story, see Stone, pp. 855–61. Of particular interest is Izhak Englard's analysis of this phenomenon over a quarter of a century ago. See "Majority Decision vs. Individual Truth: The Interpretations of the 'Oven of Achnai' Aggadah," *Tradition* 15 (1975), pp. 137–52.

63. Stone, p. 859.

64. Levinas tends to conflate the Bible and the Talmud, just as Strauss tends to conflate the Bible and the medieval philosophers. It's an interesting question as to which is the more problematic stance.

65. DF, p. 101.

66. "Why We Remain Jews," JPCM, p. 340.

67. As quoted in Chapter 4.

68. As quoted in Chapter 4.

69. Stone, p. 684.

70. Stone, p. 865, emphasis added.

71. Stone, p. 865.

72. My point here is not to suggest that a justification of Jewish law is a criterion for acceptance into the canon of modern Jewish thought but only to point out the irony of contemporary receptions and perceptions of Strauss and Levinas.

73. Isadore Twersky's "The Shulhan Aruk: Enduring Code of Jewish Law," Judah Goldin, ed. The Jewish Expression (New Haven: Yale University Press, 1976) eloquently describes this interplay.

74. Paul Ricoeur comments on a parallel tension in Levinas's thought in which Levinas eschews history, but nonetheless explicitly dedicates his work to the memory of the victims of National Socialism. See Ricoeur, "Otherwise: A Reading of Emmanuel Levinas's Otherwise than Being or Beyond Essence," Yale French Studies 104 (2004), pp. 82–99.

75. See Peter Ochs's description of postcritical scriptural interpretation in The Return to Scripture in Judaism and Christianity, Peter Ochs, ed. (New York: Paulist Press, 1993).

76. "Why We Remain Jews," JPCM, p. 343.

77. In making this claim, I would qualify Kenneth Hart Green's suggestion that Strauss's thought offers a model for a return to Maimonides for the purposes of a constructive Jewish thought. In my view, Halevi and not Maimonides is the model of constructive (i.e., theological) Jewish thought, for Strauss. On Strauss's reading, Halevi left philosophy and in so doing was able to live the relationship with the divine by way of the language of Judaism. Maimonides, in remaining a philosopher, on the other hand, was not able to remain true to the prephilosophical life world of Jewish texts and instead distorted these texts in his philosophical world view. I agree with Hart that Maimonides is the model of medieval rationalism for Strauss because, on Strauss's reading of him, Maimonides's dilemma is Strauss's own. But this is the dilemma of someone who is simultaneously loyal to Judaism yet unable to move beyond philosophical doubts. Halevi, in contrast, on Strauss's reading recognizes the tension between the believer and the philosopher, but is nevertheless able to believe. Strauss's appraisal of Halevi in this regard is consistent with his positive appraisal of Aristophanes as an alternative to Socrates (see SA).

78. As Strauss puts it in connection with Rosenzweig, "when speaking of the Jewish experience, one must start from what is primary or authoritative for the Jewish consciousness and not from what is the primary condition of possibility of the Jewish experience: one must start from God's Law, the Torah, and not the Jewish nation. But in this decisive case, Rosenzweig proceeds in the opposite manner; he proceeds, as he puts it, 'sociologically.' He notes that the Jewish dogmatists of the middle ages, especially Maimonides, proceeded in the first manner: traditional Jewish

dogmatics understood the Jewish nation in the light of the Torah; it was silent about the 'presupposition' of the law, viz. the Jewish nation and its chosenness.... [I]f the Jewish nation did not originate the Torah but is manifestly constituted by the Torah, it is necessarily preceded by the Torah which was created prior to the world and for the sake of which the world was created." In my view, this is a very perceptive description of the underlying premises of Rosenzweig's thought and also links Strauss's thought in interesting ways to Hermann Cohen's.

79. A recent exception to this trend is Jonathan Cohen's *Tevunah ve-temurah: panim be-heker ha-filosofyah ha-Yehudit.*

80. This, of course, is a paraphrase of Strauss's concise statement of the matter in *Natural Right and History*: "Historicism asserts that all human thoughts or beliefs are historical, and hence deservedly destined to perish; but historicism itself is a human thought; hence historicism can be of only temporary validity, or it cannot be simply true. To assert the historicist thesis means to doubt it and thus transcend it" (p. 25). For a recent discussion of the problem of historicism in modern Jewish thought see David Myers, *Resisting History: Historicism and its Discontents in German-Jewish Thought.*

CHAPTER 10. CONCLUDING THOUGHTS: PROGRESS OR RETURN?

1. JPCM, pp. 95–6.
2. "The Modern World of Leo Strauss" *Political Theory* 20(3) (1992), pp. 448–72, reprinted in Robert B. Pippin *Idealism as Modernism: Hegelian Variations* (Cambridge: Cambridge University Press, 1997, p. 213).
3. Pippin, p. 213.
4. Pippin criticizes Stanley Rosen for positing a direct line from Kant to Nietzsche (Pippin, p. 214), a point we considered briefly in the conclusion of Chapter 6. Pippin's criticism notwithstanding, I would argue that Rosen's analytic point nevertheless remains intact in considering the relation between Hermann Cohen and Levinas.
5. Pippin, p. 223.
6. OT, p. 196.
7. See for instance Leon Kass, *The Beginning of Wisdom: Reading Genesis* (New York: The Free Press, 2003).
8. CM, p. 11.
9. There certainly are practical solutions (i.e., people have to act and perhaps one good reason that everyone is not a philosopher is that if this were the case, coherent social action could well be all but impossible).
10. An acknowledgement of such a break would not, of course, bring with it an obvious answer to where the future of Jewish life lies. We have already mentioned Mordecai Kaplan's contention that the Jewish past must, in most cases, be left behind. Yet it is also possible to imagine a response to Strauss that affirms an orthodox approach to Jewish law, but that argues that Judaism in the twenty-first century must engage with, while still not affirming theologically, Christianity. Such a position is one represented by David Novak, who is much influenced by Strauss.
11. Some contemporary Christian thinkers actually argue along these lines. Perhaps significantly, many of them tend to be Protestant and not Catholic—compare Stanley Hauerwas, George Lindbeck, and others. This is an interesting issue not just

theologically but politically and historically as well, especially in the context of debates about the American Founding.

12. Again, David Novak's recent work attempts to engage these conundrums. Having studied with Strauss, Novak takes his inspiration from him, but nevertheless breaks with him in arguing both for natural law and for a rethinking of the Jewish-Christian relation. See especially *Natural Law in Judaism* (Cambridge: Cambridge University Press, 1998).

13. Pippin's teacher, and Strauss's student, Stanley Rosen, has argued in greater detail and more persuasively than anyone that the details of Strauss's analysis of many ancient texts are wrong. Yet Rosen does not dismiss Strauss for he understands that Strauss's legacy lies in the questions he asks about the very possibility of philosophy and its meaning. I would concur with Rosen that the best way to extend Strauss's legacy is to question and engage with Strauss's readings of philosophical texts and to argue with Strauss on the basis of detailed readings.

14. William Galston, in *Leo Strauss, the Straussians, and the American Regime*, Kenneth L. Deutsch and John A. Murley, eds. (Lanham, MD: Rowman and Littlefield, 1999, p. 430).

15. This phrase is Galston's.

16. See, for instance, the many impressive essays in *Leo Strauss, the Straussians, and the American Regime* that argue favorably on liberal democratic grounds for Strauss's view of liberal democracy.

17. Again, see Galston's "A Student of Leo Strauss in the Clinton Administration."

18. The phrase is Pippin's, p. 213, referring to Hegel's notion of *Versöhnung*. A matter for further study would be to consider the relation of Hermann Cohen's rather different notion of *Versöhnung* to Strauss's thought. Compare *Religion of Reason*'s discussion of atonement, which is probably a better translation of *Versöhnung*.

19. Steven Lenzner and William Kristol, "What Was Leo Strauss Up To?" *The Public Interest* 153 (fall 2003), pp. 19–39. See especially p. 38: "President Bush's advocacy of 'regime change' – which avoids the pitfalls of wishful global universalism on the one hand, and a fatalistic cultural determinism on the other – is a not altogether unworthy product of Strauss's rehabilitation of the notion of regime." The direct link between Strauss and Bush seems dubious at best, as even Lenzner and Kristol indicate with the phrase "not altogether unworthy product." Nonetheless, Nicholas Xenos's claims, based on Lenzner and Kristol's comment, about Bush and Strauss strike me as fantastical at best (compare "Leo Strauss and the Rhetoric of the War on Terror").

20. "Progress or Return?" JPCM, p. 93.

21. Letter to the Editor, *New York Times*, June 13, 2004. Lear's letter is a response to Jenny Strauss Clay's op-ed page in the *New York Times*, June 7, 2003 in which Clay wrote "My father was a teacher, not a right-wing guru." I would agree with Clay's description of the recent obsession with Strauss when she writes: "Recent news articles have portrayed my father, Leo Strauss, as the mastermind behind the neoconservative ideologues who control United States foreign policy. He reaches out from his 30-year-old grave, we are told, to direct a 'cabal' (a word with distinct anti-Semitic overtones) of Bush administration figures hoping to subject the American people to rule by a ruthless elite. I do not recognize the Leo Strauss presented in these articles."

22. GN, p. 362.

23. In Strauss's words, "just as our opponents refuse respect to unreasoned belief, we, on our part, with at least equal right must refuse respect to unreasoned unbelief " (IPP, p. 148).

24. GS 3, p. 635.

25. This comment is in keeping with Strauss's criticism of Weimar Germany's weakness with regard to law (see Chapter 6). The reference to the cross of liberalism and the preference of the ghetto is also in keeping with Strauss's continued criticism of what he claimed was Christianity's contribution to the ills of modernity. Again, Strauss's comments parallel recent work in anthropology and the work of Talal Asad in particular, which attempts to criticize an unduly myopic vision of the modern state with reference to religious law. See Asad, *Formations of the Secular*, especially Chapters 6 and 7. In terms of current controversy about Strauss, Xenos connects this 1933 letter to the war with Iraq. I find this connection rather dubious in terms of Strauss's thought and also a pretty odd argument in terms of the "neoconservatives" who, given their own ideological commitments, would surely reject Strauss's unfortunate comments to Löwith.

26. CCM, as quoted in Chapter 6, n. 40.

27. "Strauss's Generalized Agnosticism and American Liberalism," *Leo Strauss, the Straussians and the American Regime*, pp. 129–41, at 129. For Strauss's criticism of Isaiah Berlin's "Two Concepts of Liberty" in this context, see p. 131.

28. "Strauss's Generalized Agnosticism and American Liberalism," pp. 138–9.

29. This, of course, is Strauss's criticism of modern conceptions of natural right and of Burke in particular. See NRH, pp. 294–323.

30. See Ronald J. Terchek's interesting discussion of Strauss's relation to communitarianism in "Locating Leo Strauss in the Liberal-Communitarian Debate," *Leo Strauss, the Straussians, and the American Regime*, pp. 143–56.

31. As we saw especially in the discussion in Chapter 8 of Strauss's conception of the continually ambiguous relationship between the wise philosopher's quest for wisdom and his affirmation of a broader political community, Strauss affirms neither the priority of an absolute individual nor an absolute community. In this sense as well, liberal democracy, as described by Botwinick, coheres with Strauss's wise philosopher's skepticism about his own individuality in relation to a larger political community.

References

Adelmann, Dieter. 1997. "H. Steinthal und Hermann Cohen." In *Hermann Cohen's Philosophy of Religion*, Stéphane Moses and Hartwig Wiederbach, eds. Hildesheim, Zurich, and New York: Georg Olms Verlag, pp. 1–33.

Asad, Talal. 2003. *Formations of the Secular: Christianity, Islam, Modernity*. Stanford: Stanford University Press.

———. 1993. *Genealogies of Religion: Discipline and Reasons of Power in Islam and Christianity*. Baltimore: Johns Hopkins University Press.

Bacry, Henri. 1999. "La Bible, le Talmud, la connaissance et la théorie du visage de Levinas." In *Emmanuel Levinas Philosophie et judaïsme*, Danielle Cohen-Levinas and Shmuel Trigano, eds. Paris: In Press Éditions, pp. 13–19.

Bagley, Paul J. 1992. "On the Practice of Esotericism." *Journal of the History of Ideas* 53 (2) (April–June): 231–47.

Batnitzky, Leora. 2004. "Dependency and Vulnerability: Jewish and Feminist Existentialist Constructions of the Human." In *Women and Gender in Jewish Philosophy*, Hava Tirosh-Samuelson, ed. Bloomington: Indiana University Press, pp. 127–52.

———. 2001. "Love and Law: John Milbank and Hermann Cohen on the Ethical Possibilities of Secular Society." In *Secular Theology*, Clayton Crockett, ed. New York: Routledge Press, pp. 73–91.

———. 2000a. *Idolatry and Representation: The Philosophy of Franz Rosenzweig Reconsidered*. Princeton: Princeton University Press.

———. 2000b. "On the Truth of History or the History of Truth: Rethinking Rosenzweig via Strauss." *Jewish Studies Quarterly* 7 (3) (September): 223–51.

Beck, Lewis White. 1969. *Early German Philosophy: Kant and His Predecessors*. Cambridge: Harvard University Press.

Behnegar, Nasser. 2003. *Leo Strauss, Max Weber, and the Scientific Study of Politics*. Chicago: University of Chicago Press.

Ben Sasson, Haim. 1961. "Dor golei safarad 'al 'atsmo." (Hebrew) *Zion* 26: 23–64.

Bernasconi, Robert. 1988. "The Silent Anarchic World of the Evil Genius." In *The Collegium Phaenomenologicum: The First Ten Years*. G. Moneta, J. Sallis, and J. Taminiaux, eds. Dordrecht: Kluwer, pp. 257–72.

Berns, Walter. 1991. *Taking the Constitution Seriously*. Lanham, MD: Madison Books.

Bishop, Joel Prentiss. 1882. *Commentaries on the Written Laws and Their Interpretation.* Boston: Little, Brown, and Co.

Bouretz, Pierre. 2002. "Leo Strauss devant la modernité juive." *Raisons politiques* 8 (November): 22–50.

Bowlin, John A. 1999. *Contingency and Fortune in Aquinas's Ethics.* New York and Cambridge: Cambridge University Press.

Braiterman, Zachary. 2004. "Against Leo Strauss." *The Journal of the Society for Textual Reasoning* 3(1) (June), http://etext.lib.virginia.edu/journals/tr/volume3/braiterman.html.

Brauge, Rémi. 1988. *L. Strauss, Maimonide: Essais rassemblés et traduits de l'all.* Paris: PUF.

Burns, Michael. 1998. *France and the Dreyfus Affair.* New York: Bedford Books.

Burnyeat, Myles and Michael Frede, eds. 1977. *The Original Sceptics: A Controversy.* Indianapolis: Hackett.

Chalier, Catherine. *What Ought I to Do? Morality in Kant and Levinas.* Jane Marie Todd, trans. 2002. Ithaca, NY: Cornell University Press.

———. 1993. *Lévinas: l'utopie de l'humain.* Paris: A. Michel.

Cohen, Hermman. 2003. *Ethics of Maimonides.* Almut Sh. Bruckstein, trans. Madison: University of Wisconsin Press.

———. 1977–87. *Ethik des reinen Willen,* vol. 7. Reprinted in *Werke.* Helmut Holzhey, ed. Hildesheim: G. Olms.

———. 1972. *Religion of Reason Out of the Sources of Judaism.* Simon Kaplan, trans. Leo Strauss, intro. New York: Frederick Ungar.

———. 1924. *Jüdische Schriften III.* B. Strauss, ed. Berlin: C.A. Schwetschke and Sohn Verlagsbuchhandlung.

———. 1919. *Religion der Vernunft aus den Quellen des Judentums.* Benzion Kellerman, ed. Leipzig, Germany: Fock.

———. 1877. *Kants Theorie der Erfahrung.* Berlin: Dümmler, Reprinted in *Werke,* vol. 1, 1987.

Cohen, Jonathan. 1997. *Tevunah ve-temurah: panim be-heker ha-filosofyah ha-Yehudit* (Hebrew). Jerusalem: Mosad Bialik.

———. 1995. "Strauss, Soloveitchik and the Genesis Narrative: Conceptions of the Ideal Jew as Derived from Philosophical and Theological Readings of the Bible." *The Journal of Jewish Thought and Philosophy* 5(1): 99–143.

Cohen, Richard. 2001. *Ethics, Exegesis and Philosophy: Interpretation after Levinas.* Cambridge: Cambridge University Press.

———. 1994. *Elevations: The Height of the Good in Rosenzweig and Levinas.* Chicago: University of Chicago Press.

Cornell, Drucilla. 1992. *The Philosophy of the Limit.* New York: Routledge.

Cover, Robert. 1992. "Violence and the Word." In *Narrative, Violence, and the Law: The Essays of Robert Cover.* Martha Minow, Michael Ryan, and Austin Sarat, eds. Ann Arbor: The University of Michigan Press.

———. 1987. "Obligation: A Jewish Jurisprudence of the Social Order." *Journal of Law and Religion* 65(5): 65–90.

de Boer, Theodore. 1997. *The Rationality of Transcendence: Studies in the Philosophy of Emmanuel Levinas.* Amsterdam: J.C. Gieben.

Derrida, Jacques. 1998. "Faith and Knowledge." In *Religion,* Jacques Derrida and Gianni Vattimo, eds. Stanford: Stanford University Press, pp. 65–6.

———. 1978. "Violence and Metaphysics: An Essay on the Thought of Emmanuel Levinas." In *Writing and Difference.* Alan Bass, trans. and intro. Chicago: The University of Chicago Press, pp. 79–153.

Descartes, René. 1971a. "Discourse on Method." In *Descartes: Philosophical Writings.* Elizabeth Anscombe and Peter Thomas Geach, trans. Indianapolis: Bobbs-Merrill.

———. 1971b. "Meditations on First Philosophy." In *Descartes: Philosophical Writings.* Elizabeth Anscombe and Peter Thomas Geach, trans. Indianapolis: Bobbs-Merrill.

Deutsch, Kenneth L. and John A. Murley, eds. 1999. *Leo Strauss, the Straussians, and the American Regime.* Lanham, MD: Rowman and Littlefield.

de Vries, Hent. 1999. *Philosophy and the Turn to Religion.* Baltimore: Johns Hopkins University Press.

Drury, Shadia. 1998. *The Political Ideas of Leo Strauss.* New York: Palgrave Macmillan.

England, Izhak. 1975. "Majority Decision vs. Individual Truth: The Interpretations of the 'Oven of Achnai' Aggadah." *Tradition* 15: 137–52.

Etkes, Immanuel. 1993. *Rabbi Israel Salanter and the Mussar Movement.* Jonathan Chipman, trans. Philadelphia: The Jewish Publication Society.

Ferrari, G.R.F. 1997. "Strauss's Plato." *Arion* 5(2) (fall): 36–65.

Finnis, John. 1980. *Natural Law and Natural Rights.* Oxford: Oxford University Press.

Gager, John. 2000. *Reinventing Paul.* Oxford: Oxford University Press.

Galli, Barbara. 1995. *Franz Rosenzweig and Jehuda Halevi: Translating, Translations, and Translators.* Montreal: McGill-Queen's University Press.

Gaston, Lloyd. 1987. *Paul and the Torah.* Vancouver: University of British Columbia Press.

Gibbs, Robert. 1992. *Correlations in Rosenzweig and Levinas.* Princeton: Princeton University Press.

Gordon, Peter Eli. 2003. *Rosenzweig and Heidegger: Between Judaism and German Philosophy.* Berkeley: University of California Press.

Green, Kenneth Hart. 1993a. *Jew and Philosopher: The Return to Maimonides in the Jewish Thought of Leo Strauss.* New York: State University of New York Press.

———. 1993b. "Religion, Philosophy, and Morality: How Leo Strauss Read Judah Halevi's Kuzari." *Journal of the American Academy of Religion* 61: 225–73.

Guttmann, Amy, ed. 2001. *A Matter of Interpretation: Federal Courts and the Law.* Princeton: Princeton University Press.

Guttmann, Julius. 1971–6. "Philosophie der Religion oder Philosophie des Gesetzes?" *Proceedings of the Israel Academy of Sciences and Humanities* 5: 143–76.

———. 1933. *Die Philosophie des Judentums.* München: E. Reinhardt.

Halevi, Judah. 1998. *The Kuzari: In Defense of the Despised Faith.* N. Daniel Korobkin, trans. Northvale, NJ and Jerusalem: Jason Aronson Inc.

Handelman, Susan. 1982. *The Slayers of Moses: The Emergence of Rabbinic Interpretation in Modern Literary Theory.* Albany: State University of New York.

Heidegger, Martin. 1991. *Nietzsche.* David F. Krell, ed. San Francisco: Harper Collins.

———. 1983. *Gesamtausgabe. Nietzsche: Der Wille zur Macht als Kunst,* vol. 43. Bernd Heimbüchel, ed. Frankfurt: Vittorio Klostermann.

———. 1962. *Being and Time.* John Macquarrie and Edward Robinson, trans. San Francisco: Harper Collins.

Herzl, Theodor. 1960. *The Complete Diaries of Theodor Herzl* (vols. 1–5). Harry Zohn, trans. New York: Thomas Yoseloff.

Hunter, Ian. 2001. *Rival Enlightenments: Civil and Metaphysical Philosophy in Early Modern Germany.* Cambridge and New York: Cambridge University Press.

Husserl, Edmund. 1977. *Cartesian Meditations.* Dorion Cairns, trans. The Hague: Kluwer Academic Publishers.

———. 1965. *Phenomenology and the Crisis of Philosophy: Philosophy as a Rigorous Science, and Philosophy and the Crisis of European Man.* Quentin Lauer, trans. New York: Harper & Row.

Jaffa, Harry V. 1999. *Storm over the Constitution.* Lanham, MD: Lexington Books.

———. 1993. *Original Intent and the Framers of the Constitution: A Disputed Question.* Washington, DC: Regnery Publishing.

———. 1984. *American Conservatism and the American Founding.* Durham, NC: Carolina Academic Press.

———. 1973. *Crisis of the House Divided.* Seattle: University of Washington Press.

———. 1952. *Thomism and Aristotelianism.* Chicago: University of Chicago Press.

Kant, Immanuel. 1965. *The Critique of Pure Reason.* Norman Kemp Smith, trans. New York: St. Martin's Press.

———. 1960. *Religion within the Limits of Reason Alone.* Theodore M. Greene and Hoyt H. Hudson, trans. New York: Harper and Brothers.

Kaplan, Mordecai. 1994. *The Meaning of God in Modern Jewish Religion.* Detroit: Wayne State University Press.

Kass, Leon. 2003. *The Beginning of Wisdom: Reading Genesis.* New York: The Free Press.

Katz, Claire. 2003. *Levinas, Judaism, and the Feminine: The Silent Footsteps of Rebecca.* Bloomington: Indiana University Press.

Katz, Jacob. 1993. *Tradition and Crisis: Jewish Society at the End of the Middle Ages.* Bernard Dov Cooperman, trans. New York: New York University Press.

Kielmansegg, Peter Graf et al., eds. 1995. *Hannah Arendt and Leo Strauss: German Emigres and American Political Thought after World War II.* Cambridge: Cambridge University Press.

Kochin, Michael. 2002. "Morality, Nature and Esotericism in Leo Strauss's *Persecution and the Art of Writing.*" *The Review of Politics* 64(2) (spring): 261–83.

Kornberg, Jacques. 1993. *Theodor Herzl: From Assimilation to Zionism.* Bloomington: Indiana University Press.

Lagarde, Georges de. 1956–70. *La naissance de l'esprit laïque au déclin du Moyen Age,* vols. 1–5, 3rd ed. Louvain, Belgium: E. Nauwelaerts.

Lagarde, Paul de. 1891. *Deutsche Schriften.* 2nd ed. Göttingen: Dieterich.

Lambert, Laurence. 1996. *Leo Strauss and Nietzsche.* Chicago: University of Chicago Press.

Lenzner, Steven. 2002. "A Literary Exercise in Self-knowledge: Strauss's Twofold Interpretation of Maimonides." *Perspectives on Political Science* 31 (4) (fall): 225–34.

Lenzner, Steven and William Kristol. 2003. "What Was Leo Strauss Up To?" *The Public Interest* 153 (fall): 19–39.

Lescourret, Marie-Ann. 1994. *Emmanuel Levinas.* Paris: Flammarion.

Lingis, Alphonso. 1994. *A Community of Those Who Have Nothing in Common.* Bloomington: Indiana University Press.

Locke, John. 1980. *Second Treatise of Government.* Indianapolis: Hackett Publishing.

Lom, Petr. 2001. *The Limits of Doubt: The Moral and Political Implications of Skepticism.* Buffalo: State University of New York Press.

Lorberbaum, Menachem. 2001. *Politics and the Limits of Law: Secularizing the Political in Medieval Jewish Thought.* Stanford: Stanford University Press.

Luther, Martin. 1989. *Disputation against Scholastic Theology in Martin Luther's Basic Theological Writings.* T. F. Lull, ed. Minneapolis, MN: Fortress Press.

Luz, Ehud. 1991. "Yahaduto shel Leo Strauss" ("Leo Strauss's Judaism"). (Hebrew) *Da'at* 27: 35–60.

_____. 2001. *Jerusalem and Athens: A Selection of Essays.* (Hebrew) Jerusalem: Mossad Bialik, pp. 54–6.

Maimonides, Moses. 1981. *Maimonides' Commentary on the Mishnah Tractate Sanhedrin.* Fred Rosen, trans. New York: Sepher-Hermon Press.

_____. 1963. *Guide of the Perplexed.* Shlomo Pines, trans. Chicago: University of Chicago Press.

Mansfield, Harvey. 1993. *America's Constitutional Soul.* Baltimore: Johns Hopkins University Press, reprint.

Marion, Jean-Luc. 1999. *Cartesian Questions.* Daniel Garber, trans. Chicago: University of Chicago Press.

_____. 1975. *Sur l'ontologie grise de Descartes: Questions cartésiennes II.* Paris: J. Vrin.

McDaniel, Robb A. 1998. *The Philosopher's Jeremiad: Prophecy and Political Philosophy in Leo Strauss and Emmanuel Levinas,* Ph.D. diss., Vanderbilt University.

Melamded, Abraham. 2005. "Is There a Jewish Political Thought?" *Hebraic Political Studies* 1:1 (fall) 24–56.

Mendelssohn, Moses. 1983. *Jerusalem.* Allan Arkush, trans. Hanover and London: University of New England Press.

Merrill, Clark A. 2000. "Leo Strauss's Indictment of Christian Philosophy." *Review of Politics* 62(1) (winter): 77–105.

Mortley, Raoul, ed. 1991. *French Philosophers in Conversation: Levinas, Schneider, Serres, Irigaray, Le Doeuff, Derrida.* London and New York: Routledge.

Mosès, Stéphane. 1982. *Système et révélation: La philosophie de Franz Rosenzweig.* Paris: Les Editions du Souil. Translated by Catherine Tihanyi as *System and Revelation: Philosophy of Franz Rosenzweig.* Detroit: Wayne State University Press, 1992.

Moyn, Samuel. 2005. *Origins of the Other: Emmanuel Levinas between Revelation and Ethics.* Ithaca, NY: Cornell University Press.

_____. 2003. "Emmanuel Levinas's Talmudic Readings: Between Tradition and Invention." *Prooftexts* 23(3) (fall): 338–64.

_____. 1998. "Judaism against Paganism: Emmanuel Levinas's Response to Heidegger and Nazism in the 1930s." *History and Memory* 10(1) (spring/summer): 25–58.

Myers, David. 2003. *Resisting History: Historicism and its Discontents in German-Jewish Thought.* Princeton: Princeton University Press.

New, Melvyn, Robert Bernasconi, and Richard Cohen, eds. 2001. *In Proximity: Emmanuel Levinas and the Eighteenth Century.* Lubbock: Texas Tech University Press.

Nietzsche, Friedrich. 1967. *The Will Power.* Walter Kaufmann and R. J. Hollingdale, trans. New York: Random House.

Norton, Ann. 2004. *Leo Strauss and the Politics of American Empire.* New Haven: Yale University Press.

Novak, David. 1998. *Natural Law in Judaism*. Cambridge: Cambridge University Press.
————. 1995. *The Election of Israel*. New York: Cambridge University Press.
Oberman, Heido. 1963. *The Harvest of Mediaeval Theology*. Cambridge: Harvard University Press.
Ochs, Peter, ed. 1993. *The Return to Scripture in Judaism and Christianity*. New York: Paulist Press.
Orr, Susan. 1995. *Jerusalem and Athens: Reason and Revelation in the Works of Leo Strauss*. Lanham, MD: Rowman and Littlefield.
Pangle, Thomas. 2003. *Political Philosophy and the God of Abraham*. Baltimore: Johns Hopkins University Press.
————. 1990. *The Spirit of Modern Republicanism: The Moral Vision of the American Founders and the Philosophy of Locke*. Chicago: University of Chicago Press.
Pawel, Ernst. 1989. *The Labyrinth of Exile: A Life of Theodor Herzl*. New York: Farrar, Straus, and Giroux.
Peperzak, Adriaan. 1993. *To the Other: An Introduction to the Philosophy of Emmanuel Levinas*. West Lafayette, IN: Purdue University Press.
Pines, Shlomo. 1963. "The Philosophical Sources of *The Guide of the Perplexed*." In Maimonides's *The Guide of the Perplexed*. Shlomo Pines, trans. Chicago: University of Chicago Press, pp. lvii–cxxxiv.
Pippen, Robert. 1992. "The Modern World of Leo Strauss." *Political Theory* 20(3): 448–72. Reprinted in Robert B. Pippin, *Idealism as Modernism: Hegelian Variations*. Cambridge: Cambridge University Press, 1997.
————. 1989. *Hegel's Idealism: The Satisfaction of Self-Consciousness*. Cambridge: Cambridge University Press.
Poma, Andrea. 1997. *The Critical Philosophy of Hermann Cohen*. John Denton, trans. Albany: State University of New York Press.
Popkin, Richard H. 1964. *The History of Skepticism from Erasmus to Spinoza*. Berkeley: University of California Press.
Preller, Victor. 1967. *Divine Science and the Science of God: A Reformulation of Thomas Aquinas*. Princeton: Princeton University Press.
Raleigh, Erik Root. 2000. "A Strauss Divided." *Clarion* 5(1) (October/November): 26.
Ravitzky, Aviezer. 1996. *Messianism, Zionism, and Jewish Religious Radicalism*. Michael Swirsky and Jonathan Chipman, trans. Chicago: University of Chicago Press.
Ricoeur, Paul. 2004. "Otherwise: A Reading of Emmanuel Levinas's Otherwise than Being or Beyond Essence." *Yale French Studies* 104: 82–99.
Robbins, Jill. 1994. "Facing Figures: Levinas and the Claims of Figural Interpretation." In *Transitions in Continental Philosophy*. A. Dallery, S. Watson, and E. M. Bower, eds. Albany: State University of New York Press, pp. 283–91.
Rockmore, Thomas and Joseph Margolis, eds. 1992. *The Heidegger Case: On Philosophy and Politics*. Philadelphia: Temple University Press.
Rogers, Melvin L. 2004. "Rorty's Straussianism; Or, Irony against Democracy." *Contemporary Pragmatism* 1(2) (December): 95–121.
Rorty, Richard. 2003. "Religion in the Public Square: A Reconsideration." *Journal of Religious Ethics* 31(1) (spring): 141–52.
————. 2001. *Richard Rorty: Critical Dialogues*. Matthew Festenstein and Simon Thompson, eds. New York: Blackwell.

Rose, Gillian. 1993. *Judaism and Modernity: Philosophical Essays*. Oxford and Cambridge: Blackwell.

Rosen, Stanley. 2003. *Hermeneutics as Politics*, 2nd ed. New Haven: Yale University Press.

———. 2002. *The Ancients and the Moderns: Rethinking Modernity*. South Bend, IN: St. Augustine's Press.

———. 1974. *G. W. F. Hegel: An Introduction to the Science of Wisdom*. New Haven: Yale University Press.

Rosenzweig, Franz. 1994. *Scripture and Translation*. Lawrence Rosenwald and Everett Fox, eds. and trans. Bloomington: Indiana University Press.

———. 1976. *Der Stern der Erlösung*. The Hague and Boston: Martinus Nijhoff. Translated by William W. Hallo as *The Star of Redemption*. New York: University of Notre Dame Press, 1985.

———. 1974–84. "Das neue Denken." In *Zweistromland. Kleinere Schriften zu Glauben und Denken*, vol. 3 of *Franz Rosenzweig: Der Mensch und sein Werk: Gesammelte Schriften*. Boston and The Hague: Martinus Nijhoff. Edited and translated by Alan Udoff and Barbara Galli as *Franz Rosenzweig's "The New Thinking."* Syracuse: Syracuse University Press, 1999.

———. 1965. *On Jewish Learning*. N. N. Glatzer, ed. New York: Schocken.

———. 1923. "Apologetic Thinking." *Der Jude*, Jahrgang VII: 457–64. Translated in *The Jew: Essays from Buber's Journal Der Jude*. Arthur A. Cohen, ed., Joachim Neugroschel, trans. Tuscaloosa: The University of Alabama Press, 1980.

Sagi, Avi and Daniel Statman. 1995. "Divine Command Morality and Jewish Tradition." *Journal of Religious Ethics* 23 (1) (spring): 39–67

Said, Edward. 1996. *Representations of the Intellectual*. New York: Vintage Books.

Schneewind, J. B. 1998. *The Invention of Autonomy: A History of Modern Moral Philosophy*. New York: Cambridge University Press.

Schwarz, Moshe. 1978. "Enlightenment and Philosophy: On Jewish Philosophy in the Modern Era." (Hebrew) *Da'at* 1: 7–16.

Schwarzschild, Steven. 1970. "F. Rosenzweig's Anecdotes about Hermann Cohen." In *Gegenwart im Ruckblick: Festgabe für die Jüdische Gemeinde zu Berlin 25 Jahre nach dem Neubeginn*. H. A. Strauss and K. Grossman, eds. Heidelberg: Lothar Stiehm Verlag.

———. 1955. "Two Modern Jewish Philosophies of History: Nachman Krochmal and Hermann Cohen," D. H. L. diss., Hebrew Union College, Cincinnati.

Shapiro, Marc B. 2004. *The Limits of Orthodox Theology: Maimonides' Thirteen Principles Reappraised*. Oxford and Portland: The Littman Library of Jewish Civilization.

Sheehan, Thomas. 2001. "A Paradigm Shift in Heidegger Research." *Continental Philosophy Review* 34: 183–202.

Sheppard, Eugene. 2006. *Leo Strauss and the Politics of Exile: The Making of a Political Philosopher*. Lebanon, NH: University Press New England/Brandeis University Press. Forthcoming.

———. 2001. *Leo Strauss and the Politics of Exile*. Ph.D. diss., University of California at Los Angeles.

———. "Raising Zionism to the Level of Antisemitism: Reflections on Leo Strauss as a Young Zionist." *Jewish Studies Quarterly* (forthcoming).

Smith, Steven B. 1997. *Spinoza, Liberalism, and the Question of Jewish Identity*. New Haven: Yale University Press.

Sparn, Walter. 1986. "Das Bekenntnis des Philosophen. Gottfried Wilhelm Leibniz als Philosoph und Theologe." *Neue Zeitschrift für Systematische Theologie* 28: 139–78.

———. 1976. *Wiederkehr der Metaphysik: Die ontologische Frage in der lutherischen Theologie des fruehen 17. Jahrhunderts.* Stuttgart, Germany: Calwer Verlag.

Spinoza, Baruch. 1982. *Ethics.* Samuel Shirley, trans., Seymour Feldman, ed. New York: Hacket.

———. 1951. *A Theologico-Political Treatise.* Unabridged Elwes translation. New York: Dover Publications.

Stern, David. 1988. "Midrash and Indeterminacy." *Critical Inquiry* (15): 132–61.

Stone, Suzanne Last. 1993. "In Pursuit of the Counter-Text: The Turn to the Jewish Legal Model in Contemporary American Legal Theory." *Harvard Law Review* 106(4): 813–94.

Stout, Jeffrey. 2004. *Democracy and Tradition.* Princeton: Princeton University Press.

Stowers, Stanley. 1994. *A Rereading of Romans: Justice, Jews, and Gentiles.* New Haven: Yale University Press.

Tanguay, Daniel. 2003. *Léo Strauss: Une biographie intellectuelle Essai.* Paris: Grasset.

Tarcov, Nathan. 1983. "Philosophy and History: Tradition and Interpretation in the Work of Leo Strauss." *Polity* 16 (fall): 5–29.

Thomasius, Christian. 1979. *Summarischer Entwurf der Grundlehren, die einem Studioso Iuris zu wissen und auf Universitäten zu Lernen nötig sind.* Aalen: Scientia Verlag.

Twersky, Isadore. 1976. "The Shulhan Aruk: Enduring Code of Jewish Law." In *The Jewish Expression.* Judah Goldin, ed. New Haven: Yale University Press.

Udoff, Alan, ed. 1991. *Leo Strauss's Thought: Toward a Critical Engagement.* Boulder, CO: L. Rienner Publishers.

Walzer, Michael. 1987. *Interpretation and Social Criticism.* Cambridge: Harvard University Press.

Walzer, Richard. 1985. Commentary in *Al-Farabi on the Perfect State.* Richard Walzer, trans. and ed. Oxford: Oxford University Press, pp. 8–13 and 425–9.

Wiedebach, Hartwig and Annette Winkelmann, eds. 2002. *Chajm H. Steinthal: Sprachwissenschaftlicher und Philosoph im 19 Jahrhundert.* Leiden, The Netherlands and Köln, Germany: Brill.

Wolterstorff, Nicholas. 2003. "An Engagement with Rorty." *Journal of Religious Ethics* 31 (1) spring: 129–40.

Wyschogrod, Edith. 1980. "The Moral Self: Emmanuel Levinas and Hermann Cohen." *Da'at* 4 (winter): 35–58.

Xenos, Nicholas. 2004. "Leo Strauss and the Rhetoric of the War on Terror" *Logos* 3(2) (spring): 63–81, special issue on "Confronting Neoconservatism."

Zac, Sylvain. 1965. *Spinoza et l'interprétation de l'écriture.* Paris: Presses Universitaires de France.

Zuckert, Catherine. 1996. *Postmodern Platos.* Chicago: University of Chicago Press.

Zuckert, Michael P. 2002. *Launching Liberalism: On Lockean Political Philosophy.* Lawrence: University of Kansas Press.

Index